this is Japan

By the Same Author

BALI & BEYOND
OFF TO ASIA
THE NEW AUSTRALIA
PLUMES & ARROWS
THE VIKING CIRCLE
ADAM IN OCHRE

colin simpson
this is Japan

An extended and updated coverage incorporating **The Country Upstairs** (published in Britain as **Picture of Japan**)

angus & robertson publishers

Angus & Robertson Publishers
London · Sydney · Melbourne · Singapore
Manila

This book is copyright. Apart from any fair dealing for the purposes of private study, research, criticism or review, as permitted under the Copyright Act, no part may be reproduced by any process without written permission. Inquiries should be addressed to the publishers.

First published by Angus & Robertson Publishers, Australia, 1975

Incorporating *The Country Upstairs*, first published by Angus & Robertson Publishers in 1956, reprinted in 1957 (twice), 1958, 1959 and 1961, with revised and enlarged editions in 1962 and 1965 and reprints in 1966 and 1969.
Published in Britain under the title *Picture of Japan* and in the United States as *Japan: An Intimate View*.)

© Colin Simpson 1975

National Library of Australia
card number and ISBN 0 207 13259 3

Photosetting by Thomson Press (India) Limited, New Delhi

Printed in **Hong Kong**

foreword

Author's answer to
Is this a new book?

The straightest answer to that question has to be a *Yes and No*. As writing, more of the book is new than not new, and what is not new has been updated and clipped into what I hope is better shape. This is certainly not just another revised and enlarged edition of *The Country Upstairs** (which was first published in 1956 and after five printings was revised and enlarged in 1962 as it was again for another edition in 1965, by which time it had sold nearly fifty thousand copies).

The American author Edwin O. Reischauer faced much the same problem with his revised-and-enlarged 1946 book *Japan Past and Present*. He re-wrote a lot and added a lot and his book is now *Japan: The Story of a Nation*, a book "so thoroughly changed from beginning to end as to deserve a new title".

As to changes in this one, two more trips to Japan, in 1973 and '74, have added quite a lot of new material. Kyushu, the attractive south island, is included as a four-chapter new section. The tourist track has also been extended to take in Nagoya, Gifu and its cormorant fishers, Ise and its shrines, the Ise Peninsula and its pearls. And I've gone off-track in Honshu to include the west coast's "other Kyoto", Kanazawa and, up north, Matsushima, which is a scenic gem of a place, better than the Inland Sea. I've taken further looks at much-changed Tokyo and gone back once more to such places as Kyoto, Nara, Hiroshima. In some other ways the book is nearer to being a definitive one: so I feel that the new title, *This is Japan*, is in order.

Yet, though there is more content, the book is not as long. The compact format imposed quite a task of crisper coverage in a leaner style. Perhaps the result is a better book, in today's terms, than the best-seller that first appeared in 1956.

COLIN SIMPSON

---

*In Britain the book's title was *Picture of Japan*; in the U.S.A it was *Japan: An Intimate View*.

To the memory
of a good friend in Japan,
TORAO ("Tiger") SAITO
(1910–1970)
who was distinguished as an architect
as well as a journalist, author, photographer,
and was foundation editor of Asahi Shimbun's
fine English-language annual
This is Japan.

Exchange Rate of Japanese Yen

The first thing the visitor has to get used to in converting Japanese currency is that the sums are so nought-y : ¥1,000 being less than three Australian dollars or two English pounds; a million yen being no more than the price of an unpretentious car; one unit of our currencies being worth hundreds of units of theirs.

The following rates are as given by a well-known and world-wide travel organization, Thos. Cook & Son, in late August 1975:

Australian dollar	**¥378**
U.K. pound	**¥630**
U.S. dollar	**¥296**

Intending travellers should get not only the latest exchange rates but seek advice on which currency to take to Japan (in Travellers Cheques, always safer than notes). If the yen is in process of hardening (i.e., the rate is going down, costing us more) then there can be advantage in taking TCs in yen.

The yen is the one Japanese money unit now. There used to be the *sen*—and even the *rin,* which was one-tenth of the sen that was one-hundredth of the yen that is worth now, say, one-third of a cent. The yen was worth about 50 cents American before the First World War, and before the last war it was around three to the U.S. dollar. After Japan's defeat and economic collapse the Americans, in 1949, fixed a rate of 360 yen to their dollar. Japan's remarkable recovery, with some weakening of the U.S. dollar, has reduced that rate to around 300.

The Australian-dollar rate was as high as 450 in 1974 before devaluation reduced it to 386. Conversions in this book are based on the round figure of ¥400 to the $A.

JAPAN

SHOWING THE AUTHOR'S TRAVEL

SCALE		
KILOMETRES	160	320
MILES	100	200

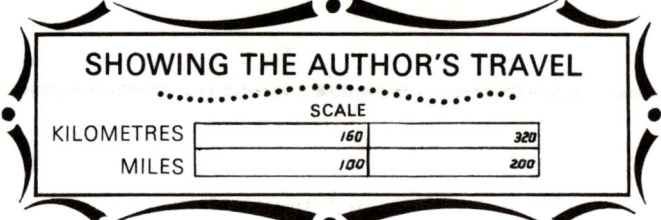

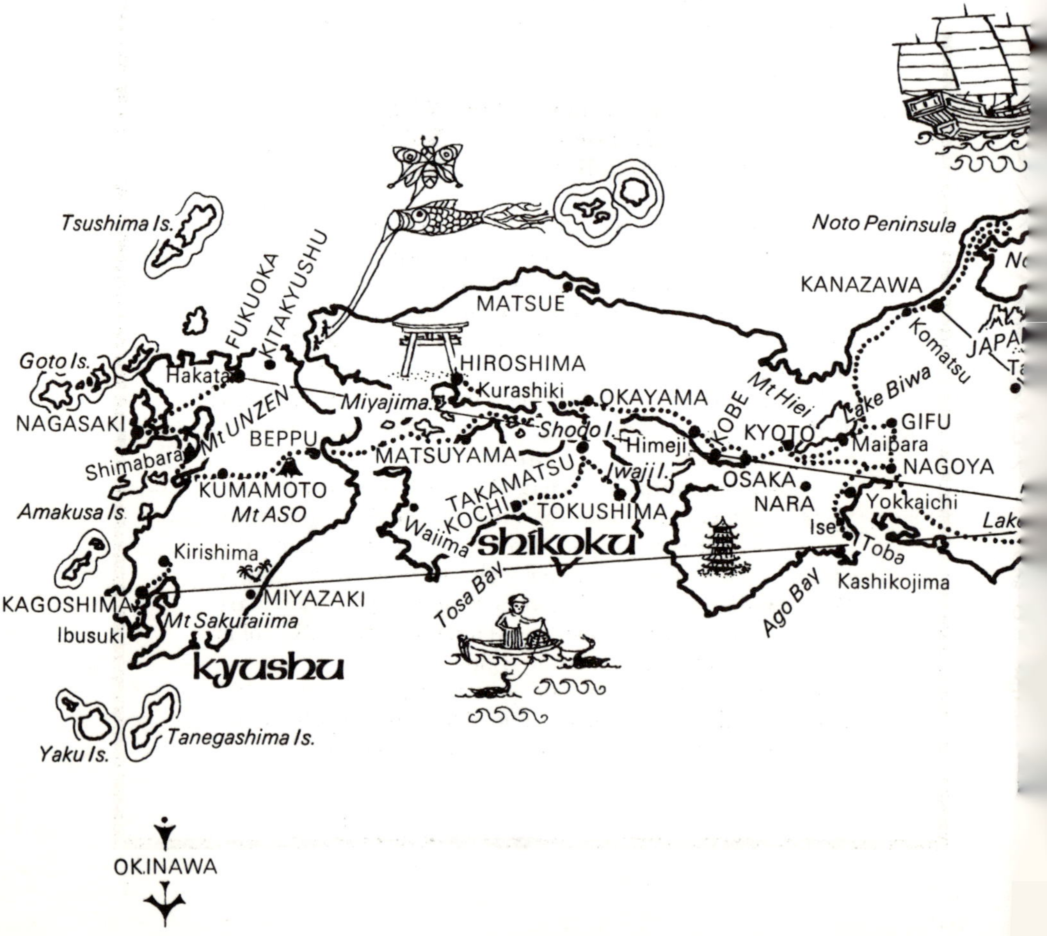

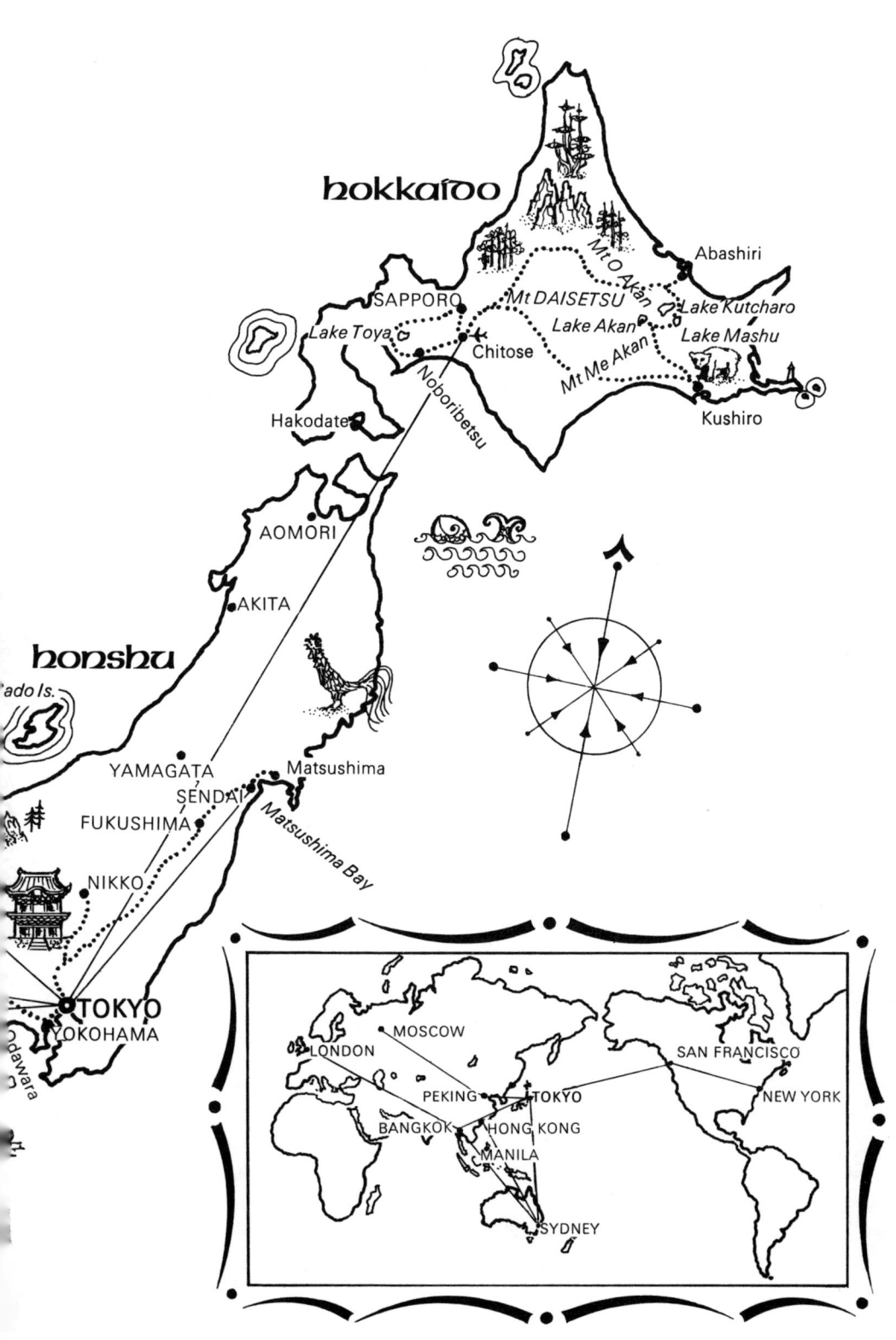

contents

THE JAPANESE

Their train runs on a different line	3
But their eyes are NOT slanted	8
"The rady rost her brue umblerra"	13
Love of company, and change of shape	16

THIS *WAS* JAPAN

A shrine is built, for the sixtieth time	23
The chrysanthemum and, alas, the sword	28
"We can beat these big white softies"	33

TOKYO

The biggest city and its quiet heart	39
Hotels, a Japanese inn, and food	42
What to do by day in the megalopolis	52
Sampling night-life the tour way	62
Michiko, a hostess, and bars to beware of	66
A "love hotel", and the massage girls	73

THE PERFORMERS

Geisha party: What really goes on	81
Theatrical Kabuki, classical Noh	85
An art of melodrama done with dolls	90
Sumo's ritual of huge wrestlers	95

KYOTO, NARA & NIKKO

First Nikko, then the "bullet" train	101
Kyoto has the style and the savour	111
More Kyoto: Stones make a garden	118
Nara is more than a big Buddha	124

FUJI AND BEYOND

The Fujiya lived on a tycoon's love	129
Viewing Fuji-san and the pearl places	134
Nagoya, epitome of postwar Japan	143
The money-bringing birds of Gifu	146

INLAND SEA SHORES

Going Japanese at Miyajima	153
Hiroshima: So you knew about the bomb?	159
Shikoku, and along the Inland Sea	165

OFF-TRACK IN HONSHU

Kanazawa, in its way, is another Kyoto	177
Why the poet wrote "O! Matsushima"	185

KYUSHU, THE SOUTH

Steamy Beppu and Aso's volcano	193
Kumamoto, a sexy old stronghold	196
Nagasaki: A flavour of foreigners	201
The new gateway is Kagoshima	205

HOKKAIDO, THE NORTH

The top island is another Japan	213
Strange lakes and the bear-cult Ainu	221

REFERENCE NOTES	233
INDEX	235

List of Illustrations

COLOUR PLATES (a) *indicates author's photograph*

Girls and war veterans (a)	18-19	Kenrokuen Park, Kanazawa (a)	98-99
Schoolboys clowning (a)	18-19	Dance mask, Nara	98-99
Torii gateway to shrine	18-19	Matsushima Bay (a)	130-131
Soka Gakkai Hall	34-35	Curious rock forms (a)	130-131
Two geisha	34-35	Kabuki costume	130-131
Gold Pavilion (a)	50-51	Mount Aso summit (a)	146-147
At Katsuga Shrine (a)	50-51	"Sun Flower" ship	146-147
Autumn at Miyajima (a)	50-51	Kabuki Lion Dance	146-147
Spring at Odawara (a)	66-67	"Sand Baths", Ibusuki	178-179
Marriage	66-67	Iso Gardens, Kagoshima	178-179
Air hostess	66-67	Tea ceremony	178-179
Costumed children (a)	66-67	Hara-San's pictures	178-179
Sumo wrestling	66-67	Mount Akan, Hokkaido	194-195
Miyajima shrine (a)	82-83	Ainu headman	194-195
Torii in the sea	82-83	Wooden utensils	194-195
Gagaku musicians	82-83		
Dance at Miyajima (a)	82-83		
"Moon" Bridge, Takamatsu (a)	98-99		

BLACK AND WHITE PHOTOGRAPHS

"Bullet" train leaving Tokyo	18-19	Hiroshima survivor (a)	82-83
Planting the ricefield	18-19	A-Bomb devastation	82-83
Shinto shrine at Ise	18-19	Long-tailed rooster	98-99
Ginza by night	34-35	Cormorant fishing, Gifu	98-99
Kokusai theatre	34-35	Matsushima Bay (a)	130-131
Meguro "love hotel"	34-35	Other formations (a)	130-131
Bed with mirrors	34-35	"Wedded rocks", Noto (a)	130-131
Nikko mausolea	50-51	Dummy policeman (a)	130-131
Festival at Nikko	50-51	Potter (a)	130-131
Ryoanji stone garden	50-51	Mikimoto pearl oyster rafts	146-147
Katsura Imperial Villa	50-51	"Restful Cottage", Fujiya Hotel (a)	146-147
Bunraku puppet theatre	66-67	Nagoya Castle	146-147
Geisha dancing	66-67	Akasuka Lantern Gate	178-179
Byodo-in Temple	66-67	Kamakura Buddha	178-179
Horyuji Pagoda	66-67	Lake Mashu	194-195
Entrance, Japanese inn	82-83	Snow festival, Sapporo	194-195
Art Exhibit, Tokyo Biennale	82-83		

ILLUSTRATIONS ACKNOWLEDGMENTS

The author and his publishers gratefully acknowledge illustrations made available by the following: ASAHI SHIMBUN Publishing Company, Tokyo: Colourplates of Sumo Wrestling, Torii in the Sea, Gagaku Musicians, Kabuki Costume, Dance Mask, Mt Akan, Ainu Headman, Wooden Utensils.

JAPAN NATIONAL TOURIST ORGANIZATION: Colourplates of Torii Gateway, Two Geisha, Tea Ceremony and black and white photographs of Planting the Ricefield, Shrine at Ise, Ginza at Night, Kokusai Theatre, Nikko Mausolea, Geisha Dancing, Japanese Inn, Long-tailed Rooster, Akasuka Lantern Gate.

JAPAN AIR LINES for the colour transparency used on the front of the jacket, and the Air Hostess subject and the monotone Nagoya Castle.

FUJIYA HOTEL CO. for the colour transparency showing Mt Fuji, on the back of the jacket.

KAGOSHIMA TOURIST FEDERATION for the colour transparencies of "Sand Baths" at Ibusuki, Iso Gardens at Kagoshima and the "Sun Flower" Ship.

THE SOKA GAKKAI, Tokyo, for the colourplate of its Sho-Hondo.

MIYAKO HOTEL, Kanazawa, for the Shinto Wedding in colour.

MR TAKESHI HARA for colour transparency of his flower pictures.

JAPAN INFORMATION SERVICE, Sydney: Black and white photographs of the "Bullet" Train, Nikko Festival, Ryoanji Stone Garden, Katsura Imperial Villa, Bunraku Puppet Theatre, Byodo-in Temple, Horyuji Pagoda, Kamakura Buddha, Lake Mashu, Snow Festival at Sapporo.

GIFU PREFECTURE, Sightseeing Office for the two photographs of Cormorant Fishing.

ORION PRESS, Tokyo, for the Meguro "Love Hotel" photographs.

K. MIKIMOTO, Inc. for the Pearl Oyster Rafts in Ago Bay.

the japanese

日本人

Their train runs on a different line

THIS JAPANESE friend of mine was on his honeymoon. Suzuki-san, as we can call him, was driving a hired car in Kyushu when he came to a railway line with a level crossing.

He stopped the car and looked for an approaching train. He could see none, nor could he hear one coming. There was no barrier, no red light, no clanging bell, no warning he could see. A notice was obscured by bushes, Suzuki-san says, and his view of the line was clear only on the right, which is the car driver's side in Japan as it is in Australia. The train came from the left, and without any warning whistle.

The train's driver must have hit the brakes fast. Even so, the car was pushed forty metres along the track. Suzuki-san's injuries were fairly superficial, but his bride had fractures that put her in hospital for a week and incapacitated her for a month.

Suzuki-san went to the office of Japan National Railways and humbly apologized for delaying and causing damage to the train. He was told that the train's locomotive had been damaged to the extent of ¥500,000 (say $A1,250) and he was liable for this amount. Suzuki-san was a rather junior accountant in a semi-government department in Tokyo on a salary equivalent to $A40 a week, which bonuses would bring to $A60.

If such an accident had happened to me in Australia or in Britain or in the United States I would have sued the railway for negligence and expected to get substantial compensation. But the Japanese situation was that Suzuki-san knew that he, not the railway, was regarded as the guilty party; he was the one who would be expected to pay compensation.

Suzuki-san told me that he was "very lucky" in the matter of the compensation he had to pay: the sum was reduced to ¥2,400 ($A60). This was because the organization he worked for was associated, as Japan National Railways is, with the Ministry of Transport, and executives of his organization were on very friendly terms with executives of JNR. Otherwise, he said, he would have had to pay something like the full amount claimed, ¥500,000, which was equal to his earnings for five months.

TO THAT STORY, which instances a significant difference between what happens in Japan and what happens in a Western-minded country, our reaction may well be that the Japanese system is weighted in favour of the big corporation and against the individual; or, in this case of the *national* railways, in favour of the State and against the citizen. And that is true enough, although not as true as it used to be before the 1941 war.

At the same time we have the difference that nowhere has the individual, as employee, held the big corporation in such high regard as has been the

4 The Japanese

case in Japan. The worker commonly shows the company a degree of diligence and loyalty that is not at all characteristic of our industrial society. Bound up with this is the Japanese corporation's being prepared to provide the worker with a job for all his working life.

Industrially, Japan has become Westernized. Only by means of the Western technologies it adopted could it have become the world's third-largest (after the U.S.A. and the U.S.S.R.) producer in terms of gross national product. Only by becoming the Britain of Asia, industrially, did it become the world's biggest builder of ships.

The Japanese themselves, however, are not as Westernized as many people think. Most may wear Western clothes, but by no means all of them have put off the kimono—and where else in the world is such centuries-old dress still everyday wear? In fact, there is a new pride in nationalism and Japanese tradition, and it is instanced in more Japanese men choosing kimono formal dress to be married in.

The average Japanese does not live in a Western-style house but in a flimsier one where he takes his shoes off at the door. He eats more Western food than he did, such as meat; he drinks beer and Coca-Cola: but his breakfast is still likely to be rice, soup, seaweed and bean curd, not eggs and bacon. He still likes raw fish better than grilled steak, and prefers chopsticks to cutlery. He still begins a book at the back and reads top to bottom and right to left. If he uses a handsaw he doesn't push it but pulls it. He still doesn't shake hands (except with foreigners), but bows. His attitudes to women, and to the company that employs him, are distinctly different from the Westerner's. He has a different concept of what is his duty, and a different outlook on many matters, including sex—and if what is customary to a Japanese seems topsy-turvy to us, yet it may be no less reasonable. In sexual intercourse, one Western partner may say to the other, "I'm coming!" The Japanese equivalent is, "I'm going!"

So I didn't tell the story of Suzuki-san's railway accident because it was hard to find another illustration of East-West difference, but because it showed a Japanese authority maintaining the traditional position of non-change in relation to the operation of the very thing that has done so much to bring about Japanese change—the railway.

THE FIRST TRAIN the Japanese ever saw was a miniature one but nevertheless marvellous to them. It came with the Americans' so-called "black ships"—four frigates, two of them steam driven—under Commodore Matthew Perry, who came to demand of the *shogun* (generalissimo) at Edo (later Tokyo) a treaty of commerce with the United States, which Perry got in 1854. Perry presented to the Shogun, Iyesada, a model railway. Bernard Rudofsky says in his book on Japan[1]: "Until rickshas made their appearance the Japanese had never seen a wheeled vehicle." In fact, they had a dray-like cart called a *daihashi*, a passenger ox-cart like a palanquin on wheels, a *gissha*, and a four-wheeled tower used in festivals and called a *hoko*—but that appears to be all. No use was made in war of the chariot, which was used in China in the 14th century B.C., and no coaches are depicted in old woodblock prints of traffic along the main route to Edo, the Tokaido Road: the nobility are shown

---

[1]. Author and publication are given in Note 1 of Reference Notes at the back of the book, just before the Index.

being carried in a *kago*, something like a sedan-chair, or borne in a large litter called a *norimon*.

After seeing a horse carriage that was brought in, a Japanese named Yasuke Izumi and two co-workers invented the *jinricksha* (human-power-vehicle). They were rewarded by the government for their invention, and a small monument was erected to them. The rickshaw, as it came to be called, was soon in use in other parts of Asia.

A variety of wheeled vehicles had been for so long in use in nearby China, with which Japan had been in fairly constant contact since the fifth century, and it seems strange that the Japanese did not get more wheeled vehicles from the source their civilization drew so much else from. One writer[2] on the country has listed no less than twenty-six "borrowings" from China.*

Three centuries before the Americans came in through Japan's Pacific front door, Europeans had entered Japan by the southern gate from the China Sea, at Kyushu. Portuguese came with the first guns in 1543, the first Jesuit missionary Francis Xavier in 1549; the Dutch arrived in 1609; the English in 1613. Then the door was slammed on the Christian powers except the Dutch, for whom a chink was left open at Nagasaki.

Japan came out of its feudalism after the shogunate—the military dictatorship that had governed the country for nearly seven hundred years—handed back to the emperors the power the warlords had taken from them. In 1868 what is called the Meiji Restoration brought in a fifteen-year-old emperor who took the name of Meiji (meaning "Enlightened"). He had progressive advisers and he said, "Knowledge shall be sought throughout the world." It was not only sought but applied to the extent that *within five years* these things happened: Telegraphic communication was opened between the new capital, Tokyo, and Yokohama. Postal service began. The solar calendar was adopted. The first shipping company and four banks were founded. A new educational system increased the number of schools to eight thousand. And in 1872 Japan got its first passenger railway.

Emperor Meiji rode with the first train, and the railway had enormous prestige from the presence of the *Tenno*, the Emperor, who said in his imperial message: "The whole people will wish to use this means and, thanks to it, commerce will prosper." He was so right.

The Japanese were to become the world's most inveterate train travellers. Railways brought to seaports the export goods that flooded across the world. The country that had been so backward in its transportation, and was so heavily defeated and devastated in the Second World War, developed the Tokaido Line "bullet trains", the world's fastest.

ANYTHING as prestigious as the epoch-making new railway was sure to array itself in more than ordinary authority. A railway station-master, with us, hasn't much status: in Japan he is a dignitary. The first one I saw was sending

*The list of "borrowings from China" as given, alphabetically: acupuncture, architecture, Buddhism, Confucianism, copper coins, cormorant fishing, fire-crackers, flower-arrangement, food, government, lacquerware, lanterns, massage, musical instruments (*samisen, koto, biwa*), painting, paper-making, paper-windows, poetry, pottery, printing, puppet drama, rock gardens, sculpture, silk culture, tea culture, writing. Japanese civilization's debt to China is undoubtedly very great: but, then, so was Britain's indebtedness to the civilization of Rome, and Rome's indebtedness to Greece.

6 The Japanese

off a train from Tokyo Central. The station-master's cap was banded with red and gold stripes and he wore white gloves. He stood at attention near the edge of the platform, just outside the carriage I was in, and he gazed solemnly at the outsize pocket watch he held before him in his white-gloved hand. On the tick of 8 a.m. the train began to move. The station-master and his two assistants bowed.

That was a tourist train going to Nikko. Nearly all the tourists on it weren't foreigners like me: they were Japanese. Wherever you go by train in Japan there are likely to be crowds of these travelling Japanese. As Maraini[3] says: "Every school organizes one or two excursions a year ... nearly all children who receive secondary education know the famous places of their country."

Yet of the 260 lines Japan National Railways operates only seven in 1974 were not running at a loss, despite the extraordinary numbers of commuter passengers crammed, by physical force, into every carriage of every Tokyo suburban service in the rush hours. Husky students are hired by the railway to be passenger pusher-inners, called *shiri-oshi* (buttocks-shovers).

A railway system that more than a million people depend upon to get them into and out of Tokyo every morning and evening, however uncomfortably, is in real trouble if any of its trains are delayed or don't run. So the railway does everything in its power to see that nobody causes any train delay. As a deterrent it severely penalizes anybody who does—so far as that is possible. In an average year about fifteen hundred persons are not deterred, and the delays they cause are classified as due to "obstructions" on the line. So many Japanese suicides end their lives by throwing themselves in front of trains.

Suicide is not a subject one would choose to dwell on, but its incidence and methods do tell us something about the Japanese character. In the year I first visited Japan, 1955, its suicide rate was the highest in the world, with Austria and Denmark equal second. It was a time of lingering post-war disillusion, of a reconstructed economy still getting into high gear, and the main reason for the suicide rate running at over twenty thousand a year was given as "difficulties of earning a living".

By 1973 things were very different. The Suzuki-sans read in their Tokyo newspapers that they were wealthier than the average Englishman, and half as well off again as the average Austrian. Austria's suicide rate had stayed at the top, with Hungary's: Japan's, like Denmark's, had fallen—but was still eighteen thousand in 1972.

There is nothing in Japanese religious beliefs (Shinto, Buddhist, Confucian) that forbids taking one's own life, as there is in the Christian and Moslem creeds. Moreover there is a long tradition of what is thought of as honourable self-sacrifice by committing *hara-kiri* (a word that, incidentally, is not in my Japanese-English dictionary[4]: *seppuku* is the preferred term).

A story and stage drama the Japanese have long found most moving is *The Forty-seven Ronin* (masterless samurai warriors). Their Lord Asano was forced to commit suicide for allegedly insulting another lord, Kira, against whom the *ronin* swore vengeance. Eventually they killed Kira and cut off his head and put it on Asano's tomb. Then the forty-seven—who are regarded as paragons of loyalty, selfless super-heroes—gave themselves up, and were allowed to commit *seppuku*. That happened historically, back in 1703. In 1945, after Emperor Hirohito announced surrender, seven Army officers committed suicide in protest in front of the Imperial Palace; the Minister of

War wrote a poem and then shot himself; the Chief of the Eastern Defence Command shot his wife then himself; and many other officers followed their example, mostly at the Niju-bashi (Double Bridge) of the Palace. "Their bodies lay tidily in a row, face downwards; the requirements of etiquette must be scrupulously observed even in death."[3]

Perhaps no non-Japanese can hope to understand fully the death in 1970 of Yukio Mishima, the renowned author of twenty novels and thirty-eight plays. He was aged forty-five, a handsome zealot of physical fitness, yet a heavy smoker and whisky drinker at weekends. At nineteen he had published stories that "revealed with extreme frankness his homosexual tendencies"[5], but was married, with a son and a daughter. Mishima was intensely a patriot who saw the Emperor as "our source of glory", and he once described himself as a Japanese Don Quixote. He commanded a private army he called the Shield Society (to "shield" the Emperor) and was a dedicated opponent of Japan's national policy of peace: he was a believer in *bushido* (way of the warrior). He also believed in reincarnation. He wrote in English to an American friend that he had come to wish to "sacrifice myself for the old beautiful tradition of Japan which is disappearing very quickly day by day".[6]

On 25 November 1970 Mishima and four disciples, carrying samurai swords, thrust their way into the office of a general of the Self-Defence Forces. With the general tied up, Mishima harangued from a balcony a crowd of Self-Defence soldiers about the evils of Japan's Westernization and its no-war Constitution. Saying "I don't think they heard me very well", he went back inside, knelt, stabbed his abdomen and had made a very long sideways incision before the companion standing behind him swung a razor-sharp samurai sword and struck off his head.

But their eyes are NOT slanted

I FIRST came to Japan in late October 1955 on a Qantas flight from Australia that ended at Tokyo's airport on a tarmac lacquered with rain. From the car that took me into the city centre I looked mainly at the pedestrians.

Side-street Tokyo is full of exoticisms and night-time Tokyo is a fascinating city, but main-road Tokyo by day is not particularly eyeworthy. There is a splashy sort of differentness given the street scene by the advertising signs and hoardings in bold Kanji ideographs, the Japanese writing that looks like and derives from Chinese. But no other big city I've seen is so devoid of notable civic buildings as this biggest city in the world.

Looking at the pedestrians, there was some show of Japanese national dress. A few old men shuffled along in dark kimonos and *geta* (wooden sandals). An occasional workman wore the ideographed dark-blue *hapi* coat. Nearly all the males wore Western clothes. Of the women, the kimono-wearers were mainly middle-aged or older. The young ones generally were wearing skirt, blouse and cardigan under a plastic raincoat.

At the Marunouchi Hotel, which is in the commercial heart of Tokyo (Marunouchi means "at the centre of things") bell-boys swung open the front doors, bowing. A smiling desk-clerk booked me in. A diminutive young porter protested politely that he was strong enough to carry my outsize suitcase. It was such a burden to him that I insisted on carrying the heavy brief-bag. When we got out of the elevator on the fifth floor three maids, even smaller than the porter and looking like midget nurses in their white headcloths, descended on me. They chirruped Japanese consternation, as though it were unthinkable that a six-foot male, a guest, should be allowed to carry any of his own baggage. Tugging and laughing, they got the brief-bag out of my grasp and then bore it off between them in triumph to my room. Two bowed and departed, the other maid stayed. Her smiling face was like a pleasant moon, of a colour between peach and ivory. She regarded me with great good humour and finally said, "I—help—unpack."

I said that that would be an excellent idea—after I had had a whisky. I went to undo the brief-bag. She beat me to it, produced the bottle, conjured up a glass and a silver pitcher of ice-water and set all this before me on a tray. I sat down to it, and she was immediately on her knees removing my shoes. She slipped my feet into a pair of bedside slippers. The slippers had had a paper band round them, to indicate that they were perfectly clean. While I drank my Scotch the maid stood back and giggled with gratification at having made me comfortable.

Service. Japan had it the way wood had grain. It still has; but not to the extent one commonly encountered when labour costs were much lower and hotels could afford more staff. Also, in the decade after the war, there was an air of subservience. Today the Japanese have recovered their pride and they stand up much straighter than they did in 1955. Servility has gone, but civility still prevails.

THAT FIRST AFTERNOON I was in Tokyo I had to go to the Foreign Ministry, the Gaimusho. The hotel desk-clerk wrote the name and address on a slip of paper for me to hand to a taxi-driver. But when a bell-boy sprang out the front door to get me a taxi I said no. I had a street map and I'd walk. People are not realized by being glimpsed from a car window. You have to get out and be with them on common ground, literally, rub shoulders with them.

Now as I walked the pavements of Tokyo among the Japanese I was conscious of how they were different superficially from our Western kind. I told myself it was silly, and then that it was *not* silly, really, to say that they looked alike. Although this chunky little bullet-headed quick-shambling workman was quite a different-looking person from this smoothly-walking, studious-looking, young man there was still a marked degree of uniformity in features and physique. Racially, the Japanese are a "purer" people than we are.

We are accustomed, when we walk down the street of some city of ours, to seeing fair men and dark men and all the complexion-shades between, from ruddy to blue-chinned. And we are not likely to look twice at a six-foot, seventeen-stone bookmaker pushing his paunch past a whipper-snapper of a jockey. In Japan you do not see this big variation from the average colouring and height and weight (except in the case of *sumo* wrestlers).

The girls, and the men, who go by in Melbourne or London or New York are brown-haired or blonde or brunette, with the occasional redhead. One of my first impressions of the Japanese was that they all had black hair—black as Indian ink. Their hair thins and greys, of course, but not as soon as ours does.

Where we are used to seeing blue eyes and grey eyes as well as brown or hazel, there all the eyes are dark; not black, but seal-brown or darker. The foreigner is more conscious of Japanese eyelids than he is of Japanese eyes, because the "Mongolian fold" draws the lids together and the pupils are less visible. How that relative flatness between brow and cheekbone saves even the tiredest Japanese from having a hollow-eyed look and from bags and circles under his eyes! At death's door he may still look "bland".

Looking at Japanese eyes—and this applies to Oriental eyes in general—I soon began to doubt the commonest of Western assertions about them, and on the evidence of my own eyes came to the conviction that we have been nurturing a myth. The Japanese are *not* slant-eyed. Owing to the pull of the taut Mongolian fold of the upper eyelid, the lids of the open eye are closer together than ours. This narrowing can produce an attractive shape, like an almond with one point slightly hooked, or it can produce what we regard as an ugly slit. The modern Japanese don't like the slit look, either, and their own favourite movie stars are all notably wide-eyed—which is often the result of surgery. But a narrowed eye is one thing; a slanted eye is another. Whatever their shape, Japanese eyes are usually set straight, or so near to straight that they cannot be called slanted.

Why is it, then, that we think of their eyes as slanted? In making the same observation—that the Japanese are not slant-eyed—the American writer James Michener (who said it was probably futile to claim they are not, so ingrained is the belief that they are) put forward a reason. In his book on Japanese colour prints, *The Floating World*[7], Michener says we have thought of Japanese eyes as slanted because "Japanese artists adopted the pleasing convention that they were." Depicting the eyes as slanted, and sometimes string-thin, gave the favourite actor or courtesan a look that was found appealingly sophisticated. I think artists also used it to make the Japanese face appear longer than it is.

Another convention of Japanese ukiyoe artists was to show a desirable woman with a tiny mouth and with hands no bigger than a child's—and still another was to depict women as taller than they were. They were greatly assisted in creating the illusion of height by the fashion of the trailing kimono.

AVERAGE HEIGHT of Japanese women in the early nineteenth century was under five feet. Today it is five feet five inches. Average height of the men has increased, since feudal times, from five feet three to five feet eight.

Some of the increase in height is attributed to the schoolchildren's legs growing more and not becoming bowed since they have been seated at Western-style desks instead of on the floor. Boys and girls are also notably heavier. Classroom seats are now made larger, and doorways higher, than they used to be.

"The Japanese," it has been drummed into us, "are yellow-skinned." Japanese males' skin colour appears to me to range from ivory to what might be called a bloodless brown. The women, I thought, looked almost a different race. They have pink in their cheeks, which the men hardly ever have. When you look at any bunch of Japanese schoolgirls you notice not only that they have darker faces than their elder sisters who use make-up, but that many of them have a bright russety redness in their faces, as though their cheeks were wind-chapped.

High school girls still wear navy-blue middy uniforms with large sailor collars. Male students wear a black uniform with gold buttons, with a round peaked cap of the same black material (though the majority now go bareheaded). All boys of all schools wear the same sombre black-cloth uniform.

The sac-suited businessman may shed his Western clothing when he gets home in the evening and relax in a kimono. Those who use public baths (a great many houses have no baths) will always go there in kimono and geta—a padded kimono in the colder weather, over a light *yukata* or cotton kimono. Even the padded kimono is not a very good garment for warmth because all kimono sleeves are so wide that they admit draughts of cold air.

While the kimono itself is free-fitting and comfortable, the *obi*, the long waist-band or sash a woman wraps round her kimono in cummerbund-style, is distinctly uncomfortable because it binds the body so tightly. It constricts the upper abdomen and also the breasts. Which raises the question of whether Japanese women are markedly small-breasted because of the atrophying pressure of the obi, or whether they wear the obi because they are congenitally so small-breasted they can do so.

A woman who has worn a tight obi for many years will have a distinct band of discoloration round her body. But comfort has never had much to do with fashion or, for that matter, with dress aesthetics. A Japanese woman in a beautifully patterned kimono and an obi of rich brocade is one of the world's most graceful and ornamental figures. She should not be wearing, also, the short-coat *haori*. It cuts her shape into three—she is already cut in half, pleasingly enough to the eye, by the obi—and the haori makes her look dumpy, thus counteracting the kimono's lengthening effect. And the coat comes out over the obi's back-fold in a way that makes the wearer look humpbacked. But she needs the haori for warmth.

How MANY Japanese? The 1975 official estimate showed an increase to 110 million. Among nations' populations in today's world Japan's ranks sixth. Of the more populous nations China has roughly eight times as many people as Japan. India has five times, the U.S.A. twice and the U.S.S.R. more than twice as many. Indonesia has a quarter as many more.

Japan's population has been increasing in the past decade at little more than a yearly 1 per cent, a rate that is very low. Contraception is practised by nearly all marrieds and abortion has been legal since 1948. The birthrate at nineteen per thousand is not much more than half what it was just after the Second World War—which only one Japanese in five remembers. Three quarters of the population were born during or after the war.

The average household now has under four (3.7) members. This indicates not only the trend to smaller families, with only one or two children, but that parental in-laws are not part of the household to the extent that they used to be. Filial duty does not prevail over other feelings as much as it did. Some Japanese girls now say a good catch is a boy who is "*iye tsuki, car tsuki, baba nuku*" ("with a house, with a car, without an old lady").

The birthrate has been going down, but fewer Japanese being born has been counterbalanced by more Japanese living longer. The lifespan has stretched remarkably. Compared with what it was in 1900, it is twenty-eight years longer for men, who can now expect to live to seventy. Women's life expectancy has increased this century by twenty-eight years to seventy-six. The Japanese are now, like the Scandinavians and the Dutch, one of the longest-living people in the world.

Yet they are also a people who become old, economically speaking, when they are relatively young. Most big companies retire their employees when they reach 55, with a sum of money equal to about two years pay. The still-vigorous average retired men might find some other low-paid employment, but the over-55 people constitute an economic problem that is most acute in terms of the over-65s. Japan has been spending only 5 per cent of the national income on social services compared with Australia's 15 per cent. The elderly received only about a quarter as much of their income from the State as old people did in Britain and the U.S.A.

Seven hundred thousand aged Japanese lived alone. The suicide rate among aged Japanese women was the highest in the world.

If the causes of death remained constant, approximately twenty-eight of every hundred Japanese born in 1973 would die of diseases of the cerebral blood vessels (conditions such as apoplexy and thrombosis), eighteen would die of cancer (which was likely to be cancer of the stomach), and only fourteen would die of heart disease which is the West's major killer and the cause of thirty-nine out of every hundred deaths in the United States.

Another contrast is that New York has, I should think, at least a thousand psychoanalysts whereas Tokyo had, at the last count—six.

This is not to say that the Japanese are not given to anxieties: their cerebral

12   The Japanese

haemorrhage incidence and suicide rate attest that they are. One source of stress was indicated by an elderly guide I had. He said, "We are a peculiar people. We like to do difficult things."

This old man, who was highly literate, asked me if I knew the writings of James Joyce. I assumed that he was acquainted with Joyce only because he knew English, since Joyce expressed himself so often in terms of associated word sounds—as when he used "lemoncholy" for "melancholy"—and that same associativeness simply would not occur in another language.

The guide said there were two Japanese translations of Joyce's *Ulysses*, which is untranslatable.

"The rady rost her brue umblerra"

THE CHAPTER HEADING spells out how some Japanese might say, "The lady lost her blue umbrella". From the difficulty they have with the *l* and *r* sounds, and the way they invert these, the traveller derives some innocent amusement. We may even feel an inclination to applaud when we hear "telephone" turned into *terrorphone* and television spoken of as *terrorvision*.

In Tokyo I was late for a dinner engagement because a taxi-driver couldn't understand where I wanted to go when I said, "Imperial Hotel". After that I always carried in my pocket a matchbox from the hotel (pronounced *hoterru*) I was staying at.

Why does this inversion of *l* and *r* take place? An Englishman I met in Kyoto said, "It's perfectly simple, my dear fellow. They say *rady* for 'lady' because they haven't got an *l* to say 'lady' with. No *l* in the Japanese alphabet."

There is no such thing as a Japanese alphabet. They have ideograms, not letters—and when they romanize their language they use our alphabet. But in my Japanese-English dictionary there is not one word beginning with *l* (or with *v* or *x* or *th*).

So it seems odd when your Japanese guide, pointing out the train window at the tawny October cropfields, tells you that the rice is ripe and what you hear is, "The lice is lipe".

Ah, you say to yourself, this is the way the Chinese pronounce. 'Very' becomes *velly*. So you say to the guide, "Minoru-san, I'm told the harvest is *very* late this year." He replies, "It is rate, but not *berry* rate." Lacking *v* he uses *b*. But he doesn't lack *r* as the Chinese do: I've never heard a Japanese say *velly* or speak of the *chelly* blossom. But *brossom* some do say. Quite commonly, they turn *l* into *r*. So a Suzuki-san who had a lovely holiday in Honolulu may tell you that he went to Honoruru and had a rubbery horror-day.

"Your name Corin-san," a bar hostess would say, looking at my name card. "You come from Austrayria. Rong way."

"Long" we often hear as *rong* (and at times you may think something is being described as wrong); "blue" becomes *brue*, the "cloudy" day *crowdy*. I remember the air hostess, when I was returning from Hokkaido to Tokyo in 1960, telling her passengers that she hoped they had all had a good *fright*—and that the airline looked forward to having us aboard again "the next time you fry". It doesn't happen nowadays; at least it doesn't on the international services of Japan Air Lines, which is very conscious of its image as a suave and sophisticated carrier.

In Japanese speech there is a sound that is like a combination of *r* and *l*. When a Japanese, speaking our language, says the word "plank" we expect the *l* sound and, missing it, our ears detect the other part of the combination sound, the *r* part, and we hear "prank." Conversely, when a Japanese says

14   The Japanese

"prank" we may hear "plank". But the *l* sound is more likely to be heard as *r* than *r* is to be heard as *l*.

MANY JAPANESE are now speaking English with few lapses into what we might call the *umblerra* idiosyncrasy. They can do this, just as Dutchmen get round to saying *job* and *Jesus* instead of *yob* and *Yesus*; a few Englishmen even manage to speak French as the French do; and Torres Strait Islanders get over their inversion of *p* and *f*—which caused a rude-sounding rendition of an old hymn when they tearfully farewelled a beloved missionary with *We Parted on the Shore*.

The consonant *f* is another one the Japanese don't pronounce quite as we do. There is the story of an American lady golfer on a course in Japan who was shocked to hear a man in the Japanese foursome playing behind her call out in her direction, "Whore!" She felt stunned by the epithet—and very nearly was by the golf ball of the Japanese player who had sliced his drive and shouted in his best English a warning "Fore!" Their *f* has a lighter, blown sound with something of *h* in it.

We run consonants together, two and even three of them as in my name *Simpson*. The Japanese like their consonants separated by vowels. So I become (with the *p* discarded) Simison. They borrowed from English the word *strike*, to describe what to them was industrially unknown, a stoppage by workers: *strike* became *sutoraiki*. But there are exceptions to the rule. A case where the vowel between consonants is dropped is in the name of the beef dish that is first favourite with Western tourists in Japan, *sukiyaki*. Naturally enough, foreigners ask for *sookiyaaki*, which has come to be the expected pronunciation. But to the Japanese it is *s'keyaki*.

Our pronunciation style is to accent one syllable of a word: the Japanese usually stress the parts of a word evenly. *Hiroshima* isn't Hirro*SHEE*ma; and tourists who've heard about that being wrong are apt to call it HirOSHima. But that isn't quite right either—though it is better than the SHEEma pronunciation. It is He-rosh-ee-ma, evenly accented.

A convention of Japanese speech is that it is all right for a man to bid someone "good morning" with *ohayo* (pron. as Ohio), but not for a woman: she must add a polite expression and say *ohayo gozaimasu* (pron. go-zah-e-mahss). In expressing thanks she will not say simply *arigato* (pron. ah-re-gah-tow) but *arigato gozaimas'*. "Please" is *dozo* (that first *o* is dragged out).

There is the honorific *o*. One's own house is merely *uchi* but the house of another is politely referred to as *o-uchi* (honourable house).

The most commonly used honorific is *san*. It hyphens on to surnames (and, with friends, forenames) irrespective of sex and whether the person would be, with us, a Mr or Mrs or Miss. *San* is properly said, with the broadened *a*, more *saan* than *san*.

THE MOST IMPORTANT WORD in any foreign language can be, on occasions of urgency, the one that means lavatory. The tourist should forget that polite euphemism "toilet" which the Japanese turn into toiret (or *otearai*, which means "honourable wash-basin") and say *benjo*. It may be about as genteel as "loo" or "john" but it will get you there—and probably faster if you add a polite *dozo* or *kudasai* for "please".

To know a few words of the language of the country you are travelling in is—well, I almost wrote "essential". It isn't quite, if your language is English and you can afford to stay in first-class hotels where, invariably, some English will be spoken, and if you take tours with English-speaking guides. Better far than being born with a silver spoon in the mouth is to be born with an English tongue. We are the Lucky People whose language other peoples have to learn, which makes us the Lazy People because the same necessity is not there for us to learn another language.

Doubtless I should try harder; but most of the words I acquire seem to melt in my mind between one trip and the next. Also, I feel that I mustn't learn the language because doing so would turn me into the atypical traveller, something other than the *tourist* that I am; and I could no longer identify with the reader who hadn't learnt Japanese, nor could that reader identify with me. Nobody who sets out to learn Japanese should understimate what he or she is in for. The first time I was in Japan I met a Japanese woman writer who had written this: "In Japanese language exactness of expression is purposely avoided."[8] Lafcadio Hearn, who lived many years in Japan and took a Japanese name and a Japanese wife, never learnt the language because, as Hearn wrote: "Could you learn all the words in the Japanese dictionary you would not make yourself understood in speaking unless you learned to think like a Japanese—that is to say, to think backwards, to think upside-down and inside out."[9]

Japanese, says Fosco Maraini, is a language of extraordinary wealth, but of the most infernal complexity. It is "an exquisitely subjective language ... a magnificent language for love ... a language made for poetry or allusion, as well as for invective, panegyric, solemn discourse, for expressing feelings, and for underlining individual or social circumstances". But it is "incapable of constructing sentences of unequivocal meaning".[3]

Spoken Japanese has some structural kinship with the Korean language but it is very different from Chinese, which is monosyllabic, concise, uninflected; whereas Japanese is polysyllabic, diffuse and richly inflected. True, the Japanese took in a lot of Chinese words, for the same reason that English took in a lot of Greek and Latin—to express ideas, technical and abstract, that the indigenous language couldn't cope with—but they changed the words' meanings and pronunciations.

There is not one kind of Japanese writing but four: Kanji, the square-looking Chinese ideographs that run into thousands; Kata-kana and Hira-gana, two scripts which are quite different, the first looking a bit like shorthand and the other very cursive; and Romaji, which is Japanese written in our roman alphabet. Nearly all books are written in a mixture of Kanji and Kata-kana or Hira-gana.

Whereas our children learn word formation with a twenty-six-letter alphabet, "a Japanese child spends the first six years at school learning to read and write more than a thousand signs. It is true that learning an ideogram means learning an idea at the same time, and that the process is therefore not so time-wasting as it might seem. Nevertheless the strain on the eyes and the memory is great."[3]

In addition to mastering the three Chinese-based syllabaries and roman-style Japanese, the high school student learns English as well, or tries to.

Love of company, and change of shape

OF THEIR ECONOMIC CONDITION it was said in 1972 that the Japanese had "never had it so good"—even though a quarter of the eleven million people in Tokyo still lived in tiny flats where they had to share lavatories and bathrooms or go out to a public bath.

By 1974 there was economic recession, but nearly every Japanese home already had its washing machine and the ratio of colour television sets, higher than in the United States, was the highest in the world.

Two indicators that the Japanese the world was still inclined to think of as living frugally were consuming conspicuously were given in the book by Kakuei Tanaka[10] published in mid-1972 just before Mr Tanaka became Prime Minister: (i) Whereas the peak period of demand for electric power used to be December (mid-winter) for heating, the peak was now August (mid-summer), so widespread had become the use of air-conditioners for cooling; (ii) Japan entered 1972 with 21 million privately owned motor vehicles—the second largest number in the world. Not that Japan was, overall, a great country for the motorist. New York's ratio of road space to city area was three times Tokyo's. All Britain's roads were paved but only one-eighth of Japan's were.

The need for more and better highways, so that industries could be decentralized, was stressed by Mr Tanaka, who pointed out that 33 million people lived within fifty kilometres of the centre of the three largest cities, Tokyo, Osaka, Nagoya. A third of the population was living on 1 per cent of the land.

Japan in the early seventies was described as the third richest nation on earth, next to the U.S.A. and the U.S.S.R. The West's stock phrase for Japan's production performance was "an economic miracle". That performance was most impressive in terms of IPI (Industrial Production Index), relating 1972 production to the base year of 1960, which rated as 100. Japan's production had so increased that its index figure was 284—way ahead of the U.S.A.'s 150 and West Germany's 170. It had boomed to more than twice Britain's 130.

In 1972 the *boomu* balloon that had soared so high began descending. The extent of Japan's exports to the U.S.A. had provoked cutbacks. Then in 1973 came the Arab countries *shokku* of shocking oil prices. Japan was hardest hit of any major country because virtually every drop of oil it used had to be imported. It had to pay billions of yen more for its oil. So, in 1973 the price to the industrial consumer rose by 50 per cent, and household electricity went up by almost as much.

In mid-1974 Japan was, for the first time in six years, in the red as to its balance of payments, (but by the year's end it was back in the black). Its economic growth rate was in process of slowing from around 10 per cent a year to (depending on which economist you read) 6 per cent or $3\frac{1}{2}$ per cent

Love of company, and change of shape 17

or 2 per cent or zero. As to inflation, Japan's was among the highest in the world (only Iceland, Greece and Portugal had worse) with a rate of 23.2 per cent for the year ended May 1974. Prices had risen steeply, but so had wages, which rose by nearly 30 per cent in 1974 (but the "spring offensive" wage rise in 1975 was only 14 per cent).

The July 1974 elections made it plainer than ever before that the Liberal Democratic Party's prop, stay and virtual partner in government was the *Zaibatsu*, the Big Business plutocracy of companies. Mighty Mitsubishi fielded one of its employees as an LDP candidate, and spent an estimated $A2 million of company money on his campaign. Other LDP "corporate candidates" had the backing of the steelmaker-shipbuilder Nippon Kokan K.K., the Sumitomo Bank, Toyota the car-maker, and the electricals giant Hitachi.

Predictably the Socialist Party said, "The LDP is the political arm of big business", and that the corporations would expect Government pay-offs for their support. The LDP was returned, though with a reduced majority. The Socialist, Communist and Komeito ("Clean Government") parties made solid election gains.

A test case on the employee's right to hold dissident political views was taken at the end of 1973 by one Tatsuo Takano, aged thirty-three, who ten years earlier had been on a three-month management-training course with Mitsubishi Plastics. When the firm heard that, in college, Takano had taken part in an anti-government demonstration, Mitsubishi refused to have him on its staff. The Japanese Supreme Court upheld the firm's right to do this if it disapproved of his politics.

The company argued: "When we employ someone it is for life. Loyalty to the company is to be expected, like loyalty to the family, of which the company may be considered an extension."

IN THE MITSUBISHI group of companies one, Mitsubishi Heavy Industries, was ranked by *Fortune* in 1974 as the fourteenth largest company in the world outside the United States. In the same big league were Mitsubishi Chemicals, Mitsubishi Rayon, Mitsubishi Metal, Mitsubishi Petrochemical, Mitsubishi Mining and the Mitsubishi Bank. Subsidiary companies numbered thirteen hundred.

Mitsubishi's real estate company owns forty acres of Marunouchi, the main business district of Tokyo. (Street bowls of pansies and pavement beds of flowers made the street I walked from my hotel to the Foreign Correspondents Club the most comely street in Tokyo. But the city council didn't pay for its being so; Mitsubishi did.) Mitsubishi built much of the weaponry Japan used in the Second World War, including the Zero fighter plane. The American Occupation authorities, in their crackdown on the Zaibatsu, declared illegal both the name Mitsubishi and the famous triple-diamond trademark.

I have met Mitsubishi employees who wore the three-diamond lapel badge proudly. Their families could have lived in Mitsubishi apartments with rent as low as $A10 a month, electricity included. With the employee earning $A400 a month his housing was costing him only one-fortieth of his income, whereas Western workers commonly pay one-fifth. At Toyota, the car-maker, employees were likely to come off the Toyota tennis courts on a Sunday morning, go home to lunch in their low-rent Toyota apartment, then take a Toyota bus to a Toyota-provided afternoon concert. Or they attended the company's *ikebana* (flower-arrangement) classes or played chess at the Toyota Chess Club. There were five Toyota seaside resorts for holidays.

Mitsui, one of the biggest corporations, was also highly paternalistic. I talked to a Mitsui employee, a university-educated and most pleasant man, during a train journey on my first trip to Japan in 1955. Harada-san, aged thirty, said he was prepared to work very hard for promotion in a firm he felt fortunate to be with, and expected to be with for twenty-five years more until he retired at fifty-five. His salary at that time was only half his Australian counterpart's. He and his wife would have liked a second child, he said, but could not afford another. Food cost Harada-san a higher proportion of his income than it would have in Australia. Clothing was bought at bonus time: the twice-yearly bonus was equal to about ten weeks' pay. He smiled and shook his head when I asked if he had a car. He said he used a charcoal *hibachi* for heating because it was less expensive than an electric radiator.

The Harada-sans of 1974 could afford not only a radiator but a small car. The Australian worker still got a bigger pay cheque, but the Japanese worker's biannual bonuses and the low-rent company housing brought his "real" income close to parity with the Australian's. Indeed, when it came to owning a car the Japanese worker was better off, according to a survey made by Australia's *National Times*. It found that in order to buy a Corolla two-door sedan the Australian would have to work for nearly six months, whereas the Japanese could earn the in-Japan price in under four months.

But when it came to buying a house the Australian worker was far more likely to achieve his modest "dream home"—and on a sizeable block of land such as only a rich man in Japan could afford.

IN A POLL of twenty-eight thousand workers taken by the Labour Ministry no less than 37 per cent said they felt happiest, "when I am devoting myself to my work and when the result of my work has been appreciated by my superiors".

Yet many Japanese companies gave only three days of paid holiday a year— one in four did not grant a paid vacation—and only a quarter of Japan's leading companies provided for two days off at the weekend. Many employees still worked six days a week. By 1974 the five-day week had spread to about half all businesses with more than a hundred employees.

Because the paternalism of the Japanese company shields workers from unemployment (which in late 1974 was 1.5 per cent in Japan, 3 per cent in Australia, 6 per cent in U.S.A.) it might be assumed that the company is, at least, spared labour troubles and demands for high wages by trade unions. Such an assumption caused Herman Kahn, the author of a 1971 best-seller *The Emerging Japanese Superstate*,[11] to write confidently that the Japanese worker would never rock the boat and jeopardize Japanese competitiveness by making wage demands of more than an affordable 20 per cent a year, certainly nothing like 32 per cent—which is what Japanese unions demanded, and got, in their "spring offensive" of 1974. In pointing out how wrong Kahn was, one of the most astute of Tokyo foreign correspondents, Gregory Clark, wrote:[12] "Many workers identify the trade union rather than the employer with the firm."

Unions are usually related to one enterprise—to the factory, not to the

High school girls at Kumamoto pass by a legless supplicant and a concertina player, veterans of a war that only one in five of today's Japanese remembers.

On a railway platform at Maibara some schoolboys, seeing my camera, struck attitudes that reflected movie-TV violence; others just grinned attractively.

"Bullet" train streaking out of central Tokyo through the Ginza region. These expresses, the fastest in the world, reach speeds of 260 kilometres an hour.

Ricefields cover much of Japan's one-sixth-arable land. Harvesting is mechanized but planting seedlings is still a back-aching task, for women and men.

The purest form of Japanese religious architecture is beautifully typified at Ise by this sanctuary building, part of the most sacred of all Shinto shrines. Of natural wood with straight thatched roofs (lacquer and curved roofs came later), the Ise shrines complex is rebuilt every twenty years to the pattern that was set 1,300 years ago. Furnishings also are made anew.

The torii is the gateway to every Shinto shrine. Legendary origin of its shape is that a perch was set up for roosters to crow on at daybreak, outside a cave where the Sun Goddess had hidden. By this pretence that the people had another goddess to bring the sunrise, Ameratasu was lured out, and the light of the sun was restored to the world.

Love of company, and change of shape   19

industry or craft. There are thousands of them, and about twelve million Japanese, a quarter of all the workforce, are unionists. The biggest and most potent federation of unions, Sohyo, is closely allied with the Japan Socialist Party.

A JAPANESE CAR MAKER, Mazda, was in 1974 running an advertisement for its cars in Australian papers with the heading "OUR IRON ORE COMES HOME IN GREAT SHAPE". It said that Australians had bought 125,000 Mazdas, in which the steel was made from Australian iron ore.

That Japan bought $A427 million worth of that ore in the 1973-74 fiscal year was a big factor in the special trade relationship that had developed between Japan and Australia in the decade that began in 1964. Japan was importing more than half of all the minerals mined in Australia. It took 90 per cent of exported Australian coal, and 80 per cent of the iron exports. It had also been buying 40 per cent of Australia's wool and 18 per cent of Australia's beef—about 85 per cent of all the beef Japan imported—before its 1974 ban on beef imports to give Japanese meat-growers more market. Japan was also a big buyer of Australia's bauxite, manganese, nickel, copper, zinc, lead, sugar, salt—and was the biggest potential customer for Australia's big reserves of uranium and natural gas.

Australia's Prime Minister Whitlam said in October 1974, "Japan is our largest export market, taking 31 per cent of all Australian exports". Japan bought three times as much as Australia's next-best customer, the United States. So Australia's "special" relationship with Japan was much as an arch's is to its keystone. Without the Japanese market the Australian economy and living standard would lose the support Australia depended upon even more than Japan depended upon the supply of Australia's raw materials.

Australia could have more difficulty in finding alternative markets for over $2,000 million worth of its raw materials a year than Japan could in getting more iron from Brazil, more coal from Siberia, more copper from Congo, more bauxite from Jamaica, enough uranium from Africa, and greater access to undeveloped resources of iron, coal and oil in China.

Because Japan would evidently be a tremendous customer for Australia's coal in 1975 and had contracted to buy 73 million tons of Australian iron ore in that year in order to produce an anticipated 120 million tons of steel (which is getting close to what the world's biggest steelmaker, the U.S.A., has been producing), the tendency was to assume that there was next to no chance of the chill to the Japanese economy developing into a serious and highly infective malady.

If such a Japanese depression should happen it will come as no surprise to an economist of the notable Waseda University in Tokyo, Professor Haruo Naniwada. He wrote in early 1974 that Japan's rate of growth had been so recklessly high that it had put Japanese industry in hock to the banks to the extent that 84 per cent of capital was borrowed. This debt to the banks was beyond industry's capacity to repay, he said, and economic Doomsday was just round the corner. Professor Naniwada predicted an end to Japan's modern era so disastrous that it would be, he said, comparable to the fall of the Roman Empire.

On the other hand the president of the Japan Economic Research Centre, the respected Mr Hisao Kanamori, had little doubt that Japan would fly through the economic turbulence and become the world's richest nation by 1985. And MITI (Ministry of International Trade and Industry) appeared to share his view.

But, even if the Japanese economy revitalized and continued to bound ahead, it might well do so in a different shape. The planners at MITI and EPA (Economic Planning Agency) proposed a Japan that relied less on oil and more on atomic energy (there was a plan to build about fifty nuclear power plants by 1985), less on heavy industry using coal and ores and much more on sophisticated manufacturing where the prime input was not materials but knowledge. From such an economy one would expect more airliners and fewer oil tankers, not so many cars but a lot more computers and contact lenses.

That kind of economy would also reduce Japan's problems of industrial pollution, be more in line with a society that increasingly values higher education (Japan now has four hundred universities) and is much less agricultural and blue-collar than it was a decade ago, much more technology-minded and white-collar.

A Japanese economy of that altered shape would not, however, be nearly as complementary to the Australian economy as it has been, and it was not to be expected that from it the same degree of mercantile prosperity would rub off on Australia.

this was japan

昔の日本

A shrine is built, for the sixtieth time

"SINCE THIS LAND OF ISE is a land where no turbulent tempests blow, and is a peaceful land where the twang of the bow and the hiss of the arrow are never heard, I desire to rest in this land."

So, in Japanese mythology, spoke the Sun Goddess, Amaterasu. She, more than any other deity, was the symbol of the Japan that is called the Land of the Rising Sun, the nation with the big red round of the sun on its national flag. And the *Jingu*, the Grand Shrine of the Shinto religion, was built at Ise (pron. Eesay), which is down the east coast of Honshu from Tokyo, about three hours by train.

This shrine at Ise—which is actually a number of shrines—is said to have been founded in 4 B.C., in terms of our calendar; not that any historian will vouch for any date in Japanese history before the seventh century. However, Shintoism's exact age as the native religion of Japan doesn't much matter. Clearly it was a going religion for some seven hundred years before India's Buddhism came in from Korea-China.

The Japanese solved the problem of choosing between two religions in a unique way. They retained the old while adopting the new. So, at the last count in 1970, the number of Shintoists was 83 million and Buddhists 87 million, making 170 million: yet the population then was only 105 million. Most people were adherents of both faiths.

To the shrines of Ise come four million visitors a year; but they are referred to not as "visitors" but as "pilgrims", Ise being a Japanese Mecca of a kind. I was certainly no pilgrim, but I felt a certain gratification at getting to Ise at last. It was not that on five earlier sojourns in Japan I had been unaware of these shrines and their significance. But Ise is not a place the Japanese tourist people urge upon the foreign tourist, to whom it can't be the spiritual experience it is to the Japanese. Apart from that, Ise has nothing spectacular like the big Buddha at Kamakura, nothing vivid like the vermilion Katsuga shrine at Nara, nothing opulent like the Tokugawa mausoleum at Nikko. Ise is a subtle place, a very Japanese place, and the Japanese are right, I think, in feeling that the average Westerner can't understand it.

Ise is religion, and religions are not for understanding, anyway: they are for believing in. A Moslem who believed that if he died for Allah on the battlefield his reward was to go straight up to a heavenly whorehouse of houris could hardly be expected to understand the Christian's non-copulatory God whose Son had to be born free of all stain of sexual intercourse by having the Virgin for His mother. In Shintoism, too, there is this acceptance of sexuality from which Christianity turns away. The Japanese creation myths, which used to be spoken by reciters, didn't get written down until the seventh century when writing came in from China. The old chronicles describe the couplings and creations of the gods with what Fosco Maraini calls "magnificently solemn obscenity".[3]

Yet the early form of the church of this religion, which we see at Ise, is a simple but beautiful wooden structure built in a style that is remarkable for what one can only call its purity. But that is hardly as extraordinary as the fact that the Japanese, who brought the Shinto shrine to this aesthetic form thirteen hundred years ago, have been, ever since then, *rebuilding the Ise shrines anew, exactly in that form, every twenty years.*

They were rebuilt for the fifty-ninth time in 1953, and now there are the new shrines that were completed in 1973.

SHINTO (*shin* = gods, *to* = way of) is a religion without scriptures or ethical commandments. It evolved out of nature worship. It endowed natural forces and objects and certain humans with a kind of godhead called *kami*. Its pantheon increased until it was said to have "800 million" gods.

The progenitors of these, and of physical Japan, were Izanagi, whose form was that of a handsome young man, and his beautiful sister, Izamani. She said of her body, "It grows and grows continually, only there is one part that does not grow." Her brother Izanagi said, "My body, too, grows and grows, and there is one part that grows to excess," and he suggested the insertion of that excessively growing part of his body into that part of hers that was not growing. From this incestuous union the islands of Japan were born along with gods of trees, mountains, rivers and the elemental forces.

In giving birth to the god of fire Izamani was so badly burned that she died and went to the afterworld. Here the distraught Izanagi sought her and, feeling polluted by his contact with the nether regions, bathed to purify himself. (Purificatory rites are very much part of Shinto. Especially is this so for the priests, whose garb is white—not that they are celibates. Before entering a shrine the worshipper washes his hands and rinses his mouth with water. The cleanliness so characteristic of the Japanese is founded in their native religion.)

Izanagi purified himself by bathing in the sea. His diving in caused the birth of sea gods. When he washed his left eye the goddess of the sun, Amaterasu, was born; and, from washing his right eye, the goddess of the moon, Tsukiyomi. Washing his nose produced a god who, later, turned out to be a holy terror, Susanowo.

Susanowo joined with his Sun Goddess sister Amaterasu in creating some children, though not in the usual way. Amaterasu took her brother's sword, broke the blade into pieces and "after having chewed them blew a light mist from her mouth which gave birth to three goddesses".[13] Susanowo then took the strings of jewels his sister was wearing and, after cracking them between his teeth, blew a light mist from his mouth that gave birth to five masculine deities—which Amaterasu claimed as her children because they came from her jewels.

The eight were to become venerated as the ancestors of Japan's most noble families, including the imperial family—and that peculiar piece of myth was the basis of the claim that the emperors of Japan were descended from the Sun Goddess. And because the Imperial Household still reverences Amaterasu as its ancestral deity, the Emperor has the closest relationship with the Grand Shrine of Ise. Four times a year he sends an envoy with a

A shrine is built, for the sixtieth time

splendid offering of clothes to the goddess—who, incidentally, receives daily offerings of food and rice from the priests.

To return to the legend: Amaterasu hid in a cave, because brother Susanowo had run amuck. The disappearance of the Sun Goddess plunged the world into darkness. The other gods determined to get the light back. So they set up, first, a bird perch for cocks to crow on and convey that, Amaterasu or no Amaterasu, dawn was breaking. This perch was the origin of the *torii* that is the gateway to every Shinto shrine.

Then the gods made a mirror of polished metal (Japan had no looking-glasses until Europeans came, nor had China) and hung the mirror on a tree. Then a goddess named Ama no Uzume danced on top of a drum-like tub. Ama no Uzume got carried away and threw her clothes off and made her dance a lewd one, causing all the assembled gods to roar with laughter (which sounds like a record response to a striptease performed in pitch darkness, but perhaps the Moon Goddess, Tsukiyomi, was present and lent some light).

Amaterasu, in the cave, wondered what on earth was going on—with all this ribaldry, and shouts that the gods had found someone they liked better than the Sun Goddess. Peeking out, she was fascinated to see her reflection in the mirror, and on another tree a fine string of jewels. She came right out, and the world was bathed in light again.

The Sacred Mirror (it is always written of like that in English, with capitals) is said to be preserved to this day and is the holiest of all Shinto objects because, having once held the reflection of Amaterasu, it is supposed to retain something of the goddess's image. It has not been seen by anyone since the Emperor Meiji had it sealed in a box which is borne by a procession of priests to the newly rebuilt inner shrine of Ise when the sacred objects are removed every twenty years. The removal is always made under cover of darkness.

Among Shinto's other treasures, next to the Sacred Mirror is the jewelled Sacred Sword called Kusanagi. This came, according to legend, from Susanowo who stopped making a nuisance of himself for long enough to kill a marauding eight-headed serpent, and he found the wondrous sword in the serpent's tail. The precious sword is never exhibited either, but is kept at the Atsuta shrine in Nagoya, which I had visited on my way to Ise. Then there are the Sacred Jewels that were hung on the tree outside Amaterasu's cave. They are in Tokyo, at the Emperor's palace.

There are other treasures—one is the model of a man with an elaborately caparisoned horse, and others are swords—and there are 525 kinds of garments made in the style of the Nara Period (A.D. 710–794), 1,085 items altogether that are all refashioned anew every twenty years. The "old" ones are destroyed by burning, lest pollution attach to them, I was told by the Director at the Grand Shrine, a priest in secular dress who was introduced as the "Reverend" Hagiwara.

Director Hagiwara had all the figures and costs on the whole renewal operation that was completed in 1973—but those remarkable statistics we can come to.

THE SETTING at Ise is grander than the shrines, if we see nature as grand when it pillars the sides of gravelled paths with great-trunked cryptomeria-trees, the pines that are called Japanese cedars, or *sugi*, and soar to a height of forty metres. The shrines and the many pilgrims don't quite dispel a sense of the "forest primeval".

From a plane flying over—and this would not be allowed at low altitude—one would have trouble in discerning the shrines amid the trees. Nothing is coloured with paint. This is Japanese woodwork as it used to be before it took on the lacquer of Chinese vermilion.

Natural wood expresses the primal Shinto aesthetic. Not that wood, natural or painted, was chosen for reasons of aesthetics so much as for reasons of earthquakes. Building in stone was out: a Japanese Parthenon would soon have been shaken to the ground. For the same seismic reason Japanese castles, though based on massive stoneworks, were built of wood.

Japanese taste saw virtue in simplicity of design—the austerity of the straight line was preferred to the sensuousness of the curve—and refinement was equated with restraint, whereas Chinese taste ran to opulent embellishment. In part, this had to do with Japan's being a poorer country and Chinese civilization's being more advanced in technical resources. To that extent the Japanese made virtues of necessities. But there was more to it than that. Culturally, the Japanese never became offshore Chinese, however much they took in from China, because they never let go of their indigenous artistry and craftsmanship.

The main (inner) shrine is not large, hardly more than eleven metres long by five and a half wide. The greater part of it is raised two and a half metres off the ground on round wooden columns, supporting a "veranda". The larger columns go through to the roof, which is very thickly thatched and has long overhanging eaves. Along the ridge of the roof six log-like round billets of wood project in a quite distinctive style. From each end of the ridge thin beams project skyward at an angle that accords with the slant of the roof.

The walls of the shrine are of the same wood as the columns, pale blond *hinoki* (Japanese cypress), plain unvarnished planks finished to satin smoothness. The effect, especially when a shrine is just newly built, is one of pristine beauty arising from a simplicity of forms finely harmonized and amounting to Japanese classicism in design. The effect of "purity" is such that an Ise shrine makes a baroque Spanish cathedral of the Blessed Virgin look positively sensual by comparison.

The only embellishments are of gilded copper, beautifully fashioned and laid flatly on the timbers, in places where they provide an accent of artistry like some elegance of jewellery setting off a superbly simple gown.

Not that one can inspect the *Naiku* (inner shrine) building closely, because only the specially privileged are allowed beyond a gateway. In the precincts photography is forbidden, as is smoking and talking loudly. At some distance from this shrine of the Sun Goddess Amaterasu is the *Geku* (outer shrine) dedicated to Toyouke, the goddess who presides over foodstuffs, clothing and dwellings, the material necessities of life. Then there are the *Bekku* (affiliated shrines) and there are 14 of these together with 109 lesser shrines. So the number of buildings—which include treasuries where the sacred clothing and objects are kept, purification halls, storehouses, the hall where ritual dances and sacred music are performed, the quarters that accommodate a legion of priests, the kitchen for the preparation of the Sun Goddess's food (the fire is still started in the "pure" manner by the friction of two pieces of wood), and the stable where two sacred horses are kept—*all* of

A shrine is built, for the sixtieth time

these buildings are rebuilt anew every twenty years.

Director Hagiwara said the sixtieth rebuilding completed in 1973 was spread over eight years and took 122,535 man-hours of work. When I wrote down this figure he went off and came back with an exercise book from which he read out that the wood used accounted for 13,671 *hinoki*-trees, and into the thatching of the roofs went 25,800 bundles of the pampas-like *susuki*-grass. Renewing the fences required 12,300 poles of bamboo; and 8,713 hours of metal-working used 37 tonnes of copper and eleven kilograms of gold.

"And what did it all cost?" I asked the director.

He gave the figure of Y4,587 million (over $A11 million).

Some say there will never be another rebuilding of the Ise shrines. Not only will twenty more years of modern thought have eroded religious belief in Japan and laid new emphasis on expenditure priorities in a country lagging behind Western societies in its spending on social welfare; it is further argued that the craftsmen to do the work in the traditional ways will not be around in the years preceding 1993.

I don't expect to be around then either, to see whether there is another rebuilding of the Ise shrines, at a cost inflated to some astronomical figure. But I wouldn't be too surprised if it all happened again for the sixty-first time.

The chrysanthemum and, alas, the sword

THE EMPEROR of Japan remains, in a world that pays less and less attention to monarchies, a monarch whose dynasty is the oldest in the world. Probably it goes back to the third century, historically. But legend sometimes shaped itself as history in the Japanese mind.

So on a day in 1940, the year before the country Pearl-Harboured its way into the Second World War, fifty thousand people gathered in front of the Imperial Palace in Tokyo to celebrate the 2,600th anniversary of the founding of the Japanese empire by the first emperor, on a precise date which was 11 February 660 B.C.

No Japanese historian who wanted to keep a teaching post at a university, or simply stay out of jail, would have pointed out that there was no historical basis for this celebration. Nor was there historical evidence that Emperor Hirohito was descended from a first emperor whose name was Jimmu and who was regarded as being descended from the Sun Goddess, Amaterasu. However, in dealing with myths it is as well to remember the dictum of Robert Graves that "whatever happens among the gods above reflects events on earth" and that myth can be "a dramatic shorthand record of such matters as invasion, migrations, dynastic changes, admission of foreign cults and social reforms".[13]

To the historian Storry[14] this mythology suggests that there were "perhaps two main streams of migration from Asia to Japan", and Jimmu was the leader of a migrant expedition that conquered the region known as Yamato, where the Ise shrines are, to the south of modern Kyoto; the other stream went to Izumo on the western side of Honshu not far from modern Matsue. Here the Earth God, Susanowo, not the Sun Goddess, was the paramount deity; and this is said to reflect a real historical rivalry between two peoples, of whom the Yamato Japanese produced the emperors. As Tomlin says, "Even today the Emperor, whose personal shrine is Ise, may not enter the inner precincts of the Izumo shrine."[5]

Racially, the Japanese are Mongoloid relatives of the Koreans and the Chinese—at least that seems to be the view of most ethnologists. When I was first in Japan I met a knowledgeable man who described the Japanese as "basically South Sea Islanders invigorated by a cooler climate". He didn't deny that some had come direct from the Asian mainland, just as, he contended, the Oriental-eyed islanders of Micronesia had originally. The islanders who migrated to Japan, he said, came in via the Philippines and got mixed up with the Malays on the way. He thought Emperor Jimmu's family were probably Okinawa pirates who plundered into Kyushu.

WHOEVER the first Japanese were, the aborigines they dispossessed were a pale-skinned, rounder-eyed, Caucasoid people. The Ainu—often called the "Hairy" Ainu because they are very hirsute compared with Mongoloids—may have spread all over the Japanese islands, judging by the widespread Ainu place names: *Fuji*, the famous mountain, is an Ainu name. Like Australia's aborigines the Ainu were driven from the best land to the less desirable regions. The Ainu remnant have become, rather sadly, a tourist attraction in the least-populated, coldest, wildest part of Japan, the northern island of Hokkaido (which we'll come to).

Of the little that is known about prehistoric Japan, the main statements come to us through the archaeologists and are made in clay. Pottery of a ruggedly impressive kind called Jomon (meaning "rope-design" or "cord-marked") has been carbon-dated back to 5000 B.C. for the decorative kind, and purely functional pots are said to go back to 10,000 B.C. and be the most ancient prehistoric pottery so far known.

Some scholars won't have it that the primitive Ainu culture was capable of producing these strongly designed Jomon pots. A decorative Ainu plate that took my wife's eye and we bought in Hokkaido is design of a high order—most distinctive and quite unlike anything Japanese. Not as old as Jomon ware is Yayoi (clay-tube) pottery, which *does* look Japanese and expresses itself mainly in figures and clay horses for tomb decoration. (Good examples of Yayoi can be seen at the National Museum in Tokyo.)

A QUICK CLIMB up the ladder of Japanese history can aid the tourist's view of Japan. The bottom rung of the ladder is in the fourth century A.D.: here recorded history begins.

The earliest records are Chinese, and they tell of a Japanese Queen Himoko who rules not only the state called Yamato but thirty smaller states as well. At this stage rice cultivation has been going on for about four centuries and bronze and iron have been in use for three. There is contact with China and Korea. In the fifth century when a *Tenno* (emperor) dies a huge tomb is built, rather in the shape of a broadened keyhole, with a great mound in the middle and a moat all round.

Midway through the sixth century Japan gets Buddhism, from Korea. The scholarly and devout Prince Shotoku, regent in 593, not only advances Buddhism but introduces the Chinese system of administration and the Chinese calendar. There are now a hundred thousand Chinese and Koreans living in Japan.

A new capital is built, modelled on the T'ang dynasty's capital of Ch'ang-an. This, in 710, becomes Nara. Just as the T'ang dynasty in China is synonymous with artistic excellence so is the Nara period in Japan and the Heian period that follows, taking its name from Heian-kyo, the city that succeeds Nara as the capital, and becomes Kyoto. Japan is no longer a cultural dependancy of China: it is breaking out of the Chinese mould and making its own pattern.

Not only is there innovation in temple architecture, in sculpture, in painting, but a remarkable Japanese literature begins—and the main writers are women, ladies of the luxurious Court. Most notable is Lady Murasaki, whose *Tale of Genji* (about "Shining Prince" Genji) will come to be regarded as the world's first psychological novel. It is written, about the year 1000, not in Chinese (which men study but women are not supposed to) but in the

Japanese syllabary. Poetry is so much part of the Heian nobility's life, and professional poets are in such demand in order to have sensitive tributes brushed onto scrolls, that the Court has to set up a Bureau of Poetry. "Perhaps at no time has life been lived so consistently at the level of aesthetic refinement."[5]

AFTER THE CHRYSANTHEMUM, the sword .... The flowering of artistry at the Heian Court withers during the twelfth century, in the hot breath of civil wars. Two great family factions, the Minamoto and the Taira (also called the Genji and Heike), each seek the kind of influence at Court that was long enjoyed by the Fujiwara family, through marrying its daughters to emperors' sons. The samurai spirit now dominates Japan, and what distinguishes the samurai from other men are his swords.

The samurai (the name means "one who serves") has had his beginnings as a bodyguard, necessary because the desperate poverty of peasants has driven many of them to brigandage. The samurai role expands to that of professional warrior, of something akin to Europe's knight (whose chivalry was much overstated), and sometimes it rises to that of *daimyo*, feudal lord. The samurai has two swords, his long curved weapon and his short dagger-like one, which has ritual use for disembowelling in the honourable suicide of *hara-kiri* or *seppuku*. Even a lesser samurai is entitled to cut down any commoner whose demeanor he considers insulting. One reason that civil war is constant is that sword-power begets aggression, and no samurai who lives by the sword wants to see it sheathed.

The Minamoto-Taira struggle ends in 1192 with a Minamoto being appointed *shogun* (generalissimo). He rules not from Kyoto, where the emperor remains a figurehead, but from Kamakura. This military government is called the *Bakafu* (literally "tent government"). Control of the country is to be held by whoever can hold it by military strength for seven hundred years before power is returned to the Imperial House. In Kyoto one emperor is reduced to selling specimens of his calligraphy.

The Kamakura period sees the samurai becoming more civilized, concerned with the fine design of his sword as well as its head-lopping capability, giving thought to elegance in his armour, and to character composure through the disciplines of Zen (meaning "meditation") Buddhism. So the arts thrive.

Meanwhile the midwives of the poor paste paper over the mouths and nostrils of infants that families cannot afford to feed. Farmers live in houses with thick thatched roofs and, often enough, nothing but earth for the floor. The town élite have houses more heavily timbered than those we associate with Japan: not until the fifteenth century does the style of house with sliding paper doors and floors of *tatami* appear—a new architecture whose serene simplicity owes much to Zen.

Buddha's image is reared enormously in bronze at Kamakura. Kublai Khan, the mighty Mongol butcher, strives to invade Japan, and just fails to do so. Marco Polo, who does not set foot in the country, tells the West that Japan exists, calls it Zipangu and suggests that it is stiff with gold. For several centuries Japan is riven with more civil wars, which are still going on when in 1543 a Portuguese ship, blown off course, puts in to an island south of Kyushu. Its arrival is epochal, because it has what the war-minded Japanese have never seen before—guns. So impressive are their firearms that the Portuguese are allowed to come again, and bring Christianity.

It is 1560. The shogunate, back at Kyoto from Kamakura, is government without control. Japan is a clutch of mini-kingdoms, each daimyo fortifying a castle town to defend his domain—or to launch assaults on his neighbours, as the daimyo Oda Nobunaga does victoriously when he puts aside the bow and arrow and makes full use of the new weapon, the musket. Nobunaga emerges as the strong man, with the Shogun as his puppet. When enemies contrive Nobunaga's death, his leading general, Hideyoshi, makes himself master of the entire country (except the northern island, Hokkaido, which is left to the barbarian Ainu).

Hideyoshi, being of lowly birth, cannot be a shogun. So he brings the Emperor out of the shadows and rules in the role of prime minister or regent. Although he is the son of a peasant foot-soldier, Hideyoshi sees class rigidity as essential to national unity, and he forbids peasants to possess swords, and farmers to become merchants, though he encourages commerce almost as much as he cultivates the arts. Dwarfish and monkey-faced, he is devoted to the Noh play and the tea ceremony. He smashes martial Buddhist monasteries and is tolerant of Christianity until, suspecting European designs on Japan, he bans the missionaries and has some of them crucified. Dreaming of a Peking capital to a Japanese empire, Hideyoshi launches invasion against China. His forces cruelly ravage Korea, but the only apparent benefit to Japan is that some Korean war prisoners bring in techniques to make better ceramics. From Korea, too, comes printing—and copper cash in place of rice as currency.

Hideyoshi dies in 1598. His heirs quarrel. The head of the powerful Tokugawa family, Ieyasu, seizes control and rules as shogun, from his castle at Edo (which is to become Tokyo, meaning "eastern capital").

TOKUGAWA Japan is to have unprecedented peace (apart from peasant risings and some slaughter of Japanese Christians) for 250 years. Tokugawa-brand feudalism makes it virtually impossible for the daimyos to overthrow the shogunate. Daimyos have to live off and on at Edo and, when they are not in residence, leave their wives and children there as hostages. They have to contribute so heavily to Tokugawa projects they are not left sufficiently rich to finance trouble. And they are under the eye of the world's most efficient secret police.

Loyalty and obedience are further inculcated by encouragement of Confucianism. Isolating Japan from the outside world is also good for the primacy of the Tokugawas. So the door is closed on Europeans (except that it is left slightly ajar for the Dutch).

As well as feudalism and isolationism, national disasters—earthquakes, tidal waves, the Great Fire of Edo in 1702, then Mount Fuji's last eruption—play some part in hobbling Japan's social progress. Midway through the nineteenth century it still has to enter what we call the modern world.

America, for commercial reasons, wants the Japanese door opened. Its first mission ignored, the United States sends Commodore Perry in 1853 and, when he returns in the following year with his potent-looking "black ships", he gets a treaty. This the Imperial Court does not welcome, but the shogunate, accepting realities, ratifies it.

32   This *was* **Japan**

Then, after internal ferment and fighting, it is the shogunate that falls and, ironically, the great changes are ushered in with restoration of power to the emperor. "A return to antiquity," say tradition-loving Japanese as they espouse the transformation of their feudal state into a modern one.

"We can beat these big white softies"

OF WHAT HAPPENED during the reign, from 1868, of the Meiji ("Enlightened") Emperor enough has already been said about such measures as the introduction of the railway. A modern Japan did not obliterate the old Japan: it was superimposed on it, and Japanese characteristics showed through. The chrysanthemum of artistry continued its flowering. The sword—although the samurai were ordered in 1876 to stop wearing swords—was certainly not beaten into a ricefield ploughshare.

The martial spirit of the Japanese expressed itself in two wars during the Meiji era, with China (1894-5) and Russia (1904-5). Both were decisively won and paid dividends. When the First World War broke out Japan was already a power, one of the "Big Five", a useful ally.

"It goes back to that 1914 war," Longman, the knowledgeable old-hand Englishman I met on my first visit to Japan, said when we talked about why Japan launched itself into the Second World War. "If you remember, it was a white man's war. Brown men were not to kill white men. The Japanese Navy could escort, but it couldn't fight. They felt badly about that. But when they were admitted to the League of Nations they felt that their place in the world was secure. They soon found out it wasn't. They looked for access to raw materials and they looked for markets; and they ran up against trade-tariff barriers. They wanted more living space, but no one was likely to give it to them—they were just a lot of Japs. So they took Manchuria. And then they began to think, 'We're only little blokes, but we're the sons of the gods, and if we train hard enough we can beat these big, white softies.' And how they trained, how *hard*! Forced marches, ruthless regimentation, bravery to order—their soldiers had it drummed and bashed into them that they were expendable in the cause of *Dai Nippon*, Greater Japan.

"The military had the whiphand of government. They whipped and whipped and they couldn't stop. It became government by assassination. 'Put our general into that ministry,' they'd demand. And if he wasn't put in, the politician who was would be bumped off. Or if they didn't get their way they wouldn't supply a War Minister to the Cabinet."

In 1934 the Director of Military Education didn't please the war-pathers (Longman went on). A sergeant walked into his office and killed him in cold blood. The sergeant didn't resist arrest. He had carried out a "divine mission". When the police grabbed him, his military cap fell off. He cried like a child at the disgrace.

"We talk about 'Japan'," said Longman. "Who was then 'Japan'? It was the Army. And who was the Army? It was mainly career officers, who were far from being Sandhurst and West Point types; not the sons of the old samurai families, but more often than not the sons of poor farmers. They hated the aristocracy, whom they identified with the absentee landlords who had ground their fathers into poverty and caused their sisters to be sold into brothels. They hated the intellectuals. They hated Western culture. They were earthy little brutes as hard as nails, who imagined themselves to be the new-day samurai. They loved to bust the nose and break the glasses of any new recruit who showed any sensibility.

"A lot of people in Japan didn't want that war. There were the mothers who hid their sons. And the sons were dragged out and shot before their eyes as a warning to other mothers not to try the same thing. There was hate of the Army—but it was in a people trained to subservience and obedience to the will of the Emperor, for whom the militarists professed to speak.

"The Emperor was God, if you like, but he was just as remote. He'd been put back in his box, as he had been before the Meiji Restoration, to be brought out when it was necessary for him to utter some edict. All he knew was what his advisers told him—he was literally out of this world. The Emperor at that time was no more than an idolized talking doll on the knees of the military clique.

"The Prime Minister at the time, Prince Konoye, did not want a Pacific war. When General Tojo replaced Konoye there was no hope of the Pearl Harbour plan not being put into effect. The Army was hell bent for war. The Navy didn't want it."

AS A RESULT of that war Japan lost some two million killed, one in three of whom were civilians. The Allies bombed 119 Japanese cities and 60 were, in aggregate, destroyed to the extent of 40 per cent. Tokyo was more terribly devastated than it had been by the Great Earthquake of 1923; appalling fires engulfed its wooden houses and so many people fled the capital that its population went down from nearly eight million to three million. Ten million Japanese lost their homes, and one factory in every three was destroyed. The Japanese Navy was eleven-twelfths sunk or smashed, and of ten million tons of merchant shipping only one million tons remained afloat. Lost, too, was a small empire of island possessions—Formosa (Taiwan), the Marianas, the Pescadores, even Okinawa (since returned). Japan, as Longman said, was "battered half to death".

"Look at Japan today. They're an astonishingly resilient and diligent people," he said, speaking in 1955. At that time, only ten years after the surrender that followed the atomic-bombing of Hiroshima and Nagasaki (dealt with in chapters on those places), the war was still fresh in our minds and theirs. A brilliant young doctor I called Senri-san who was my guide in Osaka and Nara (and is, as I write, a cardiologist and Associate Professor Hirakawa at Gifu University) was at school when the war began. At fifteen his high school lessons stopped and the boys went to build wooden planes for the training of fighter pilots who would bring down those emissaries of all evil, the B-29 bombers that were unloading death and destruction on nearby Osaka.

"We were taught," Senri Hirakawa said, "that we were fighting the forces of evil—'Satan' America and 'Devil' Britain."

When a B-29 got hit by anti-aircraft fire and the crew had to bale out and land in a ricefield the military police had great trouble in preventing the angry farmers from killing the American "devils".

The largest religious building in the world doesn't look enormous against Fujiyama (snowless in summer), but it is said to be as remarkable in its architecture as the Sydney Opera House; and it cost about as much, over $A100 million. It is the Sho-Hondo (meaning Great Hall) of the Soka Gakkai (meaning Value-Creating Society), a neo-Buddhist sect that was founded in 1937, suppressed during the Second World War and, since then, has built up a membership of ten million. The Sho-Hondo, completed in 1972, consists of a plaza called the Garden of the Law, a Pavilion of Perfect Harmony, a Temple of Purification, and a vast Mystic Sanctuary which is covered by a suspension roof without pillars. Says the Soka Gakkai: "The ideological basis of our movement is respect for humanity and nature, and its major aim is the creation of an absolutely peaceful society in which to develop world-wide happiness and prosperity". And: "The image behind the artistic conception of the building is that of a beautiful crane with its wings outspread, as if about to soar into the sky."

The Ginza's neon brilliance was dimmed after the 1973 Arab oil crisis cut electricity, but in 1975 this major spectacle of night-time Tokyo was much restored.

Renowned for its lavish and dramatic stage presentations is the Kokusai (International) Theatre in Tokyo.

Not a castle in Disneyland but what is called a "love hotel"—the Hotel Meguro Emperor in a Tokyo suburb.

Below: A mirror-walled room with round revolving bed, fitted with gadgetry, cost ¥25,000 for the night.

Two geisha entering a high-class, traditionally-Japanese restaurant, where they entertain guests. "Geisha" means "art person". Geisha parties are very expensive.

The nation was completely mobilized. Everyone was part of a unit, of five or six families, which had its appointed leader. As the war went on most boys came to wear an austerity suit of brown cloth that was virtually a uniform. No longer were neckties worn—"necktie was Western and, so, devilish".

"My elder brother practised throwing himself in front of a dummy wooden tank with an armful of dummy dynamite," Senri-san told me. "He was taught to do that."

When Allied invasion was thought to be imminent, bamboo was distributed to make spears.

"We expected American paratroops to come down, with machine guns," Senri-san said. "The order was that when a paratrooper landed ten of us must attack him with our bamboo spears. Nine of us might be killed by his gun. But the tenth man would kill the paratrooper. So, in the end, Japan would prevail." He added that when the surrender was announced he felt "paralysed".

In explanation of the bitterness which still existed in Australia against Japan at that time, I gave Dr Hirakawa some facts (which I'd gathered on the spot) about prisoner-of-war treatment in Sandakan camp in Borneo and what happened on the death marches there. I didn't spare him the grim details.

He said, quietly, "Yes, I know such things did happen. Evidence in war crime trials was published in our papers—it was compulsory for them to print it. I read it, I know it must be true, and I have no excuses to make for what Japanese soldiers did. If I say something to you please not to regard it as an excuse. If you are taught, as we were taught, that your own life does not matter at all, then it is not to be expected that you will consider the lives of the enemy who are your prisoners to matter very much."

Another guide I had, Minoru Murofushi, must now be in his mid-forties and is, I think, an executive in the big import-export firm of C. Itoh. The bright-minded son of a middle-class family, Minoru was a ten-year-old schoolboy at the time of Pearl Harbour. Zealous to play his part in what seemed to him Japan's glorious adventure, he studied hard to become a naval cadet officer.

"When I was still certain that Japan must be victorious, the war ended with surrender. I was like—a plicked barroon," Minoru said. "All my purpose was lost. For two years I could not study at all."

The American Occupation forces came to Numazu, where Minoru lived. Minoru had been told that the enemy was likely to do cruel and terrible things to the conquered Japanese.

"When first I saw American soldiers in the street I expect them to kick me. But they smiled to me. I lost my fear and tried to speak with them in the little English I learnt from school before English teaching was stopped. They gave me some chocolate. I walked home, meanwhile thinking, 'Why have we been told so much lies about these Americans. They are kind. I am sure the girls do not have to run into the mountains so they will avoid to be raped.'"

THE OCCUPATION was primarily American. All the Allies were nominally represented but almost the only non-Americans were British Commonwealth personnel who were, in the main, Australians. The United States "displayed a magnanimity and far-sightedness such as few conquering nations have exhibited".[5] With that view (Tomlin's) I would now agree. At the time I did not think that General Douglas MacArthur's men were likely to do as good a job of founding democracy in Japan as, one must concede, was done.

I was among those who felt that leaving the Emperor on his throne posed the gravest danger to the peace of the future because it maintained a nucleus, imbued with semi-divine attraction, round which the samurai-Shinto-Bushido ("way of the warrior") fanaticism could again coalesce. But it now appears that the surrender worked and the Occupation worked and even the democratization measures worked because the monarchy was maintained, and would not have worked if it had not been. And MacArthur—a vain and aloof figure of such cultivated charisma—was the most acceptable of Americans to the Japanese because he had the mien of a shogun.

We incline to forget just how much of a transformation was achieved, or set in motion, during the Occupation:

-Under the new Constitution of 1946 the elected parliament, the Diet, became supreme as the organ of government. The Emperor, reduced to a symbol, renounced any divine or semi-divine status.

-The Shinto religion with its "divine mission" ideology was divorced from the State.

Japan was forbidden to have armed forces or a munitions industry. ("Self Defence Forces" have subsequently been fostered.)

-Purged for having been exponents of aggressive nationalism were about two hundred thousand Japanese civil servants and others, including politicians. Twenty-five war leaders, including General Tojo, were tried and sentenced to death or imprisonment. Of lesser war criminals, five thousand were found guilty (in Tokyo or Singapore trials) of gross cruelty, and over nine hundred were executed.

-Women were given the vote, the right to inherit property and to marry without parental consent.

-New labour laws guaranteed workers' rights, and trade unions (which had been disbanded when war came) were encouraged to re-form and be active. Communists were released from jail and given legality.

-Land reforms eliminated most of the absentee landlords who had controlled half of Japan's arable land: 4,600,000 farmers got land of their own.

-The industrial oligarchy known as the Zaibatsu was broken up and 200 million shares in the family-controlled combines were put on the open market.

-Education was extended from six to nine years at school. "Moral Science" teaching that exalted martial patriotism was banned. Boards of education were established in a greatly extended area of local government.

Inflation, shortages of goods and rampant black marketing came close to destroying the Japanese economy. But the American stabilization plans eventually worked, though the road was rough indeed for Suzuki-san until 1950 brought a burst of economic prosperity arising from orders from the Americans for supplies to fight the Korean War.

By the time the peace treaty was signed in San Francisco in 1951 the rebirth and rebuilding of Japan was under way. And another decade of unprecedented endeavour was to see the beginnings of the "economic miracle" and, in terms of trade, a defeated Japan doing better than a victorious Britain.

tokyo

東京

The biggest city and its quiet heart

Tokyo in 1973 was not only the biggest city in the world, with 11.6 million people; it was the only big city that had been rebuilt *twice* in fifty years.

In 1923 there was the Great Kanto Earthquake, which happened on a very windy first day of September and just when the midday rice was cooking on all those lit stoves. The resultant fires that raged through collapsed and largely wooden buildings caused horrendous damage. And then there was the Second World War destruction that reduced so much of the city to charcoal and rubble.

So Tokyo has been re-created twice, and not in its own image. The earthquake and accompanying holocaust left little trace of the old Edo of the Tokugawa shoguns except the walls that enclose the Imperial Palace. The residential and industrial districts were to an extent relocated, and in the mercantile sectors of the city late-nineteenth-century Western buildings were replaced with early-twentieth-century ones that were as un-Japanese as Tokyo Central Railway Station, which looks like a great red-brick import from Amsterdam. The National Diet (Parliament) building and some office blocks in the Marunouchi business area were left standing after the March–May 1945 bombing that was so intensive it wrought even wider havoc than did the atomic bomb on Hiroshima.

After the post-war rebuilding a great deal of Tokyo was still wooden and in the habitual style of small houses and shops in narrow streets, but a lot more of it was a product of what one Japanese architect christened the New Stone Age: the "new stone" was concrete (in Japanese, *konkuriito*). A feature, then, of the century's third Tokyo was the number of apartment blocks and slab-sided concrete buildings: functionalism was the ruling form during the vast and feverish task of rebuilding. But construction could be functional only up to a point, and that point was thirty-one metres above street level; because of the earthquake danger, regulations forbade any building of more than nine storeys (which is really only eight storeys in our terms because the Japanese always call the ground floor the first floor). In that nine-storey Tokyo, there was no vantage point from which you could look down on the remarkable domain that lies at the city's heart, the Imperial Palace.

The beginning of the breakthrough which has changed the profile of Tokyo was the building in 1957-8 of the Tokyo Tower (at Shiba Park, a couple of kilometres from the Imperial Palace). Some sort of ultra-high structure *had* to be built to provide the antennae for television transmitters, and it couldn't be sited on some nearby mountain because there aren't any. The fact that a tower over 300 metres (1,092 feet) high could be so anchored and constructed that it was earthquake-proof, and that it had two observation galleries with people walking around in them, posed the question: Couldn't buildings be, safely, higher?

The height limit was increased to sixty metres, and in 1965 I found myself staying in a seventeen-storey hotel, the New Otani. Since 1971 there has been the Keio Plaza Hotel of forty-seven storeys. In its Shinjuku vicinity the Sumitomo Building is even higher. Tallest of all would be the Mitsui Building of fifty-five storeys.

TOKYO'S FIRST SKYSCRAPER, built in 1968, was the thirty-six-storey Kasumigaseki Building, and high up in it is an excellent Prunier restaurant where I was having lunch on a May day in 1974 with the executive director of All Nippon Airways. I said something to Mr Ryotaro Nakatsuka about being able, from our window-side table, to see into the Imperial Palace grounds. My host said that a much better, closer view could be had from the Tokyo Marine and Fire Insurance Building, the tallest in Marunouchi. With typical Japanese courtesy he telephoned to executives he knew in this insurance company his airways did business with, and the next morning I went there and from its thirtieth floor had this remarkable view.

The imperial domain was like an island of quiet green, so wooded that the sparse habitations were half lost in trees, an island set in a rocky and rather dirty urban sea—except that a sea would have been lashing at the island's stone-wall cliffs, whereas the walls were mirroring themselves in the still water of a moat, with swans. Part of this unreality at the heart of frenetic Tokyo was that about a fifth of the 250-acre royal preserve was a park, with roads and pathways curving through its lawns, and here, as elsewhere on this moated "island", nothing moved; there was not a human figure to be seen. (This was a Friday, and on Mondays and Fridays the Higashi Gyoen park is as closed as it used to be every day until, in 1968, the Imperial Palace East Garden was opened to the public.) There was almost a mirage quality about it as one's focus moved from this preserve of peace to the roaring traffic racing round its perimeters and, away from the main avenues, to the denser pattern of little dun-coloured streets too narrow to have footpaths.

There were more buildings within those moated walls before American B-29s targeted the palace in May 1945. A temporary palace was built and still has its flat roof visible in the central wooded area. The new Imperial Palace, a ferroconcrete building low in line and serenely Japanese in character, was completed in 1968. The roof of copper blends darkly with the green of the pines in the grounds.

Looking down on the imperial "island" one is inclined to wonder whether the sovereign figure on it has been marooned, as it were, by history. It is difficult to know how much the sovereign means to the average Japanese nowadays. From being regarded before the Second World War as the Son of Heaven, descended from Shinto's gods, the Emperor—who, it will be remembered, renounced his legendary divinity in 1946—has become a person, a most exalted person to be sure and highly respected, but not reverenced.

As a person, His Imperial Majesty Hirohito is not a charismatic figure. Born in 1901, he has at no stage sought a self-expressive role—although when, in 1946, the Supreme Council split three-three on whether to accept the Potsdam Declaration terms for ending the war, the Emperor decided for surrender. For years he has given the impression that what he most wants to do is to continue to concern himself with his hobby, marine biology, There is a laboratory in the palace grounds, and in this branch of science Hirohito has some renown: he is credited with discovering eighty new species and has written eight books to do with marine biology and two on botanical subjects. He came to the throne at the end of 1926 on the death of his father, Emperor Taisho—who for years had not been strong in body or mind, and his son had been Regent—and 26 December 1976 would be his fiftieth anniversary.

Hirohito's son, Crown Prince Akahito, who unprecedently married a commoner, was a popular figure—but no more than that.

There was critical public reaction to a report that the Imperial Family was fed exclusively with food grown under conditions where it could not be affected by pollution. Among Japanese women there was widespread disappointment that the beautiful commoner who became Princess Michiko had lost the independence of mind she was so much admired for, and become just another subservient Japanese wife in her royal role.

One cannot but feel that the Japanese imperial system—though perhaps no more than the British monarchy—is slowly passing into desuetude, and that the view from some higher Marunouchi skyscraper in the 1980s could be of a central domain still moated and walled but looking much more like Central Park in New York or Green Park in London or Sydney's Botanic Gardens.

THE TOKYO TOWER does not provide anything like as "intimate" a view of the Imperial Palace grounds as I had from the insurance building in Marunouchi, but it does show you Tokyo—or as many miles of Tokyo in as many directions as haze and smog allow. The view does not enchant the eye as does the view of Paris from the Eiffel Tower, of which this one is blatantly an imitation; and, of course, it had to be made a bit higher, about 20 metres. Paris is the handsomest of cities to look down on because it is patterned to Haussmann's great plan: Tokyo is a chaotic sprawl, an ugly city.

As to air pollution (as apart from sea pollution and river pollution) in Japan, I found conditions in 1973 and 1974 not as bad as I had been led to expect, in fact not bad at all. True, I was in Tokyo in the fairly good weather common to late autumn and late spring; but I gained the impression that the Japanese Government was doing more about air pollution than we were giving it credit for. Indeed, it has taken up a stance that might put Japan in the position of doing more than any country. The restrictions planned to reduce carbon monoxide and other pollutants emitted from cars and trucks, to go into effect in 1975, were particularly tough and called for reductions of up to 80 per cent of what was allowable in 1974. Also to begin in 1975 was a punitive new program to further control the sulphur oxide emissions from factory chimneys.

Air pollution is measured from the Tokyo Tower, which not only is topped with the antennae of the capital's seven television transmitters and its two FM radio stations, but is the big communications facility of Government and of Japan National Railways with its radio-directed "bullet" trains.

In the tower a number of leading electrical firms provide striking displays and show their latest electronic products. There are gaudy "fun" attractions and a waxworks that boasts that its figures (historical, horrible and Brigitte Bardot) were supplied from London's Madame Tussaud's. All in all the Tokyo Tower is possibly the least Japanese thing about Tokyo.

Hotels, a Japanese inn, and food

THE FIRST THING the foreign traveller needs in any city, apart from transport, is accommodation. Tokyo is not short of hotels, and it has some very good ones.

Hotels are naturally more expensive in central Tokyo than elsewhere in Japan but their rates were not exorbitant when compared with what Australians and Americans paid for the same standard of accommodation in their own big cities. The 1974 problem was not the cost of staying at a three-star Tokyo hotel but of affording to eat there. Food costs were fierce.

Half a dozen Tokyo hotels I can speak of from personal experience, and I like best one of the two places I have stayed at twice. The first time I was in Japan, and the last time in 1974, I stayed at the Marunouchi (which has now dropped the second *u* from its name and become Marunochi, one syllable less than the pronunciation (Mah-rue-no-ou-chee) of the spelling that still applies to the business district where the hotel is). Since 1955 many newer and larger hotels have been built and the Marunochi would no longer be in the top-rate ten. Even twenty years ago it hardly rated as "expensive"; although I didn't have much money and it seemed so. Moreover, as an author writing about the country I wanted to do the Japanese thing wherever possible. So I had very much in mind what an American I sat next to in the Qantas plane from Sydney had said: "Why don't you stay at a Japanese inn?"

This American, who got off at Manila, had never stayed at a *ryokan* (pron. r'*YO*kan) himself, but friends of his had. "And they loved it. They said it just made their stay in Tokyo. And I'm sure it was a whole lot cheaper than a Western-style hotel."

I got the name of a good Japanese inn and in the late afternoon of my second day in Tokyo I set out for it. This *ryokan* was in Akasaka (Ah-kah-sah-kah), a well-favoured residential and nightclub district which is in the southwest of the city and is sometimes confused with Asakusa (Ah-suk-sah), the big downtown amusement centre.

I had the address written in Japanese and this I handed to a taxi-driver with the blithe expectation of being delivered there in about fifteen minutes. Taxis have changed since then—nowadays the driver opens and closes the rear door by moving a lever beside the steering column, and many drivers wear white gloves—but it is still as difficult as ever it was to find an address in labyrinthine Tokyo. Major thoroughfares are named but most streets are nameless, and the numbering system for houses is not related to streets, anyway. The taximan asks passers-by and usually ends up at a police box in the area where he thinks the address is. A policeman gets out a chart and they pore. By this tortuous process the *ryokan* was finally located in a narrow street at dusk when the advertising lanterns were coming on in the shops and men in cotton kimonos, *yukata,* were clack-clacking in their *geta* wooden sandals to the public bathhouse.

A path of stepping-stones led through a small green garden to a vestibule, stone-floored. Below a step, some shoes; above it, slippers and a half-open paper-covered sliding door. In the doorway a young woman in kimono appears, drops on her knees and bows her forehead almost to the floor. She is joined by a second maid who does the same. I stand there feeling foolish and respond to all this genuflection with a bit of a bob. I make my inquiries about accommodation. Both maids blink at me gravely; neither has a word of English. One gets up and goes off at a discreet run, her heels flipping up in snow-white *tabi* socks beneath the back hem of her kimono. She returns with a gold-toothed woman I identify as the proprietress, the mamma-san. I ask whether she speaks English.

"Little bit I can speak. *Dozo* (please) come in."

Shoes off, slippers on, along polished wood to what is the inn's reception desk where I establish that it has a vacant room. But the tariff is on the basis of breakfast and dinner included and, with the cost of these meals added, I'd be paying more than if I kept my hotel room and ate economically. And my room here would have no attached bathroom. There was a telephone, but I should go mad trying to make calls, what with mamma-san's minimal English and my six words of Japanese. At the Marunouchi when I lifted the receiver a voice said, "*Moshi-moshi*" (the Japanese "hello") but as soon as she heard me the girl switched to English. Another thing: Akasaka is not exactly central and I'd be spending a lot of yen on taxis.

All the same I was strongly tempted to stay there when I saw the room I could have had and where, I found, I could have dinner. All meals are served in the room at a *ryokan*: there is no dining-room, and no menu; you have the meal the inn has prepared.

The room was appealing in its aesthetic simplicity. The floor was of *tatami* mats, which are not mats in our sense of the word, but rectangular pallets of rice straw covered with finely woven reeds. Each mat is of a standard size, about two metres long by one metre wide. Usually *tatami* is straw-coloured, but when mats are new (and these were fairly new) they look specially good because the reed covering is the palest of pale hues of green. As I shed slippers (you must never walk on *tatami* except in bare or stockinged feet) and stepped admiringly through the paper door a maid slid open, I bumped my head on the lintel. Low doorways in Japanese inns and houses are a hazard the sixfooter has to learn to look out for.

The ceiling was of plain wood, the grain of the pristine pine boards contributing to an effect of artistry derived from nature. Two of the walls were *shoji,* paper on rectangularly patterned frames of thin woodwork, in the form of sliding doors. Outside one of these was a pane of glass, a modern innovation that made it possible to view the garden without letting in cold air. One wall had an alcove, the *tokonoma,* hung with a scroll, the *kakemono,* which may have on it a picture or, as I discovered this one had, a very short poem done in brush calligraphy. At its base stood an *ikebana,* flower arrangement, consisting of a pot with a long stalk of red berries and one yellow gerbera, nothing more. A slim round post of polished wood made one corner of the *tokonoma* alcove.

Apart from a black-lacquered central table that was less than knee-high and at which one sat, on a floor cushion, the only furniture was a lovely paper-shaded lamp. The bedding, called *futon*—a roll-up mattress, sheets, quilt and a straw-stuffed pillow—would have been in the cupboards behind a *shoji* door, and the table would be moved aside to lay it in the middle of the floor.

Even as I admired the room's uncluttered day-time look and its air of serene cleanliness, I could visualize what would happen to its appearance if I moved in with the normal Western traveller's luggage, which is so much more than the Japanese travel with. They go off for a week with no more than an overnight bag.

Seated with my back to the *tokonoma*—which is the honoured guest's position—I was propped up by a gadget that, slid under the cushion and providing an arm-rest, was designed to aid the muscle-bound *gaijin* (foreigner). My un-foldable, too-long legs were straight out under the table, the stockinged feet protruding oddly on the other side. I consumed, while I waited for my dinner, a small bottle of Japanese beer—which is lighter than Australian beer and good (particularly the Kirin and Sapporo brands). With the beer the maid brought in a steaming handtowel, rolled up and resting in the smallest wicker basket.

The *tempura* dinner was very good. *Tempura* is one of the two dishes (*sukiyaki* is the other) that Westerners enjoy most in Japan. You could call it "bits of fried fish", but the seafood morsels, dipped in the lightest of batter and then cooked very quickly in boiling vegetable oil, are more than that, and crisply delicious. The soup that came in its lacquer bowl was thin as any *consommé*, subtle in flavour, decorative with floating strands of green and having in it what looked like a piece of sponge rubber—dried bean curd—which is not one of the easiest things to pick up with *hashi*, chopsticks.

On using chopsticks the rule is this: Hold the lower stick rigid, never try to move it. Get this lower stick rested down at the base of the thumb and across to the ball of the middle finger. Anchor it there with pressure of the thumb. Top stick is the one that does all the moving, the pincering to pick up things. Top stick is held between the ball of the thumb and forefinger; and they move it. Try this with two long pencils, the sharpened ends protruding an inch or so at the back of the hand. Practice touching the tip of the top one to the tip of the stationary one. If you are doing it right you can pick up a rubber.

Getting to use the *hashi* adroitly is not something that happens in five minutes; but it really isn't much sweat. You can, of course, get a spoon and fork, but don't give up easily, for I'll swear that Japanese food tastes better off chopsticks. Rice is hardest; but you are allowed to hold the bowl of rice at mouth level and "shovel" it with the sticks held together.

So, in came my dinner, its lacquerware dishes and its arrangement a delight to the eye. What to eat first? I start on a tiny dish of pretty pickles, thinking they are appetizers: they are for eating later with the rice, or as palate fresheners. Soup is there, but to take it at the start is not the Japanese way. It will stay, in its lidded bowl, hotter than the *tempura*. However, the Japanese are much more concerned with food's taste than its temperature. So nearly all the dishes come at once.

You *drink* the soup, holding the bowl lightly in two hands. You won't slurp, but the Japanese consider it quite mannerly to do so; they feel that a bowl of soup or *soba* (noodles) is not properly savoured if it is taken silently. Rice comes, at a dinner like this, in a large lacquer pot, and when the lid is removed the quantity usually looks sufficient to feed a starving Indian family. I thought I should take some, replete though I was, and, having begun eating rice, did what is considered a wrong thing: I continued to drink *sake*.

Sake (pron, sah-ke), the Japanese rice wine, I liked so much with that first Japanese meal that, thereafter, I hardly ever took a Japanese dinner without it. *Sake*'s taste could be described as being like a weak dry sherry that isn't dry enough—but it is redeemed, utterly, by being served *warm*.

To preserve its warmth a good restaurant will always serve it in a vase-like bottle standing in a bowl of hot water. From this it is poured into cups so small that they hold only about as much as egg cups, and properly so because a larger quantity would cool before being drunk. Yet a problem, I found, remains. *Sake* cooled being *sake* spoiled, when it is poured it should be drunk. But the maid was solicitously kneeling beside me throughout the meal and as soon as I emptied my *sake* cup she filled it again. Well, you don't really need another *sake* right away, but you don't want to see it cooled and spoiled. So you drink it, and the maid promptly fills the cup again, and it wouldn't do to let it lose its warmth, so . . . . *Sake* is 15 per cent alcohol (Scotch is around 40) and I am not a very strong drinker, but on a number of occasions I have consumed two "vases" of *sake* at dinner without effect other than a warm feeling of euphoria.

Back at the Marunouchi Hotel I had gone to bed about midnight and was hardly asleep when I was awakened by the blare of a car horn. I lay listening to another sound, a thin bugling that was plaintive and rather sweet—as though one of the horns of an Oriental elfland was being faintly blown by an elf who was just learning. I heard it on other nights and inquired. It was a *soba* seller, a street vendor of noodles who announced his presence and the progress of his handcart through the back streets by blowing his call on a tin flute.

THE SECOND TIME I was in Japan my wife was with me and the tourist authorities put as at the Nikkatsu Hotel, which no longer exists. The Tokyo hotel that had the name was the Imperial, and after dinner we had to go there. It was early April, cherry-blossom time—and there in the Imperial Hotel's foyer, growing from earth surrounded by plush carpet, was a large cherry-tree in full bloom. I don't know how they moved a whole, blossoming cherry-tree into the hotel—but it was a very Japanese thing to do.

The importance of *sakura* (cherry blossom) as a tourist attraction had been evidenced as soon as we got off the Qantas plane at Haneda airport. I had asked the man from the tourist organization who met us, "Is the blossom out yet?" and got this answer: "It is out about seven-tenths in Tokyo, and is best at the moment in Ueno Park, but will not be perfect for a few days. Rain is expected at weekend but we do not think there will be strong wind to blow blossom away." He consulted our itinerary solemnly. "At Myanoshita you will be too soon for blossom. But Kyoto, yes, though Kyoto this year is early. Blossom is now at its best there according to latest advice by telephone this afternoon from JTB [Japan Travel Bureau] Kyoto office. Nara also is about at perfection."

Along the Ginza there was cherry-blossom everywhere, twigs and branches of it, tied to light standards—plastic and very pink. Next day we went to see the "seven-tenths" blossom in Ueno Park. It was much paler than we expected, a very pale shell-pink that, as Claire said, was lovelier than the bright-pink variety. Japanese we spoke to shared our preference for the paler kind.

Tourists often ask about the cherries—are they the "black" variety or the red? There are no cherries on the trees that are grown so widely in Japan for the beauty of *sakura*.

The Imperial Hotel used to be an earthquake-proof (it withstood the 1923 'quake) building "floating on mud", architecture by the famous Frank Lloyd Wright. It was of strikingly interesting design but I never wanted to stay in one of the rooms off the endless low-ceilinged passageways of a building that was once described as the world's only three-storeyed basement. The next visit to Japan saw us accommodated in the Imperial's annexe, then new, a functional matchbox of a building but comfortable and with good sound-proofing against the nearby trains. Frank Lloyd Wright's building was demolished in 1968 as uneconomical and there is a huge new Imperial, at which I stayed in 1973. The foyer looks only slightly smaller than the concourse at Sydney's Central Station; and the style is international rather than Japanese.

A more aesthetically designed and decorated hotel is the Okura. It was built by a tycoon, Baron Okura, with the intention of putting Mr T. Inamaru, president and general manager of the Imperial, out of business. Baron Okura died before his grand hotel opened, and Inamaru-san easily survived its competition. But the Okura is often spoken of as the best hotel in Tokyo.

The forty-seven-storeyed Keio Plaza is an Inter-Continental hotel that is the Tokyo Tower of hotels, a little taller than the Eiffel of New York hostelries, the American. So it is the tallest hotel in the world—in earthquake-prone Tokyo! Two professors of Tokyo University took part in the design of vibration-causing equipment that used a huge revolving iron ball to check laboratory computations which indicated that the Keio Plaza structure would stand up—although the walls would crack—under an earthquake five times that of the 1923 'quake's intensity. Science triumphant, in 1971 the building was opened—with three Shinto priests in white robes and black lacquered hats chanting a thousand-year-old prayer as they solemnly shook twigs of the sacred *sadaki*-tree on the forty-sixth floor and called upon the Shinto gods to bless the Keio Plaza, its eleven hundred rooms, eight restaurants and seven bars. The Tokyo Hilton is another hotel of good repute. I know only that its Keyaki Grill serves excellent food.

I have stayed at the New Japan in Akasaka. Outside one glass end-wall of the main dining-room a waterfall cascaded from the rocks and greenery of a hillside garden into a pebbly pool. The New Japan was good, but not central enough to be convenient.

The seventeen-storey New Otani, where I stayed in 1964, was "international" in style right up to its revolving Blue Sky Lounge on top, but the grounds were very Japanese, and not only in their landscaping with a tea-house and a little stream crossed by an arching vermilion bridge. The grounds were studded with marvellous rocks. The hotel's owner, Mr Yonetaro Otani, a magnate of heavy industry, collected rocks. His hobby was not uncommon in Japan; the prime minister at the time, Mr Ikeda, was a rock collector and so were two of his Cabinet ministers. Otani-san had a staggering collection worth more than a million dollars. Two of his most valuable rocks were enormous boulders of red agate. One of these stood nearly three metres high in the hotel garden, with all its natural contours highly polished.

HOTEL FOOD PRICES were rising at the rate of $12\frac{1}{2}$ per cent a year when in late 1973 I came away from the Imperial Hotel with a room-service menu from which I quote some items with the 10 per cent service charge added: Orange juice ¥308 (a fresh orange cost ¥660, about $AI.60); eggs and bacon ¥605; pot of coffee ¥396; chicken sandwich ¥770; hamburger ¥990; cold roast sirloin ¥3,300; filet mignon ¥4,180 (over $A10 when the yen was at 400 to the $A). And any bill over ¥1,200 was subject to addition of a further 10 per cent in tax.

I wasn't the only guest who sometimes forwent the morning luxury of room service and walked across the road to a coffee shop or a block away to an unstylish little cafe where you could have a full breakfast for less than half the ¥1,400 the big hotels charged.

Of course, the ten-dollar steak is no ordinary cut of the rump. Its quality was exemplified in a rib eye of Kobe beef I had when I was taken to the Porterhouse steak restaurant at the Marunochi Hotel when I was staying there in 1974. Cattle carefully reared for the table get beer in their diet and are massaged to spread the fat so that the meat is marbled with it, and the farmer may take a mouthful of *sake*, or potato-spirit *shochu*, and spray it over the rump he is massaging. Mr Kiyoshi Kobayashi, who was both managing director and manger of the Marunochi, was proud of the standard of the Kobe beef served at the Porterhouse.

When I had first known the Marunouchi (with the second *u*) Hotel of almost twenty years before, Kiyoshi Kobayashi's father was running it. And, in his eighties, there Taro Kobayashi was still, in his upstairs office every day, and with the same courtly manner I remembered. Clearly he had passed to his son a sense of dedication still manifest in the hotel's management.

Some businessmen felt that they just had to stay at the more prestigious Okura or Imperial. Others stayed at the Marunochi (which could be 25 per cent below the Imperial's rates) because it was right in the business district—especially Australian businessmen. From the time of the Occupation the Marunouchi/ochi has been Tokyo's "Australian" hotel. It still has a yearly festival occasion centred on 26 January, Australia Day.

For tourists the Marunochi's location was hard to beat—right next door to the main office of Japan Travel Bureau and close to Tokyo Central where tourists start their train trips. Yet it was quiet, and within walking distance of the Ginza's shops. In 1974 a twin room cost, with taxes and service, about ¥10,000 for two.

If you wanted to eat very economically—and could manage to ignore the Marunochi's three elegant restaurants, Samurai lounge-bar and summer roof garden—there was a quick-service restaurant across the road, owned by the hotel, called the Maruhotei. It was priced for its main trade, the office workers, and not much English was used, but I found I could get by there; you could point to what you wanted, in the display case of sample dishes, such as many restaurants have, with the food modelled realistically in wax.

Ramen is the "economy" dish many Japanese eat for lunch and some meals of ramen could save the budget traveller sufficient yen to splurge on a good Japanese dinner. Ramen is Chinese noodles in Japanese soup. A JTB booklet on Tokyo refers to it as "the most popular dish in the nation", especially popular with young people. There are chains of ramen restaurants where you sit on a stool at a counter and order a bowl of the ramen of your choice—*shio* (salt), *batah* (butter), *miso* (bean-paste) or the one I tried, *shoyu* (soy) flavoured, which had a slice of ham in a biggish bowl of tasty noodles that cost (in 1974) under ¥200.

But nobody, surely, *wants* to be economical when there are such memorable meals to be had in Tokyo. Let me recall a few in a rundown on the Japanese cuisine.

JAPANESE CUISINE? Some there are who say that Japanese food isn't worthy of being spoken of in the same breath as Chinese. And nobody whose taste buds are working would deny that the Chinese are culinary masters. But so are the French. And it was from a Frenchman, a Parisian who had spent seventeen years in Asia, that I first heard eloquent tribute paid to Japanese food.

Robert Guillain was Far Eastern correspondent for the French newspaper *Le Monde*. He wrote: "I, a citizen of France, sane of mind and gourmand of stomach, dare to profess that Japanese cooking may be classified immediately after French and Chinese cooking .... Japanese cooking ranks, I believe, as one of the Big Three in cooking." He went on: "The day will come, after you have left Japan, when you will mourn the fact that only in Japan is Japanese food to be had."[19] Since M. Guillain wrote that about forty Japanese restaurants have opened in New York. One of them, in the Waldorf Astoria Hotel on Park Avenue, is Inagiku. The Inagiku at Kayabàcho in Tokyo was regarded by the executive director of the Japan National Tourist organization who took me there as "perhaps the best restaurant in Japan". Its proprietor, Mr Nobuo Asano—who is himself the chef at the number-one Inagiku—told me that he was proposing to open an Inagiku in Australia, in Sydney (where there are already some good Japanese restaurants, notably the Suehiro at North Sydney). Inagiku's specialty is *tempura*.

—TEMPURA (pron. tem-poor-a) was what I had as my first Japanese dinner, at the *ryokan* mentioned earlier: but more needs to be said of this notable dish. At Inagiku, the lightly battered morsels are fried in Asano-san's special blend of sesame oil and camellia oil, in front of you as you sit at a circular counter. As each piece is cooked it is placed on rice paper and you take it up with the *hashi* and dip it into a mixture of lemon juice and salt or into a sauce made from soy, *mirin* (a sweet *sake*) and horse-radish. If everything Inagiku uses for its *tempura* were in season at once, and available fresh and to Asano-san's standards, then you could expect a morsel each of: (seafoods) prawn, eel, cuttle-fish, scallop, flathead, whitebait, goby and *risu* or kiss-fish, and (vegetables) mushroom, lotus root, eggplant, ginger-root, gingko-nut, green pepper, Japanese onion, Japanese celery and asparagus. This place is the tops, and expensive, about ¥5,000 a person. You can get good *tempura* for ¥3,000 and less at many places. With *tempura* you drink warm *sake*.

The traveller may be told, "The average Japanese doesn't eat *tempura* and *sukiyaki*—those are tourist dishes, not Japanese food." It is true that the average Japanese rarely eats these dishes, but it is because he can't afford to; it isn't that he doesn't like them. As to their being non-Japanese, I am told by Japanese that they got the *tempura* style of frying from the Portuguese four hundred years ago—long enough for it to become naturalized, surely; and long before there were tourists. One thing that distinguishes Japanese food from Western (a distinction it shares with Chinese) is its use of soy sauce (*shoyu*). The soybean wasn't grown in Western Europe or in the United States until about a hundred years ago. The use of soy (and sweetened *sake*) in its preparation is sufficient to make *sukiyaki* a Japanese dish.

Japanese cuisine is based on fish whereas ours is based on meat. Buddhism proscribed the eating of animal flesh; but some ate it. *Suki* means a plough-share and *yaki* to grill. A Japanese book published early last century says, "*Sukiyaki* is to grill chicken seasoned in soy, on a ploughshare over the fire."

Beef-eating came into favour in Tokugawa times after Townsend Harris, America's first consul in Japan, hungering for a steak, had a cow slaughtered at Shimoda in 1885. A monument to the cow was erected in 1931, and was paid for by the Shimoda Butchers' Guild.

—SUKIYAKI (*skeeyahkee*, but *sookiyahkee* is much used) is made with thin slices of beef—prime Kobe or Matsuzaka or Omi beef at the pricier restaurants—cooked in an iron pan, usually over a gas ring, in the middle of the table before you. Typically, the maid or waitress greases the pan, rubs it with a leek-like Japanese onion, pours in a little *dashi* (soup stock) and the sweetened *sake*. She puts in first a few slices of beef, then the other ingredients that are standing by attractively on a platter—mushrooms, leeks, bamboo shoots, yam noodles, bean curd (*tofu*), chrysanthemum leaves, with soy sauce. It smells very good as it cooks. In front of you is a bowl in which a raw egg is beaten up (unless you signify that you don't like raw egg—which would be a pity) and the maid puts slices and pieces of the piping hot meat, etc., into this raw-egg "sauce", which cools it and makes it taste delectably smooth. As more meat and vegetables go into the enriched liquor in the pan the flavour gets better and better. Again, *sake* is the drink. Expect to pay about ¥3,000 a person for *sukiyaki* at a first-class restaurant. It is also done with chicken, but beef *sukiyaki* is much better.

—MIZUTAKI is chicken (or beef) stewed at the table in an earthenware pot. You finish the meal with the rich broth.

—SHABU-SHABU. Very thin slices of beef, held in your chopsticks, are swished in a pot of boiling stock until cooked, then dipped into special sauce. Vegetables and bean curd are cooked in the meat-flavoured soup.

—YAKATORI means "grilled poultry", and the grilling is the better for being done over charcoal. Delectable chunks come on bamboo skewers—chicken, duck, pork, with bits of pimento and Japanese onion. Specially good is a roasted chicken leg that has been basted and re-basted with soy. Side-street *yakatori* shops can serve you excellent fare that doesn't cost much. For a superb full meal, costing around ¥2,500 for fourteen "sticks", a 1974 place of note I went to was Toricho in the Rippongi area. More centrally, Torishige in the Ginza was said to be as good.

—KABAYAKI is eel dipped in soy sauce and then grilled. It is so flavoursome it needs the accompaniment of rice.

—SASHIMI is sliced raw fish. Westerners often go "Ugh!" at the idea of eating fish raw; but I have come round to relishing a few slices of tender young tuna, dipped in soy, as an *hors d'oeuvre*. At least try a rosy slice or two.

—SUSHI (rhymes with "cushy") is again raw fish, or shrimp, clam, even octopus, but with the slices placed atop thumb-sized patties of rice that has been flavoured with vinegar and may be wrapped in seaweed like tissue paper. JTB advises *sushi* beginners to start with *ebi* (boiled shrimp), *tomago* (cooked egg) and then proceed to raw fish with *maguro* (lean tuna). You eat *sushi* with the fingers, dipping the fish side only in soy sauce (without letting the slice slide off into the soy and splash clothing; soy stains are bad).

—FUGU (foo-goo) is blowfish, which is poisonous. It is a gourmet dish with Japanese and is considered "lucky". For *fugu* to be eaten safely it must be prepared in a certain way, and to serve it requires a special licence. I had never had it until, in 1973, an old friend, Frank H. Agui (another executive director of JNTO) took me to a restaurant called Fukugen Kudan. (*Fuku* is the Kyushu name of the fish, and the choicest *fugu* comes from Kyushu: Kudan is the area of north Tokyo where the restaurant is.) It is open from late September to late March: only in those months can *fugu* be fished and served. The meal begins with *sashimi* (raw) *fugu*, sliced paper thin and looking most decorative whorled on a glass plate. Cooked, the fish is bony, the taste good but not as remarkable as the price of it is high. But have no fears about its being safe to eat. The proprietor's grandfather came from Kyushu and opened the restaurant and the family has been preparing *fugu* ever since.

—SUPPON is turtle. Turtles (not the big ones of tropical seas) are raised in tanks to die for Japanese gourmets, who may precede the meal with a cocktail of *sake* and turtle blood. I was not offered this, I am glad to say, when I had a (*very* expensive) meal of turtle soup (some turtle meat was served, but the soup was the thing) at a Tokyo restaurant with this specialty (Dai-Ichi, No. 1 Tanga-cho, Akasaka). My host was the late Torao Saito, the friend to whom this book is dedicated. "Pour a little *sake* in your soup," he said, and I said, "Tiger, I don't want to. The flavour is wonderful as it is." He said, patiently, "The flavour is partly due to *sake* being already added. It will be even better if you add a little more." So I did, and it was.

 TIPPING: the subject is inseparable from hotels and restaurants. Japan has done more than any country in the non-Communist world to get rid of the practice of giving extra payment for servitors who are paid to serve you, in the belief that if you do this you will get better service (T-I-P, To Improve Performance). The belief, in my experience, is generally well founded. In the Soviet Union where tipping is supposed to be regarded as despicable capitalist patronage of the worker (though many a tip I've had accepted in Moscow) the service is awful. But Japan *is* different. The service you get does not depend on your tipping.

Let us be clear about who you *are* expected to tip. Porters at airports and at railway stations are not on wages and what they get is not tipping but payment for carrying bags at a fixed charge (about ¥150 a bag). Tour guides are tipped about ¥1,000 a day if they are yours exclusively; ¥500 if you are in a carload; less if it's a coach party. Chauffeurs of tour cars are given, say, ¥500 a day.

Taxi-drivers usually don't get anything, but Tokyo's traffic is such that they earn a hard living and if the fare is ¥450 and I hand over a ¥500 note I don't feel like taking the ¥50 (12 cents Aust.) change. If they carry heavy bags or you keep them waiting you should add 100 yen or so.

Direct tipping is not obligatory for food and drink waiters, whether restaurant or room service, or for maids, front desk staff or bellboys. Personally,

Gold-leaf on lacquer covers the lovely Kinkakuji (Gold Pavilion) at Kyoto, first built in 1397. Burnt by a mad priest in 1950, it was rebuilt exactly as before.

The way to the beautiful Katsuga Shrine at Nara is lined with old stone lanterns donated by rich worshippers. Among them were some of the shrine's tame deer.

At Nikko very richly embellished mausolea memorialize the shogun Ieyasu Tokugawa, who died in 1616. Below: In one of the annual festivals a palanquin is carried by priests.

The renowned "stone garden" at the Ryoanji Temple at Kyoto has not a single flower or shrub, only stones set aesthetically in rake-patterned gravel.

Built in the seventeenth century and most carefully preserved as a superb example of Japanese domestic architecture is the Katsura Imperial Villa at Kyoto.

Autumn had turned to crimson and gold the maples at Miyajima by a small bridge near the Iwaso Inn where I stayed on this very lovely island, in mid-November.

Spring had decked the roadside cherry-trees with pale pink blossom in mid-April at Odawara. Such trees bear no fruit, are planted for the blossom's beauty.

Hotels, a Japanese inn, and food

I always give bellboys at least a hundred yen for lugging bags up to a room or down to a car. Doormen who call you a taxi depend, I believe, on getting something from you.

Some hotels state very plainly, *A 10 per cent gratuity charge will be added to your bill to replace individual tipping.* I should like to think that the 10 per cent thus collected by the hotel is actually distributed to the staff, but am unable to believe that it is. That is why I incline to tip. I should like very much to feel that every kind of servitor is adequately paid and that I could, with a clear conscience, refrain from a practice which may be not only demeaning to the recipient but can be bad for the donor by making him feel superior. Moreover, tipping is a nuisance and a worry. You don't know who to tip, when, and how much of the strange currency to give—if you have the right change, and half the time you haven't.

What to do by day in the megalopolis

THE TOKYO of 11.6 million people—nearly half as many again as Sweden, nine-tenths Australia's population—is more than a city. What is called Greater Metropolitan Tokyo takes in twenty-six cities in twenty-three wards or *ku*, six towns, nine villages, a rural county and some islands.

An inventory like that can make world's-biggest-*city* description sound a bit specious, what with Tokyo's population being spread over 836 square miles. But Sydney, which Australians regard as being crammed, spreads only one-quarter as many people (2.9 million) over a metropolitan area nearly twice the size (1,573 square miles).

Tourists don't normally get involved with much of Tokyo in the two to three days that is the average time spent there as part of an average stay in Japan of thirteen days.

Tokyo is not typical Japan any more than it is natural-scenery Japan. What no other place in Japan has is such an aggregation of shops, museums, art galleries, theatres and other places of entertainment—and people. One has only to go near a railway station in the rush hours to get an impression of a moving wall-to-wall carpet of people.

The best time and place to view this passing parade when it is in a less skeltering mood is on a fine Sunday afternoon in an area of the Ginza that is then closed to traffic and becomes what is called a "Pedestrian's Paradise". The big department stores are open on Sunday, the busiest shopping day, and their escalators are filled with diagonal crowds ascending and descending between one floor's bright cave of merchandise and the next. At the foot of each *up* escalator there is likely to be a pretty girl in the store's uniform bowing her head as she says, over and over and over again, "*Irasshaimase*", which means "Welcome".

The Ginza (*gin* is "silver", and silver coins were minted here in old Edo) was an area rather than a street; but during the Occupation the street called Chuo-dori became known as Ginza Street. By "Ginza" most guidebooks still mean an area about half a square mile divided into eight blocks and split by an eight-lane avenue. The Ginza is not only the main mid-Tokyo shopping centre but the most stylish and englamoured part of the city.

The department stores are so well stocked and so given to putting on interesting exhibitions that a visit to at least one of them ranks as a "must" for the tourist, who will probably want to do some shopping anyway. Big ones in the Ginza include Mitsukoshi, Matsuzakaya, Matsuya, Komatsu and one whose wrapping paper, designed with a rose, I am fond of, Takashimaya. Another big one, Daimaru, is practically part of Tokyo Central station. If you take the subway to Shinjuku—which is, in terms of Sydney, a King's Cross and a former low-life area that has been transformed—there are two department stores in the station there, and nearby is a very good one called Istehan. Shinjuku also has a "Pedestrian Paradise" mall on Sundays.

When I last left Tokyo there was a show of hand-made glass at the Matsuya emporium, Mitsukoshi was readying its own theatre to put on *Bunraku* puppet plays, paintings by some renowned Japanese artists were being exhibited at Takashimaya, which had a folk-crafts department worth seeing, and Matsuzakaya was having an exhibition of flower arrangements by one of the *ikebana* schools.

Paper, every kind of paper from wrapping- to writing- to wall-, from wood-block prints to fans to folding paper for *origami*, is the speciality of a shop that delighted my wife Claire, who found it first, and I love it too: its name is Haibara at 7, 2-chome, Nihonbashi, just beyond the Ginza.

As to what are the best buys, there are many things beside the well-known cameras and cultured pearls, transistor radios and tape recorders (such as can actually be cheaper in Hong Kong, though there may be not the same range of latest models) brocades and dolls.

"To buy anything electrical we do not go to a department store, we go to Akihabara," said the Yukiko-san who was my Tokyo mentor on the last trip, as she steered me to the Hibiya Line at the Ginza subway station. Six stops didn't take long and we emerged opposite Akihabara station to face a line of shops, discount-type, open-fronted, all selling "electricals"—radios, tape recorders, television sets, cassette-players, floor-polishers, refrigerators, you-name-it. For a very good Sony radio I was quoted a price that was 20 per cent less than what the maker said it should retail for. In Japan, unlike Singapore and Hong Kong, one is not expected to bargain. But it pays to compare prices at Akihabara. I didn't and found I could have done as well at a shop named Kimura Camera, right in the Ginza heart of Tokyo.

In buying a radio or radio-cassette-recorder combination be sure to specify where it is to be used—usually the salesman will ask—because you could buy something that worked superbly on Japanese wavelengths but badly under home-country conditions.

FOR ABOUT A SCORE of years of writing about travel in at least a score of countries I have been at odds with the belief, widely held in literary circles, that only philistines take conducted tours. That a poet should get on a tourist coach with a bunch of "camera-carrying Americans" is apparently found unimaginable by the kind of people who are quick to pick up a fashionable prejudice but never ask themselves why it should be vulgar for Americans to carry cameras. My thanks, then, to James Kirkup, an Englishman who has lived and taught English literature in Japan and whose writings include eight books of poetry, for saying in his book *Tokyo*: "If one has only a day or two to spare for sightseeing, perhaps a daytime tour is the best way to see the highlights of the city."[16]

So, not without a slight shudder at the name Dynamic Tokyo Tour, we board the coach run by JTB/Hato Tours, having paid ¥4,800 (say $A12) for the all-day tour, lunch included. It is 10.15 a.m. pick-up at the Imperial Hotel. The guide tells us her name is Amy as we go on to pick up at the Okura Hotel, which Amy advises calling the Okula if we are saying the name to a taxi-driver. As to the *l* and *r* pronunciation, the bright Amy knows a nightclub that the proprietors wanted to call the Grasshopper: but what they gave the signwriter, who lettered the name beautifully in gold, was Glasshopper.

We go first to one of the entrances to the Imperial Palace. A bridge leads to a gate on the other side of a moat where swans glide. Atop the walls are grassy banks with pines. ("The pine-tree is the symbol of constancy."—Amy.) These crooked-limbed pines are too much clipped ever to be shaggy and, on this mild November day, many of them are already wearing girdles of straw against the coming winter's cold. All that can be seen of the Palace is a patch of roof copper, oxidized green.

"Only twice a year can we enter the Palace grounds—on New Year's Day and on April twenty-nine, the Emperor's birthday," Amy says and adds, "Volunteer workers come in from the country to clean the grounds. They get no pay, but afterwards they meet the Emperor and Empress."

Runners keep pounding past. Shorts-singlets-sandshoes is their garb and they do the Palace circuit on footpaths with few pedestrians because here we are removed from the broad streets of rat-race traffic and commercial buildings. The Japanese are keen on physical fitness. Last time I stayed at the Marunochi Hotel my room was at the back looking out across a lane to the seventh floor of a large office building. At 8.45 every weekday morning the office workers I could see, all men, all wearing white shirts (never a pink or a patterned one) would stand beside their desks and do five minutes of excercises. And I could see identical synchronized movements of arms-raising and torso-swinging and up-on-the-toes being done on the sixth floor and the eighth floor as well. The exercises came from an instructor on radio.

When the coach moved off from the Palace I noticed a young man exercising quite unselfconsciously while he waited at a street crossing for the light to turn green. Amy said the police have to learn and regularly practise *judo* and *kendo*.

Judo is the modern name for Japanese *ju-jitsu* (or *jutsu*). It uses leverage to overcome strength and force, and so has been called the "gentle art", though there is nothing gentle about the way an expert judoist can hurl an opponent to the ground or render one helpless with a hold that further leverage can make agonizing or bone-breaking. A good deal of cultist nonsense is talked about the mystique and "intellectual discipline" of judo. It was branded a "war game" by the Occupation and banned in Japanese schools right after the Second World War; but the ban was lifted in 1949.

At one end of a hall where I watched bouts of judo at Tokyo University, kendo was going on. Kendo was more of a war game than judo, and looked almost savagely martial. It is a form of fencing using bamboo staves. Opponents wear the protection of a gridded mask and thick shoulder padding. The students I watched moved with the mien and speed of demons, thwacking each other with extraordinary vigour and uttering cries that sounded ferocious. Certainly it looked as though it could be just the training to increase the skull-cracking capability of a police riot squad; but I was sorry to hear in 1974 that the Crown Prince's schoolboy son, Prince Hiro, was learning kendo.

Karate I also watched. "Tiger" Saito took me to see the Takushoku University Karate Club in action. Astonishing judgement and muscular co-ordination was attested in the way these students launched flying kicks at each other without losing balance and without connecting—if your kick touched the opponent you lost points. In the same way, you pulled your punches, for a karate punch can not only smash a plank of half-inch wood; it can kill. I examined forearms ridged with hard muscle built up by lifting iron weights. Knuckles had turned into knobby calluses that came from punching a pad of straw rope tied round a post. A body-jarring process at best, this called for a lot of hardihood because as you punched into the rough rope you were expected to *twist* the fist, which breaks the skin and builds up scar tissue. Karate's potentiality for wreaking bodily damage—and it could be used by the criminally minded or the unscrupulous—seemed to me frightening.

Afterwards I was having a drink with the late Saito-san, who was a black-belt judoist in his day (of, I think, the fourth *dan*, meaning step or grade: the highest dan is the ninth) and he said, "Judo is all right. But this karate I don't like."

THE TOURIST COACH goes on into the Kasumigaseki district where the ministries of the national government are and the building of the parliament, the Diet, rises to a pyramidal top like a ziggurat.

Five political parties had representatives in the Diet, in this order of strength: 1, Liberal-Democratic Party, the conservatives who have been almost constantly in power since the war; 2, Japan Socialist Party, whose policy is socialism, pacifism and the "peaceful revolution"; 3, Komei Party, called the "Clean Government" party, which sprang from the Buddhist organization Soka Gakkai but is now an independent political entity; 4, Japan Communist Party, which has no alliance with (and, in fact, is detested by) the Communist Party in China; 5, Democratic Socialist Party, the dissident right wing of the socialists.

The tour goes to the Tasaki Pearl Galleries where we get a quite thorough and interesting demonstration of how a pearl oyster is planted, surgically, with a nucleus that can cause it to produce a cultured pearl: but I think it would be more relevent to detail this process when I am writing of pearl production at Mikimoto Pearl Island.

We go westward through the Akasaka district, headed for the Meiji Shrine. In this region, but not visited on this tour, are two remarkable structures I saw in 1965 soon after they were built. They are by Japan's most renowned architect, Professor Kenzo Tange. One is the National Gymnasium, a marvellously designed building, its swirl of a roof entirely supported by spiral steel pipe. The other, which is opposite Chinzan-so where we go to have lunch, is a Roman Catholic cathedral like no other cathedral in the world.

The Meiji Shrine is in a 175-acre park that was planted with more than a hundred thousand trees by people from all over Japan when the shrine was erected in 1920 to honour the memory of the Emperor Meiji who came to the throne in 1867 and was regarded, almost reverentially, as the "Father of Modern Japan". In fifty-odd years the trees thus planted have turned this into an imposingly wooded place, with avenues of the curious big tree with fan-shaped leaves, which is Tokyo's symbol, the gingko-tree. But in size the gingkoes can't compare with the two tree trunks that form the uprights of the huge *torii* gateway to this Shinto shrine: they are more than a metre in diameter and are 1,700-year-old *hinoki* (Japanese cypress) trunks that were brought from Taiwan. They, and the crosspiece of the arch, are bare. The

Japanese would never apply paint to wood as notable as this.

If it is the visitor's first Shinto shrine (as it was mine), there may be the same surprise I felt at the way the priests sell "fortunes" like lottery tickets.

Go there in late June and, I am assured, you will see the famous Iris Garden incomparably abloom with more than a hundred varieties of irises. November 3rd was the Emperor Meiji's birthday, now celebrated as Culture Day, and on that day you can see (with luck, for there will be big holiday crowds) old-time archery from horseback by riders in costume. A lot of picturesque re-creation of feudal-era customs and occasions goes on in Japan. Such "festivals" are frequent and, although they may be held at shrines or temples, they will be marked much more by vigorous gaiety than by religious solemnity.

On or about 15 November autumn visitors to Japan—if they want some enchanting colour pictures or would simply like to see the world's best-dressed children—should go to a big shrine such as the Meiji in Tokyo or the Heian in Kyoto, for the festival called *Shichi-go-san* (meaning Seven-five-three). Girls aged seven, boys of five, and both boys and girls of three years are taken to a shrine wearing ceremonial dress. The girls are in brilliant kimono and little brocade obi, with their faces made up. The boys have the darker but richly stylish *hakama*, the pleated skirt that used to be worn by courtiers and samurai. Although when I was last at the Meiji the day of Shichi-go-san was still almost a week away, some mothers were already there with their elaborately garbed children—to the joy of "camera-carrying Americans" and others on the tour.

CHINZAN-SO. This is a lovely and extensive garden with restaurants and a few beautiful small places for private dining and, nowadays, multi-storeyed facilities for weddings-receptions-banquets. These last tend to overpower the charm of the place, but doubtless they, like the tourist coach parties, provide income that makes it possible for the big hotel group Fujita Enterprises to maintain such prime Tokyo acreage as a garden.

On a hill that was called Chinzan because it was thick with camellias, Prince Yamagata, a statesman of the Meiji era, had the finest landscaper of the day design him a garden. Among the shrubs and trees that arose the prince placed as an ornament a miniature thirteen-tiered pagoda, which is believed to honour the memory of a famous master of tea ceremony. When Baron Fujita inherited Chinzan-so he had a full-sized three-storey pagoda, which had stood near Hiroshima for nearly a thousand years, brought to the garden; there is also a shrine building that was brought from Kyoto and re-erected. Looking at Chinzan-so today it is hard to credit that in the Second World War it was virtually destroyed by bombing.

I ate lunch quickly in the "barbecue" restaurant in order to walk in the garden I had seen something of on my first Tokyo visit, when I went there as the dinner guest of Mr S. Hirodo who set up the Australian branch of the wool-buying firm Kanematsu. We came in the evening and had a delightful meal in a tea-house overhung with maples turned autumn-scarlet. Kimono'd maids served us at the traditional low table set on a *tatami*, and it was quiet enough to hear the running of a small stream beneath the veranda and the occasional flurry of a carp. I remember that Hirodo-san's daughter had returned only the day before from the United States where she had been at university, and she said, happily. "This is what I think of as the true Japan."

What to do by day in the megalopolis 57

THE TOUR went to spend an hour or so at the biggest theatre in the Orient, called the Kokusai (pron. Coke-sigh) in the entertainment district of Asakusa (A-suk'-sa, the one that gets confused with Akasaka). The stage is enormous and some things that happen on it are quite spectacular.

"Kokusai" means "international", and Japanese audiences want exotica no less than tourists do; so there is sure to be a high-kicking chorus line modelled on the Rockettes of New York and quite possibly rigged out in Parisian style. There are traditional Japanese costume pieces as well. But the big thing about a Kokusai show is its dramatic spectacle. I saw one show where the hero, in order to rescue the maiden who is about to be sacrificed to the Dragon Snake, braves not only an inferno but a typhoon that brings down an avalanche of rocks. The Dragon Snake threshes and coils about our hero, but he vanquishes it against a background that includes, for good measure, a roaring waterfall.

"Five years ago we put on stage a waterfall forty metres wide," the theatre manager said, and he told me how many million yen it cost to mount a Kokusai show like that.

FROM THE KOKUSAI THEATRE the tour coach returned to the hotels, but I did not go with it: I thought it would be quicker to take a taxi to the Imperial, where Agui-san of JNTO was to pick me up at six o'clock, and I wanted to shower and change before we went, at the early hour that is customary in Japan, to dinner.

The taxi-driver was the one mentioned early in the book who didn't seem to understand "Imperial" hotel. He took me to the New Japan Hotel, miles away. Then it became plain, as he kept racing round the Marunouchi district and making U-turns, that if he knew where the Imperial was—and he didn't appear to—he didn't know how to get to it: finally he made it. The fare from Asakusa should have been about ¥600. There was ¥1,500 on the clock and what should have been a fifteen-minute ride had taken nearly an hour. It was 5.50, I'd have no time to shower, I was furious as I shoved a ¥1000 note from my wallet at this fool of a driver—who never did manage to find the Imperial's front entrance—when he let me out in the street beside the hotel. I raced to my room. I'd just have time to change into a suit before Frank Agui came.

It was then that I discovered I had no wallet. In it was about $A30 in Japanese money, tickets for a tour to Kyoto and Nara, some identification, and a crop such as one soon collects of what the Japanese call their name cards.

The point of this story is that I got my wallet back. Evidently I hadn't put it properly in my hip pocket. It was picked up where the taxi stopped, by a man on his way to work at a nearby printery. He telephoned a JNTO executive whose card he found in it. When it was brought to me by a delighted Yukiko Watanabe of JNTO we went to see the finder, the printery worker. He had no English and I could only repeat "*Domo, domo arigato*" (Many, many thanks) and shake his hand and bow as I handed him an envelope. In it was ¥3,000, wrapped in paper. It would have been very bad Japanese manners to have proffered the reward in the form of naked money.

This was not the only personal experience that bore out what one hears about the Japanese being particularly honest. On my last trip to Tokyo, on

58 Tokyo

arrival at Haneda airport, I took a taxi to the Marunochi Hotel, and my luggage went into the boot—except for one small case. This I took into the back seat of the taxi along with cameras—and on the back seat of that unidentifiable taxi the small case stayed when I got out at the hotel. It was utter carelessness: I couldn't even claim that I was travel tired because on the Japan Air Lines flight, 10.30 p.m. out of Sydney, I had slept very well.

The small case contained nearly thirty rolls of Kodak Ektachrome colour film, which brings a fancy price in Japan. The taxi-driver, I gather, was on the other side of Tokyo when he found the case, connected it with me, and brought it back to the hotel—while I was out. But I thought that, this being Japan, he could well turn up, so I had left for him, at the front desk, an envelope.

THERE WERE half a dozen other JTB/Hato daytime tours, four of them full-day; and, for those who were really time-pressed, there was an Uptown Tokyo morning tour and a Downtown Tokyo in the afternoon. The morning tour, at the Happoen Japanese garden, introduced tourists to the tea ceremony. Tea ceremony could also be experienced as part of a full-day tour called Art-Around-Town.

I shall never forget my introduction to the tea ceremony. I was the only foreigner, seated with about thirty Japanese, mainly young women, of the Chuo University Tea Society in an unostentatiously elegant tea-house in Ueno Park. You sit on the *tatami* floor not in cross-legged fashion but as Japanese women sit, back on the heels. It is a position that became, for me, so uncomfortable that, twice in the half-hour that felt like eternity, I just had to move my feet to the side and cool those burning muscles. Nobody stared, of course, and etiquette forbade the commiserating smile.

The tea-master, a very refined-looking young man, came in, bowed and was bowed to by us all, walked in the decreed manner—soles not leaving the floor, hands pressed lightly against the front of the thighs—and proceeded to make tea for two young ladies who were the "primary guests". The water boiled on a charcoal fire; the dark-green tea, fine as powder, was placed in two ceramic bowls and the water poured on; then the tea was whipped to a green froth with a whisk that was a lovely thing in itself, made of a single piece of bamboo delicately cut and splayed.

The tea-bowls presented to the guests were quite unlike any fragile porcelain we might associate with taking tea. They were thick pottery of uneven contours that required more than a quick glance to reveal their subtle beauty of shape and glazing. A guest "received" the bowl, with a bow, picked it up in a prescribed way—with the left hand, the right underneath, the bowl held low—and turned it round once, admiring it. Also you had to say to the person next in line to receive the bowl, "*Osakini*", a polite apology meaning, "I shall take it before you". That also applied when tiny cakes were served. The cakes were not eaten but wrapped up in fine white *kaishi* (pocket paper) that Japanese always carry. I had none. Minoru Murofushi, who had brought me along and told me about saying "*Osakini*", slipped me some paper.

At first I was afraid that my tea would arrive before I had learnt, from watching others, just what to do with it. Then, as my leg muscles felt as though they were being stretched on a rack, I thought my turn would never come. Eventually it did. I admired the bowl, handled it so, drank from the side with the main design, took the tea in the proper number of sips (three), set the bowl down. I thought I was doing rather well.

Then the tea-container—one couldn't call anything so beautiful a tea-caddy—was passed round. It was of matt-black lacquer gloriously patterned in gold: one of the loveliest things I had ever held in my hands. To see the design better, I tilted it forward.

"Don't—tip—it." I heard Minoru's whisper as I felt his nudge. I passed it on to him, with a side-of-the-mouth "What did I do wrong?"

Minoru took the container, turned it, removed the lid and replaced that, and passed it down the line before he said, "The tea-master made a little scene in it."

The powdered tea's surface had been shaped by the master into a miniature landscape. And the *gaijin*, by tilting the beautiful container, had caused earthquake-like havoc, making the little mountains fall into the little valleys and otherwise wrecking the tea-master's work of artistry.

To be expected was an Industrial Tokyo tour. But, in the biggest of cities, the visitor was also offered a Village Life and Crafts tour. It went out to an old farmhouse and also to a "doll-making town" and a shop that specialized in making paper and papier-mâché toys and to "Bonsai Village" which raised the miniature potted trees called *bonsai*.

The technique of growing dwarf trees involves pruning the roots and keeping the tree alive on minimal nourishment of soil and water, with just enough sunshine. Lilliputian pine-trees develop gnarled and twisted trunks as they age. There was one in the Imperial Palace, only about thirty centimetres high, that was cultivated by the third Tokugawa shogun, who died over three hundred years ago. Dwarfed fruit-trees such as *kaki* (Japanese persimmon) bud, blossom, and bear fruit like trees full-grown. Trunks and branches are diminutive but leaves and fruits grow to almost normal size.

"Bringing up a bonsai," the Japanese say, "is like bringing up a child." Many a Japanese businessman comes home in happy anticipation of changing into kimono and having a half-hour with his bonsai, deciding whether to pinch off a new stem that is budding, snipping a twig to improve a branch's shape, and finally putting the tree out where it will be sheltered from the wind but refreshed by the dew. If the baby cries in the night his wife will get up to it; but if there is a rainstorm he will leave his warm bed and bring in the bonsai.

Another tour called Tokyo Seven Wonders sounded as though it were tailored for travellers whose Japan would be just Tokyo: it took in two temples, a shrine, Tange's ultra-modern Catholic cathedral, and lunch was at a farmhouse. It also went to a museum I can recommend highly to anyone who is interested in Japanese crafts—embracing pottery, metalware, lacquerware, dyed and woven materials, wooden creations—crafts merged with folk art and among the most Japanese things about Japan.

This place was called Nihon Mingei-kan (meaning Japanese Folk Art Museum) at 861 Komaba-cho in Meguro-ku, five minutes' walk from Komaba station (near Tokyo University) on the Inokashira line, which goes from Shibuya. Mingei-kan is finely housed in a Japanese-style building that used to be a mansion. (Nearly all museums are closed on Mondays.)

As to Japanese pictorial art, it is richly represented—along with superb examples of Japanese sculpture, ceramics, lacquerware and textiles—in the Tokyo National Museum in Ueno Park. This is one of the great museums of the world.

Japanese painting in its traditional forms has a number of characteristics that make it different from Western painting, and the picture collections we go to see in Japan are the more interesting if we know what those differences are. Firstly, our painters work principally in oil paint: Japanese painting has been mainly in watercolours. Western artists painted with a full palette and on to canvas: a lot of Japanese painting was done in monochrome, on white paper or silk. *Sumi-e* are pictures done only with black ink, made by mixing water with rubbings from *sumi*, an inkstone formed from lampblack and resin. Tones pale to a misty grey from black lines showing astonishing control of the conical tuft of a brush that is held, more often than not, vertically. Such pictures might be on scrolls on screens, across paper walls or sliding doors.

Landscape was an Oriental subject centuries before European painters did it. But the Japanese painter (and before him the Chinese from whom he derived his style and technique) did not look at a scene and paint what he saw. He blended imagination with observation to compose what was ideal rather than real. His was subjective rather than objective art. Also it was without the European concern with shadows and modelling (yet a good sumi-e painter could brush in a circle so that it conveyed the roundness of a ball, without a vestige of shading). The Japanese artist did not employ the same sort of perspective. He was inclined to exclude backgrounds, was highly selective of what was significant, and very perceptive of the part blank space could play in paintings that were so seldom prosaic, so often the graphic equivalent of poetry.

Scroll painting (*e-makimono*) had no European equivalent. Illustration rather than decoration was the scroll's purpose. It was unrolled and viewed from right to left, and the story illustrated was often written as part of the scroll. Scrolls illustrating sexual activities—they were held to be instructive for brides—are often talked about but seldom seen, these *shunga* scrolls being mainly in the hands of collectors. Eminent artists did shunga scrolls.

Wood-block prints gave the widest circulation to *ukiyo-e*, meaning art concerned with the common people. Ukiyo-e added a vigorous new dimension to Japanese art and impressed many Western artists even though it began in the category of "pin-up" pictures of Kabuki actors and courtesans. Sharaku, Utamaro and Harunobu were among the outstanding ukiyo-e figurative artists. They could draw marvellously, even though their women's string-thin eyes and minuscule mouths don't accord with our ideas of beauty.

Scenic ukiyo-e were just as distinctively Japanese. These prints, often of "famous views", were the forerunners of tourist postcards. They were originally popular as souvenirs of journeyings that increased greatly in the latter part of the Tokugawa era, especially along the Tokaido Highway between Kyoto and Edo (Tokyo). Two masters of this *genre* were Hokusai (pron. Ho-ka-sy) and Hiroshige (Hirra-she-gay). Both of these artists could endow a scene with extraordinary decorativeness and drama, as when Hokusai shows, from the sea, a distant Mt Fuji under the curve of an enormous wave falling in foam like dragons' claws; or Hiroshige composes and colours superbly his *Ohashi in a Shower* which has lines of rain half-curtaining a river scene and a bridge animated with skeltering figures.

What to do by day in the megalopolis   61

Looking at the scenic ukiyo-e in Tokyo's National Museum one can understand why, in the heyday of the French Impressionists, a Paris art dealer put on exhibitions of Hokusai prints, and why some European painters were influenced by such imaginative design in depicting landscape.

Sampling night-life the tour way

TOKYO is the capital of a country that employs one-tenth of its workforce in the catering, accommodation and entertainment trades, and it has more night-life facilities than any other city in the world.

This embarrassment of riches isn't quite what it sounds, though, for the foreigner. What may look like just another bar turns out to be a private club; or it is the kind of place that subsists on the expense accounts of Japanese businessmen, to whom the tax authorities are notably kind.

First thing to remember in planning your Tokyo nights is: start early. This is an early eating city where hotel dining-rooms are open by six o'clock and most restaurants open at five.

Tokyo is also a surprisingly early closing city, though it is hardly true to say, as a JTB publication does, "By 12 midnight the whole country is in bed." I have been to a "club" (entry was no problem) in Akasaka that carried on past three o'clock in the morning; but the reason I was there was that the bar I had been at in the Ginza closed before midnight. Nightclubs and cabarets were required by law to close at 11.30 p.m.

"Why this decree on eleven-thirty closing?" I asked a Tokyo-dwelling compatriot who is particularly knowledgeable about the city's night life, particularly the fleshier aspects of it: I'll call him Randolph.

"It's supposed to be in the interests of public morality," Randolph said. "I'm inclined to think it's in the interests of business efficiency. If the executive who is out entertaining doesn't have a very late night he doesn't turn up at the office bleary next day."

That made sense, I thought. The so-diligent management men of Japan could hardly have performed their "economic miracle" with hangovers. Nor did they have the Western capacity for long sessions of alcoholic intake.

Randolph said, "I think there is another reason why the nightclubs shut so early. The hostesses in a big nightclub—not the little bars, where you can 'buy them out'—cannot leave until the place closes. So if a customer comes to an arrangement with a hostess for sex afterwards—and with a lot of them you can—that arrangement's all right if he can meet the girl outside at eleven-thirty. But if it's two or three in the morning it makes it too late when he gets to his own bed."

I said, "So there would be less 'immorality' if these places closed later?"

"That's for sure," Randolph said.

Tokyo's greatest night sight used to be the free show put on by the city's lights, its neon-sign extravaganza. Perhaps, when this is being read, so it will be again. Owing to the energy crisis that rationed oil and rocketed the expense of electricity, the 1974 Tokyo I saw was as a candle is to an incandescent lamp, so sparse was the night signery compared with the spectacular show of coruscating neons that used to switch on every evening. Half the attraction, I always thought, was that you couldn't read most of the advertising injunctions to buy this or use that (some, of course, were in English) and the Japanese ideographs that sprang into coloured life against the night were just so many brilliant shapes and designs.

NIGHT TOURS of the JTB/Hato Bus kind gave a sampling of Tokyo nightlife, and two of these spent perhaps an hour at the Kabuki theatre (if it was playing) and, after the tour had visited a big nightclub, ended with what was billed as a "Geisha Party". The tour I went on—it provided no new kind of experience but I wanted to see what the 1974-type tours were like—began with a sukiyaki dinner.

Since, in the preceding chapter, I quoted the poet and author James Kirkup as saying that, for the time-pressed traveller, "perhaps a daytime tour is the best way to see the highlights of the city", it seems only right to note that he also wrote, "The night tours to geisha house, cabaret and restaurant should be avoided, as the atmosphere is usually tense, dull and phoney."[16] I know what Kirkup means, but I don't agree that their demerits are such that these tours should be avoided.

Take the one I did, called Tokyo Golden Night. It was about five hours, approximately 6.30–11.30 depending on pick-up and drop-off time at your particular hotel, and cost ¥7,500. The dinner at the Suehiro (pron. Swayhero) Restaurant—not the Ginza-branch Suehiro, and not one of its top-grade dining-rooms—was not a very good sukiyaki and none of the elegances of Japanese dining went with it. The sake came in glass bottles, as though it were ginger ale, not in any ceramic container, and there was no hot water bowl to keep it warm. To be fair to the operators, it was costing only ¥1,500 (which I work out from the fact that a tour that was identical except for dinner cost ¥6,000), including transport to and from it. The sukiyaki dinners I compare it with cost not less than ¥3,000, double.

There is nothing "phoney" about the Kabuki theatre the tour would have gone to next if Kabuki had been playing; but it wasn't so we went instead to the Nichigeki Music Hall. This theatre puts on some of the best nude revue to be seen anywhere in the world. I happened to have seen the whole show the week before. It was excellently staged, the girls had first-class bodies, and the Nichigeki was much sexier than it used to be; in fact there was rather a plethora of simulated sex acts. So I couldn't help wondering which part of the first half our tour would take in, and what some of the housewifely-looking ladies in the party, which included a number of Australians and New Zealanders, would think of it. Sure enough, we were ushered in during the man-with-two-lesbians scene.

It could have been worse, if we had arrived during the second half of the program. Scene 8, innocuously titled "A Fairy Tale", was the most objectionable performance I have ever seen. It depicted sadistic cruelty being inflicted on a prostitute, who was stripped naked and bound with rope. She was tortured by four male actors cast as "good-for-nothing fellows". Nobody spoke and the woman acted her part without any screams as the men touched lighted cigarettes to her bare breasts, pricked her flesh with knives; and she writhed as though agonized when one man thrust a bamboo pole between her legs before all her clothing was ripped off. It was the foulest kind of violence and, in my view, truly obscene (using the word in terms of dictionary definition of it as a synonym for "disgusting", "repulsive", "abhorrent"). I am shocked by this Japanese inclination towards cruel violence, the more so because it is manifested by a people who are in so many ways so civilized.

Surprisingly, the country that produces for public showing films that pander to sado-masochistic tendencies and others based on blood and pain is obsessedly censorious about pubic hair. What might be called the glossy-muffy magazines, such as *Playboy* and *Penthouse*, which present full-frontal nudity unretouched, were on sale in Japan. But wherever pubic hair appeared in a photograph there was a broad black band across the page.

A BIG NIGHTCLUB called the Golden Gessekai was the tour's next stop. We arrived in time for the 8.30 p.m. floor show, which was elaborate but in the stock international style of bare-bosoms-and-feathered-bums showgirls and the striptease specialist—nothing distinctively Japanese.

The tables we had were well placed for viewing and we were served one drink. If I had taken myself to the Golden Gessekai—where I certainly wouldn't have wanted to spend a whole evening—the cover charge would have been ¥3,200 including a small bottle of beer or one whisky, and all drinks thereafter ¥800. Our guide said the average customer spent ¥15,000. If he had a hostess at his table and to dance with for two hours that would be, with a tip, around ¥5,000 or ¥7,000 depending on whether he took whichever girl was sent to him or he made his own choice or, perhaps, nominated a hostess he had liked on a previous visit. The guide said the Golden Gessekai had a hundred and fifty hostesses. Two other nightclubs, the Crown and China Town, each had three hundred; there were a lot at the gaudy old Queen Bee, and the Royal Akasaka had six hundred.

The Mikado, advertised as the "biggest cabaret in the world" by the Tokyo Silver Night tour that went there, had over a thousand hostesses. They cost ¥3,000 an hour if you picked your own. When a girl was required she was called by a buzz on a tiny transistorized paging gadget that was fitted inside her brassière.

The two best, and most expensive, nightclubs in Tokyo, with top-quality acts and superior ambience, were said to be, in 1974, the Copacabana and the Latin Quarter (which was good when I was there some years ago). The Copacabana doesn't take tour parties and it sounded so prohibitively expensive, I didn't go to it.

THE "GEISHA PARTY" that concluded the Tokyo Golden Night tour was, in the word James Kirkup used, "phoney". It simply wasn't a geisha party (a real one will be described in THE PERFORMERS section). It was quite good entertainment in itself, with Japanese dances to music played on *samisens* (Japanese banjos), flute and drums; the several "geisha" were more elaborately costumed than any I had seen before; and there was some interestingly costumed folk dance.

For it to be a geisha party there would have had to be geisha in attendance on us at a dinner with sake (there was no food and we were served beer). Moreover, some of the dancers were men, who are never present as hired entertainers at a geisha party. The only thing this entertainment had in common with a geisha party was that, towards the end, guests were encouraged to participate in some follow-the-leader Japanese dancing up on the stage.

The "geisha" who came on stage wore uncommonly gorgeous kimonos and had very fancy ornaments stuck in their lacquered hair. These young women were described in the tour leaflet as *"oiran* (élite Geisha)". The oiran was not really a geisha but a courtesan.

Michiko, a hostess, and bars to beware of

THE BIGGEST of the capital cities was said to be the safest. "Even on dark, lonely streets in the dead of night you need not be afraid of lurking shadows," a free Tokyo weekly called *Tour Companion* assured the tourist, and added, "Mugging is unheard of." I still wouldn't have wanted to take my chance as a drunk in some back alley of Shinjuku in the early hours of the morning; and Tokyo had some vicious gangsterism. But Tokyo's crime record was astonishingly lower than New York's.

Tokyo had (in 1973) nearly two hundred murders, New York had 1,680; and 3,735 reported rapes as against Tokyo's 426. And Tokyo had only a fraction of New York's number of reported robberies.

With this relative immunity from menace in mind I was walking along a Ginza side-street, just walking and looking, about eleven o'clock on a Friday night. There were drunks about as there always were on the evening of pay-day, reeling laughing out of narrow streets where they had been long in a beer-hall or drinking the cheap and potent *shochu* spirit in one of the little eateries—so small that some had room for only four customers. These places always proclaimed themselves, by having over the door a *noren*, which is a curtain hardly deeper than a pelmet, ideographed with a name.

The side-streets were perspectives of bar signs. These thinned away into darkness where the entertainment area petered out in sober-sided regions of 8.30-to-5.30 commerce. If a bar's name was in English the bar was usually on the ground floor or downstairs from street level. Such names were likely to be as un-Japanese as Bar Montparnasse, Silver Slipper, Club Lucky, Bar Riviera, or one that I used to know fairly well called Bar Lido.

The Lido was my introduction to Tokyo bars: I had been taken there on my first night in Japan, nearly twenty years before. The last time I had been there was in 1960. As I walked about in the Ginza this night I thought of the Bar Lido. It was quite a small bar in the Nishi (West)-Ginza, well managed by an ex-geisha, Yoshiko Saiki, and her two sisters. John Fysh, son of the founder of Qantas and then the airline's manager in Tokyo, took me there, and I wrote about it.

The role of the bar hostess was my concern, and what I wrote was based on a couple of note-taking sessions at the Lido with a hostess I called Michiko. She was a slim, pretty girl of only twenty, her face not typically round but oval; in features and hair-style she was not unlike my then-teenage daughter.

Michiko had been a salesgirl in a department store, where her wages had been very low. Although at the Lido she was paid no wage at all, she was earning, on average, more than twice as much a week as at the department store, and sometimes six times as much. She said she needed this extra money mainly because her father was not living and it would make it possible for

Traditionally dressed couple being married at Kanazawa's Miyako Hotel by a Shinto priest. Below, left to right: Japan Air Lines hostess; small girl and boy dressed up for the Shichi-go-san festival.

Bunraku is the Japanese doll theatre. The manipulators handle the puppets so skilfully that the dolls take on the reality of people in the enacted plays.

At a geisha party at a restaurant geisha entertain guests with dances. They may also play music, usually on the banjo-like samisen and the small taiko drum.

The Phoenix Hall—it has wing-like colonnades and bird ornaments on its roofs—of the magnificent eleventh-century Byodo-in Temple of Uji, near Kyoto.

Four of the five storeys (pagodas' tiers are never of an even number) of the pagoda of Japan's oldest temple, the seventh-century Horyuji near Nara.

Sumo is traditional Japanese wrestling. The ring, of clay, is under a canopy like the roof of a Shinto shrine: from this hang the big coloured silk tassels. Sumo wrestlers, giants by Japanese standards, weigh as much as 160 kilos (25 stone). The man spreading his arms wears the kilted white rope girdle of a grand champion. At left is the champion's sword bearer, and the gowned figure at right is the referee. Below: Some sketched sumo action, reproduced from a refreshments bag at the Osaka tournament I attended.

her younger brother, who was finishing high school, to go to college (by which she meant a kind of university) next year. A friend who knew the night spots said, "They all tell you they're putting a young brother through college—and half the time its true".

The system was (and is) that the bar hostess is a geisha in modern dress in so far as she sits with and looks after the customer, lighting his cigarettes, ordering his drinks, conversing with him, dancing with him—the Lido had a radiogram and dance space for about three couples. To earn money the hostess had to get the customer to spend money on drinks, for her as well as for him. The hostess invariably ordered an expensive cocktail, or "imported brandy" (which she didn't get, but even if she were served kola cordial the customer still paid the fancy price). The hostess got from the bar, which kept tally, a percentage of whatever the customer spent. And the bar got a hostess fee from the customer, and she got a tip. I'd give Michiko more than she was usually tipped because I was getting information from her. I picked her because she seemed to me brighter and franker than the other three hostesses, and I stressed that I'd rather she didn't answer my questions at all than answer them with lies.

"Okkay, Corin-san," she said. "I speak you true."

I asked Michiko what was the most money she had made in a week since working at the Lido. She said it was ¥18,000, which was six times as much as she used to get at the department store (and was equivalent to about ¥50,000 in 1974). I asked did she often make as much as that.

"Never happen—only last week!" She looked at me, and she knew that I knew she couldn't make that much out of drink commissions and a share in the hostess fee and tips.

I said: "How many men did you go to bed with last week? Two?"

"Who tell you I go to bed with men?" She didn't exactly bridle at my frankness, but she wasn't happy. "Yoshiko-san tell you that?"

No, I said, I had not talked with Yoshiko-san about her. Michiko finished her brandy or whatever it was and I finished my drink and didn't wait for her to ask whether I wanted another.

Michiko smiled at me. She crossed her left arm over her right and I was looking at her bare left wrist. She said, "I have no wrist watch. I like to have."

The watchless wrist could mean several things: she was earning enough to buy a watch but couldn't because she was contributing so much at home; or she actually had a watch, but left it off and showed the bare wrist to make the customer feel sympathetic and generous (I didn't think this was the case); or she was saying, in effect, "Pay me enough to buy a watch and you can go to bed with me."

I offered Michiko a cigarette, which she took, and put it down and reached for the matches to light mine; but I flicked my lighter and held it out to light her cigarette and she said, "Thank-you, Corin-san" and let her hand touch my fingers. Clearly, she liked being treated as we treat our women rather than in the tradition of Japanese male dominance. But I don't know how much that had to do with her saying, "I like you. I no like you I don't go with you."

I ascertained that I could spend the night with Michiko, at a Japanese hotel where I would pay the moderate room charge and breakfast, and the girl would be well pleased if I gave her ¥7,000 (today they ask ¥20,000, say

$A 50), but if I couldn't afford so much I gathered that she would settle for ¥5,000.

She could not leave until the bar closed—or not unless I was prepared to "buy her out" which meant compensating the bar, perhaps to the tune of several thousand yen, for the loss of Michiko-customer earnings. Any money Michiko earned by prostitution was hers and the bar got no part of it.

Although I was writing notes from time to time, Michiko found it a little difficult to believe that I was really more interested in getting information than in coming to an arrangement with her.

"Maybe you like a girl who is more pretty, more big?" said Michiko, who wore the kind of frilly blouse that is favoured by girls who are flat-chested. "Junko-san, my girl friend over there, nice girl, is more big. I do not know if Junko-san will go with you. But I ask her if you want. I get her to come here to this table?"

No, I assured Michiko, she was very pretty, appealed to me more than Junko-san did, but . . . . She smiled and touched my hand again as she saw the hope of half the price of her wrist watch fade away. Then I wanted to know what her mother thought of her working in the Bar Lido; and whether her mother knew what she was doing when, some nights, she didn't go home to where she lived out in the suburbs.

"Mamma, she thinks I work behind bar, serve drinks. When I give her money for new kimono I say rich man give me big tip. If I don' go home I say I stay Junko's place in town. Junko-san don' live in town but my mamma don' know that." Then she asked about my family: "Corin-san, you married man, you got wife in Austrayria? That why you say no to me?" and I asked what she thought about married men having sex with girls and she said she knew that wives, even Japanese wives whose husbands did it all the time, did not like it. But it was one of those things that men did and—well, men were men, and she thought the best thing to do was to accept that. I asked if she was religious and Michiko said, "Sometimes I go to Shinto shrine. To ask for good luck."

I LOOKED FOR the Bar Lido one night in 1965 but it wasn't where it used to be in Nishi-Ginza. A man, whom I didn't pick at once as a tout, had asked me what place I was looking for and when I told him he said the three sisters who had kept the Lido had split up and two had opened a bar somewhere else but he didn't know where.

He was a middle-aged, bespectacled man who spoke good English and he persuaded me to go to a bar he knew. Before I ordered I had a look at the drinks list and the prices were as he had said, reasonable. But there was: *Under the Regulations a Tax of ¥1,000 Must be Added to Your Bill.*

I said I would have one drink and buy one for the comely hostess I had been ensconced with, but I would not pay the ¥1,000 tax, because there was no such regulation. They offered to break the "tax" down to ¥ 500, but I said no and goodnight and the bar accepted philosophically that the tout hadn't brought in a sucker this time and would have to go out and look again.

Now, in 1974 as in '73, I was staying out of hostess bars because one heard on every side that they had become quite exorbitant. And the Japanese tourist authorities, to their credit, admitted that this was so and even warned the visitor. I quote from a booklet put out by JTB: *"Since these places cater mainly to those energetic Japanese business men on a big expense account, the tab is likely to be an astronomical amount at the end of the evening. So you won't want to spend your evening here."*

There I was then, walking the Ginza, feeling nostalgic about the Bar Lido, afraid of going into any bar because of what it might cost to get out, and, meanwhile, becoming thirsty, when a short middle-aged man fell into step beside me. In first-rate English his opening gambit was, "May I say something?"

I knew he'd say it anyway so didn't answer. He said, "Would you like to have one drink at a nice bar I know. Beer is only five hundred yen. And no cover charge. With English-speaking girl hostess to enjoy."

It was no answer to ask him if he remembered the Bar Lido. The tout said, "Oh, yes. The one that was in Nishi-Ginza. Then it went to another address on the Atago-dori. Yoshiko-san, she got married. No more Lido." (A Bar Lido was listed in Fodor's '73 guide as catering primarily to foreigners, with "Amiable English-speaking hostesses. Fairly expensive".) The tout said, "Will you have one drink at my bar?"

"Where the hostess charge is how much?"

"Up to you," he said. "Up to you. No fixed charge. And, as I said, no cover charge."

I decided to put myself in the position of a lonely male tourist who is persuasively propositioned by a tout and goes along with it. Why, after all, should a first-time tourist be such a suspicious fish if he wanted a drink and maybe had ideas about a girl? So I'd let myself be hooked to find out what happens. I figured that it could cost me around ¥5,000. I was wrong.

We went to this upstairs bar—I cannot give its exact Ginza location and its name was not in English on the sign outside and, strangely, it did not have its own matchboxes or its name on the drink list (but I gathered that it was called Bar Fuji). As soon as I was seated in a cubicle, of which it had only three, a sexy-looking hostess was thigh-to-thigh beside me. She was darker-complexioned than Japanese usually are, more zestful and less passive, a girl with a mouth as wide as her skirt was short and her hands friendly. I'll call her Yoko.

I said I'd have a Suntory Old whisky and Yoko said she would like the "hostess cocktail". As soon as it was served she was toasting me "*Kampei*" (the Japanese "Bottoms up"). When we had a second drink she was clearly surprised at my asking her the price of the cocktail she had ordered. But she answered, "Three thousand" and, handing me the drink list, pointed to the printed evidence: "*Girl Hunter Cocktail*—¥3,000. Seven-and-a-half dollars Australian!

The main reason the bars can get away with outrageous prices—apart from their being tax-deductible business expenses—is that a Japanese man feels that he is losing face and looking stingy if he appears concerned about costs. In this respect I proved, in the short while I spent in this bar, very un-Japanese. And I was thoroughly chided by Yoko-san for being, in her eyes, unreasonable, parsimonious and rude.

"If you out for a good time, why don't you bring plenty money with you?" she wanted to know. If I was so poor she would have a cheaper drink, like this cocktail for ¥2,000. No? I wasn't even buying her a five-dollar drink? It was very bad-mannered of me to say that the bar was "a bloody clip-joint".

She had met other Australians and they did not swear like that. One Australian she knew owned a yacht and he spent much money in this bar whenever he came to Japan and he had bought for Yoko many things including dresses.

Yoko had an animal-like quality which probably would have made her a very enthusiastic partner in bed. I went so far as to suggest that I had some money at the hotel and ask how much would I need to come to an arrangement with her when the bar closed. But I could not have made that sound sufficiently convincing because I got the scalding rejoinder that she wouldn't tell me how much she'd want because the amount would be too much of a shock!

For this twenty-minute experience of what can happen if you let a well-spoken tout lure you to a bar I got a bill for ¥10,700, nearly $A27. If, as could happen, you didn't check on prices and had about five whiskies and the hostess as many Girl Hunter Cocktails at ¥3,000 plus (legal) tax, plus hostess charge, the amount could easily have reached a hundred dollars.

NOT ALL BARS are clip-joints. For instance, Randolph knew a square-dealing place in Asakusa with the un-Japanese name of Danny's Inn where beer was ¥300 with take-away girls ¥10,000 and the girls didn't clip you either.

A bar I liked in 1974 was Romy's Roppongi. Its *bonhomie* was good without being specially Japanese because it was run by blonde Romy Mai who had a Norwegian mother and a French father. Romy's operated until 2 a.m., in the Roppongi area of late-night liveliness, opposite the Self Defence Forces establishment. It was known for its bright bartenders, usually female and sometimes European. It didn't have what the guidebooks call "amiable hostesses". The forthright Romy told me: "You don't come here for a lay. If men want that I'll tell them where to go."

Sex in Tokyo was not offered as blatantly as it used to be. In the mid-fifties no Western male tourist could walk a block in the Ginza at night without being approached by touts saying, "You like private show, sir?" Even when Claire was with me one came up, only changing the invitation to, "You like sex education, sir, madam?"

I managed to see the Yoshiwara before the anti-prostitution law of 1957 put it out of business. We (Torao Saito took me) arrived in style in a big black limousine of *Asahi Shimbun*, with the newspaper company's rising-sun flag flying from the radiator cap until, at the entrance to Brotheland, the driver stopped the car, furled the pennant and popped a little hood over it. Men with rickshaws came running out of the darkness, soundlessly in their rubber shoes. Reaching the car, they all jabbered of what they could take us to outside the legal Yoshiwara—I gathered from "Tiger" that they offered illegal pornographic movies, live-sex exhibitions and homosexual prostitution. The car went on down a wide street of bright-lit "houses of pleasure". Girls were at all the entrances and the place looked very lively. Years later I went to see what had happened to the Yoshiwara area. It was dismally dark and squalid, with a few short-time hotels, girls outside calling to the rare passing couple, "Come in, please, to rest." A once-gaudy restaurant was shuttered and cobwebbed except for one open door that revealed a couple of candles flickering over dirty tablecloths. A grandmotherly woman and a young boy sidled up with, "You like see sekkus movie?"

What goes down in one form comes up in another. Shinjuku has cafés with names like Voluptuous Valley that charge several times the regular price for coffee but provide bead-curtained cubicles where students whose yearnings aren't matched with enough money for an hour's hotel room can take compliant girl friends. If the student has no girl he may go to a "touching bar". The girl who goes into a cubicle with him and sits on his lap will have no pants on.

The Japanese had their own taboos and areas of mental dirtiness. For men to display affection used to be regarded as so improper that kissing was considered a Western indecency, and kissing scenes were deleted from imported films up until the Second World War. After the war some cinemas began installing closed loges or "love seats" so that young patrons could indulge in this former immorality. Today's Japanese marriage manuals not only take the "deep kissing" caress for granted but commend the genital kiss as normal sexual foreplay.

TRANSVESTITES mince about some Shinjuku streets at night offering themselves to homo- or bi-sexual males.

"Sister Boys" was the Japanese description of male homosexuals, and the late fifties saw the emergence in Tokyo of "sister boy" bars (the term "gay" has since come into common usage). A lot of coffee houses had sprung up, with *chanson* singers. The Japanese have always been inclined to consider themselves the French of Asia, and the young were idolatrous of Juliette Greco and Yves Montand. Some of the most acclaimed Japanese *chanson* singers were "sister boys". The term was used tolerantly; it was not pejorative as was *pam-pam* boy, meaning a male non-transvestite prostitute.

I was taken to one of these "sister-boy" bars. We were joined at a table by two young men who gave their names as Kono and Kenny. Both wore heavy eye make-up and Kenny's cheeks showed some rouge. Kono seemed intelligent and spoke English fairly well, but said he was more fluent in French. Kenny, who had no English, was like a kittenish girl, who simpered and patted me on the knee—at which point the visit seemed rather silly and, after one drink all round, we left. It appeared that Kenny was a transvestite who often wore kimono and a wig like a geisha.

A much newer Tokyo development, one I first heard about in 1974, was called the male host club. Only males who were hosts or staff were allowed into these clubs. The unstated reason for refusing other men admittance: "Your wife might be in there."

"Foreign women can go into these clubs, but they are primarily for Japanese and they have come about because of the Japanese marriage condition," said the bright female guide on a night tour who told me about them. "Arranged marriages are not so common today, but most wives who are now middle-aged were matched by a go-between with some man who was considered suitable. Love does not come into such marriages, or rarely so. And the husband goes out with his men friends, and he has girls. The wife feels neglected and sexually frustrated. If she can afford to, she can go to one of these clubs and find handsome young men who are ready to make a fuss of her and provide not love but the next best thing. You see them shopping in the Ginza, these middle-aged women with young men you think are their sons. They are not their sons, these young men they are buying things for."

Three Australian girls went into the biggest of these male host clubs, in

Akasaka. Five good-looking young Japanese men came to their table and sat with them and were pleasant and asked what they would like to drink and ordered for them. Then one said, "Could *we* have a drink?" The girls bought two rounds, and got a check for ¥11,000.

A "love hotel", and the massage girls

MEGURO is not a salubrious suburb of Tokyo, and the car crawled past a grey factory in a narrow street and stopped beside a dirty-looking canal. We got out and, looking up, I blinked to see a medieval-style, storybook castle. It had round towers, turrets, battlements, pennants flying, the lot. I hadn't seen a more castellated castle in a day's trip down the Rhine.

"That has to be it," my companion said. "The 'love hotel' Steve Greene wrote about—the Hotel Meguro Emperor." He quoted the caption to a photograph in the *Tokyo Weekender*[17] showing the battlements illuminated at night, "Meguro's Posh Palace of Pleasure and Passion". It was taller than I'd expected.

"Nine storeys," said my friend Jack. "It was on the ninth floor if you remember that the charming proprietor, Miss—you wrote her name down—"

"Miyoko Yamamoto."

"She took the writer up to the ninth floor in a red-lighted elevator and swung open the sound-proof door of the top-price sex suite. The one with the big round bed that undulates as it revolves."

I said I liked the bit about this three-metre-diameter bed with silken sheets having a headboard with not as many dials and toggle switches as a Boeing 747 but enough to bring a blue movie on to a television screen, provide love music (with microphone if you wanted to do your own serenading), change the wall panels all into mirrors, to go with the all-mirror ceiling, and activate a closed-circuit television camera which took pictures of the bed occupants and then provided instant playback. (Another account mentioned that such pictures, once viewed, would "self-destruct".) All this for ¥25,000 (over $A60) a night. The room was also available at $A24 for two hours.

Well, we'd go in and see if Miss Miyoko Yamamoto would show it to us, so that I could write about it at first hand. This young lady was twenty-seven now and a few years younger when her rich uncle, having sold a block of Tokyo real estate, provided five million dollars so that she could realize a Disneylandish dream which uncle thought could be a good business proposition— a sumptuously romantic hotel just for people to make love in. She seemed not averse to the publicity for the place that accrued from letting writers have a look: Steven Greene, who was a *Stars and Stripes* staffer, and London's Robert Whymant of *The Guardian*, whom I'd met at the Foreign Correspondents' Club and who was also doing a piece about it.

We went through a fancy gate into a small over-decorated garden with a little fountain. The entrance hall had dim-lit glamour and smelt of perfume. When-knights-were-bold exoticism was expressed with a suit of armour beside the lift. There was no reception desk but a kind of box-office. Between us and the just-discernible young lady inside was a curtain of black lace such as Spanish mantillas are made of. Doubtless this was to indicate that patrons who did not want to be seen at all could not be seen clearly; or their lady friends subjected to no more scrutiny on entering than this through-a-lace-darkly glimpse.

My friend Jack, who runs an instrumentality of the Australian Government in Tokyo, used his fluent Japanese to say that I was a *yumeina sakka* (famous author) who had heard of the Meguro Emperor and wished to talk to Miss Miyoko Yamamoto and see her hotel. The attractive young lady behind the lace, who could have been Miss Yamamoto—and from the assured manner of her tone we thought she was—said that Miss Yamamoto was not in. Could the young lady, then, arrange for us to be shown a few rooms? No, she could not.

"I think," Jack said as we shrugged out, "we were a disappointment to her. Two men—we could have been very welcome. If you remember, Steve Greene wrote that, of all her clientele, Miyoko likes best male homosexuals. She told him. 'They're the least noisy, and they always tidy up before they leave.' "

"LOVE HOTELS" appeared on the Japanese scene about 1968 and have since proliferated and grown more elaborate. They are known as *abeku hoteru*, the first word being a very-Japanese pronunciation of the French *avec*, "with": a hotel you go to *with* someone.

Prostitution is illegal in Japan, but the love hotels are quite legal, are sanitarily inspected, and they count politicians among their clients, according to *The Guardian's* Robert Whymant who wrote: "The Westerner who crudely assumes that these are mere houses of assignation is only partly right . . . . They perform a vital service as oases of intimacy in the most tightly packed islands in the world. In a nation where half of all families live in apartments seven feet by nine, whose paper walls betray each sigh, they offer a brief chance of privacy to lovers and married couples alike."[18]

My friend Jack said that some Tokyo Americans he knew were touring the Kansai region by car, stopping wherever they felt was rewarding, and they saw a very nice-looking hotel and booked in for the night. They had their small son with them, and left him in the hotel room while they went out to do some shopping. There was television to entertain him. They returned to what they had not known was an *abeku hoteru* to find the boy sitting, fascinated, in front of a screenful of lesbian sex.

A Kyoto love hotel had a lobby with singing birds, rooms that suggested that Fellini had been brought in to do the high-camp, brothelesque décor and, as well as video-cassette erotica, the management thoughtfully provided an electronic dildo.

At the Meguro Emperor, room rates ranged up from a ground-level US$15 a night. There was an additional 50 per cent charge on each person over two who occupied the same room—and not infrequently four or five did. There was restaurant service, which ran to ten-dollar Kobe steaks and other re-invigorating fare including an allegedly aphrodisiacal drink, "Korean Carrot Juice".

There were thirty rooms, all different. One had artificial rain pattering on the bed-roof. In another the bed was surrounded by a "moat". One nasty one had an ante-room with a split swing, a black leather chastity belt and a whip.

Some had sunken marble baths, even mirror-lined baths. A very expensive bed rose three metres high into a mirrored dome. One customer had paid US$800 for a night's use of the hotel's facilities—which did not include the provision of partners: you had to bring your own.

Of course, you could order up an attractive young lady to give you a massage.

"MASSAGE" is not the word it was. In recent years it has had some of its meaning rubbed off and other meaning rubbed into it.

Whenever I am given a good massage I am always impressed by the skill that goes into the kneading, the exercising that my tissues get while I lie there inert; impressive, too, if the operator is a masseuse, is the strength that can develop in female fingers. But no such training in massage techniques is required of the girls who work in "massage parlours" in New York, London and Sydney. In these establishments the male can get a rubdown of sorts but MASSAGE is strictly for the signboard; the girls are there for, and the real money is made from, the "extra services" they perform, ranging from the masturbatory manual to oral to full sexual intercourse.

Unlike their Western sisterhood, the Asian girls have been schooled in the technique of "straight" massage, which is difficult; what else their hands do is so much more easily accomplished, and so much more expensive.

First there is the matter of nomenclature, of which name signifies what. *Sauna* is the bath description to look for if all you really want is a steam bath and a good massage. Typical, I should think, was the Phoenix Sauna I went to in Takamatsu. After I had sauna'd and showered I relaxed in the lounge in kimono with a glass of fruit juice in front of the colour television until I was called for massage. The premises were strictly open-plan, no cubicles, and the masseuse worked on me, and very expertly, alongside a man who was massaging another male customer.

Where a Japanese establishment is described as a *Turkish Bath* then— according to my Tokyo compatriot Randolph and others—the male customer can expect not only an accomplished "straight" massage at the hands of an attractive female but that this can be extended to the genital area by arrangement and for a usually hefty fee. Upon my first arrival in Tokyo, I fairly quickly acquired a hangover and thought to repair this next morning at the Tokyo Onsen, a bathplace (*onsen* mean "hot spring") which I note is listed in Boye DeMente's pleasure-guide for businessmen[19] under "Turkish Bath Houses". (It could, of course, in the many years since I was there have changed its style and practices.) This is what happened then:

I went into the Tokyo Onsen building, bought a ticket and went upstairs, where a woman supervisor bowed and bade me wait. She reappeared with an attractive girl of about twenty, clad in very short white shorts and a tied-round top like that of a bikini swimsuit. I followed my bath maiden down a corridor lined with small white-curtained rooms. We went into one, and the girl pulled the curtain across the doorway. The room had a hot-box, a tiled bath and a bench-like table. The young woman smiled at me and showed a welcome acquaintance with English by saying, "Please to take off clothes." I asked her name and she said it was Maki.

I undressed, Maki opened the hot-box front, I stepped nude into it, she closed the box so that only my head protruded and I proceeded to stew.

When my brow oozed perspiration she mopped it with cold towels. After five minutes that felt like ten Maki asked if I had had enough of that; I had. When I stepped out she motioned me, *"Dozo"*, into the tub-like bath she had filled with hottish water, which was mineralized.

Maki washed my back and knees and I washed the sweaty rest of my jack-knifed nakedness. When I got out and had dried myself she handed me another towel and motioned that I should wrap it round my loins and get up on the table-bench for the massage.

She began on the soles of my feet and worked up the leg muscles, her fingers expert and strong. With loose fists she played on my spine as though it were a xylophone. I got a good and relaxing feeling from what she did with the muscles of my neck. After about ten minutes of that Maki said, "Turn over, please". I did so under my loin towel, and she began on my feet and legs from the front. About the torso she didn't do much, except that she gave both shoulders a vigorous workout.

I asked Maki if many foreigners came to the Tokyo Onsen and she said most customers were Japanese but quite a few were foreigners. Did some customers, foreigners or otherwise, try to "get fresh" with her—did she understand that expression? *Hai.* Yes, they did.

"Maki-san, do some customers make suggestions that you do things to them?" She answered yes, they did.

"You don't do things like that?"

"Yes," Maki said.

"You *do?*"

"No," she said, digging fingers into my shoulders.

"But you said 'Yes'."

Her, *"Yes, I don't do things like that!"* was most emphatic—and my introduction to the negative yes one comes up against in Japan, along with the affirmative no. "You don't like it?" answered with "Yes" means agreement that it isn't liked. "No" to the same question can mean "I like it".

Maki said, "Some massage girls do anything man want, but not this place."

"Utamaro, that's the place you should go to!" Randolph spoke with enthusiasm. "I'd say it was named after the artist Utamaro, who was not only superb in his woodblock prints of women but did a lot of erotica, what were called *shunga* pictures, porn."

I had read of this Turkish Bath in the little book JAL puts out for its first-class (male) passengers.[19] Utamaro, it said, "caters to high-level businessmen (subscribes to *Wall Street Journal*) and charges accordingly. One hour treatment is ¥5,000 with expected tip about ¥3,000. Highly reputed for its service." I asked Randolph what kind of service was meant, involving what kind of extra charge.

"I haven't been there," he said. "As I hear it the fifty-dollar touch is common at Utamaro. It's for the visiting tycoon and the top-management men who entertain him. Out of *my* reach." Which led to the obvious question: What made him think that *I* could go there?

Next in line in Boye DeMente's highly selective list of "Turkish Bath Houses" for JAL's pocket guide[19] was the Ginza Turkish Bath, described as "where many foreign residents take visitors (who once they have experienced a Turkish bath *à la Japan* usually go back on their own as often as possible) . . . .

Open daily from noon to 12 p.m.... Twenty private rooms. Fifty rotating girls, most of whom are very attractive. All are good sports."

Yes, Dolph said, he had been to the Ginza place. He paid ¥2,500 and got the hot box, then a bath, then massage, and that took the best part of an hour. Then he had "Special Massage", which had cost ¥5,000 and was over in about two minutes.

the performers

文樂 能 相撲
芸者 歌舞伎

Geisha party:
What really goes on

RIGHT IN THE middle of what we might call the area of misunderstanding about Japan stands the pretty figure of the *geisha*. "Most foreigners do not have a correct understanding of the geisha," said a tourist publication reprovingly. "They are not prostitutes."

The name (pronounced gay-sha) is from *gei*, meaning art, and *sha*, person. A geisha, then, is an artist. Before she can appear before guests she must go through a long training in etiquette and social graces, in Japanese dancing and even Western dancing as well, and in playing on the samisen and the *taiko*, a drum, and she must be able to conduct the gracious tea-ceremony and do *ikebana*, flower arrangement.

A geisha, while she is still young, though not commonly before she has finished her training at the okiya, usually becomes the mistress of some wealthy businessman. Until she gets a patron she is not regarded as having real status in her profession. Though she continues to entertain other men in the restaurants where geisha parties are held she is, as it were, bespoken sexually. (Yet I have had a geisha say to me at the end of a party, "You stay. You stay night with me." She was the least attractive of the geisha present, and probably she had no patron.)

From her professional earnings, and with what her patron gave her, the geisha might save enough money to open a restaurant of her own: not many of them marry. If she is an exceptionally talented woman, even though she may not be especially good-looking, a geisha is not necessarily finished at thirty-five or even when she is past forty. Among Japanese businessmen and politicians who traditionally discuss business or even matters of State at banquets with geisha in attendance, there are always those who prefer the worldly-wise company of the older woman.

The existence of geisha as a Japanese institution points up differences in attitudes to marriage and to sex. According to Ruth Benedict,[20] the Japanese fence off one province that belongs to the wife from another that belongs to erotic pleasure, and both provinces are equally open and above board.

Whereas in our society, Miss Benedict says, a husband's physical attraction to another woman is humiliating to his wife "because he bestows elsewhere something that rightly belongs to her", the Japanese judge differently.

"Only the upper class can afford to keep mistresses, but most men have at some time visited geishas or prostitutes. Such visits are not in the least surreptitious. A man's wife may dress and prepare him for his evening of relaxation. The house he visits may send the bill to his wife and she pays it as a matter of course. She may be unhappy about it but that is her own affair."

At Kyoto a night tour went to an okiya where geisha trained. Dances were performed, and a geisha in the old costume with hair ornaments and the heavy make-up no longer worn—the mask-like white face and only the lower lip painted, which looks rather grotesque to Western eyes. There was also a bit of tea-ceremony with two doll-like children who are being schooled in geisha graces. As the tourists were leaving the geisha teetered out on the old-style geta that are like wooden clogs three or four inches high. Her kimono was pulled well down at the back of the neck, to expose the nape—which was considered as alluring as bosom cleavage is in the West.

However, it was unusual for tourists to get to a real geisha party.

I WAS LUCKY. I happened to know a visiting business man whom I shall call J.B. He had business with the Nikon people, the big camera company. Nikon were giving him a geisha party. J.B. asked the sales manager of Nikon if it would be all right if this author friend of his came along. Sales manager Kuratsuji said, "Of course."

So, on the appointed evening, we drove to a suburb of Tokyo where there are a number of restaurants that cater for functions of this kind. No neon lights proclaimed the restaurant we came to, just a discreet sign in Japanese characters on one post of a gateway. We went up a path through a garden to what must have been in times past the large residence of a prosperous family.

The shrubs of the garden shone in the moonlight. That night the moon was full. Looking up to it, our host said, "Different peoples see different things in the moon. We Japanese, who are fond of moon-viewing, we say that in the moon there are two rabbits."

J.B.'s Tokyo representative, who was very much an Australian, said, "If there's two now there'll soon be a bloody million."

Our host smiled politely at this strange jest—the idea of a plague of protein must seem extraordinary to a Japanese. Then we were at the door, being welcomed by the proprietress and several maids, all on their knees and bowing to the floor. We took off our shoes and were provided with soft slippers.

The room we came into, through lattice-paper doors at a corridor's end, was large and serene. A single picture, a scene of trees in greens and greys and white, hung on the tokonoma side of the room. The dining table must have been fifteen feet long and less than knee-high. We were seated on square cushions set on the immaculate tatami. For those of us who were foreigners the back-and-arm-rest gadgets that slip under the cushions were provided. Maids appeared with hot hand-towels in little wicker baskets.

When the geisha came in and, after making their kneeling bows to us, stood up against the delicate straight-line pattern of the paper wall, the room seemed to flower, so decorative were the colours and patterns of the kimonos and the obi brocades.

The brightest and prettiest of them was the youngest, the *maiko*, a young geisha who was just budding into the profession: she was only nineteen. Her name was Matsuchiyo, and her kimono was exquisitely flowered on silk that was the colour of pink sugar. At first glance she was like some marzipan confection. Then the high-piled, jet-black, lacquered hair-style showed that she was truly like a Hakata doll. The others had short hair dressed in Western style.

A geisha knelt beside each guest and served him with sake and beer, lit his cigarette, made a surprising amount of conversation out of her few words

Miyajima, the sacred island in the Inland Sea, has this superb shrine of Itsukushima.

Famous torii of Itsukushima shrine rises in the sea off Miyajima.

Entrance to a ryokan, a Japanese inn, with typical stone paving and lantern and water-holder, chaste natural woodwork and tatami floors (in the room at right).

Art exhibit I saw at the Tokyo Biennale 1974. The only living people are the two indicated. All the other figures have been modelled, with extraordinary realism.

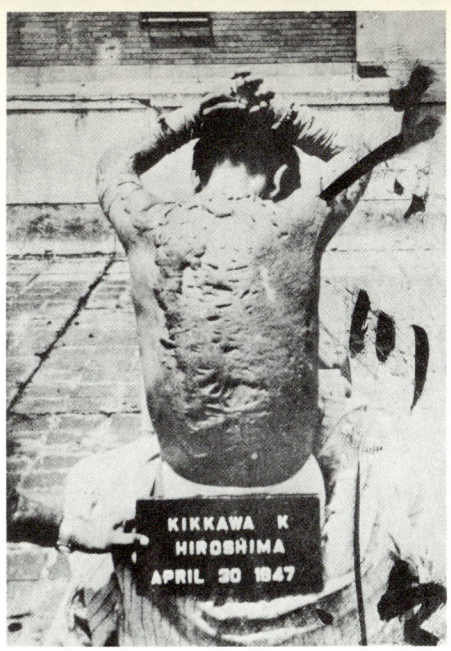

At Hiroshima in 1955 I met Kiyoshi Kikkawa. Ten years earlier, when the atomic bomb dropped, he was frightfully burned, as shown by the postcards of his back which he used to sell, autographed, at the stall where he also sold melted bottles and other A-Day "souvenirs". At Hiroshima in 1973 I was told that K. Kikkawa had left the city, after being "over-active in anti-war protests".

Section of Hiroshima as it looked after the atomic 6 August 1945. Now it is a bustling, bigger-than-ever industrial city where all the Mazda cars are made.

The court music called Gagaku, dating back to the seventh century, is still performed at festivals of the Itsukushima Shrine on the island of Miyajima.

Dances performed with masks and elaborate costumes at the shrine on Miyajima probably came to Japan from India, through China.

Geisha party: What really goes on

of English, and managed to create an atmosphere of enjoyment touched with coquetry. The geisha did not take any food or drink themselves. They had eaten before we came, a geisha named Tokuko conveyed to me. Their whole purpose was to serve, to amuse, to entertain.

Japanese cuisine's appeal to the palate is matched by its appeal to the eye. One dish held a morsel of smoked fish and a baby turnip smaller than a ping-pong ball and of the most delicate flavour. In another were two little wedges of raw fish. Tokuko indicated that I should take a piece in the *hashi* (chopsticks) and dip it into a sauce of soy mixed with horse-radish, into which she shredded the tiny leaves from a sprig of a herb that looked like thyme.

This was the first time I ate raw fish—and I never looked at it askance again. After all, we eat oysters raw, and raw beef in Steak Tartar. The fish was young tuna. Least expected of the foods we had was chrysanthemum petals, served as a garnish.

"The leaves can be eaten also—fried," the spare and elderly company secretary, Mr Wakabayashi, assured me across the table.

After this first course, the geisha left the table. Two of them seated themselves at one side to play the samisen. The instrument has been described as a Japanese banjo, but a banjo would look plebeian alongside a samisen. Fujiko knelt in front of a small and very decorative stand-drum called a *taiko* and tapped this with thick drumsticks that rose and fell in ritualized movements as the two samisen players sang and the maiko, Matsuchiyo, danced for us.

To say that it was a parasol dance conveys little, and it is difficult for a foreigner to appraise Japanese dancing in which every movement of a foot or a finger, or of the eyes or the head, has its meaning. Anyone with any appreciation of ballet would have been delighted with the grace of the young geisha and the artistry of movement of the parasol. As her body swayed gently she seemed to command every fold of the kimono and when she drew the white *tabi* of one small foot across the tatami it was with the lightness of an artist's brush tracing a delicate line.

Matsuchiyo had been apprenticed, one might say, to a geisha house mamma-san when she was thirteen, before her ordinary schooling ended. For the last two years her training had been intensive. She had to study and pass examinations in deportment and dancing, etiquette and conversation, flower arrangement and tea-ceremony, as well as the musical instruments. At the maiko stage Matsuchiyo would not have had a patron, though she may well have been marked already by some eminent client of her mamma-san, for she was appealingly beautiful. "In the old days," I was told, "a maiko's virginity was broken on the night she graduated as a geisha."

We had some more food—quail, with a little dish of two hard-boiled quails' eggs on the side. And more sake, of course. As soon as I drained the tiny sake cup it would be filled again by Tokuko from one of the porcelain bottles that stood in their hot-water containers on the table.

After the next course the company secretary went to the entertainment place beyond the head of the table. He knelt on a cushion, a small music stand was placed before him, and two geisha ranged themselves with samisen at his side. He sat very still as he sang in a high clear voice, his hands rested on his knees, his eyes half closed. Mr Wakabayashi sang two classical Japanese love-lyrics, and when I said afterwards that I should like a translation of one of them, he wrote out the words for me in English:

Rain falls gently on the lighted stream.
Two umbrellas over the dim shadows of two people
Move slowly at this late hour to the accompaniment of a street-song.
Is it Okichi who goes in the palanquin
Along the Shimoda street wet with spring rain?
Her tears run down as fall the leaves of the flowers of the camellia.
The sad street song and the willows, weeping, keep company with her heart.

Okichi was the concubine of Townsend Harris, the first American consul and, subsequently, the first United States Minister to Japan, who came in 1856. Mr Wakabayashi explained that Okichi was sad at being separated from her lover. I tried to imagine a company secretary in my country rendering something comparably poetic at a business dinner.

We had some more dances. For one of these the geisha put on flat conical hats to represent raftmen, in a song about rafting down a river. The next one, performed by Toshiko, was, Mr Wakabayashi explained to me, "a comical dance concerning the egg-plant and the pumpkin quarrelling on the farm".

"See now how she blows out her cheeks—she is the pumpkin!" It was very clever clowning, and obviously the entertainment was getting lighter and brighter; in fact, it was on its way to becoming hilarious.

Matsuchiyo, who had been looking after J.B. at the table, motioned to him to get up and join her in what is known as the Baseball Game. He had been to geisha parties before and knew what to expect, and he said to me as he got to his feet, "Here we go. Sublime to the ridiculous."

The maiko pretended to throw the baseball and he pretended to hit it. Then they were playing the hand game that is centuries old in Japan—the game of "Scissors cut paper, paper wraps stone, stone breaks scissors", the hidden hand thrust forward with two fingers extended, or the palm flat, or the fist clenched. They were uncanny the way, if you had "paper", they made "scissors", or if you made "scissors" they came up with "stone".

In one game you stand on a cushion, back to back with a geisha, and, at the count of three, bump behinds together so that one or the other loses balance. The little geisha, I found, were very adroit in their timing and, while I was still wondering if it was right for a six-footer to bump his bottom in the small of a five-foot female's back, I found myself neatly projected right off the cushion.

"You people make business a pleasure," said J.B. as the party broke up, with bows and felicitations, soon after midnight.

Though it is hardly good manners to assess costs of hospitality received, I did, for the record, get an estimate from one of J.B.'s associates on what such a party cost. The 1975 equivalent amount would be not less than $A500.

Theatrical Kabuki, classical Noh

I FIRST SAW Kabuki with Longman, who went regularly. I asked him why this Japanese theatre appealed to him so much.

"I like my theatre to be theatrical," he said. "I don't want the Tennessee Williams kind of play. The actor has the special gift of a supercharged personality and of being able to get inside a role and make it larger than life. We're cutting him down to the size of ordinary people—we don't let him *act* any more!" Longman picked up his fourth whisky. "The Japanese, thank God, don't expect the actors on the stage to be people. They expect the people on the stage to be actors." He drank to Kabuki and added: "Realism to the *benjo*!"

I said I had read a little book on Kabuki by a Japanese author who wrote, "One might as well climb trees in search of fish as expect logic in a Kabuki play." But what exactly should one expect?

"Don't expect it to be highbrow," Longman said. "Kabuki isn't. *Noh*, on the other hand, is. Foreigners usually think Kabuki is wonderful—at least they think the spectacular plays and the dance sequences are. Noh bores them—it's too slow, they say. And it *is* slow, too, and as ritualized as a church service. Maybe that's why I go to it." He smiled. "There's a kind of *purity* about Noh that an old sinner like myself needs...."

In Kabuki there are no actresses: all the female roles are played by men. And yet (I learn from Faubion Bowers[21]) it was originated by a woman. She was a dancing girl named O-Kuni, in the late sixteenth century, and she may or may not have been attached to a temple. Her act was a mixture of ritual dance and erotic by-play. She built it up into a troupe performance, adding dance-plays and farces. When O-Kuni died her type of entertainment was taken over by groups of women who were, more or less, prostitutes. Their immorality was so flagrant that Women's Kabuki, as it was called, was banned. Young men took it over—pretty boys who wore their hair in forelock style and, Bowers says, "most of the Young Men's Kabuki vehicles concerned humorous aspects of sodomy." The samurai began fighting over the boys in the theatres and the Shogun, after ordering a command performance, banned it in 1652 (shortly after a law had been passed making homosexuality illegal).

Kabuki was revived with mature men as the players. They were forced to shave the front of the head to reduce homosexual appeal and this halfbald appearance has become stylized make-up. Men's Kabuki had to make its way as valid drama, for which there was a great public appetite, and it developed into true theatre. Many of its plays were drawn from Bunraku, the puppet theatre, and were even more popular when presented by flesh-and-blood actors. The actors retained some of the puppet movements.

86 The Performers

The first Kabuki play I saw was of the genre or plebeian-life type. On the very wide stage the setting was an open-fronted house, with children playing in the street outside, and the principal character was a *taikomochi*, which the English-language programme defined as "a professional pimp". Longman explained that, though "pimp" meant procurer, a taikomochi was also a skilled entertainer, who played and sang as well as bringing the girl.

This taikomochi was being dunned by a money-lender and suspected by his wife of renewing an old affair with a geisha: he was having a miserable time. There was an interior plot involving a pair of young lovers who attempted to commit suicide. I couldn't resist asking Longman whether this was old-style Japanese Tennessee Williams. He told me to go to hell and said, "What about the acting?" I had to concede that the acting, in its stylized way, was extremely good. And the *onnagata* (actors in the roles of women) were most convincingly female.

We went out for an intermission cigarette. The beating of a wooden clapper, instead of the ringing of a bell, warned us that the curtain was about to rise or, rather, open: a man runs along the stage dragging the curtain aside.

"This will make you happy," Longman said tersely as the stage revealed its next quite remarkable setting, which was on two levels. On the higher level, in the centre, sat a villainously splendid figure with a black and white face, a gold crown and a magnificent robe of scarlet and silver. He was flanked on the right by a row of samurai who wore red capes and black-and-white-striped drawers; they had paunchy bare bellies painted lighter red, and the muscles of their calves were outlined in purple: everything about their make-up suggested malevolent force. On the lord's left sat a row of priests, and when the chief priest carried to the lord a scarlet drinking bowl the back of his robe showed a bold black design of an octopus. These were, mangnificently, the "baddies" of this play called *Onna Shibaraku*. (*Shibaraku* means "Wait a moment".)

The "goodies" were the people on the lower stage level. Their costumes and their make-up suggested virtue and innocence. The lord's plan was to lop their heads off. His samurai conveyed without a word their itching to be at this bloody deed. Now and then one of them would wriggle on his stool with impatience.

At the moment when it seems they are about to descend and massacre the virtuous a voice rings out from off-stage: "Shibaraku! Shibaraku!" Then a famous woman warrior named Tomoe Gozen appears.

She does not appear on the stage at all but on what is called the *hanamichi*, a long wooden gangway running from the stage to the rear of the theatre. Here she delivers her speech that rebukes the evil lord and saves the innocents. (This peroration brought great applause.)

As the programme said, "The composite picture formed on the stage is of primary importance, the story being more or less secondary." And the composite picture was wonderful theatre.

Then there was a play called *Shunkan*, written by Chikamatsu (1653-1725) who is often referred to as the Japanese Shakespeare. It was not only highly effective as drama—or, we might say, melodrama—but it demonstrated the remarkable mechanics of the Kabuki stage.

Shunkan is one of three conspirators whose plot against the Heike clan has been discovered and who have been exiled to a remote island. The setting is the beach, a section of the rocky shore, with sea and sky beyond. A ship appears; small in the distance, it moves across the horizon. It reaches the island; a big prow comes in on the right of the stage.

At the end the whole huge circular section of the stage revolves, turning the island and the rocks, and bringing part of the sea to the side of the audience. Shunkan climbs up on a cliff and there, shaking with grief in a manner that recalls the puppet theatre, he acts out his utter despair.

Longman said during the intermission, "I hold that there is a point at which melodrama can become genuinely moving. But with those of us who go to Kabuki regularly and know the stories well, the main satisfaction is in seeing what an actor can do with the role. I've seen a dozen Shunkans. I thought this fellow, Koshiro the Eighth, did very well—he's damned near as good as his father."

In 1974 the best Shunkan, and probably the best all-round actor in Kabuki, was Ennosuke.

IN ANOTHER KABUKI PLAY, *Kagami-jishi*, Yayoi, a maiden of the palace, performs an elegant dance for the New Year celebration. In the course of her dance she picks up a lion-head mask. The mask takes on life, the lion's spirit assumes control of her, and as Yayoi leaves the stage it is as though the lion-mask is pulling her, resistingly, away. The *onnagata* danced this role with the greatest delicacy. His every gesture was as feminine as his "melon-seed" lips—painted on after the onnagata's own lips are whitened over completely with make-up. Every movement of hand and limb had that boneless young-girl quality.

Then the lion appears. The kingly virility of the lion is accented by two small butterfly dancers flickering about the stage annoying him. His annoyance gradually mounts into rage.

The lion lowers his head and the white mane—which is as long as the actor is tall—is flung out and sent flying round and round, whirling faster and faster, until you wonder how any neck muscles can stand it. The applause that breaks from the audience takes on the same furious tempo, and then becomes a solid thunder of admiration. The actor stops as though struck. He flings back the mane and assumes the statuesque, glaring-eyed pose that in Kabuki is called *mie* and is always accompanied by a beating of wooden clappers from behind the stage. Utaemon VI, the leading onnagata of the day, was the delicate dance-maiden and the terrific lion. It is a Kabuki tradition that the same actor always plays both roles.

THE NOH DRAMA is lyrical where Kabuki is lusty. It is, approximately, as Greek poetry is to Elizabethan prose. It is philosophical where Kabuki is flamboyant. It is aristocratic where Kabuki is of the people—until the nineteenth century it was a punishable offence for anyone below the rank of samurai to witness Noh. Kabuki, with all its theatrical conventions, makes many concessions to reality: Noh is synthesis, and stylized to the point of ritual. Noh deals in symbols. It is concerned with the spirit and the senses; but never with sensuality or with active violence: it is passive and subjective. It shows no awareness whatever of the tempo of our times. A Noh play moves with the slowness of a sleep-walker. And the quality of the dream is never far away, for Noh deals in things remembered, in ghosts and gods and demons that haunt the mind and the memory. Noh, in short, is poet's theatre.

Actresses do not appear on the Noh stage, either. It preserves the man as its actor much as religion preserves him as its priest. Some wigs are worn, but make-up is eschewed entirely. The players have either masks or naked faces; and only the principal players have masks. Casts are small and the masks are most frequently those of: (i) the calmly beautiful face of a young girl, (ii) a man in his prime, (iii) an old woman, wrinkled with age and grief, (iv) an old, thin-bearded man, (v) a demon.

Such subsidiary characters as nobles, or even emperors, are portrayed by boys. Costumes have not changed in hundreds of years: they are chastely gorgeous. A gardener or a fisherman may wear priceless brocade in Noh: his character is established by some small thing he carries. The acting is so stylized that just touching the fingers to the eyes conveys weeping. A step or two to one side can signify a journey from China. The fan in the actor's hand may serve as a sword or a wine cup. An elliptical shape of bamboo on the stage is a ship, and when the actor steps inside this he is sailing away. In one play I specially remember the Lady Aoi, who lies stricken with a mysterious illness, is represented by a folded robe on the stage.

The Noh stage itself is a beautiful construction of plain, cream-white, highly polished cypress, square-pillared to a roof of perfectly cut and pressed cypress-bark, shaped after the roof of a Shinto shrine. The stage proper, about six metres square, is raised above the level of the auditorium and juts out into it, so the audience is seated on two sides of the stage as well as in front and is separated from it by a bordering of white sand. To the left is a long balustraded bridgeway or corridor. From behind a richly coloured curtain at the end of this the performers appear.

The principal performer (called the *shite*) moves out, wearing one of those superb masks made with the lost artistry of hundreds of years ago, and a brocaded costume that is usually an heirloom that has been handed down in the actor's family. The Noh performer never wears on his feet anything but the snow-white *tabi*, bifurcated socks. In a woman's role these are always visible, but a man may wear a stiff-folded divided skirt that covers his feet and trails behind them.

The performer walks in a special Noh manner, the soles of his feet never leaving the floor. Only by long training can a man do this and, without any sway or unsteadiness, hold his body perfectly erect as his feet make their precise, formal, slow glide that brings him to the stage. There he stops at a certain pillar (the "name-speaking place") and announces who he is, where he has come from, and where he is going.

On the stage is seated a chorus of narrators and musicians who tell the story in verse-chant and accompany it, usually, with hand-drums. These are held on the shoulder and struck by bringing up the palm of the hand: one drum makes a very sharp sound, having wooden ends and being struck with a metal "thimble" on the player's hand. The shrill Noh flute is played, in a way that establishes the mood of the play, as the performer is proceeding to the stage.

The "backdrop" to the stage is always the same—a venerable green pine-tree, which is painted on the rear wooden wall. There are no other "settings" and practically no "props".

The Noh play story derives from history or mythology. It is generally a god play, a ghost play, a woman play, a mad (insanity) play or a demon play. The mood is always poetic and the sentiment more often than not religious. This one is fairly typical: A Buddhist hermit, while reciting the *Lotus Sutra*, becomes aware of someone in the garden outside his cell window. It is a woman who says she is the spirit of the *basho*-tree. Having heard from the hermit's *sutra* that trees no less than creatures can attain to Buddhist salvation, she wishes to express her gratitude in a dance—which consists only of the waving of her sleeves in an elegant imitation of the leaves of the tree.

When the spirit-woman moves to a certain position on the stage and stamps twice, it signifies that the play is ended. The acoustic effect of the stamping on the stage, which is a feature of Noh dance, is heightened by a number of large empty jars placed beneath the stage to give it the property of a sounding-board.

Such a play as I have outlined may take an hour to perform. To relieve the solemnity, the Noh programme has comic interludes called *Kyogen*: these, too, are highly stylized.

The language used in Noh is as archaic as Chaucerian and Spenserian language is with us and even scholarly Japanese have to take a libretto along to the theatre to follow the lines. I was able to follow, fairly closely and with appreciation of their poetic content, two of the plays I saw because they were included in a book of verse-form translations of ten Noh dramas[22]: I bought this at the theatre.

It would be affectation to deny that there were not times, during the longer recitative passages, when I did not feel boredom at the Noh. But it was, at least, boredom made beautiful. Noh is an experience rather than an entertainment—an experience I am glad I did not miss.

An art of melodrama done with dolls

Osaka is the Manchester or the Chicago of Japan. More than a million spinning machines whirred, a third of all Japan's machines were in the making and a quarter of the chemicals. Osaka claimed to do forty per cent of Japan's business.

Amid all this bustle and smoke and noise, Osaka housed and subsidized an ancient Japanese form of theatre art, *Bunraku*, the puppet-drama. The doll-play had come to Japan in the sixth century, from Korea, but Bunraku did not develop until the seventeenth century when the great playwright Chikamatsu, the "Japanese Shakespeare", began writing for the puppet theatre. A new style of rhythmical narration was introduced. This was a recitative chant with one man—who had to be a highly talented dramatic and vocal artist—telling the story and taking the voice-parts of all the puppet cast. The reciter—a term that does him less than justice—is called the *tayu*. The tayu is regarded as more important than the *ningyo-tsukai*, the puppet-master. The manipulation of the puppets must be matched to the words, not the words to the movements.

No strings are used to manipulate these puppets. The principal dolls are bigger than half life-size. Sixteen different kinds of doll-heads attach to seven categories of bodies. Some open their mouths, some have eyebrows that raise, even hair that can be made to stand on end.

The dolls are manipulated by men on the stage in full view of the audience. The puppet-master, who manipulates the leading "characters", usually has two assistants. He appears in formal kimono, but the assistants are garbed in black with black eye-slitted hoods. The audience, I was told, "does not see" the manipulators. Across the front of the stage is a board high enough to hide the legs of the puppeteers and the top of this is the level on which the dolls move. Stage settings are classically simple and effective.

The Bunraku theatre was far from crowded and we got good seats. The special programme for foreigners was in poor English but it helped understanding. I was fortunate in having a remarkable guide whom I shall simply call Senri-san here, and say later why he was remarkable.

The curtain went up. Against a chrysanthemum-pattern backdrop samisen players were seated in line. They wore *kamishimo*, a formally elegant style of kimono caped with a stiff pleated material that projects beyond the shoulders in wide points. They brought their plucked-string music to a stirring crescendo. Then, putting down the big plectrums, two of the players took up bows and played their samisens violin-style. The rest of the orchestra sat stone-still, their faces immobile, and I was struck not only by the repose but by the refinement of their features. They played again, a livelier piece, and this time the music of an unseen flute joined with the samisens.

"Now," said Senri-san, when the curtain came down, "we have the play. But look first to the little platform to the right of the stage."

A black-gowned, black-hooded figure appeared on it, bowed and announced the tayu and the samisen accompanist. The platform revolved, taking the black figure off and bringing on the reciter and his musical-effects man, with samisen.

The tayu begins to speak in a long-drawn chant the prologue of the play. Its title can translate as *A Piece of White Banner*: it was written in 1625.

The curtain goes up on a house interior with a gate to the left and a suggestion of a lake beyond. Enter the puppet-master with two black-clad faceless assistants, one either side, and they bear a doll-figure, nearly half life-size, of a young man. The assistants work the arms and legs as he advances into the room. Two women puppets come from rooms at the back. Then an old man, a farmer, is brought on. There are now, as well as the puppets, eleven people on stage—four puppet-masters and seven all-black assistants, who remind me, distractingly, of medieval torturers. I don't think I'm going to be able to forget they are there, as the spectator is supposed to.

The young man starts with surprise as he sees one of the two women. She is, we learn, pregnant.

The old farmer tips out of a fishing net a severed arm—blood-marked and realistic. He has fished this from the lake. We hear the story behind the grisly find. It is the arm of a young woman who was carrying a white banner of the Genji clan. (Senri-san's whispered commentary makes the story clear to me.) The woman, pursued, took to the lake. The enemy caught up with her as she swam. She refused to give up the clan banner. So they chopped off her arm with a sword. She was the old farmer's adopted daughter.

The old man shakes with grief. His movements are perfectly attuned to the lamentations that seem to echo through him from the emotion-charged voice of the tayu. The tayu is an elderly man, bald and smooth-cheeked, and the muscles of his cheeks work violently. The notes of the samisen come in like plangent commas or exclamation points, or they suddenly launch a new line in the voice-drama. Perspiration is beginning to bead the tayu's forehead. And the puppets—the distraught old man and the more subduedly grief-stricken women, and the young man who is somehow cagey in his movements and not to be trusted—the dolls are beginning to give this melodrama reality, in spite of all those manipulators being on stage.

The young man leaves. He is the farmer's nephew. He is going off to inform the Heike clan that uncle is hiding in his house the wife of the Genji clan's samurai leader.

For the second act there is another tayu—a different one comes on for each act.

Act Two. Enter two samurai "generals", the largest puppets yet and wonderfully costumed. I'll call them (though it grossly over-simplifies their uniforms and characters) Red General and Blue General. Their reactions to seeing the severed arm are wonderful puppetry. The generals tell the old man they know he is hiding the wife of the enemy clan's leader. And what of the child she is bearing? The old farmer says the child has been born and he has killed it. Red General is very fierce. Blue General chivalrously urges that they take no action against the hidden woman. Eventually, Red General leaves. He does not just stump out. He stops at the door and puts on the shoes that were taken off when he entered. I can still "see" the manipulators but half the time I am not very conscious of them being there.

Act Three. There is another tayu and, on stage, a house-wall has been removed so we see into the room where the hidden woman is. Blue General is with her. He comes forward. He tells the old farmer that he was the one who cut the arm off the swimming woman who would not give up the Genji flag. The old man's reaction is, again, superb puppetry and all his anguish comes out in the voice of the tayu. The samisen player is punctuating not only with dramatic string-notes but with staccato monosyllables—sometimes he utters a sound like a dramatic hiccup.

A boy appears. He is the son of the woman whose arm was cut off. He shrilly accuses Blue General of killing his mother.

Then this woman's body is brought in, on a litter by fishermen, from the lake. The boy flings himself on the corpse (he seems to fling himself: I am hardly noticing the manipulators now) and moves there in a paroxysm of grief. Towering, Blue General approaches. He picks up the arm and places it beside the woman, as though joining it to her body. There is the small roll of an unseen drum.

The corpse revives: slowly and quite horribly the woman sits up. She cries the name of her son and falls back again, dead. I had never thought that dolls and a narrator could produce such Grand Guignol drama. I count six puppet-masters and eight black assistants on the stage. I had not been aware of half of them before I deliberately took stock, and when the dead woman sat up I was not aware of any.

The old farmer is saying that when the woman came into his family, as a child, she had a beautiful sword. She must have belonged to a noble family. He describes the sword. Blue General reacts.

A squeaking cry is heard. The woman in hiding has had her baby. A white Genji banner is hung up to celebrate the birth of the child, who is heir to the leader of the clan.

Act Four. The fierce Red General, dying, reveals that the dead woman, the boy's mother, was his own daughter, whom he abandoned to further his social position. The boy, his own grandson, should behead him for this infamy. Nothing loth, the boy cuts off the Red General's head. He picks up the head and takes it in to the woman with the baby.

"What utter bloody melodrama!" I am thinking, and at the same time: "Yet how perfectly the puppet theatre is suited to enact it. Heads can come off dolls—you can hardly have that with actors. And this last-act tayu—he is the most remarkable yet."

After the curtain, the small side-stage revolves, taking off the tayu who has given a terrific performance. His face is streaming with sweat.

"How did you like that last tayu?" Senri-san says.

I said I had never seen an actor on the stage "give" as much as he did. Did the younger tayu always do the last act?

Senri-san smiles. "No, not youngest, but best. Would you like to meet the tayu of the last act?"

TEN MINUTES LATER I was sitting opposite the last-act tayu in the restaurant on the first-floor of the theatre.

An art of melodrama done with dolls

His name was Tsudayu IV. His father, the third Tsudayu, had been the greatest tayu of his day. This son, aged forty, was very tall for a Japanese. He had just taken a shower and put on a black kimono. His skin and hair were shining with health. Tsudayu-san spoke no English but I had Senri-san's interpretation.

Yes, he said, being a tayu made great physical demands. I asked how he kept himself fit.

"He plays baseball. He used to be pitcher for the Bunraku team. In the morning he does chest-expanding exercises—a tayu is always much developed in the chest, and a puppet-master in the arms and legs and hips. He needs always to get plenty of sleep. He does not smoke."

I had suggested drinks, but Tsudayu-san took only coffee. He hardly ever drank. "One bottle of beer makes him look like boiled octopus, also makes him sleepy."

He was not very fond of sake—unlike the famous old tayu Shojo Yamashiro, who used to drink three pints of sake every day. Yamashiro's doctor warned about his blood pressure and said he should drink only five small cups. The old tayu said, "No. Once in ten days I shall drink fifty cups." He had been named as one of Japan's "Human Treasures".

Did a tayu make much money?

"No. But he says it is his art and his life's work. He makes some money working for radio and sometimes he does narration for Kabuki plays."

Were the puppet-masters also poorly paid?

Yes, they were. Bungoru Yoshida (now dead), the master *ningyo-tsukai*, got a small stipend from the government in recognition of his mastery, but his fees were not nigh. At eighty-five the great puppet-master was nearly blind and deaf, but he could still work the dolls superbly.

Which plays did Tsudayu-san consider the finest examples of Bunraku?

They talked about that. The names of the four plays Senri-san wrote down in my note-book: 1. *Sugawara Denju Tenarai Kagami*; 2. *Yoshitsune Senbonzakura*; 3. *Ichinotake Futabagunki*; 4. *Hadesugata Onnamaiginu*.

Did the tayu think there would be sufficient revival of interest in Bunraku for him to be able to look forward to better fees for his superb performances in the future?

"He says he does not think about the future," Senri-san interpreted the tayu's reply. "His father taught him that a tayu should always give everything he has in his performances today and never think about tomorrow."

AFTERWARDS I was having dinner with my guide in an Osaka sukiyaki restaurant. Senri-san had, after some persuasion, let me order beer for him too. But he left half of it.

"It makes me feel queer," he said. "We Japanese cannot take liquor the way you Western people can." He added, "Also, drink would be bad for me in my work."

I agreed that it could be awkward for a guide who drank with his tourist and found himself fuzzy or sick.

"Yes, and in my other work too." Senri-san smiled. "You see, I am a doctor." I stopped eating and said, "I thought you were a full-time guide—you're so good at it. Why didn't you tell me—you're a qualified doctor?"

"Yes, but to you, sir, I am your guide."

If I remember rightly I told him to go to hell and stop calling me sir. He laughed and handed me a different card to the one he had previously given me. It read:

SENRI HIRAKAWA M.D.

Medical Service 111
Kyoto University Hospital

"I am qualified to be in private practice now," he said, "but I wish to specialize. So I am for four years an intern at the University Hospital for the valuable experience, but I do not receive pay. So, as I must earn some money, I am a guide."

For four years Dr Senri Harakawa worked a five-day week at the hospital and at weekends was a tourist guide. He sometimes guided evening tours as well.

I hoped to see Associate Professor Hirakawa, as he had become, at Gifu University in 1974; but when I was in Gifu he had to be at a medical conference in Kyoto.

Sumo's ritual of huge wrestlers

SUMO, the traditional Japanese wrestling that isn't like wrestling as we know it, is performed by men who aren't like Japanese: they are so big.

Ordinarily, I would not walk across the street to see a wrestling match, but *sumo* (pronounced soo-mO) was strange and special, and as Japanese as a Shinto shrine dance.

JTB took parties of tourists to sumo. But it was difficult for the tourist to see sumo as I saw it, from a *tatami*. A sumo tatami—a railed-in matting about four-feet square that accommodates three or four people—is very expensive. Tatami are nearly all permanently booked by companies and organizations. The Osaka Ministry of Transportation, which had a tatami or two, rose nobly to the occasion and its Director said they would take me, on the tenth day of the sumo Grand Championship Tournament, with only five days to go and the issue excitingly in doubt. Scores of millions of Japanese were talking about it, and wanting to be there. A JNTO guide-interpreter, Miss Cecilia Arima, had to be provided for, too, as the amiable executive the Ministry sent to take us, Mr Shiro Tomita, didn't speak any more English than I spoke Japanese.

In the taxi to the Osaka City Gymnasium I asked Tomita-san, through Cecilia, how much did sumo wrestlers weigh. He gave the weight of Taiho, the reigning grand champion, in *kan* (one kan is 8.267 pounds) and it worked out that Taiho, who was over 37 kan, was 310 pounds, 22 stone, or 138 kilograms. The average Japanese adult male weighs no more than 57 kilograms, less than half the average sumo wrestler. To train for the sumo ring a young man needs to be abnormally tall and big to begin with; and he eats huge meals to put on more flesh.

The stadium was vast—and immediately impressive because there was a magnificent canopy suspended over the ring. It was like the pitched roof of the shrine the Japanese hold most sacred, the one at Ise, and hung with big tassels of coloured silk below purple bunting with a flower-motif crest.

THE HALL is almost full, the time three o'clock. The minor events that have been going on all day are ended and the big bouts for the championship will shortly begin.

A man in *hapi* coat and old-fashioned Japanese breeches appears, as though out of a Hiroshige print, with the *furoshiki*-wrapped boxes of food and carry-bags of bottles that Tomita-san ordered outside.

The lights in the stadium go down, leaving only the ring bathed in brilliance. This square arena is built up of clay, with no side-ropes. The ring itself is a thick raised rope of straw embedded in the clay.

"Now," says Cecilia after speaking to Tomita-san, "you will see the *yokozuna*, the grand champions, come in."

First comes the referee, who looks like a Shinto priest in his pointed black hat and gorgeous gown of brocade. He holds an ovoid ceremonial fan, the *gunbai*: with this he will direct the wrestlers and indicate the winner. Now they come, barefoot and near-naked behemoths of men, treading with solemn dignity down an aisle.

The reigning grand champion, preceded by his squire or second, is a huge sumo man clad only in an elaborate breech-clout wound round his great stomach. The yokozuna who comes in has this, too; but over it, and over a richly embroidered apron, he wears the insignia of his rank. This is a white rope, thick as a hawser, with a kind of kilt of white pendants; and, behind, the rope is tied up his back in a large and fancy knot. He is followed by his sword bearer. They squat, and so does the elaborately attired referee, and the grand champion spreads his arms. Then he gets up and shows himself off to the crowd.

He claps his hands—the traditional Buddhist way of attracting the attention of the gods. He stamps his feet, symbolically crushing evil spirits. He raises first one leg sideways, and then the other. His bare buttocks are huge, his stomach vast, his chest almost womanly. Under so much fat not much muscle can show—but it is there.

Four grand champions go through this ritual. Then men parade round the ring carrying advertising signs of the companies who are donating the prize-money. So the sponsors get their publicity, and, importantly, on television, where sumo is a top-rating programme.

THE BOUTS BEGIN after an official in hapi coat and breeches has walked round the ring announcing the names of the first contestants, and holding out an open fan.

Yutakayama (297 pounds) takes up from a tub, as he enters the ring, a handful of salt. He throws it out in front of him, as a man might sow seed broadcast. Each wrestler does this on entering. It is sumo ritual to "purify" the ring with salt.

Yutakayama, the former champion of Japanese universities, who now holds the rank of *ozeki* (next to *yokozuna*) has a handsome face under the black oiled so-called "topknot": sumo men wear their long hair in an upswept style on top of the head. And his face, seen close-up in my little binoculars, looks utterly calm. He confronts a less-large, next-rank-down (*maegashira*) opponent called Kiyokuni.

They get down on their haunches, facing each other, a few feet apart, braced with clenched fists on the clay (which they sometimes pound as they glare at each other). Unless they rise to grapple at exactly the same time, the referee will not allow the bout. Four minutes (the limit nowadays) passes and they do not rise. The referee signals them up; they leave the ring; come in again, throwing more salt; and squat again.

Suddenly they are up and grappling—and now Yutakayama's face in the binoculars is contorted with strain as Kiyokuni's charge thrusts him back. But, with a motion too fast for me to follow, Yutakayama whirls his opponent round and shoves him over the ring-rim and out.

Another bout that was over very quickly was described by the English-language *Japan Times* sumo writer thus: "Tochinoumi and Daigo clashed hard at the initial charge. Big D drove the little yokozuna towards the edge. Tochi turned quickly and tried to swing the No. I maegashira out of the circle, but Daigo hooked one leg round the yokozuna's and tripped him backwards into the dirt."

There are twenty-five named techniques of attack. One wrestler sidestepped his opponent's bull-like charge, grabbed the back of his girdle and sent him headlong out of the ring. Another was lifted by the inside of the legs and hurled right out of the arena into the front row of seats.

When you see a huge man lifted bodily and flung to the clay you feel that he must be injured; but they are so well trained in how to fall that broken bones are extremely rare, though knees are sometimes dislocated. I saw one slapping attack, but there is no punching or chopping or hair-pulling. The sport is conceived of as being so "clean" that blood would taint it; and if a nose should bleed from an accidental buffeting the bout is stopped at once to preserve the "purity" of the ring.

The referee's decision is never disputed. If he is in doubt he calls into the ring five black-robed judges, all former sumo wrestlers, who sit in the front row.

The big bout of the day in the tournament I saw was between the favoured yokozuna Taiho (310 pounds) and the most formidable of the lower-rank challengers, the maegashira Kairyuyama (297 pounds), who had equalled Taiho's eight victories in nine bouts.

Kairyuyama got a *morozashi* on Taiho's belt at the outset, locking the champion's left arm out of action. Suddenly he shifted into what one report called "a wily submarine position" with his head below Taiho's right shoulder. Thus locked, they strained, neither giving an inch of ground. Taiho's great strength began to tell. His opponent came slowly upright and Taiho got both hands on Kairyuyama's belt. The champion's shoulder muscles worked convulsively, and Kairyuyama went back and over the edge of the straw ring.

With that victory Taiho (also called the Golden Boy and the Big Bird) took the tournament lead. The spectators unlaced their legs and began rising from the tiers of tatami.

Bridge with a "top of the moon" curve in one of the finest Japanese gardens, Ritsurin Park at Takamatsu on the Inland Sea side of the island of Shikoku.

Even more famous as a landscape garden than Ritsurin (above) is Kenrokuen Park at Kanazawa on the west coast of Honshu, where few foreign tourists go.

Roosters called onagadori are bred—for display purposes—in very tall vertical boxes, and one unhappy-looking fowl shown me by its proud owner near Kochi in Shikoku had tail feathers that measured nearly seven metres.

Fishing with cormorants is a night spectacle that brings thousands of tourists (seen in the top background, and in the right-hand boats in the lower picture) to Gifu. Working the cord-tethered birds that catch the fish is the chief cormorant master of Gifu, Zempei Yamashita.

kyoto, nara & nikko

京都奈良日光

First Nikko, then the "bullet" train

SOME TRAVELLERS become obsessed with getting off the beaten track. Such individualism has its admirable side, but it can mean missing places that are worth seeing. The track is usually well travelled for good reasons, and there is sense in the Irishism that says the time to get off the beaten track is after you've been on it, not before.

In Japan there is a well-defined tourist track. The minimum-time visitor who is in the country for only five or six days as part of an Asian package tour will go to Tokyo, Kyoto, Nara, and probably to Nikko. Travellers who are on tour for ten days will go, additionally, to the Inland Sea, overnighting at Takamatsu on the big island of Shikoku and going on by steamer to Osaka. Back in Tokyo, they are likely to take an all-day coach tour to Kamakura to see the enormous bronze Buddha there. Probably their visit to Nikko will also be as a one-day excursion, but they will go there by train, not coach. Nikko is excluded from a few package tours because it doesn't fit into a "circuit" route; it is north of Tokyo whereas all the other places are roughly south-west.

Nikko is undoubtedly one of the scenic highlights of Japan, but it is not quite the "must" the tourist organizations and *Japan: The New Official Guide*[24] make it out to be. It is certainly not one of the most characteristically Japanese places to visit, as is the Katsura gardens and the Imperial Villa we'll come to in Kyoto. Nikko's famous shrine is so opulent in its architecture and decoration it has given rise to the much-used phrase, "Never say *kekko* [magnificent] until you've seen Nikko."

Seeing Nikko on a one-day tour seems to me rather like bolting a lunch of plum cake. The place is not just an eyeful of spectacular opulence (but to the extent that it is, it is the less digestible if one returns to frenetic Tokyo on the afternoon train); Nikko can also make a nice break. The surrounding area is Nikko National Park, and in autumn the mountainsides are particularly beautiful. I stayed overnight and was glad I did so.

The train to Nikko is not one of the acclaimed "bullet" expresses that shoot tourists down to Kyoto and Osaka at speeds that touch 200 kilometres an hour. But good trains run to Nikko, too. The Tobu Railways express does the 150 km journey in an hour and three-quarters.

I have never found train travelling in Japan tedious, because I like looking at the rural landscape. Last trip, though, I got the impression that the countryside was shrinking. Of course there are still wide expanses of ricefields—there have to be to feed a rice-eating nation of over a hundred million people, and Japan is self-sufficient in rice. But quite common was the railside sight of housing going up on land bounded by dry irrigation channels, land that had been under rice before it was sold to the developers. Many a farmer was sitting pretty on the profit of adding farmland to the urban sprawl; and there were fewer farmers.

"Agriculture, which had absorbed around half the labor force as late as World War II, now uses less than 20 per cent,"[23] expressed the early-seventies situation. In 1972 the number of farm households in Japan decreased by about 700,000. The number of people engaged in agriculture was 3 per cent less—and 70 per cent of the 13,400,000 people living agriculturally were old, sixty or over. Not that people were getting out of farming because it was uneconomic. The rural section was the one suffering least from recession in 1974. Farm incomes were well up, due to the inflated price of rice. Nor did the smaller rural workforce mean lower production. In fact, the 1973 rice crop was the biggest in Japan's history.

Fewer farmers could produce more rice because of mechanization. What I saw from the train going to Nikko on my first visit to Japan I was to write of in terms of farmers "bending to cut the rice with sickles" and, "There was no sign of harvesting machinery" and, "Where a reaped field was being ploughed again it was more often with an ox than a tractor drawing the plough". Now in the fields you see mechanical harvesters, including ones that combine reaping and threshing, and the grain goes straight through plastic piping into sacks. But you will still see men wearing the farmer's traditional wide-brimmed straw hat and *hapi* coat; and women, particularly the older ones, still in the voluminous *mompe* trousers of dark-blue with blouses that may have big coin-spots of lighter blue. And the fields will still be trestled with line upon fence-like line of stacked rows of drying rice-straw. That is the autumn scene, in late October and through November, when the fields are tawny with harvest.

Spring is a different picture, with the ricefields wet and green. You will see from the train the farming people who used to be called the peasantry planting out the rice in calf-deep mud: this hasn't been mechanized yet—but it will be. When the tourists come with the cherry blossom in April the rice is pointing up out of the watery fields in shoots of the brightest green.

The farmhouses, in contrast with the matchbox look of some urban housing, have a solid, steadfast, earth-wedded look. The roofs of the old ones are of thick dark thatch. Around a farmhouse there are usually wind-break trees. You may often see another tree clump out in the middle of a ricefield. These are hallowed spots where tablets are set up in memory of the family's dead, and there will be a Buddhist stone image of Jizo, who is the patron saint and guardian of the souls of dead children.

On the way to Nikko the train traveller will also see fields domed with dark-green, cushiony shrubs: this is tea. And many of the trees between the fields will be mulberries, yielding the leaves that silkworms eat. But rice predominates, especially in spring and autumn. In summer some fields are turned over to wheat or barley.

About thirty kilometres from Nikko an avenue of *sugi*-trees, Japanese cedars (*Cryptomeria japonica*) appears on the left of the line. These great trees, three hundred years old, were planted by a feudal lord. Like all the other daimyos, he was called upon to pay his tribute to the memory of the great shogun Ieyasu Tokugawa, and he is supposed to have figured that trees would be a relatively inexpensive contribution. Be that as it may, he went on planting trees for twenty years and planted, in all, about forty thousand. Of these some fifteen thousand remain today, and some have grown thirty metres high; the splendid coniferous avenues that run for miles are one of the most memorable features of Nikko.

JUST OUTSIDE the town of Nikko—which is of no account, unless you like copper-smelting works—is the Hotel Kanaya, and it couldn't be handier to the main sightseeing area.

The Kanaya was, when I was there, one of the nicest hotels in Japan (and I note that it is still being warmly commended in *Fodor's Guide*). I came in autumn, in the first week of November, and the window of my room framed a glorious picture of a forested mountainside splashed with the colour of maples turned crimson and other trees turning gold. To the right of this, against a blue-and-white sky, Mount Nantai rose to a summit flecked with early snow.

The story goes that, back in the eighth century, a Buddhist priest named Shodo, who belonged to an order much given to climbing mountains, climbed to the top of Nantai and there met the god of the mountain. The author of an engaging book on Nikko which I bought at the hotel has the god of Nantai saying to Priest Shodo: "I have been waiting for such a priest as you for two thousand years. I earnestly hope that you will make a great effort to open this mountain to the public." A god as tourist-minded as that would have to be Japanese.

Long before the tourists came, and even before the Tokugawas came, Nikko was an important religious centre. In medieval times it was the hub of Buddhism in eastern Japan, a Buddhism that coalesced with Shintoism. This process had begun with a move towards the nature worship Shinto is based on by the "Mountain Buddhists" of which Priest Shodo was a member, and the placing of temples in forest groves. The process ended with Ieyasu Tokugawa, to whom the main shrine at Nikko is dedicated, being deified by the Emperor as "East Illuminating Great Incarnation of Buddha". That happened soon after the first Tokugawa shogun died, in the same year as Shakespeare, 1616. And, like many another event in religious history, it served a secular purpose.

The shoguns were war-lords who usurped power and reduced to a figurehead the Emperor whom the common people revered as the Son of Heaven. Ieyasu Tokugawa was as cunning as he was capable. He seems to have arranged, before he died, the whole Nikko project as a tremendous public relations exercise. His being deified—by the Emperor—would confer the greatest prestige on the Tokugawa name and family and help perpetuate the régime. And building a shrine worthy of a shogun who had become a god—a work to which all the daimyos would naturally be expected to contribute generously—would be a most useful exercise. Not only would it further enhance Tokugawa prestige but it would require such large donations from the daimyos that they would be too poor to mount any insurrections.

So, from the point of view of the shogunate, the more elaborate and costly the shrine was, the better. And, aesthetically, that is what is wrong with the Toshogu Shrine as it is called: it is just too ostentatious, not Japanese enough, too overworked in the Chinese manner. It is still, in its overdone way, both curious and remarkable. Moreover, one is inclined to tolerance, even made susceptible to awe, by the building being merged impressively with the "nature's cathedral" type of setting, having as its columns the noble *sugi*-trees.

AFTER LUNCH I went to the shrine with a guide I had to myself, not with a tour group. When we got to a vermilion bridge that arches gracefully over the rushing Daiya River, Minoru the guide said, "This is Sacred Bridge. Only the messengers of the Emperor can cross this bridge, when they come, once in a year, to make offering at the shrine." So we crossed by a mundane bridge and climbed up a stony stretch of road between the great cryptomerias.

Soon we were in the Rinnoji Temple, in its Hall of the Three Buddhas, and Minoru was telling me how high (eight metres) the gold-lacquered wooden Buddhas were and that the one on the right was called the Thousand-Handed Buddha for arithmetical reasons to do with its having forty hands and, as the guide put it, "Each one of the forty hands has twenty-five good lucks. So he can bring good luck to thousand people at one time."

The dimly-lit hall was aromatic with incense sticks the faithful bought from attendant priests and set up to burn before the images. And the roof resounded with constant small echoes as, when a Buddhist prays, he first claps his hands to attract the attention of the god. In some temples he jangles a bell or beats a drum. There was a drum here but, where its pattern had been worn away, there was lettering in Japanese and in English that said NO BEATING THE DRUM.

A priest with an ink-brush was writing names in the temple book. Many people were paying to have this done, or to have a sick relative's name written on a piece of paper and put in a box like a child's pencil case, which would be taken home.

Behind this temple stands a bronze pillar that has to do with repelling evil influences and near this are two bronze lanterns that were donated by silk merchants, but they weren't considered worthy of being associated with the Ieyasu Tokugawa's memorial shrine because the donors were "in trade". We were to see lots of stone lanterns and other bronze ones, standing more than man-high. They were all right because the daimyos donated them.

The Toshogu shrine, further up the hill, is approached by a flight of ten steps, where the common people could stand during ceremonies, as they were not allowed to set foot within the shrine. At the top of the steps is a great *torii* gateway about nine metres high made of granite brought from Kyushu, gift of the feudal lord of Fukuoka. A greater donor was the lord of Kohama (near Kyoto) who gave a five-storey pagoda (a pagoda never has an even number of tiers) and this red one is a good example of the lovely structure that came originally from India and reached Japan via China and Korea.

The shrine is a complex of vermilion-lacquered buildings, and the main entrance to it is through the first of three famous gates (*mon*), called the Niomon. This elaborate portal has Buddhist guardians either side of it called the Deva Kings, wearing fierce expressions and showing their strength in peculiarly modelled muscles of their bare torsos. To one side of this is the Sacred Stable where the Sacred Horse used to be in case the god should wish to take a gallop. Images of monkeys were associated with Japanese stables because of a belief that monkeys possessed power to ward off horse diseases. Here, under the eaves are the most famous monkey images in the world, those moralistic, originally Chinese ones, the Three Wise Monkeys who "see no evil, speak no evil, hear no evil".

Two more flights of steps bring us to the Yomeimon, the Yomei Gate, and this is what the Japanese have particularly in mind when they say Nikko is so *kekko*, so magnificent. It is, indeed, extraordinarily opulent, architecurally and in its decoration. "Gate" hardly describes a structure that is two-storeyed, gabled, hipped, corbelled, balconied and lavishly bracketed. Its carved and coloured decoration runs the gamut from Chinese princes to peonies, dragons to giraffes and phoenixes. There are even carved clouds. "And you will notice there the pattern on one of the columns is carved upside down," said the guide. "That is mistake deliberately made so that evil powers would not be made jealous and angry by this gate's perfection."

I have a copy of the *Guide Text* from which guides learn what to say about the places they take tourists to. It calls the Yomeimon, "the most beautiful gate in Japan". Yet you won't find this gate pictured or even mentioned in *Architectural Beauty in Japan*[25] and it has been described by some Japanese writers as "excessively decorated". Maraini[3] makes the point in his book that, whereas there are superb examples of Japanese taste at Ise, Nara, Kyoto, there is another and opposite pole of Japanese taste that Nikko represents.

Among the curiosa are the Crying Dragon on the ceiling of the Yakushido Chapel ("When the hands are clapped beneath its head the echoes make it seem as if the dragon is crying"); the Dragon Ceiling of the Haiden (Oratory) whose hundred coffered sections are painted with a hundred different types of dragons; the Karamon (Chinese Gate), which is also very strong on dragons together with another fabulous guardian animal called *tsutsuga-mushi* and, along with carved plums and peonies, figures of Chinese sages, an emperor and a harp-playing fairy; and there is a coloured carving that is immensely popular with Japanese children, the Sleeping Cat.

Guides often say that a famous carver of the cat, and much else hereabouts, Jingoro Hidari, was so skilful that jealous rivals had his right hand cut off, and that Hidari carved the cat with his left hand. The *Guide Text*, though, doubts Hidari's existence; it says he was, if anything, a carpenter not a sculptor, and that the tales of his prowess were the inventions of professional storytellers.

Visitors are not admitted to the innermost sanctuary with a gold-lacquered altar where the spirit of Ieyasu Tokugawa is enshrined. He is buried on top of the hill.

The Toshogu Shrine is said to have been built in seventeen months from November 1634 and to have employed an average nine thousand men daily, including the best artisans in the country, brought from Kyoto and Nara. Official records give the total cost as a sum, tremendous for that time, of ¥8,000 million (about $A20 million at the 1974 rate). Enough gold leaf was used to cover six acres.

There are other shrines as well as many other features to the places I've mentioned. But enough Nikko opulence is enough.

A highway with many hairpin bends ascends the slope of Mount Nantai to a famous waterfall that is fed by the outflow of a lake. To view the waterfall you get in an elevator. This drops you down to where you walk through a tunnel to a vantage point where you can look up at the fall.

106   Kyoto, Nara & Nikko

The imaginative author of a booklet on the Nikko region says of Kegon Fall that it is like hundreds of thousands of white dragons hurling themselves over a cliff. He also says, "It is greatly noted for committing suicide."

Beyond Kegon Fall is Lake Chuzenji, which is very deep. Being more than twelve hundred metres above sea level, the lake is a popular summer resort. On the sunny day when I was there the scarlet *torii* of a lakeside shrine was vivid against the indigo water, and autumn maples burned on the mountains of the farther shore.

WHEN the first of the "bullet" trains hurtled down what was called the New Tokaido Line the Japanese did not claim that theirs were the fastest trains in the world. They do now.

Back in 1964 when the "bullets" began between Tokyo and Osaka there were some very fast expresses already operating in Europe: West Germany's *Rheingold* ran at 160 kilometres (100 miles) an hour, Italy's *Settebello* barrelled along at 147 km/h and France's *Mistral* (which once hit the astonishing speed of 331.4 km/h during a trial run for the world's speed record) operated regularly at 128 km/h.

In 1965 I had the kind of ride one remembers on an express of the *Hikari* (it means Light) type and saw the speed indicator showing 180 km/h. In 1966 the "commercial maximum" speed had increased to 193 km/h (120 m.p.h.), which established the Japan National Railways trains as the world's fastest. And when I was last aboard, in 1974, the speed had gone up again to 210 km/h (131 m.p.h.).

What made the 1965 run so memorable was that I was allowed to spend half an hour of the journey up in the motormen's cabin. This was an utterly different experience from sitting in one of the very comfortable carriage seats and watching through a wide window the landscape between Tokyo and Kyoto slide by so smoothly that there is more sensation of speed in a car going at 100 km/h. What I got up front was a strange experience where the primary sensation had to do not with what was going past but what was coming at me. I was inside a projectile that was slithering along on steel at a velocity that felt terrific, and was from time to time being gobbled up by tunnels.

These trains being electric, there are no locomotives. And no drivers. When I climbed up into the nose—there is a "nose" at each end and its shape half point, half ball, is near enough to a bullet's to justify the name—there was a compartment with what was like the wrap-round windshield of an airliner. There were three motormen. One was seated watching some instruments—there seemed to be very few of those, and only a couple of levers. The second man simply got up and indicated that I should take his seat. The other one was talking on the telephone. I almost had to stop myself saying, "What a way to run a railroad!"

Everything was taken very good care of—in Tokyo. There, in front of the panels of cabinets that housed electronic devices in a big room with a diagrammatic representation of the lines right round its walls, sat men called section supervisors, each looking after a certain train in a certain section, and each knowing, by lights, where that train was in that section. A supervisor had only to press a button and a motorman would pick up a telephone. This was called CTC (Centralized Traffic Control).

First Nikko, then the "bullet" train   107

There was also ATC (Automatic Train Control). This was on the train itself, and I couldn't see it because its electronic equipment was down there in the bulletnose under my feet. Its purpose was to "know better" than the motorman, who might get a signal saying "speed 160" and keep the train at 180. In that case ATC would apply the brake automatically; just as it would automatically release the brake if the motorman was told to put the speed up and didn't. It was enough to make you wonder whether it would matter very much if all three motormen left levers and instruments and telephone and went back to the buffet car and had a beer.

To this kind of automated control there was added in 1972 a unique system called COMTRAC (Computer-aided Traffic Control). A sample situation where the computer would take over communication was this: Hikari 31 is to leave Tokyo at 11 a.m. The slower Kodama 363, which left Tokyo at 10.30, is to wait at noon, when it is stopped at Shizuoka station, for Hikari 31 to pass through. But something happens to delay the fast express's Tokyo departure. Should the Kodama still wait for the Hikari at Shizuoka, thus upsetting its own schedule, or should it go ahead? COMTRAC's controller makes his decision. This goes into the computer, and when the controller presses a button the computer works out the necessary alterations in train schedules and conveys the information to trains concerned. It does this by coloured lettering displayed in what is called a Braun tube.

Sitting up there, watching through the "windscreen", it seemed unreal to be going so fast so smoothly. The line was specially built, of course, to take the speed. The 515 km (320 miles) of New Tokaido Line from Tokyo to Osaka—standard gauge, rails laid on stressed concrete sleepers with rubber pads to absorb vibration—took five years to build. With the trains, the cost was ¥80,000 million (say $A200 million). The line had to be as straight and as level as it was possible to make it, and the land along the Pacific seaboard is anything but level. So about 67 kilometres of it is underground, through tunnels.

I was up front for the longest tunnel, called the Tanna, which is nearly eight kilometres. We were through it in three minutes. When a train doing nearly 200 km/h rams the air in a long tunnel the pressure builds up, because the air cannot get out of the other end of the tunnel as fast as it is being displaced. So, even in a sealed train, you feel a slight pressure in your ears. And the tunnels have to be much higher than they would ordinarily need to be—as high as thirteen metres—to minimize the pressure build-up when two trains pass in a tunnel.

Soon after the Hikari rushed out into daylight again I had a fine view of Mt Fuji. The air was somewhat misty, as it usually is in Japan, but the sun shone brightly on the famous white cap of snow. This section of the route is picturesque with glimpses of sea and a sizeable lake, Hamana Lagoon. It has been connected to the sea since an earthquake and tidal wave wrought that change in 1498. The railway's safety precautions, incidentally, take into account the risk of derailment due to earthquake. Emergency switches at short intervals right along the line can be pressed by anyone, to cut off power in a line section. There is no risk of derailment by anything getting on to the line because it is very strongly fenced. In the ten years since the "bullet" trains began there had been not a single accident causing injury. The only derailment occurred when an empty train was being shunted.

If brakes are applied when a train is doing 200 km/h it slithers for well over a kilometre before it stops. The train has to begin its slow-down kilometres before a station, so stops cut the average trip speed. Hikari-type expresses go right through to Osaka in 3 hrs 10 mins, with stops at Nagoya and Kyoto, and Kodama-class "bullet" trains did Tokyo–Osaka in 4 hrs 10 mins with ten stops on the way. The "bullet" line had been extended in 1972 past Osaka to Okayama. The New Tokaido Line had become an outdated concept: it was now but a section of a rail system called the Shin (New) Kansen (Trunk Line)—in one word, Shinkansen.

An extension through to Fukuoka was opened in March 1975, bringing the largest city on the southern island of Kyushu within seven hours of Tokyo by rail.

However, that was little more than the beginning of a vast extension plan proposed for completion by 1985. It envisaged twelve new lines that would run north to Sapporo in Hokkaido, as far south as Kagoshima at the end of Kyushu, and across Japan to such places as Kanazawa on the west coast. Work has begun on the fifty-kilometre Seikan tunnel under the strait between Honshu and Hokkaido.

The Super-Shinkansen plan fits with the image of clever, Westernized, ever-industrious Japan putting in another burst in its race to become the world's economic front-runner. So it may come as a surprise to those who think of the Japanese as materialists to a man to learn that in 1974 plans for three sections of the line were in suspension due to the opposition of residents along the proposed routes, according to the *Japan Almanac* 1974,[26] which added: "Noise and vibration of Shinkansen trains are proving to be a serious nuisance to people living along the lines, and campaigns protesting the construction of new lines have been held in and around big cities." The Environment Agency was actively negotiating with the Transport Ministry for lower noise levels. The vibration problem could be exacerbated by the proposed increase in speed of new "bullet" trains of 260 km/h (over 140 m.p.h.).

And this is not the only major area of transportation where the quality-of-life people are at odds with the economic-growth authorities. Tokyo was to have a brand new international airport by 1974; but I still landed at Haneda. The residents who said their environment would be deteriorated by the new airport simply would not allow its construction to go on—they even managed to erect a high concrete tower on what was to be a main runway. It became evident that the new Narita airport would not open in 1975 either, because of local objections regarding the safety factor of proposed fuel storage tanks.

No less worried by environmentalists' attitudes was the Japanese plastics industry. Demand for plastic-packaged foodstuffs fell off as an increasing number of consumers, conscious of the pollution problems posed by plastic garbage, began buying unwrapped goods, and carrying them not in plastic shopping bags but in baskets made of real bamboo.

JNR was also looking at, and testing research models of, what is called a "linear" train. It doesn't run on wheels. The test train was called a "magnetic levitation and propulsion vehicle". Evidently the train is levitated on an air cushion, but not in the same way as a Hovercraft is. Anyway, it looked like working and, if such a super-speed train was developed, it was expected to whoosh down the 556 kilometres between Tokyo and Osaka in *one hour*.

First Nikko, then the "bullet" train

TRAVELLING by train in Japan can be very comfortable, as well as very fast. In what are called the "bullet" trains' Green Cars all seats are reserved, and there are Western-style lavatories. Nominally there is no longer any first-class or second-class, but Green Car travel costs extra.

The Japanese travel light, and the foreigner should try to do the same, for trains have little space for luggage, except on overhead racks that are only wide enough for overnight bags or the ubiquitous bundles wrapped in cloths called *furoshiki*.

Another reason for taking minimum luggage is that you may have to lug it without benefit of station porter. An *akabo*—the red-capped man with knickerbocker breeches on legs bowed from the weight of bags he carries three and four at a time by slipping a strap through the handles and hefting the lot—was hard to get: his tribe seemed to be vanishing.

Over the years I've noticed a change in behaviour in Japanese train travellers. They are still inveterate eaters, seemingly incapable of making a railway journey without a constant intake of snacks, fruit, confectionery and tiny pots of tea, as well as boxed lunches; but they don't toss food wrappings on the floor as much as they used to. Sensibly, they remove their shoes when travelling, and women and men are inclined to tuck their legs up on seats. I have also seen the husband recline and rest his stockinged feet on the windowsill; but I have not seen, as others tell me they have, the gentleman in the opposite seat remove his trousers, fold them and stow them on the rack, and settle down in his long underpants such as are, still, standard cool-weather wear for the Japanese male.

AS IS TO BE EXPECTED in a country where the rate of economic evolution has been so high in recent years, the railside scene is not the same as it was, either. That a considerable amount of land that used to be under rice is now under housing has been mentioned, but I probably wouldn't have found that so noticeable if the new houses had not been roofed in many cases with tiles of the brightest blue—a shade of blue about as Japanese as the old Reckitt's Blue bag. Traditionally, tiles were grey or darker, a blackish brown, and they blended with the landscape, whereas the blue ones leap at the eye.

While tiles had been turning a part of my Japan picture blue another part of it had been turned green, through golf, for which the Japanese word is *gorufu*. Japanese affluence that came in so strongly with the seventies expressed itself in golf; and it is understandable that people living constricted urban-industrial lives would want to disport themselves on the widest, greenest and nearest-to-nature form of playing field. Between seven and eight hundred golf courses have somehow been carved out of a landscape where every square metre of arable land is said to be needed for food-growing. They occupy half as much land again as the enormous city of Tokyo.

The handy-to-Tokyo prefecture of Chiba got so many golf courses its governor cried "no more!" and described as "abnormal and outlandish" a development that destroyed forests and, in the course of levelling rugged terrain, blocked streams. Although other prefectures followed Chiba's lead to some degree, golfing Prime Minister Tanaka rebutted the ecologists' talk of "golf pollution" with the declaration, "Golf courses retain greenery. Japan needs more greenery, so it needs more golf courses."

The golf-induced greenery I saw many examples of from train windows was in the form of driving ranges, which were invariably netted in with green mesh. At these places the golfer could smite a dozen or so balls for a few hundred yen and so improve his game—assuming that he could afford to play on a golf course, where a round of eighteen holes might cost him as high as ¥10,000 ($A25) if the course was a fashionable one. If it were a public course he would have to queue to tee off—some players turned up with their bags and golf buggies as early as 4 a.m.

So, many who had been bitten by the golf-bug, or felt that they must play the game to stay in line of status with their colleagues, had perforce to restrict their playing, for some or most of the time, to the driving ranges that had sprung up in every city and looked from a distance like super-sized tennis courts covered in green mosquito-netting.

These added no more to the picturesqueness of travellers' Japan than did the long strip-sheeting of plastic that shielded plants in the fields of the vegetable growers; but the railside scene still held much that was characteristic, from homely touches like laundered kimonos drying on bamboo poles poked out of second-storey windows to white-and-grey castles, tiered like wedding cakes, perched on hilltops. One of these is glimpsed after our Hikari express flashes through the city of Maibara. Then we get glimpses of Lake Biwa, the largest lake in Japan and long famous for the "eight beautiful views" it has for sightseers. And then, probably on the dot of time, we are slithering into the station at Kyoto.

Kyoto has the style and the savour

A PAMPHLET I found in my Kyoto hotel room read: *So the dream has come true and now you are in Kyoto, the old Japanese capital of the Mikado for more than a thousand years.* A brochure said I was in *Kyoto—the City of Classical Culture and Scenic Beauty where the quintessence of the Orient is enshrined.*

I went out to eat. A taxi nearly got me as I crossed the street opposite Kyoto's ultra-modern railway station. I leapt for the neon-lit pavement and went straight into a noise—a racket such as a ball-bearing factory might make in full-blast production.

The noise was a *pachinko* place. Fifty pinball machines clacked, rattled, and whirred and, from time to time, disgorged masses of steel balls with a crash as one of the gamblers made a lucky play.

I was still getting used to the idea of there being two Japans—pagoda Japan and pinball Japan—and could only hope that from somewhere behind the noise and the neons and the just-like-any-other-city look the *quintessence-of-ancient-culture* Kyoto would emerge.

It did, next morning.

A GOOD-LOOKING young man stood up at the front of the coach beside the driver, holding a small microphone. Behind his glasses his seal-brown eyes held a twinkle, and a shadow of tiredness. I was to find out later that he had qualified as a doctor, worked five days a week at Kyoto Hospital and at weekends he did conducted tours.

"I am the guide," he began. "It is a great pleasure to me to be able to attend on you on this morning sightseeing tour of Kyoto." He went on to say that Kyoto was the fourth largest city in population, over a million, but number one for the sightseer because it had been the capital of Japan for eleven hundred years from the year 794, which was in the time of Charlemagne and seven hundred years before Columbus discovered America. As long ago as that the Japanese laid out a city on the square plan (which they got from China) and named the east-west streets Ichiji (First Street) through to Ninth Street, and intersected the streets with broad avenues in what we call "New York style".

This guide's English was good. He began to drop *a*'s and *the*'s as we went along (there are no articles in the Japanese language) but that didn't matter: "We have thirteen hundred Buddhist temples and four hundred Shinto shrines in Kyoto. If you stayed for whole year and visited four temples and one shrine every day, even then you could not finish them all."

The bus got under way and went down a busy main street. Just along from one of the big department stores, it drew up outside the great curved-roof wooden gateway of the first temple. *Temple* meant it was Buddhist. Any

Shinto place of worship is a *shrine*. "This is the Higashi—that means East—Honganji temple, the headquarters temple of the largest sect of Buddhism in Japan."

We didn't go inside then, but I did subsequently. You have to get permission the day before, and then you can go through it, even to the villa of the abbot whose family is so noble that the abbot was able to marry the younger sister of the present Empress. (Neither Buddhist nor Shinto priests are necessarily celibate.) This temple had been burnt down four times since it was built in 1603, and each time the faithful had contributed to reconstruct it in the original style. The contributions included the hair of Buddhist women: this was woven into a rope to hoist the building materials. The long coiled rope of women's hair is preserved in a glass case in the temple.

The bus turned into a street with banks and life insurance offices, all very Western-style and concrete. But, such are the contrasts of Kyoto, down this Shijo Street you come to Gion, the gay quarter, the "geisha-girl town".

The guide said, "One can be Buddhist and Shintoist at the same time." He added, regarding differences between these religions and ours, "We have no baptism. There is no sabbath. Sunday is only a rest day for Japanese."

The gods of Shinto are regarded as manifestations, on a different plane, of the deities of Buddhism. Oriental theologians and philosophers do not expect Westerners to understand their faiths or their philosophies.

Suppose a Japanese philosopher like Daisetsu Suzuki (he was a Zen-sect Buddhist metaphysician who became a university lecturer in America) were to get on this tourist bus. He would say that the only way to really know anything is to rely on the "innerliness of experience". And if we asked philosopher Suzuki to give us the gist of Oriental thinking he would tell us: "When I say, 'I hear a sound', what I hear is not experientially a sound, it is '*chu-chu*' (the 'twitter-twitter' of a sparrow) or '*kah-kah*' (the 'caw-caw' of a crow). When I say 'I see a flower' and declare it to be 'beautiful' what I see is not really a beautiful flower, it is the *yo-yo* (freshness and beauty) and the *shaku-shaku* (brightness) . . .[27] The Western way of thinking is strong in generalization, which results in the vaporization of reality."

He gets off the bus and we say, "*Sayonara*, Suzuki-san. You've given us something to think about."

"Please do not do that," he says. "By thinking about it you will never understand." He smiles. "No thinking is the Oriental way of 'thinking'."[27]

Well, here are two short Japanese poems to not think about:

Since I am convinced
That Reality is in no way
Real
How am I to admit
That dreams are dreams?*

I do not see myself
Reflected in the mirror;
My self, reflected in the mirror,
Sees me.†

"WE ARE GOING NOW to Kinkakuji, the Gold Pavilion," the guide said, and added that this temple was built, originally, ninety-five years before Columbus discovered America. "Unfortunately, by wilful arson, the six-hundred-year-old temple was lost. A priest set fire to it in 1950 and it was turned into ash in one night. We are going to see reconstruction."

*SAIGYO HOSHI, translated by Arthur Waley.
†DAIGAKU HORIGUCHI, translated by J. K. Yamagiwa.

Kyoto has the style and the savour

We got out of the bus and went, with quite a crowd of Japanese sightseers, down a tree-lined path. We could not see any temple. The Japanese contrive their landscape gardens so that, if something beautiful is to be seen, it is hidden until you come to where you can see it to the best advantage. The path brought us round a corner to a lake. There was the pavilion temple, dreaming over its gold reflection in the lily-patterned water.

The Kinkakuji does not look like a temple, it looks like the romantically lovely lakeside villa of some potentate—and that is what it was. It was built, beside an artificial lake, as the villa of a nobleman of the court in the Muromachi time, and then it was taken over and improved by a shogun, who lived there in peaceful retirement and ordered that, after his death, it should become a temple. He had it covered with gold-foil on a lacquer base.

We did not go inside the pavilion, but on through the lovely garden, with the guide saying, "Japanese garden has many types. Landscape garden, flat garden, stroll garden—also we call the kind of garden at this place 'background-borrowing garden'. We borrow background of mountain and sky from nature for this garden. You will see stones, water, trees, and shrubs in this garden. Stone is something like bones. Pond may be compared to blood. Shrubs and trees are skin and muscles. There are not any flowers." (We subsequently had another guide who used to say, "Please not to be disappointed in the no flower.")

As we were leaving this garden the guide said, "You see this lots of bamboo. Bamboo is very useful to us—there are one thousand one hundred ways Japanese use bamboo. It grows quite slowly at first, then very rapidly for a few days, then it slows down. In rapid period average rate of growth is twenty inches a day."

The bus rolled on through the sunny morning, past the packed rows of dun-coloured little shops with their spill of bright wares, past high-fenced houses and telegraph poles blazoned with advertising, past the crowded street-cars and the swerving cyclists and the piled three-wheeler delivery trucks, past the ceaseless movements of pedestrian men in scruffy shoes and *geta*-clacking women with babies humped on their backs, out to where there were paddy-fields of rice either side of the Katsura River.

Here the bus stopped to let us watch an odd sight. In the shallows of the river floated lengths of patterned cloth, yard-wide strips hundreds of feet long, like banners streaming out in the current's twist and flow. They were block-printed textiles, and men and women were washing them in the river, washing out the excess dye. Other great strips of the coloured cloths were stretched out to dry along the pebble-covered banks of the river.

IN THE TEMPLE called Sanjusangen-do there is a very long hall where huge wooden pillars support the darkness that gathers in the roof and incense thickens the air, and one thousand gilded Buddhist goddesses of mercy called Kannon stand in rows raised one behind the other, like a vast choir that will never move and never sing. Doubtless this sight is very impressive to a Buddhist, but I thought the battalion of Kannons made the place look like a corner of the Property Department at Metro-Goldwyn-Mayer. The main Kannon, carved in 1254, is seated and she is taller than the others and has forty arms. Most tours include it but Sanjusangen-do is not a must-see experience. Kyoto has much better things to show. However, there are some other sculptures in this hall and one, of an old man, is quite remarkable.

Looking at the thousand Kannons all the same, an American woman in our party asked the guide, "How *tall* are they?"

"Five feet seven inches."

"I'm only five feet three and a half myself," the lady said to me, lowering her voice. "And, you know, one of the best things about being in Japan is that I don't feel *short* any more."

There was also an American girl, a schoolteacher, in the party. She must have been five feet ten if she was an inch. She had gone to stay at a Japanese inn and, she said, she was aching in every muscle. The worst part was doing her hair in the morning at the little dressing-table on the floor. "But I'm going to stick it for the week, and not only because it's cheaper than the Western hotels—this one really is. They've never had a foreigner stay there before, and they only understand about six words I say, but we get along somehow—and they're so terribly nice. It's killing me, this living on the floor, but I couldn't move into a Western hotel, I just couldn't—they're so *nice* to me...."

THAT AFTERNOON we were also taken to Nijo Castle. Japanese castles do not have the square-faced fortress look of Norman-British castles; they are more like multi-storeyed mansions protected by high walls with watchtowers and moats. The idea of the moat came from Europe, and after the Portuguese introduced the gun to Japan, in 1543, castle walls were made thicker. The most picturesque is the White Heron Castle at Himeji, down past Kobe. It is rather like four or five mansions with low white plaster walls built one on top of the other, with a great stone foundation as the base.

Nijo Castle is not like that at all. The only "castle" things about it are the surrounding moat and the plastered walls with elegantly roofed white watchtowers at the corners and massive gateways. What makes the Nijo Palace (as it is better called) memorable is the rich artistry of the seventeenth-century paintings that decorate the walls and sliding screens of the living chambers and audience rooms.

The palace rooms, with their muralled backdrops, look like so many theatre stages. If you have enough imagination, and have seen enough Japanese pictures to fill in the costume detail, you can imagine the shogun and his lords moving against these backgrounds in their great stiff-folded, pointed-shouldered Court robes—the black ones and the ones of gorgeous gold-blazing brocade—robes from which emerged only the top-knotted heads of the wearers, men who glided rather than walked across the silk-smooth boards and who cast enormous shadows behind them as they prostrated themselves before the shogun.

The wooden floor approaching the shogun's bed-chamber is so sprung that it squeaks sweetly as you walk across it. The purpose of this was protective rather than musical. The guards in the next room knew someone was approaching the shogun, and they looked to see who it was. Always there was fear of the assassin.

Some of the paintings, by artists of the famous Kano family, have backgrounds of gold-foil. A great branch of a pine-tree—symbol of constancy—may stretch right across one gold wall. Another will be delicate with cherry blossoms, or restful with a design of birds—brown geese and white-eared bulbuls, or sparrows asleep in a bamboo grove whitened with snow.

THE PLACE we now come to is called either the Katsura Detached Palace or the Katsura Imperial Villa. The "Imperial" suggests that it will be a palatial villa, and it is nothing of the kind. As the guide said, "Everything in Katsura is intended to produce the impression of graceful simplicity.

"What you are going to see in this garden is the villa building and several tea-houses, used for tea-ceremony." The roof over the gateway we entered through was a simple thatch of pressed cypress-bark, more than a hand-span thick, the edges cut as cleanly as a plug of tobacco, and about the same dark-brown colour.

"You see this square stone. This stone is for placing chair—chair borne by men with the prince carried in this chair. Now the prince comes out of chair and takes gentle stroll on this path. You see many stepping stones on this path. Please not to complain about too-narrow distance between two stones. Stones are laid out at ideal distance for kimono-wearing man.

"If it was night-time that you came this stone lantern would be lit. Stone lantern is not lit by candle but by rape oil or camellia oil in small shallow pan and burning by means of twig. There are twenty-three stone lanterns in this garden we go in now, walking carefully on stepping stones, not on moss."

Now we are in the garden, acres of it, a Japanese "nature" garden without a flower except the flowers that would star the azalea shrubs in June and deck the bare cherry-trees in spring. The only bright colour then, in November, was the red-gold of the maples. For the rest, there were the greens of trees and shrubs and grasses, the black of trunk and branch against a soft blue Japanese sky, the lichen-mottled grey of many stones, and the colours of water. The aim was that nothing should look artificial, everything should look natural. And, by and large, it did. You simply felt that Nature had been in a particularly artistic mood the day a maple seed took root over there where it could put up its autumn glow against the darkness of the hill where the first tea-house stood.

However, you might have thought that Nature could have been more considerate than grow a dwarf pine right in front of that lovely old stone lantern, almost obscuring it. The landscaper would tell you that the little tree was in just the right place there—in fact its branches had been trained out to cover the lantern. Screened light was so much better than direct light, so much more "natural". To have had the lantern out in the open would not only have been artificial; it would have been vulgar.

And that tea-house at the top of the path that wound up the hill over there had to merge into the trees, not stand out blatantly. Nor could it be pretentious in style, in any way grand or coloured. So it was small and simple as a farmer's cottage, of natural wood and bamboo with a cypress-bark thatch.

"Here is small entrance to this tea-house," the guide said when we came to it, and he indicated a square hole at one corner. "It is so small you can barely go through. This is a lesson, teaching: 'Be modest.'"

As we left that tea-house and went out through a gate in the simple bamboo fence, the guide stopped and, resting one hand on the fence, said, "Here is something else I would show you."

In the core of each piece of bamboo that formed the fence was a steel rod. You could hear the Japanese thinking: "Bamboo rots, steel endures, but bamboo is aesthetic, so we will use the thing of nature to sheath the harsh steel."

THE VILLA, at first glance from the other side of the pond, looks rather like the Australian bungalow of thirty or forty years ago. The white walls strapped vertically with wooden lathes *could* be that cheapest of building materials, fibro; it has front and side verandas, and it is raised high off the ground for coolness, on wooden stilts. The roof has the gable and pitch of the roof of the bungalow an aunt of mine had at the Sydney beach suburb of Cronulla; but this roof is of the dark and lovely cypress-pine bark, and it has the old Japanese raised ridge. No architect ever enthused about aunt's place, but they rave about this villa, and with reason. Its simplicity is beautifully proportioned. It is regarded as the outstanding specimen of pure Japanese house architecture.

The inside is almost as simple as the outside, with straight-line symmetry born of seventeenth-century Japanese taste that anticipated the "linear look" of our contemporary Western architecture. The design basis—the straight line used in the rectangular form—suits the natural grained woods and the textured paper of the sliding doors and the reed floorings of *tatami*. Moreover, the Japanese knew when and how to break a straight line. In the tea-room of the villa there is a half-wall partition, made of a plaster that has been given lovely tone and texture by being mixed with fine ash. A straight edge on this could be very dull. So a slim tree-trunk, with a slight natural bend in the middle, has been joined to the plaster as a post support. The bark remains on the tree, and has been polished.

The nature-feeling finds further expression in a rock set as a step within the house, a ceiling of boards strapped with bamboo and, in one room, no ceiling at all, so that the eye goes up to the beautiful craftsmanship of the bamboo-and-reeds underside of the roof. The plainness of a sliding door is relieved with an ornamental catch that derives from the pattern of pine-needles. In early spring this catch would be changed for one that was patterned after the camellia.

The main portion of the villa connects to what is like a separate house. In front of this is a bamboo balcony. It was for moon viewing.

Between the veranda and the lake is a hedge. When the Japanese permit themselves to be so "unnatural" as to have a square-cut hedge in a garden you can be sure there is some special reason for it. As the guide said, "Hedge causes illusion that you are at greater distance from pond."

Permits are now required for tourists to go into the Katsura Imperial Villa buildings, because these masterpieces of traditional building in wood and plaster are not strong enough to endure unlimited tourist traffic.

HEIAN (pronounced Heean) was the original name of Kyoto, which simply means capital city. Heian-kyo meant "peaceful, tranquil capital". One of the reasons the Emperor Kammu moved his palace from Nara in 794 was to get a respite from the politicking of Buddhist prelates who were trying to take over the imperial religion, Shinto, and so gain influence over emperors.

In 1894 an elaborate Shinto shrine was erected to mark the eleven-hundredth anniversary of the founding of Kyoto by the Emperor Kammu. This Heian shrine reproduced the Chinese-influenced design of Kammu's original palace. Resplendent in vermilion lacquer, the Heian is more colourful than any other shrine in Kyoto and more so than any of the hundreds of Buddhist temples. Its being so Kodachromatic—and having a huge (concrete) *torii* as its gateway—are doubtless the reasons why the Heian is one of the three Kyoto sights the one-day tourist is sure to be taken to.

Behind the shrine is an extensive landscape garden that hasn't quite the subtle beauties of the Katsura but is nevertheless lovely with its lakes and stepping-stones and across-water views. There are four lakes and the fourth is bridged by a fine covered gallery. There were autumn colours of maples when I was there, but these gardens are the more renowned for their cherry-blossoming and irises in spring. A pleasant, level walk takes you through the Heian gardens in about fifteen minutes.

More Kyoto: Stones make a garden

KIYOMIZU TEMPLE hangs on the side of a mountain just east of Kyoto. Its spectacular situation is enough to make it a tour favourite. The main hall (the Hondo) and another big hall that has the innermost temple are hoisted on scaffolding-like structures that rise to verandas that were built to stage ceremonial dancing. These make superb viewing platforms. You look down on the treetops of cherries and maples and pines that almost fill a small valley; and there is a view across to the city of Kyoto. Below the Kiyomizu's veranda is a waterfall. Pilgrims come to bathe, even in winter, under a cascade said to be purifying. (*Kiyomizu* means "clear water".)

This temple is as old as Kyoto. In 798 one of the very first shoguns enabled its founding by a novice from Nara, who said he had a holy visitation near the waterfall. In the next eight centuries the temple buildings burned, and were rebuilt, six times. The present buildings date from 1633.

The two great wooden halls of the Kiyomizu complex wear their age with a dignity that derives in part from their marvellous roofs. Tiles came into Japan with Buddhism, and they usually roof temples: thatch is associated with Shinto shrines. Here the roofs are of age-dark cypress shingles. The Hondo's is gabled and scalloped, yet in a way that doesn't detract from its expansive serenity; the other is almost plain to its upcurved corners. The halls that wear these uncoloured "hats" are either entirely unpainted or have paint that is so faded on everything from fascias to veranda railings that the whole structures merge into the mountainside. When I was there in November they appeared beautifully dun when the eye took in an autumn-painted maple and the red of a rhus-tree.

The Kiyomizu temple always rose again from its ashes because it had long been a temple that attracted Buddhists of many sects: it had no enemies. Some of the Buddhist sects used to war as violently with each other as Roman Catholics did with Protestants in post-Reformation Europe.

The Tendai sect once had as many as three thousand temple buildings on Mt Hiei, which rises north of Kyoto: today it has only the buildings that comprise the sect's temple-monastery of Enryakuji. As I looked down on Enryakuji, set in a grove of tall Japanese cypresses with trunks so thick they made the stalwart vermilion pillars of the temple look small, I thought that the place could impress any traveller as a sanctuary of ageless peace and virtue.

It was the end of the 1965 winter, with snow still lying in the shaded courtyard round the big bronze standing lanterns. In semi-darkness near the altar a group of people were sitting on the floor before a priest who was addressing them. Then the flooring of the colonnade trembled under a rush of shoeless feet that slowed, and the voices of a bus-load of children were hushed to whispers. The group got up and the children took their places. The priest began again, telling about Enryakuji—but not (I gathered from my guide) the full story. The leaflet you got at the entrance, simply said the old central hall was "destroyed by fire in 1571".

Enryakuji's history began with the foundation of Kyoto when, at the order of Emperor Kammu, the temple was built to protect his new capital from evil spirits. Centuries passed, the Tendai sect grew strong and aggressive, a law unto itself and the bane of Kyoto's rulers. So powerful was its monks' army in 1536 that Tendai razed all twenty-one temples of the Nicheren sect and slaughtered three thousand of its priests and followers.

The warlord Oda Nobunaga, who was then more potent than the emperor, had had enough of the uncontrollable bonzes on the mountain, whom he castigated as priests who "keep concubines and never unroll the sacred books". Nobunaga ordered: "Surround their dens and burn them and suffer none within to live." The warlord's armies did no less than that. The mountain blazed with burning temples, Enryakuji among them, and ran with Tendai blood.

When, eventually, Enryakuji was rebuilt the Tendai sect had renounced its warlike ways. Today its monastery on the summit of Mt Hiei is one of the largest in Japan. Monks spend years engaged in what are called Tendai's "difficult practices"—all-day walking and praying at temples, constant walking accompanied by chanting, and sweeping of the temple grounds (and, yes, walls) for six hours daily. The place is *very* clean.

IF YOU GO to Enryakuji by the Hiei (pronounced Heeay) Driveway there is a viewing place where you look out across the tops of pines to Lake Biwa. This is the largest lake in Japan.

On the soft day when I was there the pale blue lake stretched towards the foothills of the Japan Alps as though seen through a filmy silk curtain. Biwa is the lake's name because the form its 240 kilometres of shoreline takes is similar to that of a lute-like Japanese musical instrument, the *biwa*. Tradition has it that the lake was formed in 286 B.C. by a great subsidence of land, at the same time as Fujiyama bulged up to the clouds and burst as a volcano.

We went on and there were monkeys—not everyone realizes that Japan has indigenous monkeys—and then the modern-looking Mt Hiei Hotel. From Enryakuji we went down the mountain by cable car to the town of Sakamoto, where the hired car picked us up and took us to Katata on Lake Biwa.

The fading light was pearly as we walked through a temple's precincts to the lake. Twisted pines were beginning to silhouette their needly branches on the sky. Hoary stone lanterns stood against the stillest, palest blue water, lined along the bank with yellow reeds. And to one side, at the end of a pier, was what is called the Floating Pavilion. This very small temple was a boxy little structure with two doors, and only big enough to hold the altars inside them, but its unpretentious wood was topped with an ornately curved tiled roof, rather like a hat that was a bit too big and elaborate.

The famous "Eight Views" round Lake Biwa are poetically catalogued as: Evening Snow on Mt Hira, Sunshine with a Breeze at Awazu, Night Rain at Karasaki, Evening Bell at the Miidera Temple, Autumn Moon at Ishiyama, Evening Glow at Seta, Sails Returning to Yabase, and Flight of Wild Geese at Katata.

This last I saw. There they were, the wild geese winging black and arrowy against the soft grey sky suffused with evening light. I added a Ninth View by stopping the car as it was crossing the new bridge across Lake Biwa, the longest bridge in Japan, a mile of concrete that rises in one section to almost a moon-bridge arc. The water had turned beige-pink and a dark fishing boat was cutting it towards a shore that went back to mountains that glimmered with snow.

ROCK GARDENS did not originate with Zen Buddhism but the disciplines of their aesthetics are akin.

Of Zen itself it is difficult to say anything that has much meaning. A notable Zen statement is: "What is the sound of the single hand?" If you ask what is meant by that question your asking means, in effect, that you would be incapable of understanding the answer. And Zen teaches that answers are not usually expressible in words, anyway.

At a Zen temple on the outskirts of Kyoto is the most famous rock garden in Japan. The temple from which the garden takes its name is the Ryoanji. Claire was with me when I went to it and we had a private guide who said, "Most tourists like the more coloured places. The Ryoanji is a bit too tame for them."

When we had gone along the tree-shaded paths and, leaving shoes at the entrance, entered the temple there were about fifty people there, all Japanese. Yet there was hardly a sound. If people spoke they did so softly. In a room that opened on to a broad veranda two young women sat on the *tatami*, rested and still, looking at the paintings that in sparse black brushline limned misty crags on the beige-white paper walls. The other visitors were sitting on the edge of the veranda contemplating the famous garden.

There are no flowers in this garden, no trees, no plants at all except some stone lichens and a touch of moss. There is white gravel, such as might be called a coarse sand, and there are fifteen rocks. The rocks are set in a gravel-sand area about twenty-five metres wide and twice that in length, larger than a tennis court. This is flanked on the far sides by a low earthwork wall roofed with tiles. Beyond the walls, trees in the temple grounds emphasize the bareness of the oblong space.

The placement of the fifteen stones, in five groups in the raked gravel-sand, is such that one Japanese authority has been moved to write that "nothing in the world has ever expressed beauty so purely and symbolically by the deft use of space."[25]

The rake marks in the gravel were (as the photograph shows) very much part of the design. In the main these lines were straight; but some circled the stones and the whole pattern could suggest that the rocks, with currents eddying round them, were islands in a river or a sea. Other interpretations have been given: a mother tiger crossing a river with her cubs; the tops of mountains projecting through clouds; the five great temples of Zen.

The Ryoanji rock garden is what it is—at least, that is how we regarded it—an abstract spatial arrangement that seemed perfect of its kind and evoked its own aesthetic.

The Official Guide[24] says that it is "regarded as one of the masterpieces of Soami, who was greatly influenced by Zen philosophy". Another authority[28] says it is usually attributed to Soami, a famous painter and designer of gardens and buildings of that time (*c.* 1500) because many believe only he could have made it. However, there is this from Japan's eminent contemporary architect and designer of rock gardens, Professor Sutemi Horiguchi: "It was presumably made at the end of the Muromachi period (1338-1573). But beauty as composed solely by stones was first discovered in the early seventeenth century; and before that time people used to admire this garden for the beauty of the big cherry-tree that grew in this garden. The eye that found beauty in the garden of a flowering tree and stones grew to appreciate beauty in a flowerless garden of sand and stones."[25]

SOUTH OF THE CITY, and usually visited in the course of a tour to Nara, are a shrine (which has to be Shinto) and a temple (temples are always Buddhist) that are both very old, and age is not their only distinction.

The Inari shrine at Fushimi is a famous one. Its history goes back over 1,250 years to A.D. 711. The main shrine with its roof of Japanese cypress shingles dates from the year 1500. Not only is the curved dark roof extant but the vermilion-white-and-gold wooden building wears it beautifully.

At this shrine there are many images of its sacred animal messenger, the fox. But there are not nearly as many foxes at Inari as there are Shinto gateways, *torri*. If you are a good worshipper at Inari and can afford it, you donate a gate. The shrine has about ten thousand *torii*, and they are placed one behind another, only inches apart, so that they form a tunnel that runs for four kilometres, right round the hill the shrine is on. Anyone who has ever seen a fully timbered mine tunnel will have some idea of how this looks—except that mine tunnels' timbers aren't lacquered a glowing vermilion above a stone pavement striped with sunlight.

The afternoon coach tourist usually sees a *kagura*, sacred dance. It is gracefully performed on a shrine veranda by a white-clad temple maiden, with accompaniment on traditional instruments by two other girls and a Shinto priest.

The temple is at Uji, and it is a beauty. Its name is Byodo-in. It has been described as "not only the finest relic of Kyoto's golden eleventh century but perhaps the greatest architectural relic of any era in Japan".[28]

The Byodo-in began as the private villa of the head of the noble Fujiwara family, who was Prime Minister and whose son Yorimichi Fujiwara turned it into a temple in the year 1052. It was extended to a complex of twenty-six halls and seven pagodas. Today, after more than nine hundred years, only three buildings remain; but one of them is the central eleventh century construction, the grandest of all the halls, the Ho-odo, the Phoenix Hall.

The building's shape is, for no functional reason, like a bird's. Colonnades stretch emptily on either side, as wings; a corridor running to the rear is the tail. A sculptural phoenix in bronze is perched at each upcurved end of the main roof ridge. In front, the Phoenix Hall is reflected in a large pond. Only remnants of its vermilion lacquer, dulled with age, give the pillars and woodwork under the wide eaves any more colour than the grey tiles of the roof sections that have, of themselves, a wing-like sweep.

Inside, the time-eaten gorgeousness of decoration centres on a cypresswood sculpture of a Buddha, three metres high. The serene figure—attributed to a famous sculptor of the Heian period, Jocho—is seated on lotus leaves with a superbly decorative back panel that is carved with thirteen small

Buddhas and swirls up to a richly-carved canopy.

The coffered ceiling used to shine with round mirrors of polished bronze; curtains draped the canopy; walls were muralled with paintings—only traces remain—depicting Paradise; even the platform of the Buddha was inlaid with gold and mother-of-pearl, which has all been picked away during eras of neglect following wars. Nine centuries ago it must have been one of the most gorgeous temples in the land and, as Gouverneur Mosher says, "It is not difficult to believe that these surroundings, seen through incense in the mirrored candle-light, must have convinced Yorimichi that he was indeed close to Amida and the Western Paradise."[28] (Amida, or Amitabha, was one of the religious heroes raised to Buddhahood. Most Japanese Buddhists believed that by adoration of Amida they could be reborn into the paradise called the Pure Land.)

AT THE END of a day of coaching and walking from temple to garden to shrine to temple the tourist may feel a sense of inner welcome towards his evening victuals—and also, perhaps, may feel too tired to go beyond his hotel for dinner. Which would be a pity because there are some very good restaurants to be found in Kyoto.

One that served specially good tempura I was taken to years ago by Cecilia Arima of JNTO; and in 1973 the Yotaro was still maintaining its reputation and reasonable prices. A dessert there was ice-cream flavoured with powdered green tea.

The last time I was in Kyoto I asked at the desk of the Kyoto Grand Hotel, where I was staying, "What's a really good restaurant you can recommend for dinner?" The answer was Junidanya, if I liked the specialty of the house, *shabu shabu* (very thin slices of beef dipped in a pot of boiling stock to cook and then dipped in a sesame-seed sauce).

I set out for this *shabu shabu* but when I got to the place in the dimly lit Gion quarter, Junidanya was about to close at nine o'clock. Which was just as well because I found out later that Junidanya's excellence is matched by its expensiveness—it cost about ¥8,000 a person. Equally expensive was Dai-Ichi, which specialized in turtle stew such as it had been serving since the latter part of the seventeenth century. And the Japanese *haute cuisine* experience for the plump-walleted connoisseur is said to be the succession of mainly vegetarian titbits called *cha-kaiseki* (tea-ceremony dinner) such as Princess Margaret was served in a 350-year-old room at an uncompromisingly Japanese restaurant that is in a class by itself, Hyotei.

Anyway, the late-comer at Junidanya beseeched the servitors who turned him away and they pointed just up the street and he found this tempura bar that doesn't get into any guidebook he's seen, called Yuranosuke. It served, as well as tempura, the best crab I have ever eaten. The best and also the biggest. Not only were the claws king-size, the specimen back shell, displayed in a glass case, was huge. Only minimal English was spoken at Yuranosuke, but I gathered that the delicious crab was *matsuba kani*, and it was not available in the summer months.

Gion has always been the geisha quarter of Kyoto. Now the number of geisha was declining. The guide of the coach had said, "This year only nineteen *maiko*, as we call junior geisha, are training in Gion."

Asked why this was so, the guide said that most of the training was acceptable—the music and other artistries and even the table-serving part that makes the geisha little more than a glorified waitress: it was the "complete obedience" part of being a geisha that modern girls didn't like.

Naturally enough, the touring *gaijin* are interested in the doll-like creatures they may see teetering on high-soled *geta* along a Gion street. The 1974 situation was that the Kyoto visitor, for about ¥6,000, could be taken to a Japanese-style restaurant for a sukiyaki-and-sake meal served by geisha, who afterwards danced and performed music, and guests and geisha played games.

Spring in Kyoto brings on the Miyako Odori. *Odori* simply means "dance" but what you go to see is a lavishly colourful presentation in which, for the opening number, the whole ultra-wide stage is filled with geisha; and in each of the two galleries coming out from the proscenium are about fifty geisha seated in line, with *samisens* on one side and with *taiko* drums on the other. All, on the stage and in the orchestra-chorus, wear the traditional high-piled lacquered hair that frames in jet their mask-like faces. The effect of flowery brightness is heightened by rows and rows of glowing paper lanterns.

As to shopping, many tourists feel that Kyoto's being the "heart" of Japan makes it the appropriate place to buy the art or craft object that will remind them always of their Japanese journey.

And so it is, but if you are looking for something antique it is as well to heed what the Japan Travel Bureau has put in print, with commendable honesty: "The visitor is warned that so many junks [*sic*] are on sale nowadays. And because of the antique boom in the domestic market, bargain hunting is now a thing of the past.... The overseas visitor is advised to buy traditional arts and crafts (simple thing like pottery) still turned out by some of the best artisans in the world."

The best shopping is usually in the by-ways, but for the tourist with very limited time there is the Kyoto Handicraft Centre. Here everything from silks and cloisonné ornaments and porcelain dinnerware to dolls and damascene, lacquered things, carvings, woodblock prints and music boxes are available all day and every day from shops under one roof.

Our cherished souvenir of Kyoto is a small pot that was a "presento" to Claire from a distinguished Kyoto potter named Kusube. At his house after Mrs Kusube had served us tea, Kusube-san showed us some of his pieces. They were chastely beautiful in shape and colour and motif: Claire, who knows about pottery, could well understand why Kusube vases had won some of the highest awards. Neither the potter nor his wife spoke any English, but we learnt through our guide that he made all his own glazes, and that he gained certain effects in the kiln by mixing with his clay the ashes of the *isu*-tree and, sometimes, powdered glass.

I wondered whether he lived by selling his pottery privately or through special shops or in the department stores, so I asked the guide to put the question to him. What did he do with most of his work?

The question was put and the answer came from Mrs Kusube who, perhaps, did not always see why her husband should be such a perfectionist:

"He breaks it."

Nara is more than a big Buddha

NARA, as has been said, was the capital before Kyoto was. Before Nara was founded, in the year 710, Japan got a new capital whenever it got a new emperor: the old capital was abandoned as an act of purification.

Nara became the first permanent capital because there was a shift in religious belief after the introduction of Buddhism. Religion, and the arts that flowered from religion, is what Nara is about. Nara never took on industrial growth and it has only about one-seventh Kyoto's population. No factory chimneys poke at the sky, only pagodas.

The Horyuji which lies twelve kilometres outside of Nara is the oldest Buddhist temple in Japan and has some of the oldest wooden structures in the world—but you won't see it on any regular one-day tour. The place that most tours go to first might be said to misrepresent Nara—and to the extent that you can almost hear some awful spruiker saying, "Yessir! Texas, U.S.A., takes off its ten-gallon hat to Nara, Japan—place of the World's Biggest Bronze Statue in the World's Biggest Wooden Building!"

The Daibutsu (Great Buddha) in the Todaiji (Great Eastern Temple) is undoubtedly an extraordinary achievement in bronze casting—it would be if it were done today and is the more extraordinary because it was done in the eighth century. The four-year job of casting it, to the design of a Korean-Japanese sculptor, began at Nara in 745. Guidebooks often give its weight as 551 tons, but the image could never have been weighed. A lot of pure gold was used in the gilding, and it is said that the country was almost bankrupted by the Todaiji and its Buddha that stands (or, rather, sits) 16.2 metres (over 50 feet) high on its lotus pedestal, has a face nearly five metres long with eyes more than a metre wide, and the palm of its upraised blessing hand is longer than a six-foot man.

In an 855 earthquake the image's head fell off. The restored head and one hand were melted in an 1180 fire. In another fire in 1567 the again restored head was again lost. This time it was not restored for more than a century, and the image we see now is the 1692 model. The temple hall, called the Daibutsuden, rebuilt after the fires (and restored again in 1914), dates from 1708.

A great work of craft the enormous Daibutsu may be, but it doesn't rate at all highly as a work of art. The Great Buddha at Kamakura, about two-thirds the size of Nara's, is much better than this rather squat and square-faced figure—the face is hardly a compassionate one, more the chief-executive-type visage. As to the reconstructed building it is in, a leading authority on Japanese architecture Professor Horiguchi[25] wrote that it has "a low artistic value" compared with the original structure.

Nara is more than a big Buddha

NARA was cherry blossom, floating, its pale confetti fallen from the trees on to the lake behind our hotel. For me Nara connects with spring the way Miyajima does with autumn maples.

I have been back again to Nara, in 1973, in the autumn. Not that the maples aren't lovely there too, but again I felt (as I had felt when I was first there, briefly, in the autumn of 1955) that Nara was for seeing in the spring. It was, after all, the budding place of the new Buddhist faith and the arts that went with it, the place where, right back in the seventh century, a concept of Japanese culture brightened on this bough of islands and began to burgeon.

In the park just up from the willow-ringed Sarusawa Pond, there were raised wooden platforms where picnic parties sat crossed-legged under the lovely canopy of blossoms. In this season everyone goes out cherry-blossom viewing. The men were mainly drinking sake and looking happy. Women with children by the hand or babies on their backs wandered slowly. Strolling musicians were about, and there was an old woman with a samisen playing to a man who lay half asleep on the grass. And once we saw a *shakuhachi* (bamboo flute) player, who wore a strange headgear like a wastepaper basket woven of reeds.

Past the second-highest pagoda in the country, the one of the Kofukuji temple—there is another fine pagoda to the north of the pond—we went on to the farther reaches of the park where there are more trees and fewer people and the tame deer come up nuzzling and nibbling for biscuits.

Between the parklands are artificial lakes, and one of these, flanked with the pale-pink mist of a cherry-blossom avenue, was just over the quiet hill where the Nara Hotel stood, a comfortable old *gaijin's* castle with a bar of solid mahogany, high ceilinged rooms of Edwardian furniture and a view across the tiled roofs of the town.

Except for the Utsukushima that projects from the shore of the island of Miyajima and seems to float on the water, I do not know of a more beautiful Shinto shrine than the Kasuga. And as memorable as the shrine itself is the approach to it. This is up a road from the second *torii* gateway to where the shrine stands in its own domain of quiet woods.

The shady road is lined, either side, with stone lanterns, mossy with age. These are all gifts to the shrine, and the more decorative for being cut with the ideographs of the donors' names. There are said to be 1780 of them. On two nights of the year, one in early February and the summer's night of 15 August, all the lanterns are lit.

Among the lanterns you are likely to see some of the hundreds of deer that wander the shrine precincts—sacred deer that are said to be descended from a white deer that was the steed of one of the Kasuga shrine deities. At the shrine there are many, many more lanterns, in bronze, some standing, others hanging from the eaves and verandas. They may look alike, but peer closely and you find that the metal is cut through with patterns of a wondrous variety.

There is a considerable difference between the lacquered and colonnaded pavilions we see here and the shrines of Ise with their purity of form and natural wood. What we have at Kasuga is what the Buddhist architecture, that came in from China, did to Shinto. It curved the straight roofs. It put in more struts and pillars than were necessary to keep the roof up, but which were very decorative. It painted red oxide on what had been plain timber, and this became the vermilion that makes shrines so vivid.

The overhang of one of the shrine's roofs has a large leaning tree growing right through it: rather than cut down the tree the roof was built round it. In a courtyard there is a tree that is virtually seven trees, or trees and shrubs: grafted to one trunk are cherry, maple, camellia, *isu, niwakoto* and *nanten*.

The Kasuga (the name means "of a spring day") was founded in 768 as the family shrine of the Fujiwaras, who were for three centuries the most powerful family in Japan and at times were virtual rulers of the country. Immensely rich, the Fujiwaras provided for the shrine's reconstruction, whether necessary or not, every twenty years. However, the present building dates from 1863.

WHEN we go out of Nara to the oldest Buddhist temple in the country, the Horyuji, we see a pagoda that was constructed in the year 607; it is the oldest building here and is said to be the oldest wooden building in the world.

Built before there was any Japanese modification of the florid Chinese style, it is by no means the most beautiful of pagodas but, because of its great age and because it is a symbol of Japan's spiritual and cultural renaissance under the influence of Buddhism, it is regarded as the most precious. So much so that during the Second World War this pagoda was taken down and its ancient timbers carefully stored until the war was over, when it was re-assembled.

In the year 522 a king of Korea presented the Emperor Kimmei of Japan with a bronze statue of Buddha Shaka. The Emperor gathered his courtiers and they admired the image and discussed whether they, too, should worship it. This particular statue has disappeared, but the principal object of reverence in the Horyuji is a Buddha Shaka statue dated 623. The whole temple is a reliquary of Japanese culture as it began to flower from the new seed of Buddhism. There is a long and slender image of a goddess of mercy, the Kudara Kannon, that Claire considers the most beautiful thing in wood sculpture she has ever seen.

Fuji and Beyond

富士以遠

The Fujiya lived on a tycoon's love

THE RICHEST MAN in Japan was (in 1974, his fifty-seventh year) Kenji Osano. Next to the Transport Ministry he was the biggest shareholder in Japan Air Lines; he operated a few transportation companies of his own; he owned thirty-eight hotels including the Surfrider, Moana and Princess Kaiulani hotels in Hawaii.*

Among the hotels Osano-san owned in Japan were the five of the Fujiya (pron. Foojeea) chain. This takes its name from the Fujiya Hotel which rises above the mountainside village of Miyanoshita. It is not far from Lake Hakone, across which I had my first view of that superb mountain Fujiyama.

The Fujiya dated back to 1878 and was the oldest Western-style resort hotel in Japan. The face of today's tourism does not reflect in such hotels, and it is hard for them to remain commercial propositions. But Kenji Osano did not only own the Fujiya: he loved it.

He spent nearly every weekend up on the quiet mountain that was sixty-three car miles from frenetic Tokyo, or playing golf on the Fujiya's own eighteen-hole course, the course where Emperor Hirohito first hit a ball when he used to stay at the lovely imperial villa, Kikka-so, which the hotel purchased and made into its Japanese annexe in 1953. That was two years before I first stayed at the Fujiya.

There was the matter of upkeep. The Fujiya had so much ground, apart from the golf course; so much garden, beautiful garden with banks of flowers to small streams crossed by little stone and wooden bridges. A mossy old waterwheel turned near the swimming pool. Groves of maples mantled in scarlet in autumn; cherry-trees were a picture of pale pink blossom in spring. There were ponds and a pool that flashed the colours of carp, and a little stream purled down the forest slope to drop into the pool as a waterfall—this

*I knew that Mr Osano was a big backer and close friend of the then Prime Minister, Mr Kakuei Tanaka, but when the foregoing was written the "revelations" regarding their association had not appeared in *Bungei Shunju*, a reputable Japanese monthly magazine. Evidently they struck up a friendship in 1947 in prison. Mr Tanaka was awaiting trial on a charge (of which he was found not guilty) of accepting a million-yen bribe. Mr Osano was in jail for illegal dealings with the Occupation Forces' gesoline. In 1964, according to *Bungei Shunja*, Mr Osano bought from Mr Tanaka, at what the magazine says was an inflated price a financially ricketty real estate company, Nippon Denken, just when Mr Tanaka needed funds to make his political run to the top. This generous gesture by Mr Osano was linked with the fact that in 1953 the Finance Ministry had, against regulations, allowed Mr Osano to take dollars out of Japan to buy a hotel in Hawaii. The Finance Minister at the time was Mr Kakuei Tanaka.

The scandal forced Mr Tanaka to resign the Prime Ministership in December 1974.

sight and sound was just outside the conservatory where generations of Britishers had taken their afternoon tea. A private greenhouse grew orchids for table decoration in the dining-room that had a carved frieze of all the animals of the Japanese zodiac.

The Fujiya had so many buildings to service and, seemingly, miles of corridors, which were partly picture galleries where you found yourself saying, "That sketch *is* signed Degas." And the elaborate spa-baths, the Mermaid and the tatty Aquarium, which used to be walled with live goldfish behind glass. The Fujiya piped natural hot-spring water right into your own private bathroom, and was the only hotel in Japan that did so.

Nothing was too good for—to name some of the notables who have stayed at the Fujiya, in chronological order from 1912—Prince Heinrich of Germany, Prince Arthur of Connaught, the Crown Prince of Sweden, the Duke of Gloucester and (when the Allied Occupation had the hotel) Generals MacArthur and Eisenhower, and John Foster Dulles and, post-war, the Prime Ministers of India, Burma, Australia and New Zealand, Crown Prince Akihito and Princess Michiko and in 1966 the Emperor and Empress of Japan.

THE FUJIYA had been operated for nearly a hundred years by what might be called a Yamaguchi dynasty of hoteliers. In 1871 a young man named Sennosuke Yamaguchi was one of the first Japanese to visit the United States, and he came back with the idea of opening a foreign-style resort hotel. He did that, in 1878, and it catered not only for Americans and Europeans resident in Tokyo but for the British on the China Station. It offered Japanese exoticism with Western conveniences.

The hotel was doing well, when, in 1884, it was burnt to the ground. A new Fujiya soon arose and prospered until it was badly damaged in the Great Kanto Earthquake of 1923. By that time the founding Yamaguchi was dead and his son was president and the management was successively in the hands of two sons-in-law of the founder who, instead of giving their names to the Yamaguchi girls they married, had taken the name Yamaguchi themselves and became, in effect, adopted sons.

One was H. S. K. Yamaguchi, who cultivated moustaches that grew a wondrous nine inches on either side. The other was K. M. Yamaguchi, whose upper lip was as hairless as ivory, and who told me that he was once a purser on an N.Y.K. ship running to Sydney. K.M. was presiding over the Fujiya when I was there in the autumn of 1955 and in the spring of the following year. He was past seventy then, but still playing golf. He has since died, and in 1974 the very personable executive manager was the young hotel man who had married K. M. Yamaguchi's daughter and, in the son-in-law tradition, taken the surname and become Yuji A. Yamaguchi.

H.S.K. was the Fujiya's great innovator. In the mid-thirties he added the de-luxe wing called the Flower Palace—each of its forty rooms had the name and decoration motif of a flower. This was a great success, so H. S. K. put up two more wings—four-storeyed with vermilion balconies and sweepingly curved temple-style roofs pronging out to fancy finials.

Then, it seems, Yamaguchi-san was smitten with doubt. Was he overdoing the Japanese exotica? And putting too much stress on luxury? Were these new wings too ostentatiously alien, not homey enough for those big-nosed English colonels in plus-fours and their chinny, tweedy wives?

Many curiously shaped islands and rock forms have been sculptured by the sea in Matsushima Bay. One on a headland gives the impression of a presiding stone idol. Below: Very odd in form is the islet of Neojima. Matsushima is a richly scenic place, as the Japanese well know, but I saw no other foreign tourists there.

Two more of the picturesque formations (see previous page) photographed on a launch cruise round Matsushima Bay, north-east Honshu. Pine-trees grow photogenically out of rock clefts on many islets, though some are just sculptural bare rock. Below: A sea-carved archway.

Sometimes islands get "married" in Japan. Meota-Iwa (Wedded Rocks) represent a god and goddess near Toba, and these two were roped together off the Noto Peninsula.

Dummy policeman, made of plastic, acts as a roadside warning to speedsters.

Still making fine pots at age seventy-seven was Kosen Toshioka at Kanazawa.

So, underneath each elaborate portico of these multi-storeyed twin Oriental mansions he put up two little rustic-type nameplates, which are still there.

One says RESTFUL COTTAGE; the other, COMFY LODGE.

The Fujiya's foreigners didn't want to feel at home. They showed such avid interest in things Japanese that H. S. K. Yamaguchi produced, for sale to guests, a book in English called *We Japanese*.[29] Foreign guests were fascinated that the Japanese should stir their tea anti-clockwise and beckon by waving the hand away from them. Religious oddities included the annual Buddhist service for dolls damaged beyond repair, and another service to comfort the spirits of needles broken during the year.

The book, which K. M. Yamaguchi enlarged, explained such customs as *O-jigi*, the Honourable Bow, and said, as to characteristics, "The Japanese are trained to suppress their emotions of joy and sorrow, which they express by a simple smile. When telling about the death of his father, his wife or his child, a Japanese will often smile, his face in no way evidencing the grief he feels. He strives to suppress all signs of emotion so as not to inflict his grief on the other person."

H. S. K. Yamaguchi was the founder of the International Moustache Club. In Japanese this was *Bankoku Hige Kutabu*, which raised a delicate problem: *hige* means a growth of hair beneath the nose, and in view of this imprecise definition the club had to admit beards. So, while the gallery of photographs to be seen in the Pagoda Tower shows some magnificent moustache growths— Lord Wyfold of England and Herr Roleff of Germany holding their own with the finest handlebars sported by Japanese generals—the show is rather stolen by S. G. Brinkley, Esq., of England, who had an astonishing beard that could have nested a flock of finches and that reached right down to his feet.

COMING TO THE FUJIYA most people take one of the "bullet" trains from Tokyo that, every half hour, shoot down the New Tokaido Line in forty-three minutes to Odawara. From there you take a car, or a bus or a rail-motor called a tram that climbs up to Miyanoshita.

On the spring visit Miyanoshita was still chilly when we stayed in the Kikka-so annexe, the Fujiya's Japanese part that used to be an imperial villa. A tatami mat in the middle of our room was removed to reveal a *kotatsu*. This is a very cosy heating arrangement. In a cemented box-like hole about a metre square the maid places a pot of burning charcoal and over it an arched arrangement like a bamboo cage. You sit on the edge of the hole, your feet rested on the fire cage. A table is positioned and covered with a thick quilt that spreads on to the floor and keeps the heat in. Thus, with legs uncramped and stockinged feet on the footwarmer, we had our evening meal of sukiyaki most comfortably. And afterwards slept soundly on the bedding spread on the tatami.

An exhibition of lacquerware was being held at the hotel. There were superb pieces that we wanted but couldn't afford. We did buy a slim black-lacquer cigarette-box—it was only ¥2,900 and would have been cheap at twice the price. Consider the process of making it:

The whole surface of the box is first treated with lacquer juice, which is the sap of the *urushi*-tree (and is poisonous, so lacquer workers sometimes suffer from a ptomaine-like sickness). Three coats of lacquer juice mixed with pumice powder are applied, each is left to dry and each one is rubbed smooth

gnificent costume of a dancer in Kabuki theatre.

with a whetstone. Two more coats are put on, dried, whetstone-polished. Then more coats of lacquer juice are rubbed in. Now the first coat of colour is applied. This is dried, then polished with magnolia-tree charcoal. As many as ten coats of colour are applied. Drying between each coat must be slow, in a cupboard where the air is kept damp. Surface polishing is with magnolia charcoal, deer-horn powder and vegetable oil. Drying can take two months to make the surface extremely hard.

The exhibition included what are called inkstone boxes, containing Japanese writing sets. The perfection of fit of the lid was gauged to a hair's breadth. It was such that when the lid was placed on the box it just floated down.

The last time I was at the Fujiya I bought something more remarkable than lacquerware. I bought a stone—a stone that is found in only one part of Japan, at a place in the north of Gifu Prefecture. This *kikkaishi* (patterned stone) is flamboyantly described on a piece of paper that came with my purchase as "Miracle Chrysanthemum Stone". The patterning does take the form of a stiff-petalled flower and is so extraordinary that kikkaishi rock has been Government-designated a National Treasure and, thus protected, no more of it can be mined for sale. Existing stock could be sold and this was in the hands of a dealer who operated only from the Fujiya. The largest kikkaishi there was priced at one million yen (say, $A2,500). Mine was relatively small and cheap, but it is a fascinating thing, unlike any other rock I've seen and marked with a cluster of four distinct flower-forms. The stone is said to have formed on the sea-bed from material exuded by submarine volcanoes.

I WENT BACK in May 1974 to the Fujiya to see how it had changed. Structurally, there was the addition of Forest Lodge, in which I had an excellent double room: its rate, for two, was ¥10,000. The hotel's top suite was in Forest Lodge, at ¥35,000. But you could go into a Comfy Lodge twin-bed room for ¥5,500.

Away from the hotel there were such major changes as the new-to-me Skyline Driveway. This fine road ran along the top of an ancient outer crater of the volcano that blew out to form Lake Hakone. Yuji Yamaguchi used to be a racing driver and he handled beautifully his powerful Datsun sports coupé. We drove first to the lake, where the Fujiya chain has the Hakone Hotel, right at the lake's edge.

The Skyline Driveway is a toll road that offers look-down viewing of the blue spread of Lake Hakone and, though the road is as high as its name suggests, from it there is look-up viewing of Mt Fuji. But Fuji was reluctant to show its face, even on this cloudless day. Such was the haze that nothing at all could be seen of the mountain's base. The summit, though, hung as a ghostly cone in the sky. It was still impressive, as Fuji-san is in every mood—but nothing like the breathtaking first sight I had across Lake Hakone.

On the way back to the Fujiya by a circular route that crossed the floor of the valley, we passed the hotel's Sengoku golf course, The public could play there, at ¥10,000 (that was $A25) a round. Golf is like that in Japan. At another place tourists could swing across the valley in a cable car. The view included a mountainside where sulphur whiffed the air and steam fumed out of vents in the region's volcanic netherworld.

What I particularly liked seeing was an old farmhouse—or it would be better called a farm mansion—which the hotel owned and could make available to guests who wanted very-Japanese seclusion. Its gable front was three-storeyed and its steeply-pitched roof of bark. Called the Country Resthouse Futagami, it towered quietly in a lovely garden with arbors of utter peacefulness.

Next day Yuji Yamaguchi had to attend a wedding in Tokyo, and he drove me "home" to the Marunochi Hotel. We stopped at the town of Yumoto on the way down to Odawara and I was shown the chain's so-modern Yumoto Fujiya Hotel. It had such features as a "soaring see-thru elevator" of glass, hot-spring swimming pools and, in the games department, not only billiards, bowling and something called beam rifle but (believe me) electronic archery.

The young Japanese love the place. I wondered if it represented the shape of things to come at Osano-san's Fujiya at Miyanoshita.

Since then I have had (in 1975) a letter from Yuji Yamaguchi that says: "Let me assure you definitely that there is nothing to change the Fujiya's traditional management policies, as well as its unique facilities, for which I have full responsibility as managing director under the immediate direction of Mr Kenji Osano, present owner, and his younger brother, Mr Sakae Osano, present president ...." Mr Yamaguchi also declared in this letter: "Mr K. Osano is not such a man as rumoured in the revelations written in the magazine *Bungei Shunju*."

Viewing Fuji-san and the pearl places

FOREIGN TOURISTS, when they move on from the Fujiya Hotel, do not usually travel to Lake Hakone by bus. They take "private automobile", and that way it does not matter how much luggage you have.

The bus got to Hakone-machi (*machi* is town) in forty-five minutes and went into a depot. The smiling conductress stood at the step as the passengers alighted, thanking them individually for their patronage. I lugged out my suitcase and said, "Hakone Hotel, where, please?"

"Bus will take you," the conductress said. I got back in the bus which eventually moved off again. It ran along a road beside Lake Ashi, which foreigners always call Lake Hakone. The bus went on for half a mile. I kept wondering where the Hakone Hotel was.

Then I saw it—not the hotel, but Fujiyama. The mountain was enormous and wonderful beyond the olive-coloured hills as the drifting clouds unveiled it, a towering triangular cut-out against the sky, blue with haze and beautiful, its cone capped white with snow.

The bus ran into a street of shops, and the buildings cut Fuji from view. I peered and craned for another look at this magnificent mountain. The bus stopped and I thought, "Yes, it *would* stop here, where all I can see is a bed-quilt hung out for airing!"

Then the conductress was bending over me and saying, "Please, you no want hotel, yes?" Feeling foolish, I realized that I was staring into the Japanese section of the Hakone Hotel. I got off and, lugging my suitcase towards the three-storeyed white building at the lake edge, looked up at its flat roof edged with blue tiles. A white-coated bellboy came running out and took the bag. I said to him, pointing to the roof, "*Ichiban* view, Fujiyama?"

"Yes, sir, very nice view, indeed, of Fuji from roof here. I will take you." He swung open the door, checked my bags in the cloakroom when he found I was staying only for lunch, and led me up to the roof. He waited while I gazed my fill. "Very nice weather today, sir, for seeing Fuji-san."

Their sacred mountain is, to the Japanese, simply *Fuji* or *Fuji-san*. Only foreigners call it *Fujiyama*, though that is correct enough: *yama* is "mountain"; so is *san* mountain, as well as a personal honorific. It is, of course, Japan's highest mountain (12,395 feet, 3,776 metres).

Volcanic Fuji's crater has been quiescent for over five hundred years, but in 1770 an eruption burst thunderously from the side of the mountain and Edo (Tokyo), seventy-five miles away, was covered with six inches of ash. This blow-out formed a thousand-foot-deep peaked crater which, at a distance and from certain angles, puts a pimple on the side of what is still one of the two most beautiful conical mountains in the world. (The other is the South American volcano of Cotopaxi in Ecuador.)

Viewing Fuji-san and the pearl places 135

Fuji is best viewed from a distance of between ten and twenty miles, according to the official guidebook.[24] Closer than that the irregularities of the mountain mar its purity of form, and beyond about twenty miles it begins to lose its majesty—though, looking at it from Lake Hakone, about twenty-five miles off, I thought it superb.

Nearly a million climbers ascended Fuji in 1973. Many a Japanese will proudly produce from a corner of his house the wooden staff he bought at the foot of the mountain and had branded at each of the ten "stations" along the route, or routes: there are six tracks, and climbers can usually get to the summit in from seven to nine hours—they climb through the night to arrive for the sunrise.

Even children make the ascent, and, nowadays, women. Before 1868, the year of the Meiji Restoration, no Japanese woman was allowed to ascend sacred Fuji. The British envoy's wife, Lady Parkes, went up the year before that.

Doubtless it is interesting to see the alpine flora and to peer into the crater that is six hundred yards across, but I never felt much urge to climb Fuji, particularly since reading that "the snow will be replaced by a carpet of empty beer cans, plastic wrappers, paper and all kinds of throwaways", and there are so many climbers "you are just like one bead on a long, long string".

Who wants to be, when they can watch her pose,
The fly that crawls on fair Diana's nose?

LUNCH AT THE lake-edge Hakone Hotel gave a view of the lake, where a big white excursion launch was gliding, crowded with trippers. Beyond the boat and the high shore rose Fuji-san, its snowcrest as white as the cap and apron of the waitress who set each dish down gently and smilingly before the late, last luncheon guest. This would be, I thought, a pleasant place to stay. But I was due that night at Atami, which lies across the hills to the south, on the coast.

The road to Atami went over the Ten Province Pass. From there, two and a half thousand feet up, I was able to see not only the spread of ten Japanese provinces, but more of Fujiyama than could be seen from lake-level.

THE BUS GOT to Atami about seven o'clock. I had to stand all the way, and couldn't see much except the drop at the side of the road. Then when we got into the streets of Atami I could see shoes—shoes and *geta* lined up in the porches of Japanese inn after Japanese inn. Atami is a famous resort town.

My itinerary said *Atami Hotel* and when I eventually got there I felt greatly in need of a Scotch. Having drunk the whisky I was about to order another when I saw the price the barman was writing on the check—and changed to beer. The barman, who spoke English well, said simply that prices at top resort towns such as Atami were thirty per cent higher than in Tokyo.

The barman spoke of Lafcadio Hearn. The Japanese still love the memory of this Irish-Greek writer who was so enamoured of their country he became naturalized and took a Japanese name, Yakumo Koizumi. For the last six years of his life—Hearn died in 1904 and his grave is in Tokyo—while he was still a professor of English at Tokyo University, he used to spend his summer vacations at the little fishing port of Yaizu, his home a fishmonger's shop, his delight the high waves that roll in against the Yaizu shore, for

Hearn was a strong swimmer. Yaizu, the barman said, means "Burnt Creek", and it got its name from when a great samurai was surrounded by his enemies there and they tried to kill him by setting fire to the grass. But he cut the grass with his sword, and escaped.

"As he sworded the grass, he made a poem," the barman said, polishing a glass. "I know that poem. It has very deep meaning. But very hard to translate."

While I was sitting at the bar three other people came in. One of them was an Englishman I was to see again when I decided that now was the time to take a hot-spring bath. When I came to the bath ante-room where you put off your kimono the Englishman who had been in the bar was just getting dressed. I asked if the bath was very hot, and he said no. Some were so hot Westerners couldn't stand them, but this one was all right. Had I taken this kind of bath before? No. Then there was something I should know—or I could make myself quite unpopular.

"One never soaps oneself in the bath," the Englishman said. "Wash yourself first under the shower at the end—that's ordinary water. *Then* get in the pool. The bath is for making you warm and making you feel good—it's *not* for getting you clean."

His name was J.M. Jerwood, he was a pearl merchant from Tokyo, and he was in Atami for the pearl auction which would be held next day, and which he thought I might be interested to see. We made a date for the following morning at eleven.

The bath was an oval cream-tiled pool about thirty feet long. A thin cloud of steam rose from the translucent spa water. I soaped and showered first as directed. It was so good that I lay about and floated round for half an hour. The warmth stayed with me long after I had gone to bed.

IN THE MORNING SUNLIGHT the sea glistened at the foot of the cliff. The cliff was one wall of a tiny cove where a long-prowed fishing-boat rocked at moorings and spilled the reflection of its yellow sides among the sliding lights in the water. You looked down on this through the frame of an old pine-tree's branches. It was a very lovely spot, a deep well of peacefulness.

"Yeh!" said a tourist beside me. "This is what they call Suicide Cliff."

"I guess so," his companion said. "This must be it."

"Ninety-two people gone over here so far this year. Still early November, and they tell me at the hotel there's sure to be the hundred before the year's out."

"That's more than throw themselves. . . ."

I got away from them fast and walked along the main drive of the Nishikigaura, which translates as Brocade Beach; but it is not a beach, it is a strip of picturesque coastline that forms one side of an ancient volcano that sank the other side of its huge crater out there in Sagami Bay.

I went back into the town. Men in kimono were strolling on their way to the hot-spring baths or coming back from them. I went off into the little streets that climb and twist among the houses and shops that cling to the side of the hill. There were food shops that sold everything from golden Atami mandarins and bean-paste flavoured with apricots to fish that stood out in the sun and was patterned with flies. You could buy the local camphorwood ware, and a papery cloth with a twist of wild silk through it—and countless

Viewing Fuji-san and the pearl places 137

souvenirs that were cheapjack proof that you had been to Atami.

You see relatively few animals in Japan, but at one shop I had a good look at the Japanese breed of cat. The tail is oddly bent and has a kind of knot at the end.

When it was eleven o'clock I went to the hotel my bath acquaintance, Jerwood, had told me to come to. The pearl auction was being held in a large well-lighted room. There must have been over a hundred buyers and attendants there. The buyers sat at long trestle tables. Bowls of pearls and bunches of necklaces were passed along in front of them. They bent over these, sometimes taking pearls from the bowls and putting them in the palms of their hands, then writing their bids on little slips of paper.

"D'you know anything about pearls?" Jerwood asked. I said I knew the Australian pearling ports and had written a novel with a pearling background, but the mainstay of the industry had become not pearls but pearl-shell. At Thursday Island or Broome (this was before pearl culturing began in these regions) you might not see half a dozen good pearls in a whole season. Here I was seeing pearls by the bowlful. Jerwood said the year's Japanese production would be about ten tons.

"Tons! Ten *tons* of pearls?"

Jerwood smiled. "Yes, tons. Of the ten tons my organization will probably buy about four."

Before I left I said to Jerwood, "Would you join me in a drink?"

"Thanks all the same," he said. "I should rather like a Scotch but—well, you won't find anyone here today drinking anything stronger than orange juice. Might put the eye out. And if a buyer makes a mistake about the quality of pearls he's buying, the drink could be shockingly expensive."

CULTURED PEARLS are quite as good as "natural" pearls and only an X-ray can tell the difference, and then the difference is only at the core. They are produced in Japan in millions, to the value of millions of dollars, because of the dogged resourcefulness of a man who was the son of a poor noodle seller and who became the "Pearl King".

Kokichi Mikimoto was characteristically Japanese in his diligence, but in not much else. A pacifist, he was a conscientious objector throughout the Second World War; he drank no sake or other alcohol; he detested the taste of raw fish; he contended that Japanese were much too dependent on rice, and his usual lunch was a pancake made from wheaten flour; he wore a black bowler hat with his kimono; and in his eighties he could still stand on his head and walk on his hands. He was aged ninety-six when he died in 1954.

Mikimoto's father had a noodle shop at Toba, which is a small port city, notable now as a tourist centre, on the Shima Peninsula. I came to Toba along a scenic drive from Ise, the place of the most sacred Shinto shrines. Mikimoto was born in 1858, only five years after the coming of Perry's "black ships". When he was about thirteen some British warships berthed at Toba. Kokichi got aboard by doing juggling tricks, and he sold the *gaijin* vegetables. He also hawked abalone and lobsters for a living.

He was thirty-three and still poor when he saw a marine exhibition that explained how oysters produced pearls by covering irritant foreign bodies, such as grains of sand that lodged, inside them, with protective layers of nacre, or mother-of-pearl. Mikimoto wondered whether, instead of pearl production being an accident of nature that happened to one oyster in a thousand, it could be made a matter of artifice, by introducing into the shells of oysters *en masse* the kind of nuclei that would be turned into pearls. For centuries the Chinese had been inserting tiny metal Buddhas into oysters and recovering them years later covered with mother-of-pearl. Experts agreed that to grow pearls in this way was possible, theoretically. Practically . . . ? Mikimoto seems to have been the sole optimist.

Mikimoto began prying open oysters and introducing grains of sand and shellgrit. He worked for months waist-deep in Toba Bay and did not look like producing so much as a single seed pearl. When he employed divers to insert pellets of clay, glass, and copper in different places in the shells of oysters that were then submerged at different depths, Mikimoto's relatives called him crazy, a "pearl maniac"; and his ever-faithful wife, Ume, who looked after the noodle shop, said it was easier to get rid of the creditors when he was away peddling marine products in Hokkaido.

In 1893, two years after he began, Mikimoto and his wife spent six days opening some thousands of oysters that had been implanted, and Ume found in one a half-spherical pearl that was worth something. They were able to lay five such pearls on the family altar and thank the gods for success.

His real success didn't come until 1905, when Mikimoto was forty-seven. He had a million implanted oysters growing on the bottom of Ago Bay, to the south, when he learnt that the dreaded "red tide" of algae that is fatal to shellfish was coming into the bay. He hired two hundred divers and they brought up 850,000 oysters—all dead or dying. Mikimoto had them all opened and they produced five fine, perfectly round pearls.

When Mikimoto saw where in the oyster these five precious little spheres had formed, he knew what he had to do: place the foreign body not between the flesh of the oyster and the shell but within the oyster's flesh. But much more trial and error was involved before Mikimoto and his son-in-law perfected the operation that introduced the bead of nucleus in such a way that the oyster did not reject it and was not killed by the operation.

The operation is demonstrated by skilled technicians at what is called Mikimoto Pearl Island at Toba; but I had seen it earlier, on the JTB-Hato bus tour in Tokyo. A membrane is removed from a three-year-old oyster and cut into tiny pieces less than half a centimetre long. The operator takes a two-year-old oyster, prises it open slightly, and inserts into its gonad section a small spherical bead cut from the shell of a freshwater clam called the pigtoe, found in the Mississippi River (all the nuclei are imported from the U.S.A.). On top of this bead the operator then inserts the sliver of (still living) membrane from the sacrificed three-year-old oyster.

"Now the oyster pregnant and able to become mother of pearl," was how the operator put it. "Such oysters are placed in wire baskets that are attached to rafts and submerged in the sea three years. Baskets must be raised and oysters cleaned periodically and each month the rafts are moved to where waters are warmer, as water colder than about eight degrees Celsius can kill the oysters. Today as much a menace as the 'red tide' is the industrial pollution of the sea that kills the plankton the oyster lives on. Normally we lose sixty per cent of oysters—this year we lost seventy per cent. When the oysters are five years old they are opened. Only about three oysters in every two hundred produce high quality pearls."

Viewing Fuji-san and the pearl places 139

To the women in the tour party the operator said, "Love your pearls. Polish them lightly with a soft cotton cloth when you take them off, otherwise in five or ten years they will begin to fade. It is bad for pearls to be in contact with any perspiration of the skin. And their worst enemy is perfume."

PEARL ISLAND, just off shore at Toba, is now joined to the town by a bridge. On the island Mikimoto lived in seclusion during the war he opposed, after an Army officer sent him a samurai sword and suggested he commit hara-kiri. Now the island has the full tourist setup of pearl museum, demonstrations of how pearls are cultured, pearl jewellery shops. And you can sit in comfort and watch, through a pavilion's glass front, the *ama* women diving.

Some tourists still come to Toba expecting to see bare-breasted girl divers bringing up pearl oysters. In fact, the divers are clad neck-to-knee in white cotton suits, and nowadays they have nothing to do with the pearl industry. They dive for abalone, seaweed and lobsters.

"There are about seven thousand *ama* in this region of Mie prefecture," said the guide at Pearl Island. "They start training when they are schoolgirls, they get jobs as divers when they are about eighteen, but don't become really good until they are thirty. On average they reach their peak about forty and some go on diving until they are sixty. The more experienced older women go down to thirty metres. They can hold their breath for two minutes."

Instead of gathering "wild" oysters from the seabed the ever-ingenious Mikimoto thought out ways of cultivating his own. He invented a wire screen coated with lime-cement to which the spats, the oyster larvae, adhered.

Toba is on open water at the entrance to big Ise Bay. Mikimoto found better conditions for his oysters in more sheltered Ago Bay, which is formed by the hooked extremity of Shima Peninsula. This, like the Toba region, is a picturesque part of Ise-Shima National Park, and I went to spend a night down there at a first-rate tourist hotel, and afterwards returned to Toba to spend a night there at another. I had been provided with two guides by Mie Prefecture authorities and, before taking me down to the island of Kashikojima in Ago Bay, they had been instructed to give me lunch at a famous (and, I'm sure, expensive) restaurant at Toba called Ise Ebi.

Ebi is lobster, the specialty of the house. Dishes that preceded it included *awabi* (abalone) cooked in aluminium foil and very good king prawns, but the lobster was what I looked forward to, especially when the guide said, "Here it is so *fresh*."

When the lobster was brought in I looked at it with horror and said I could not eat it. I didn't mind it being raw—it was shelled to the extent that the tail section of the carapace had been removed and the flesh sliced into pieces that could be removed with the chopsticks—but I minded very much that the lobster was *alive*. Its long feelers were still, quite actively, waving.

The young lady who was one of the two guides said with a half-embarrassed smile, "So *fresh*!" and that she had not previously eaten raw lobster and, when she had taken some, "It has good taste, a little sweet." She and the other guide accepted with perfect Japanese politeness what to them was, doubtless, peculiar squeamishness. Behind this there could have been the kind of innocent incomprehension of cruelty to creatures such as I've encountered all too often among peoples living primitively—but the Japanese are not primitives and they have no excuse for being so uncivilized.

I disagree with most of the denigration in a book about the Japanese by a distinguished fellow author, Hal Porter; but I go with him all the way when he castigates Japanese eating habits that include the serving of "*odori-zushi* (dancing rice-balls) each one with a shrimp that has been skinned alive twitching in agony on the top".[2] And anyone who doesn't think that shrimps, or lobsters, can experience agony needs to be asked, "Where is the evidence that they don't?"

ROOM 525 at the Shima Kanko Hotel—which rises on top of Kashikojima, the biggest island in Ago Bay—had wide views of a waterway that was as indented as Sydney Harbour but unlike any waterway I've seen outside Japan. It was patterned with the neat geometry of oyster rafts in long rectangles and with dotted lines of the bobbles of floats—these were the markers of wire baskets of pearl oysters on the seabed.

The view is famous for the way it appears at sunset, when the whole picture turns into black silhouettes on ruddy gold. But that I saw only in photographs. Rain was the order of the day while I was at Kashikojima. The sky stayed as grey as the shell of an oyster and the sun was as locked away as a pearl inside one.

I arrived in the late afternoon, the management presented its compliments with a pot of green tea and a bowl of strawberries, and I learnt that the Shima Kanko was one of the Kintetso Miyako hotels (I was to stay at two others of this chain and found all three good). Most of the two hundred rooms were Western style; but when I went down to the dining-room the faces at the other tables were all Japanese except for a party of Germans. However, the manager, Tanaka-san, said that more and more foreigners were finding their way to the peninsula end of Ise-Shima National Park.

In the Shima Kanko's dining-room I had well-prepared, fresh seafood that evening, and again for lunch next day. With dinner I tried a half bottle of Japanese white wine, Mann's, made from Semillon grapes grown near Mt Fuji, and found it less than recommendable.

Next morning drizzling rain made the worst of sightseeing days, but the launch cruise on Ago Bay was still interesting, as befitted the biggest pearl-producing place in Japan. The other main pearl-growers are Tanable Bay, away to the west, and Omura Bay near Nagasaki in Kyushu.

Mikimoto grew his first cultured pearl in Toba Bay but, he once said, "In order to make my second dream come true, I started my life of sweat and tears on Tatoku, a small island in Ago Bay." This island is still where the Mikimoto company has its main factory. As the launch passed it, the hotel's under-manager Mr Ishii, who had come with me, said that the "red tide" (the sea appears to be dyed red with the poisonous plankton) and the cold water that sometimes invaded the bay were not the only oyster killers the pearl growers had to cope with. "If a typhoon comes the oyster baskets have to be raised," he said, "and also after very heavy downpours of rain, because oysters cannot live in fresh water."

The launch threaded its way between countless rafts, some of pinewood, others of bamboo, and line upon line of black ball floats made of plastic. They are not all owned by K. Mikimoto, Inc. The pioneer's patents on pearl culture ran out in 1921, and soon Mikimoto had a couple of hundred competitors. Many of these put on the market such poor-quality pearls that, to demonstrate that he would never sell them, Mikimoto in 1933 bought up three quarters of a million inferior pearls and had them publicly incinerated in a furnace set up in one of the main streets of Kobe.

At one "factory" the cruise party landed and some people bought pearls—for as little as Y800 for a small fancy-metal pearl brooch. Ishii-san said that pearls were even cheaper here than at Toba, cheaper than anywhere else in Japan.

Ashore again, we went to a big aquarium called Shima Marineland, which is housed on a headland in a brutally modern building. Some of the fish tanks inset in the walls were gaudily over-designed, or too small for the number of creatures in them, but there were some remarkable exhibits. The giant crab of Japan hoists itself on legs like articulated stilts, which can measure as much as two metres between the extended tips. The "run" of fish of many kinds inside a huge ring of glass, round and round at eye level, was amazing, with sharks and the great cod dwarfing smaller species, and the manta (or "devil") rays seeming to fly by on black rubber wings.

After lunch I went back to Toba on the bus, which takes longer than the train, an hour and a quarter; but it is a more scenic route.

SUITE 1033 in the Toba Hotel International—which stands a modern seven storeys on a headland and commands the widest water views—was good accommodation that was also unusual. Not only was it an agreeable combination of Western-style bedroom with Japanese sitting-room that could also double as a bedroom, but it had another room that literally pointed at the view: it was triangular. You sat in one of the easy chairs by a drinks table and looked to left and right through floor-to-ceiling glass. Up to four persons could have shared this suite for Y15,000.

Pine-trees grew tall from the water's edge and took segments of the view in the crooks of their branches, in very Japanese fashion. Down through the right-hand angle of glass I could see a vessel moored, its funnel gay and decorated with the hotel's symbol, twin seahorses. The ship *Seahorse* turned out to be a restaurant, where I was to have a very satisfying meal of seafood. It was all barbecued on an oiled plate—sea snails, clam, mussels, abalone, *inokai* (a shellfish), shrimp and fish called *hamachi*, and served with a good salad.

That was after I had been dashing round Toba Bay in a speedboat such as could be hired, with driver, for a very reasonable Y1,000 an hour. The hotel manager, Mr Kato, came with me to point out places. We sped past Dolphinland, where diving *amas* as well as leaping dolphins performed for the primarily Japanese tourists. There were few bayside villas but many hotels; only the Toba International had Western-style rooms. From time to time the wave-thumping speeding stopped so that I could take pictures of islets with pines silhouetting decoratively at odd angles on tiny capes.

Just up the coast at Futamigaura a couple of rough pyramids of rock stick out of the sea and are known as the Meoto-Iwa (Wedded Rocks). They are identified with the earlier-mentioned mythological creators of Japan, Izanagi and his sister-spouse Izanami. The two rocks, regarded as sacred, are joined by having looped round their pinnacles a very stout straw rope. This rope symbol of union is renewed with ceremony every January by agile young men wearing suits of pure white with the red sun disc, Japan's symbol, on the backs of their coats.

THE TRAIN I took from Toba to Nagoya passes through two places of some note. The first of these, reached after Ise, is Matsuzaka, where the famous beef comes from. Yet I didn't see from the train a single specimen of it on the hoof. Again I was reminded that animals are relatively rare in Japan: rurally, it is a land of crops, not creatures. I don't recall ever seeing a herd of cattle, and I never saw sheep or a paddock of horses until I went to Hokkaido.

Some gourmets prefer Matsuzaka beef to the famous Kobe beef. As to the difference, only a rich man or a big expense-account business entertainer could afford to eat enough Japanese steak to be authoritative about it.

The other place of note is the city of Yokkaichi. The guide I had had at Ise and Toba, the young lady who liked the taste of living lobster, was from the Yokkaichi Port Authority, and she had given me a brochure about the port. I opened it at the back and blinked at photographs of Sydney Harbour and the Sydney Opera House. A born citizen of Sydney, I had not known that Sydney's sister city in Japan is Yokkaichi.

This sisterhood happened because Yokkaichi takes in more wool than any other port in the world, and the wool is Australian. But wool is by no means the chief industrial concern of the city. Its main industry is vast manufacturing of petrochemicals. It was getting over its problem of smoke-and-worse pollution that gave rise to an ailment called "Yokkaichi Asthma".

Nagoya, epitome of postwar Japan

IN TERMS of modern civic planning the most impressive city in Japan is certainly not the capital, Tokyo; nor is it the second-biggest city, Osaka, or the third, Yokohama. It is Nagoya.

Japan's fourth city was, in the Second World War, a centre of aircraft building and munitions making, so it became a prime target for the American bombers. Almost half of all Nagoya was laid waste, and its population reduced by nearly two-thirds. With so much of the old Nagoya demolished, the civic authorities decided to rear the new Nagoya to a design the visitor is soon conscious of.

Right in the city's centre rises a 180-metre television tower. From the observation platforms of this you look, to both north and south, along what must be the widest thoroughfare in all Japan: it is referred to as the Hundred Metre Parkway. A great band of trees and gardens, interspersed with fountains, is flanked on either side by four-lane trafficways.

The plan put commercial Nagoya in the middle, residential areas in the east and west, industrial zones to the north and south. At the two ends of this mighty mall that bisects central Nagoya there were such industries as these: the main factory of Japan's biggest maker of cars and trucks, Toyota; another big car maker, Mitsubishi, turning out its Lancer; Noritake chinaware and other makers of 80 per cent of Japan's export ceramics; cotton spinning and other textile mills; huge manufacturing based on plywood; confectionery, plastics, sewing machines, electric motors, bicycles, clocks. Nagoya, the postwar epitome of "industrious Japan", was a major contributor to the "economic miracle".

Nagoya knows that industry is poor bait to catch tourists with. So the first place it takes the visitor to is its castle. This is an imposing example of the picturesque Japanese style of castle, rising tier on tier pyramidally for five storeys on high foundations of stone and having white walls and curved roofs of tile and copper, the whole edifice and its grounds bounded by stone ramparts and moats.

The castle's original construction was finished in 1612. It was built at the order of the famous shogun Ieyasu Tokugawa for his ninth son, Yoshinao, who was made lord of the province and given this fortress for defence and as a base for attack on the forces of the rival Toyotomi family. In the last war bombs and, principally, fires destroyed Nagoya Castle—but there it is, as handsome as ever, in fact better-looking than it was before 1945. It rose from its ashes in ferro-concrete, at a cost of about $ A12 million, of which $ A100,000 went in recreating the two golden dolphins that ornament the ends of the topmost roof ridge and each weigh more than a tonne.

Ironically, the dolphins were supposed to give the building protection against fire—a legendary dolphin extinguished a fire by spouting seawater from its mouth. The wartime fire that destroyed the castle was so fierce that it melted the gold exterior of the original dolphins. The new dolphins were given scales of 18-carat gold, and the melted gold of the originals was gathered up and formed into a solid gold tea kettle that is used to serve tea in the teahouse in the garden adjoining the castle.

A palace that stood within the inner moat was also destroyed by the bombing-raid fire. Some of the *fusuma-e* (paintings on *shoji* sliding doors) for which the palace was famous were saved, and these and other National Treasures are on exhibition in the castle, which is virtually a museum.

A greater repository of paintings, lacquerware, ceramics, Noh masks, costumes, armour, and swords is the Tokugawa Art Museum. The Tokugawa's is the second largest museum collection in Japan, next to the National Museum's in Tokyo.

Nagoya's modern pride is its Civic Assembly Hall, planned to mark the city's population passing the two million mark, and completed in 1972. It is regarded in Nagoya much as, in Sydney, the Opera House is. I was able to see through it when the main hall was empty, in the afternoon. This hall doubles as a splendid theatre—the stage is twenty metres deep—and concert hall. The foyers have large and striking sculptural works in marble and ceramics and notable ceramic tiling.

Some tourists want to visit a ceramics factory, and regular tours go to where Noritake dinnerware is made. Or they may go to the Ando cloisonné factory to see the process that takes its name from the French *email cloisonné*, meaning "enamel in cells". The "cells" are contrived with thin strips of metal on a metal vase or whatever object is to be decorated by filling the shapes made by the strips with coloured enamels. Cloisonné (which the Japanese call *shippo*), came to Japan from China, but it was known much earlier in the West.

I went to the Atsuta Shrine, which the Japanese regard as next in sacredness to the shrines at Ise. This is because it has the Sacred Sword that (with the Sacred Mirror at Ise and the Sacred Jewels in the Imperial Palace at Tokyo) is one of the three Sacred Treasures of Shinto. It is not, of course, on view. The tourist who cannot get to Ise can see in the inner precincts of this Nagoya shrine the same style of purely Japanese architecture in similar buildings.

The chief deity enshrined under the name Atsuta-no-Akami turns out to to be Amaterasu the Sun Goddess. There are some very large *torii* gateways, as one would expect. Not so expected, outside the main shrine, was a fowlyard. The fowls were all roosters, for whom the first torii was a perch, and their crowing from this was contrived to suggest to the Sun Goddess in the cave that dawn was breaking without her light. The roosters are there because of this sacred association with Amaterasu. Which did not prevent a worshipper's small boy from aiming a kick at one that was squatted in the dust.

In a two-storey concrete building called the Culture Hall are the shrine's treasures, including some superb old masks used in Bugaku, the ancient court dance. Bugaku is still performed at an annual service held on 1 May.

The best time to be in Nagoya is mid-October, when the city has its festival. There is a procession representing three famous feudal lords—Nobunaga Oda, Hideyoshi Toyotomi and Ieyasu Tokugawa—in costume, a parade of traditional floats, and lots of fireworks.

Nagoya, incidentally, has an American sister city, Los Angeles.

Nagoya, epitome of postwar Japan

THE INTERNATIONAL HOTEL was Nagoya's largest and most luxurious. It had three hundred rooms, ranging from singles at about $A10 a day to the Royal Suite at ¥10,000 a day, which Crown Prince Akihito would be occupying in three weeks time. For my one night in Nagoya I had it, gratis.

It sometimes happens that a national tourist organization, trying to facilitate an author's writing about a country and at the same time minimize his travel expenses, finds a first-class hotel willing to take care of him. The hotel figures it can impress the travel writer, and at the same time not lose a night's occupancy of the kind of good room that is in high demand, by putting him in one of its luxury suites—which are vacant most of the time, anyway. So there I was, all alone with dining facilities and a kitchen, all the space of a three-room apartment, and two bathrooms with such refinements as upholstered lavatory seats and the only bidet I ever saw in Japan.

As to food, the International was proud of the cuisines of its five restaurants, and justifiably so if one could judge by the steak I had, the Matsuzaka sirloin. I can't say that I was impressed with the half-bottle of Japanese red wine, a Mercian Cabernet, I had with the steak. Nippon does better with whisky. Scotch comes at such prohibitive prices that I drank Suntory Old: I find it a very tolerable whisky. Nagoya's International Hotel had a whisky of its own called Big 0, in honour of the hotel's president, Ogawa-san.

Another thing that was international was Nagoya's airport. Three days a week a Japan Air Lines service came in from Hong Kong, via Taipei; and you could leave for Hong Kong on JAL from Nagoya.

The money-bringing birds of Gifu

FIVE NIGHTS before I arrived in Gifu in mid-May there was a coloured explosion of fireworks over the Nagara River where this not-too-large city is set at the foot of a forest-clad mountain. On 11 May every year fireworks signal the opening of Gifu's cormorant-fishing season.

As a tourist spectacle the cormorant fishing continues until 15 October, every night except when the moon is so bright that the "fire baskets" on the fishermen's boats cannot be relied upon to attract the fish, or when storms have left the river flushed with muddy rainwater.

Gifu was getting about 300,000 tourists a year. Some came for the Nagaragawa spa, which is at the riverside; but the big drawcard was the cormorant fishing. Not more than 1 per cent or three thousand of the visitors would have been non-Japanese, and if it hadn't been for this curious practice of using cormorants to catch fish Gifu would have had no foreign tourists.

I made a rough calculation that as many as ten thousand people—not only fishermen and boatmen, but hotel staffs and food suppliers, taxi-drivers and tour operators, along with shopkeepers selling everything from souvenirs to sake—were living off an operation based on a hundred or so fish-catching birds.

Conversely, if there had been no tourism there would have been no cormorant fishing. The catch of fish no longer justified it as a commercial proposition. The fishermen had to be subsidized from the tourist proceeds of a picturesque activity that provided a lot of yen. But, when I had found out just what was involved in cormorant fishing I felt quite sure that, however many livelihoods might be affected, its cessation would be all right with the captive cormorants.

WHY fish with cormorants instead of with a line or a net? The modern answer to that may be, "Because tourists will pay to see it," but the practice is old—a thousand years old in Japan, older than that in China. And in England it used to be a Court sport, a sort of angler's falconry. In Stuart times an official of the Royal Household was called the Master of the Cormorants.

A smallish fish called *ayu*—the Japanese refer to it as a river trout and also as a "sweetfish"—is highly esteemed for its flavour, and is reluctant to take bait and, so, hard to catch with a line. Emperors were being supplied with cormorant-caught *ayu* back in the tenth century, and this partiality came to be shared by the Tokugawa shoguns who began being the overlords of Japan in 1603. The local feudal lord at Nagoya was a Tokugawa, and he saw to it that *ayu sushi* (ayu with boiled rice) could be enjoyed regularly at Edo. The cormorant fishermen of the Nagara were subsidized and given the run of the river. After the Meiji Restoration cormorant fishing passed directly

Mount Aso, Kyushu's most active volcano, has a jagged crest of five peaks, one of which erupted seriously in 1958. In the foreground is susuki grass.

"Sun Flower" was the name of this engagingly painted white liner that went cruising south from Tokyo along the east coast to Kagoshima—where I went by air.

At right: The opulent Fujiya Hotel at Miyanoshita had two multi-storeyed, mansion-like wings, one of which was named "Restful Cottage", and the other "Comfy Lodge".

Kokichi Mikimoto, a noodle seller's son who was Japan's "Pearl King" when he died at ninety-six. He perfected techniques of growing pearls by introducing nuclei into oysters which hung in wire baskets from rafts (below) in Ago Bay.

Japanese castles are nearly all in this style—tier-upon-tier on a great stone base, white walls (which used to be wooden) under curved gable roofs of grey tiles. This one is Nagoya Castle. Like a number of others it was destroyed by American wartime bombing, and has been rebuilt in ferro-concrete.

In Kabuki theatre these richly costumed actors perform the Lion Dance. Men take all the roles, female as well as male, in Kabuki, which has changed little since the eighteenth century. Domestic dramas of genre Kabuki usually prove less interesting to foreigners than the spectacular entr'acte performances.

into the protection of the Emperor. It is still under direct control of the Imperial Household Department. In fact the front-ranking *u-sho* (master cormorant fisherman) of the six masters at Gifu still has the title of Ceremonial Officer of the Imperial Household Department.

I talked to this master, Zempei Yamashita, a striking-looking man with a goatee beard, at his house, where he keeps his cormorants in a spacious concreted yard. We talked in his tea-house overlooking the river. He was wearing the u-sho's traditional dress—a kilt made of heavy straw, a blue-black shirt-like garment of interesting cut, and headgear like a neckerchief knotted into a shape with a peak. His bare legs ended in straw sandals. Although he was an eighteenth-generation fisherman, Yamashita-san had graduated from Gifu University in agricultural science. He spoke good English and had written an informative paper, *Cormorant Fishing on the Nagara River*.[30]

First catch your *u*—which is the one-letter word for cormorant. The sea cormorants (*umi-u*), the biggest species, come down from Kamchatka and Hokkaido in mid-winter to a place named Hashiyama, across from Gifu on the eastern seaboard. The *u* is caught when it perches on a stick covered with bird-lime. Its sharp beak is bound, with a piece of wood stuck in it. The point of the beak is pared so it can't inflict peck wounds on its captors. Then the bird is rendered temporarily sightless—to aid the taming process— by a thread being stitched through the edge of the lower lid of each eye: the threads are tied on top of the head. I said that this eye-sewing was, surely, cruel. Why couldn't a plastic blindfold be slipped over the bird's head? It would scratch that off, Yamashita-san said.

The wild birds are bathed, and powdered plaster is put all over their bodies. When this dries "nasty things" as well as lime fall off with the plaster. The birds grow less wild-tempered under this treatment, and when they have calmed down the eyelid threads are loosed and they can see again. One wing is cut and they are put in wicker cages and brought to Gifu.

There, in a couple of the coldest weeks of the year, the cormorants learn: Pecking at the Man is useless with a stick of wood in your blunted bill. You can't fly, you just fall down. The Man, who takes you out of the wicker prison and massages your head and stomach, means you no harm. He unbinds your bill and feeds you fish—then puts the stick back. When he hauls you, by the neck, out of the basket you share with three other prisoners—no use pecking at them, either—he makes a sound which he does not make to other *u*, only to you (the sound is your name and in time you will learn to come to the Man when that sound is made). He has other, older birds, *tooshi-u,* trained ones. With these seniors you go, in a couple of weeks, to water that runs through land and is not salt like your vanished sea. The Man puts a string round your neck and lets you go into the unsalt water, the river, and catch fish. This is better. You begin to accept that you belong to the Man and his company of birds that feed in the river with other bird companies.

When you accept, then you are allowed to feed free without a neck string. But if fish are scarce and, while you catch ten another bird catches only two, the Man will squeeze you so that you throw up some of your fish for the other bird to eat.

Between 15 March and 10 May the fish in the river are protected; they are going up-river to breed. The Man has to buy other fish to feed you. Then, on 11 May, the season of *ayu*-catching at night begins. Not that you'll feed on *ayu*, except the little ones.

148 Fuji and Beyond

The narrow, flat-bottomed boat is thirteen metres long, and usually carries four men. The master is at the prow, where there hangs overside an iron fire-basket, full of wood, blazing. Perched on the for'ard gunwale are twelve cormorants, which the master will work. Each has a string round its neck and the strings—more than three metres long—are gathered in the master's left hand. In the middle of the boat an assistant fisherman will handle four to six other birds. Between these two men is the for'ard boatman, who plies a single oar. Another paddler is at the stern.

Proper binding of a cormorant's neck is one of the two most difficult things a *u-sho* has to do. As Zempei Yamashita puts it, "The neck-band must be tied exactly right, and not only to let a portion of the bird's catch go down its throat and into its stomach. Each neck tying has to suit the physical condition of each cormorant, and that can vary from day to day. You look at its gullet, the way it flaps its wings, the expression on its face, the condition of its feathers, and you consider how much work it has to do. If you don't treat your birds properly they won't fish well for you."

Attached to the thick neck-band is a thin belly-band, and attached to that is a tail-to-neck piece of whalebone. This keeps the neck-band in place and enables the master to get the cormorant to the side of the boat to give up from its beak the fish it catches underwater without its being pulled about and fatigued.

A PICNIC ATMOSPHERE prevails at the river bank as people carrying their supper in boxes and bottles go on board the lined-up spectator boats. It is early evening, about six o'clock, and the last sunlight of a fine day spangles the Nagara River.

The boats, open-sided and with long prows, are of unpainted wood, but paper lanterns and bunting show under their canopy roofs. They have no engines to intrude vibrant mechanical chatter on the evening's peacefulness. Boatmen will pole them a short way up this shallow river, aided by other men hauling, rope over shoulder, leg muscles straining as their feet grip the smooth river stones that line the bank. All these bare-legged men are decorative in *hapi* coats patterned light-on-dark with good designs that, worn with a wrap of cloth round the head, suggest the feudal Japan. These men's task isn't light. The boats they pole and haul take a load of thirty people.

On going aboard, you remove your shoes. Spectators seat themselves, back-to-gunwale, either side of a raised section that makes a continuous table down the middle of the boat. On this is put the food and drink, most of which will be consumed before darkness falls and the cormorant fishing begins. I am to have the best of suppers. It comes from the Nagaragawa Hotel where I am happily accommodated, and the hotel's under manager, Mr Yoshitumi Katagiri, has come with me, bearing this box dinner, which is not the standard dinner the hotel puts up in boxes for tourists for ¥2,000. We have ayu. So small is the catch nowadays (and for this some blame pollution of the water from the cutlery works up the river) that ayu have become very expensive. This dinner-box for two, with six of the slim fish about nine inches long, costs ¥6,000. Grilled ayu, even when cold as now, is a tasty fish—and so it should be at ¥1,000 apiece. The cost of the boat trip was ¥1,500.

Katagiri-san says that being a cormorant fisherman is a full-time job—far more time is spent finding places where the birds can feed on fish than in fishing for ayu with them—but some of the boatmen are farmers earning extra income. Tonight we will see six masters each handling twelve birds. Katagiri-san doesn't think the ayu are likely to be numerous enough to warrant assistants working other *u* from the boats, which are up-river now and will be coming down when it gets dark. Meanwhile, will I please help myself to another ayu, says Katagiri-san as he refills my sake cup.

Now it is dark and high on the summit of Mt Kinka, the mountain that peaks beside the town, a luminant cameo hangs in the night sky. It is a castle, Gifu's feudal castle in concrete reconstruction, most effectively distanced and floodlit.

From the river darkness beyond the line of boats we hear music plucked from the samisen, sounding small and plaintive in the vast black hall of night. A canopied barge appears, festooned with lanterns, a drifting stage on which kimono-costumed girls are dancing.

When the cormorant boats appear each is signalled by a flag of flame. So flaringly vivid are the buckets of breeze-waved fire hanging out from the prows that it is rather difficult to detect just what goes on at the ends of the lines the dark-shirted *u-sho* holds in his hands like reins. Then, as a boat comes abreast of us, the picture resolves itself as one of astonishingly quick action. The birds move flashingly, dart and disappear. So different from ducks in their swimming and diving, cormorants speed about the water submerged to the neck, and their necks would hardly be visible except that their throats are white. They appear to work right underneath the blazing cage, from which wood embers fall constantly. In water dyed with fire reflections and constantly rippled by the birds' darting and diving it is difficult to focus precisely a scene that passes all too quickly.

One should, I suppose, refer to the diving cormorants reappearing with "silver shapes wriggling in their beaks" but in point of fact I did not see a single fish caught. Doubtless some were—it is unthinkable that so much flashing energy should have been expended without reward of ayu, even if they were only very small ones of swallowable size which, from the birds' point of view, are all the better.

For the record, there is also cormorant fishing on the Kiso River at Inuyama, which is not far from Gifu, from 1 June to 30 September. Farther off, outside of Kyoto at the resort town of Uji, *u-kai* is a tourist spectacle on the Uji River: here the season is from the beginning of June to the end of August.

Gifu, though, is regarded as the best place to see it. Not that cormorant fishing is all that I think of when I think back on Gifu.

ON ARRIVAL from Nagoya at Gifu railway station I had been met by a charming woman from the tourist section of the prefectural government, Mrs Hiro Nishimura. When she asked me if I knew anything of the attractions of the prefecture apart from Gifu's cormorant fishing I said I had heard that the region had some marvellous old farmhouses, very big ones.

"Shirakawago is the place," she said. It was about four hours away by bus. "But you can still see one of those big farmhouses."

Her Toyota turned off the main road and we went out of the town for about twenty minutes. A hillside road flanked with lush vegetation led to a large pond in an utterly peaceful place where the only bright colour was some azaleas. A white swan glided over the reflection in the pond of this great old farm-house. It was four storeys high, and three of the floors were in the gable front formed by a steeply pitched roof of the thickest thatch I've ever seen. This huge old house—it probably used to accommodate six or seven families—had been turned into a restaurant: not that the tranquil atmosphere was disturbed by any sign that said so. If ever I go back to Gifu I want to have a meal there; its name is Iwafuneso, at Matsuoike.

We could not have dinner there then because Mrs Nishimura was taking me home to dine with her family—who, it turned out, included two very nice teenagers and a mother-in-law who cooked superb tempura. The dessert we had needed no cooking; I had no sooner shed my shoes at the Nishimuras' front door than I was being invited to put on *geta* at the back door and pick plump red strawberries from the garden. Except for the shoe shedding, it was like going into a Western sitting-room, a tastefully furnished one with settee and chairs and several bookcases. It was a very pleasant, as well as a most hospitable, introduction to Gifu.

A STRETCH of the Kiso River is acclaimed as the "Japanese Rhine", and to go down this in what is rather like a whaleboat "shooting the rapids" is touted touristically as a thrilling experience. I must report that the only resemblance between the rivers Kiso and Rhine is that they both have water in them; and although the current was strong the so-called rapids did not provide any experience I felt thrilled by. Perhaps it is better if the river is lower. Scenically, the ride is not remarkable.

The taped music on this hour-long boat run was so loud that I was glad when it changed to the Japanese "good-bye song" which sounds like *Auld Lang Syne*. Journey's end was at Inuyama, where my guide took me to see the castle. Inuyama's is the real thing, not a ferro-concrete reconstruction. It was built in 1440 and is the oldest castle existing in Japan.

inland sea shores

瀬戸内海沿岸

Going Japanese at Miyajima

MIYAJIMA MEANS "Shrine Island". To me it meant, the first time I was there, the most beautiful place in Japan.

The Japanese used to regard Miyajima as a sacred island, as Fuji is a sacred mountain. In feudal times no one was allowed to defile Miyajima by being born on it or by dying on it; the pregnant and the mortally ill were hurried off to the mainland. Nowadays births are permitted to take place on the island, and you can even die on it; but for burial—or, more usually, cremation—the body must be taken over to Ono on the opposite shore, and the relatives and friends who go to the funeral must stay at Ono until they have been through ceremonial purification.

The electric train-car from Hiroshima took forty minutes to Miyajimaguchi, where the guide-office telephoned across to the Iwaso Inn on the island. This is a famous Japanese inn—even the Emperor has stayed there.

A sleek white ferry put out in the mist of the evening on its quarter-hour run to Miyajima. The jutting little islands of the Inland Sea looked very soft, as though seen through a grey gauze curtain. The colour of the famous wooden torii I could discern only dimly. The tide was right out. There was just enough light from the pier to see how huge the torii's tree-trunk pillars were where they went into the sand. A few lights glimmered from the great Itsukushima shrine, showing chiaroscuro patches of vermilion.

A young man from the Iwaso Inn was at the pier to meet me. He put my bags in the box-cart behind the bicycle he wheeled, and we set out for the inn. Stone lanterns stood along the shoreline road, under the pines. The crisp-cold air smelt of sea and faintly of woodsmoke, the pines were as moveless as the old stone lanterns, and it was so quiet I could hear the bicycle's rubber tyres on the road. Motor traffic was not allowed.

I was looking for a shop that sold Fuji colour-film. At the Iwaso Gift Shop a woman spoke English. "I have not that size of film you want," she said, "but I can get it. Where you stay, please? Iwaso Inn. Ah, so. I will bring it to the inn." I told her not to bother, I'd pick it up in the morning, and we went on to the inn close by.

It was not very welcoming. The mamma-san, when the boy-san found her, looked thin and worried. She bowed and smiled, of course, but I got the impression that she was worried at having a foreigner as a guest. For this there was reason. She spoke no words of English, so far as I was able to discover, except "one" and "whisky". I began to feel the need of a whisky when, having shed my shoes, I was shown upstairs to my room and it became plain that the maid didn't speak any English either.

Mamma-san held up a finger questioningly and said, "One".

Ah, she means, do I want one whisky or a bottle? The bottle for God's sake! I began saying "whisky" and sketching bottles in the air with my hands. This seemed to get across. The maid departed for, I hoped, whisky. Emboldened, I added, "Dinner, tempura." Mamma-san immediately called the maid back. There was a long discussion. Finally mamma-san said, "Whisky, tempura?" I said, "Hai!" The maid departed again. I realized with a groan that now I probably wouldn't get the whisky until I got the tempura. (I didn't either.)

"One," said mamma-san, holding up her finger again. She indicated the room. I looked blank.

She looked at me and sighed. I looked at her and said "*Wakarimasen*".

"*Wakarimasen*," mamma-san echoed sadly. At least we understood each other's saying that neither of us understood.

At that point, providentially, there was a call from downstairs, and the English-speaking woman from the Iwaso Gift Shop came up, bringing the camera-film.

We sat down on the floor, the inevitable tea appeared, and Mrs Iwamura straightened things out. What mamma-san was trying to tell me was that she could accommodate me for only *one night*. There had been some mix-up about my reservations. Other people were coming tomorrow and the inn would be full. Would one night be all right? I said it would—unless Mrs Iwamura moved in as interpreter.

Dinner was ordered and bacon and eggs for breakfast in the morning, with bottle of Suntory whisky coming right up. Mrs Iwamura got my heartfelt thanks as she bowed out with mamma-san.

Now that I was alone in the room I could look at it. There were really two rooms and a small balcony-veranda, a "suite". A paper-covered door opened into a small room furnished with only a dressing-table, legless, its two tiny drawers at floor level, with a narrow mirror in which my reflection ended off at the chest. More shoji doors could be closed between this and the main part of the room, or suite. They were lovely doors of plain soft-cream and they slid perfectly. The walls were pale brown, rendered in a kind of plaster which, I believe, is mixed with finest ashes. The *tokonoma* alcove had, of course, its hanging scroll picture, and a flower-arrangement of chrysanthemums. Above the *tokonoma* a piece of gnarled natural wood, fretted with age, had been lovingly stained and polished and set up as a lintel.

There was a chaste hanging rack—for, and with, kimono. I hung two suits on it: then it looked terrible. I was dithering round in stockinged feet with my second pair of shoes, which I wanted cleaned, in my hand when the mamma-san came in. She registered horror at the idea of shoes near her tatami and bore them away as though they were a pair of asps.

It was too dark to see anything except some foliage. Down below a stream flowed by, I could hear it.

The maid came in and found the crazy *gaijin* standing in a draught of cold air sufficient to offset the effect of a dozen hibachi. I didn't care much what she thought as she closed the glass doors and drew the curtains, because she brought the Suntory, along with the first courses of the dinner. She also brought the back-rest for the floor cushion and the arm-rest. And sake.

Chizuko-san cleared away and when she returned she slid open a wall cupboard and pointed to the bedding in it. Did I want my bed made up now? "*Hai, dozo*", Yes, please. She rolled a thin sort of mattress out on the tatami, then another, added sheets and covered this with a very thick quilt of checked silk. The pillow was filled, I think, with rice straw. It felt as though they hadn't taken the rice out of the straw, but it was all right. Not that I slept on it until later. I wanted a bath.

I made motions of soaping myself and drying. Chizuko-san understood. I pointed to my watch and indicated that I would have a bath in half an hour. "Hai," she said.

HALF AN HOUR LATER I was all kimono'd and waiting. The maid appeared, bearing slippers and what appeared to be a washrag—it was hardly bigger than one. What I needed was a towel. *How To Speak Japanese Romanized* yielded *tenugui* and also *taoru*, the latter word being the Japanese pronunciation of "towel". When I said this Chizuko-san said "Hai" and pointed to the washrag thing. It was a Japanese towel. I fished from the suitcase my own towel—it was small, too, but it was three times as big as the Japanese one the maid brought. I gathered up soap and followed Chizuko-san. I was quite sure that I was going just down the corridor and to a bathroom. I was not at all sure whether the maid would deem it part of her duties to scrub my back.

But we went downstairs to the front porch. There, it was indicated, I should put on geta. I put on the wooden geta, thinking, "Detached bathroom", and followed the maid. She went out the front gate, turned right and proceeded up the street. I clattered after her as best I could in what must be, surely, the world's worst form of footwear. It was no use saying, "Where the hell are we going?" but I said it anyway. "*Dozo*," said the maid encouragingly, and what could I do but follow?

At the top of the street she turned sharp left and, with a smile and a bow, pointed to the doorway of what turned out to be a Japanese public bath-house.

I went in, and there was no one in the ante-room where you disrobe and leave your clothes in a wicker basket. From the next room, behind closed opaque-glass doors, came sounds of splashing, voices, and laughter. Well, they were going to have something to laugh at in a minute, I reckoned, as I peeled kimono and undergarments from a frame that was by Japanese standards too long and too lean, and particoloured from Australian beach-going.

The Japanese are indeed a polite people. When I stepped naked into that steamy room there were five or six men in the bath-pool and a couple more sluicing and soaping on the sides. Nobody stared or betrayed any interest. They just went on soaking and talking and washing as though it were the most natural thing in the world for a foreigner to come in. (Of all the foreigners I asked in Tokyo later, including men who had lived for years in the country, only one had ever been in a Japanese public bath-house.)

I already knew, from Atami, that you never soap yourself in the bath. So I soaped and sluiced on the side, and then got in. The water was *hot*. I had heard that the trick is to duck down quickly. I did that and it was still very hot but it was bearable. I had the inn "towel" as a washer. That seemed to be the right thing. The other men, immersed to the neck, floated their towels out in front of them, occasionally wiping their brows. They soaked and talked. In Japan the bath-house is like a club where the news and gossip of the day is exchanged, in perfect relaxation. I was surprised by the bodily modesty. A man entering or climbing out of the bath did so with one hand cupped over his genitals. Another thing is that, having wrung out his washer, he then dries himself with this rag that is no bigger than a hand-towel and still wet, by rubbing vigorously; and I am assured that he would rather dry himself in this manner than use our kind of towels.

The self-conscious *gaijin* in the bath finally became too much for one young man. He gave me a wide grin and his one word of English, "Okay!"

"Okay!" I responded and added approvingly, "*Ichiban.*"

This gave the young man excuse to vent his bottled-up amusement in a peal of laughter. It is okay to laugh when a foreigner uses Japanese experimentally; in fact it seems to be a kind of compliment. Everyone smiled and nodded, and I felt accepted into the community of the bath.

Bath over, I got back into kimono and the wretched geta. The young man who said okay and his friend left at the same time, we clattered down the road together and, with a great exchange of okays, Japanese good-nights and hand-shakings, parted at the gate to the Iwaso Inn.

As at Atami, the warmth of the bath was still with me after I had written my notes in bed and turned out the low stand-lamp that was beautifully made of paper and bamboo. There was then no sounds of geta from the street, only the murmur of the stream out there below my balcony, running through the quiet Miyajima night.

IN THE MORNING I got up before the maid appeared with the bacon and eggs and coffee the Japanese are convinced every Westerner must have before he can get moving for the day.

It was eight o'clock when I woke and the white linen-like curtains were soaked with sun. I drew them and the sun came in on the tatami and I had a look from the balcony. My stream was a little creek that gurgled round rocks and fell over a tiny man-made waterfall and got lost under the greenery that leant out from a hillside splashed with the colour of maples. Where the sun came through the scarlet ones they were lit to glory and the maples that had turned yellow were a burning gold.

The balcony hung out over the creek and all I could see of the rest of the inn was a corner of grey roof tiles, so there was the feeling of being in a house on your own, remote and next-to-nature—and that is the mood the Japanese seek to create in such lovely corners of their crowded land.

I went for a walk after breakfast and took some pictures near a little bridge that must have once been red but had faded almost to white: no paint could compete with the colour of the maples blooming over it, and I don't think I have ever seen any trees more beautiful than these were with the sun through their leaves.

Then I went down to the Iwaso Gift Shop and said good morning to Mrs Iwamura. Her husband came out; and he spoke English, too. When Mr Iwamura heard that I was without a guide he just took the day off from his shop and showed me round.

We went first to a wooden building so big it is called the "Hall of a Thousand Mats". Unlike most wooden buildings in Japan, it has never been burnt and rebuilt; the camphorwood timbers are four hundred years old and look it. Tied to some of the pillars were hundreds of what look like ping-pong bats or the wooden spoons that come in ice-cream buckets, made large. They were rice scoops, each inscribed with the name of a soldier. The soldiers who were going off to the China War back in 1894 offered their rice scoops to the gods, because of a play on words. Apparently *meshi-toru*, meaning "rice-taking", can also mean victory.

Next to this old temple-hall is a pagoda which, I was not surprised to learn, has been designated a National Treasure. From the foot of a cherry-treed slope beside the old hall, you can look up this red pagoda with its black-edged roofs sweeping out in curves as graceful as an archer's bow to points as sharp as an arrow's.

From the brow of the rise where the red pagoda stands I looked out, through a frame of old pines, on the Inland Sea. In this 250-mile waterway that is bounded by Honshu and Shikoku and Kyushu, the island of Miyajima is only one of six hundred, and there is a scatteration of several thousand islets, some so small they are no more than a rock and a pine. Miyajima is nineteen miles round—worshippers often walk the circuit calling at seven shrines on the way. The island rises to the peak of Mt Misen where there is a shrine with an eternal flame. I should have gone up there, for the panorama of the island-patterned Inland Sea. But I wanted to see in daylight the great shore-edge Itsukushima shrine. I was thinking, as we came to it, of how it looked in the film *Gate of Hell*.

Almost the first thing I saw as we entered its vermilion colonnades was—a movie camera. A Japanese film-unit was at work and, now that the light conditions were perfect and the tide was right in, so that the shrine really had the effect of floating on the sea, they were shooting and recording sequences of the ancient dances and the shrine musicians. By this stroke of luck I was to see ceremonies that are not ordinarily held at that time of the year.

There was the music-dance called *Gagaku-Bugaku*. Gagaku music and Bugaku dance came to Japan from China in the seventh century—and here it was being performed in the noonday sunlight of the twentieth. Gagaku had continued to be the Court music of Japan—it is still performed in the Emperor's palace in Tokyo—for thirteen hundred years.

The Gagaku musicians placed their beautiful decorated gong and ranged themselves in line behind it on the planking just in front of a red pavilion at the end of one of the pier-like stages that run out from the shrine. They were robed and helmet-hatted in a fashion that went right back to the Tang dynasty of China. They played plaintive flutes, the sharp little *taiko* drum and the wind-instrument called *sho*.

The Bugaku dancer came out arrayed in a red robe fronted with brocade and having trousers wide as skirts and so richly patterned the gold thread flashed in the sunlight. His gilded mask was tigerish with open mouth and bulging eyes—and something more like a baby dragon than a bird was perched on the animal head. The performer danced and postured with stylized grace to the long-drawn woody vibrance of the music, on a stage flanked with two old bronze guardian images from Korea.

In the background the most famous *torii* in Japan reared fifteen metres out of the pale-blue sea, its pillars the red-pained trunks of camphorwood-trees, and the cross-piece that forms the top of its arch even longer than the pillars are tall.

158　Inland Sea Shores

The Itsukushima shrine itself dates back some eleven hundred years. It has been reconstructed several times.

At the back of the shrine, in a rather tourist-worn park, is a museum that contains some priceless treasures, including Buddhist *sutras* (scriptures) in slim scroll-boxes with beautiful end-ornaments of gold and glass. Here, too, are old samurai costumes of armour, with mask-like covers of thin metal that fitted over the warrior's face. There are fans of paper-and-bamboo still preserved after eleven hundred years.

From a track that winds up the lower slope of the mountain you can look down on the tiled-roof town with its red pagoda and its great shrine stretching out towards the torii in the sea. The path brought us back eventually to where the colour of the maples was richest, at the back of the Iwaso Inn.

I WENT BACK to Miyajima in 1973, with a tour party. Undoubtedly it is better to see it as a day tripper than not to see it at all; but it can be a mistake to thus revisit a place of special memory where you have stayed. I knew that, but felt obliged to see how the island had changed in eighteen years.

It was still traffic-free. There were many more souvenir shops than I remembered: Miyajima was now getting two and a half million tourists a year. So there were more inns—still none that was fully Western, but one large hotel had Western-style bathrooms and toilets. At this hotel, the guide said, English was spoken.

The Iwaso Inn I felt drawn back to, and from the outside it looked just the same. The little bridge over the stream that had faded to pink had been re-painted vermilion. Again it was November and the leaves of the maples that overhung the bridge were dying their autumn death very beautifully, but their red was not quite as bright as I remembered.

I went down a path to photograph the bridge looking up from beside the stream. Two deer, a doe and its fawn, came along the rocks, their small hooves delicately picking the way, and the fawn stopped to drink from a pool.

There are tame deer on Miyajima as there are at Nara. And on the island no dogs are allowed.

Hiroshima: So you knew about the Bomb?

It is 8.15 a.m. in the city's getting-to-work rush hour of an autumn morning in 1973. Our tourist coach is bogged in traffic and takes a quarter of an hour to move four blocks.

The guide on the coach, which is taking us down to Hiroshima's harbour on the Inland Sea to go across to the island of Miyajima, tries to relieve his tourists' tedium. He says things like, "The young people, they have cars now, and they all want to bring their cars in—look, even that fellow there with the sticker with an arrow, that sign means 'greenhorn driver'."—He goes on: "The Mazda company makes seven to eight thousand cars a month here in Hiroshima. This is the big factory of Mazda. It has thirty-six thousand people making the rotary-engined car."

The guide has already told us such things as that *Hiro* means "wide" or "broad" and *shima* is "island", and the original town took its name from a castle built in 1593 on river-delta land and called Hiro-shima-jo (Broad Island Castle). And there, you can see it—he points to the right—is the Hiroshima Castle of today, a picture-postcard pile of white walls under curved grey-tile roofs. It was re-created in concrete in 1958 as a tourist attraction.

At the harbour—we reach it eventually—land is being reclaimed from the sea. Where a hillside is being cut away, to provide the reclamation fill, the land so levelled is already being built on as a new housing estate in this burstingly busy city of over half a million people.

Hiroshima in 1945 had about 350,000 people, civilians and military. Its population was approaching that figure again when, ten years after the Bomb, I was there in 1955. Now it had about 200,000 more people than it had then and much more industry, and the regeneration—even the change from the city I had known eighteen years earlier—was amazing.

It was 8.15 a.m. in the city's getting-to-work rush hour on the cloudless summer morning of 6 August 1945. From one of three American B-29 bombers flying very high above the city four parachutes floated down.

Three of the parachutes carried automatic signalling apparatus that was to signal the detonation of the bomb carried by the fourth parachute. The atomic bomb was about 570 metres above a central part of the city—to be precise the epicentre was over the Shima Hospital, run by a Dr Shima—when it detonated. The noise was not particularly loud, but the flash was terrific and then there was a ball of fire like an exploded sun.

The down-blast was such that concrete pillars at the entrance to Dr Shima's hospital were driven straight into the ground. The patients, the doctors, the nurses in the hospital were all killed.

The heat from the incandescent fireball came at light speed and, even before the blast hit, began to roast people and animals, melt glass, put bubbles in roofing tiles, start fires, char telephone poles three kilometres from the hypocentre (ground point below the bombs explosion point) and burn the skin of people who were at a distance but in the open.

It was school-going as well as work-going time and most of the fifteen thousand schoolchildren who had not been evacuated from Hiroshima were in the open. Of those within four hundred metres of the hypocentre about 90 per cent became casualties. Of those who were in the open up to twelve hundred metres away over 50 per cent were burned. If they were two miles away they were unlucky if they became casualties.

Casualties were of many kinds: the burnt-small dead whose bodies lay in the streets near the hypocentre; the dead soldiers whose hair was not burnt at all because it was under their military caps but whose noses and lips were burnt off and their ears melted and, because they were working with their shirts off, the skin had been raised from the torso as a great blister, which the blast had peeled away to the wet red flesh. An eyewitness named Katsutani said he saw many soldiers like that, dead, and, "One soldier whose features had been destroyed and was left with his white teeth sticking out asked me for water...." There were two Army divisions at Hiroshima.

Some civilians had sought escape from the heat by getting into reservoir tanks. A Dr Hanaoka said that they looked as though they had been boiled alive, and when they died they had no room to fall over. He saw a man gone mad drinking the blood-stained water. He passed tramcars full of blackened, faceless dead. A Dr Tabuchi, who lived in an outer suburb, said that many burnt refugees passed his house, making for the hills, and "their skin hung down like rags on a scarecrow".

Thousands of casualties were people who had been indoors and whose worst external injuries came from the blast that not only crushed people under masonry but flung things at them—tiles, bricks, window-frames and broken wood such as the great splinter Dr Michihiko Hachiya pulled from his thigh, and a fragment of broken glass from his neck after his house fell in. I had talked to Dr Hachiya in 1955. He had been the Director of the Hiroshima hospital of the Ministry of Communication and he gave me a copy of his book, *Hiroshima Diary*[31].

Dr Hachiya's hospital's reinforced-concrete walls had withstood the blast but it was a shambles. Three nurses who were standing near windows were dead, some doctors and other staff injured, and while the Director's wounds were being treated the hospital caught fire. A high wind had followed the Bomb's explosion—a black rain had fallen from what had been a clear sky.

Only a night operation by the light of car lamps saved Dr Hachiya's life. In five days he was on his feet and had resumed charge of one of the only three civilian hospitals remaining out of forty-five—and the two large Army hospitals were no longer usable.

Dr Hachiya's account of the hospital conditions was stomach-turning: "Everything was in disorder.... Patients who could not walk urinated and defecated where they lay." Common symptoms were bloody dysentery and sputum and uterine haemorrhage. Inflamed mouths turned to gangrenous tonsillitis. *Petechiae*, small blood spots, appeared beneath the skin. Gamma-rays had destroyed the clotting organisms called platelets. These rays also destroyed blood-cells because they destroyed cell-building bone marrow.

When patients' hair started falling out Dr Hachiya ascribed this at first to poor nutrition: there was enough rice but protein was so scarce that old men used to hawk frogs at a hundred yen each. Microscopy showed that hair follicles were atrophied. One woman's bald head Dr Hachiya described as like a yellow pumpkin. Chest hair, underarm hair, pubic hair fell out as well.

Typical of patients dying of "radiation sickness" was a Miss Tanaka, aged twenty-eight: vomiting, diarrhoea, white-cell count low, falling hair, *petechiae* developing in the chest until they were as big as thumb-tips before she died. Radiation took seven weeks to kill Miss Tanaka.

Five days after the A-bomb fell at Hiroshima, two days after the horror of Nagasaki, word spread through the Communications Hospital that Japan had this awful new bomb, too, and a special Japanese attack squadron had flown across the Pacific and dropped atomic bombs on three American cities, San Francisco, San Diego and Los Angeles.

This "news" had a tonic effect on the patients in the Communications Hospital. Those who weren't vomiting or stricken with diarrhoea at the time or were not too agonized by their burns and other injuries "cheered and made jokes", Dr Hachiya wrote in his book, and "some began singing the victory song."[31]

Dr Hachiya was a most likeable, warmly human man with a mild bespectacled face, and he is now dead. When I talked to him in Hiroshima I asked him what he thought of the A-bombing. He said: "It occured in war. Such things are unavoidable in war. It was none the less a crime because it was in war. War is a crime."

CASUALTIES were stated in figures that varied greatly. The official American survey[32] gave: 92,133 dead and missing; 37,425 injured.

Japan: The New Official Guide[24] which came out in 1966 gave the deaths as "estimated to be more than 200,000". A detailed publication[33] I got at Hiroshima in 1955 stated: "More than 240,000 persons are believed to have been killed, of which the citizens, students, patriotic corps and others numbered about 170,000 and military personnel aggregated to about 70,000". It gave 51,012 persons as seriously injured, 105,543 as slightly injured and 6,738 as missing.

The city itself was about four-fifths destroyed. Photographs show it reduced to an "atomic desert" with few buildings standing.

Near the hypocentre there was only one building not flattened apart from the Industrial Promotion Hall, which was shattered. The central part of this, a four-storeyed structure of brick and concrete, has been preserved in its bombed state. Known now as the Dome Building, it was topped by a dome the blast reduced to skeletal steel webbing. A plaque put up by the Hiroshima Cultural Association says it is "being preserved to symbolize our wish that there may be NO MORE HIROSHIMAS".

One could say "Amen" to that. But, I reflected there, if this kind of horror ever happened again it would not be "another Hiroshima" but something much worse. The atomic bomb dropped at Hiroshima was a uranium-fission device in which about 100 pounds of isotope uranium (some of it mined in South Australia) had the explosive force of 20,000 tons of TNT. The A-bomb has been superseded by the H-bomb, in which is triggered a thermonuclear explosion of substances derived from hydrogen. A hydrogen bomb the United States exploded in 1954 was said to be at least *six hundred times* as powerful as Hiroshima's A-bomb. And now the potential horror is even greater than that.

AT THE BACK of the Dome Building ruin when I was there in 1955 a lot of weeds grew, some of them waist-high. (So much for the story I remembered reading that the Hiroshima earth would be so poisoned by radiation that nothing would grow there for seventy years.) Beyond the weeds a makeshift wooden shop stood and I made my way to it. It had a signboard crudely lettered in English:

ATOMIC SOUVENIR SHOP OF A-BOMB
VICTIM NO.1, K. KIKKAWA

A woman came out of the shop and helped pick grass-seeds out of my tweed suit. Then the man came out. He was a big man, for a Japanese, in a brown kimono. He picked off some grass-seed, too, but he had only one good hand. On his other, his right hand, the fingers were claw-like, bent upward from his wrist. The guide said this was Mr K. Kikkawa, "A-Bomb Victim No. 1". He had been on his way to work in the tramways office when he was struck down with half his body terribly burned. He had spent six years in hospitals and undergone sixteen operations.

He had to earn a living, and with one hand useless, so he had set up the little shop where he displayed and sold to tourists bits of heat-twisted roofing tiles, glass bottles that had been melted almost flat, and postcards. I bought some postcards, and one was a medical-records photo of K. Kikkawa's back. His back was a mass of keloids, raised scars like blisters gone solid. The keloids covered all his back and sides except under his left arm.

Afterwards when I thought of Hiroshima—and it is a place you think of—K. Kikkawa would come into it, with his back and all the pain that must have gone with six hospital years and sixteen operations. So, when I went back to Hiroshima in 1973, I asked about Kikkawa-san. No, he wasn't there, he was no longer living in Hiroshima. He had moved away—and I got the impression that he might have been pushed.

"He became a bit of a radical," I was told. "He got over-active in anti-war protests."

THE GUIDE I had the first time was a little, oldish man in a scruffy suit. I asked him if he was in Hiroshima when the bomb came and he said, "No, I was not here, but my family was. My wife was killed and my daughter injured." I said I was very sorry and asked, "What do you really feel about the dropping of that bomb?"

He said, "It was all right to drop the bomb—that is war. But there should have been a warning."

That the atomic bomb "should be used without prior warning" was one of three recommendations that went to President Truman of the United States in June 1945 from a committee of six headed by U.S. Secretary of War Henry L. Stimson. One of the committee dissented from the no-warning recommendation. He was U.S. Navy Secretary Ralph A. Bard.

Stimson said in historic article, "The Decision to Use the Atomic Bomb", he wrote for *Harper's* magazine[34]: "The ultimate responsibility for the recommendation to the President rested upon me and I have no desire to veil it. I felt that, to extract a genuine surrender from the Emperor and his military advisers, they must be administered a tremendous shock which would carry convincing proof of our power to destroy the Empire." Stimson saw the A-bomb as averting the necessity to go ahead with the planned invasion of Japan, which it was estimated would cost one million Allied (and just as many Japanese) casualties because it was considered that the Japanese would fight to their last ditch in their homeland. In justification of the atomic bombing of Nagasaki three days after Hiroshima, Stimson said, "The surrender came next day."

In his broadcast to the nation announcing the surrender, Emperor Hirohito said, "The enemy has begun to employ a new and most cruel bomb," and that continuance of the war would "result in the ultimate collapse and obliteration of the Japanese nation".

Unquestionably the dropping of the atomic bomb on Hiroshima was the most potent factor in Japan's decision to surrender, and the bomb on Nagasaki and fear that Tokyo would be the next atomic target hastened that decision. But I cannot believe, any more than could U.S. Navy Secretary Ralph Bard, that it was necessary to drop such bombs without warning.

STILL ACTIVE in its study of the effects of atomic radiation, after nearly thirty years, was the Atomic Bomb Casualty Commision at Hiroshima where in 1955 I had talked to the then Director. Dr Robert H. Holmes had told me there was a continuing increased incidence, among people who had been exposed to the radiation, of leukaemia and eye cataracts. On the other hand, Dr Holmes said, sterility had proved transient and, no genetic effects had been observed in the first generation. Fifteen mothers who were less than five months pregnant at A-day had given birth to microcephalics (children with abnormally small heads) and these children were of sub-normal intelligence. "But this was damage *in utero*—not genetic effect," said Dr Holmes. He added that six of these mothers had subsequently borne children that were normal.

The Commission was closed when I was revisiting Hiroshima in 1973: the tour was there on a Sunday. But I was able to gain some understanding of the present situation from the guide we had, Richard Nishimura, who learned his good English working for the Americans, who called him Dick-san.

Dick-san was fifty-seven, and had been twenty-eight when in the early morning of the fateful day he came home from working night-shift at the arsenal. He was knocked unconscious and when he came to, the house was gone. He had no external injuries, but for three months he could hardly move, he vomited at intervals, his gums bled and his top teeth fell out. His hair did not fall out—and he thinks he did not suffer depilation because he was not exposed to the "black rain".

"We who were here at the time are known as the Exposed People," Dick-san told me. "Some are very comfortable because the city has doubled in size, and those who had property have made money. We also have a certain status as old-timers, veterans. But we have two big worries. About one-in-three suffer loss of vitality which usually turns out to be from loss of red blood corpuscles, incipient leukaemia.

"The other worry is rejection. Other people are afraid that, if they get friendly with us, our children and their children may want to marry. They don't want their chidren marrying those of the Exposed because they are afraid of genetic effects coming out. There is no solid evidence that any taint will transfer and persist—but there is this rejection. It is hardest on girls, and some of our daughters are having difficulty getting married."

FROM THE HILLTOP called Hijiyama Park where Richard Nishimura was telling me about the worries of the Exposed, and where the Atomic Bomb Casualty Commission is, you look out over Hiroshima. The guide described it, and not without pride, as "a city re-born".

At night Hiroshima's regeneration was to look just as astonishing as I gazed out over its neon-lit brilliance from the Sky Bar of the Hiroshima Grand Hotel, which towered many storeys higher than the Hotel New Hiroshima where I had stayed previously, and which was now regarded as old.

From the panoramic hilltop we went down through what is almost a forest of cherry-trees that have grown again to the riverside Shukkeien Garden, which was laid out in 1620 in imitation of a famous Chinese garden. There the regeneration of trees was remarkable. You could still see blackened stumps that some of the trees were reduced to by the bomb blast—but new shoots had grown into thicker trunks than the original ones.

Six rivers still make Hiroshima a delta city. Where one stream divides, in the centre of the city, a large point of flat land has become the Peace Park. It is bounded on one side by wide Peace Boulevard. Hiroshima calls itself, understandably, Peace City.

In the middle of Peace Park is the Cenotaph. Its design is simple, saddle-shaped from the side, and it arches as an open vault for a stone chest that contains the names of all those who were killed by the atomic bomb. The Cenotaph's arch frames the shattered Dome. The designer of the Cenotaph was Kenjo Tange, the contemporary master of Japanese architecture. Tange's hand is also to be seen in the rectilinear dignity of the Peace Memorial Museum.

I was there soon after the museum opened in 1955. The photographs of the burnt dead and the peeled-raw injured were too much, and after about five minutes I said to the guide, "I've had enough".

I may not have gone back to the museum had I been on my own, but I was with a tour and the tour went there. Also, I thought it may have changed. There were the same terrible photographs and tatters of clothing and tiles welded together by the heat and the big circular model of the city as it looked after the A-bomb destroyed most of it. But now the museum had a film. It showed such things as a human bone in a melted brick, the burns on the feet of a girl whose feet became embedded in molten asphalt, and a young mother dead from radiation-caused cancer.

I had the feeling that the city that had least need of the Hiroshima Peace Memorial Museum was Hiroshima. This city really knew about the atomic horror. It and Nagasaki were the only cities that did. In Sydney I *thought* I knew about it. I didn't until I went to Hiroshima.

Shikoku, and along the Inland Sea

SHIKOKU is the fourth-in-size island of the Japan archipelago, and it forms with the main island, Honshu, and the southern one, Kyushu, what the Japanese call the Seto Naikai, which they translate as "Sea within Channels"— which is a bit of a stumblebum semantically, so it is translated to the tourist as "Inland Sea", although it isn't inland or a sea as near to landlocked as the Mediterranean. It is a long waterway or *seto* (strait). What matters, though, is not what it is called but how good it is.

It is good, but not as good as the tourist literature makes it out to be. If I were asked to nominate the Hyperbole of the Year perpetrated by the laureates of the tourist leaflets I'd have to hand it to the one that describes a steamer trip by the Kansai Line through the Inland Sea as "like a journey through a 270-mile Japanese garden". Furthermore, I'd nominate the Kansai Line as the Japanese Tourist Facility Most in Need of Improvement.

The usual tour that takes in the Inland Sea is a continuation of the Kyoto–Nara tour, going on by train to Kurashiki and thence by bus and ferry to Takamatsu. Kurashiki isn't on the Inland Sea, but it has more attraction than many places that are. A section of the city has been preserved as an oasis of charm in what is otherwise industrial desert, for Kurashiki is a great manufacturer of such things as matting, machinery and cement.

Willow-trees line an L-shaped canal that runs down the middle of two Kurashiki streets that meet at right-angles. The canal was once a dirty trafficway for goods moving to and from the industrial plants. Now the water is placid and the only flotsam is some leaves fallen from the willows. Trafficless, too, are the two streets; and there is also a blessed absence of the usual urban gaudiness—not one shopfront shouting its wares in coloured advertising signs. Just a line on either side of the canal of some of the nicest and most Japanese buildings in Japan. Many are renovated or reconstructed granaries: none has more than three storeys. All have white stucco walls, roofs of grey tiles, doors of unpainted wood. So there is this harmony of quiet colours—grey, white, some black and wood-brown.

Four old granaries have been combined with architectural grace to make the building of the Kurashiki Folkcraft Museum; and opposite this, just across the canal, another building houses an archaeological museum. To my chagrin both were closed, as happens on Monday afternoons. There were, though, some very good folkcraft toys in a shop in this charming area.

Kurashiki has another notable museum, though not a very Japanese one— the Ohara Art Gallery. Its building is modelled on a Greek temple and the collection of the late Ohara-san includes works by El Greco, Corot, Rodin, Gauguin, Van Gogh, Picasso, Miro and Klee.

166   Inland Sea Shores

TAKAMATSU (pron. Takamats) is a city of about 300,000 people, the second largest on Shikoku—Matsuyama is slightly larger—and the ferry to it from Uno took about an hour. It was a moonless night and nothing could be seen of the vaunted beauties of the Inland Sea.

I had come to Takamatsu years before in much more interesting fashion, by train from Kochi on the other side of Shikoku. Claire was with me and we flew to Kochi from Osaka with ANA (All Nippon Airways) and I remember thinking that the aircraft, a DC3, was primitive. ANA's fleet in 1974 included twenty-eight Boeing 727s, and by 1976 it expected to have twenty-one 306-passenger Tristars.

Flying into Shikoku showed it to be a mountainous island, ridgy as a concertina. There were forests cut by the timber-getters' swathes and great fans of lowland fertility. Not that the ricefields didn't reach up the sides of the mountains—or rather, step down them in terraces—but where we saw these most effectively was from the train that brought us from Kochi (which I'll come to) to Takamatsu. And that is a journey worth taking for the rock formations in the Koboke Gorge, where swirls of cloud-mist were veiling and unveiling the tops of the wooded cones of mountains.

Takamatsu makes a lot of lacquerware and is a good place to buy it, especially if you fancy the kind called Kimma which has twenty coats of black lacquer cut through with elaborate patterns that have been filled in red with cinnabar. Parasols of every kind are here—Takamatsu makes more parasols than any other place in Japan. It is also a top producer of drainpipes, whose durability is attested with the brand-name *Eternité*.

What we go to Takamatsu to see are Ritsurin Park, which is one of the finest specimens of the Japanese landscape garden, and Yashima Plateau for the spectacular view it provides across the Inland Sea at sunset.

Ritsurin Park was designed as a setting for the villa of the seventeenth-century lord of Takamatsu, and the Matsudaira family is said to have spent a hundred years perfecting its landscaping round twelve hills and six ponds, against the background of a forested mountain. Flowerless, or almost so, the gardens derive their attractiveness from trees, stones and water. Pines are everywhere, some lopped and clipped so that a writhing bough reaches out like a dragon's neck. Boulders sculpturally eroded are matched with smaller stones bordering pools. Artificial lakes of subtle form mirror the maples that were turning scarlet when I was last there. And across one pond there is a beautiful bridge with a top-of-the-moon curve.

As I admired this again on the '73 trip I remembered how Nishiyama-san had said the cultured samurai used to float their sake cups from a shore beyond the curved bridge, and each would try to compose a *waka*—a poem of thirty-one syllables—before his little cup sank from bobbing against a ripple or a water-lily.

Nishiyama-san had been the proprietor of the inn we stayed at, the Kawa-roku (meaning Six Rivers) which had a few Western-style rooms. (Reports said it was still a good place.) He had taken us to a tea-house in the gardens, one that Claire specially loved for things like the bent tree-bough that formed the portico of its wicket gate, the tinkle of windbells attached to tiny lanterns, and the tea-bowls of subtly irregular form we were handed after the ritual of the tea-house mistress's turning the bowl round three times.

We emerged from lovely Ritsurin Park and there was a shop window displaying a model of the local emblem, the Lucky Badger, always depicted standing on his hind legs, but between those legs you could not see because the badger had down-to-the-ground testicles. A modified souvenir version has been produced for sale to Western tourists.

YASHIMA means "Roof Island". A high tableland projecting from the sea, a roof-like viewing place it certainly is, but a channel no wider than a river is all that makes it an island. Nowadays, you can drive up over that to the plateau by a toll road. A cable car provides a more scenic ascent.

When I was first there and we cable-car'd to the top, in the late afternoon, we were met by *kago* carriers. Claire was installed in one of these and borne off at a gentle jog; she later described the kago ride as creaky but comfortable. Nishiyama-san and I walked behind, down an avenue of pines so dark in outline I thought all the day's sun must have gone. We came to the head of Yashima just as the sun was going down in the Inland Sea. A lovelier sunset sight, with black islands on the burnished water and purple clouds as grates to the fireplace sky, I have yet to see.

It was dusk as we left a Buddhist temple where the good Nishiyama had persuaded the priests to let us go, shoeless, down interior corridors that held some fine old paintings. There was also a curiosity called the shrine's "Snow Garden". Overhung by dark trees, it was an expanse of pure white rock.

How different was the return visit to the plateau years later. The tour party went up—by coach, not cable-car—in mid-morning. The foreground of the view was geometrical with squares of land being reclaimed from the sea for industrial purposes. There were more shops; and a very ugly hotel; and crowds of schoolchildren. The sun shone brightly, a nice breeze wafted in from the sea—and there was no atmosphere, nothing of enchantment in the view or anything else.

Why did we go to Yashima, the sunset plateau, in mid-morning? Because the tour schedule read: "1.30 p.m. The bus picks you up from your hotel and takes you to the pier." And "2.00 p.m. The steamer leaves the pier for Kobe/Osaka affording you a thrilling cruise of the Inland Sea." And before 1.30 we had to be fed lunch at the Takamatsu International Hotel, which was indistinguishable from scores of other first-class glass-and-concrete rectilinear hotels in Japan. The Kawaroku, with its kimono'd proprietor, had been more memorable.

Another inn where we had stayed on the first visit to Shikoku was not as good as Nishiyama-san's as to appointments and food, nor was it as expensive, but Claire still talks about its garden. Actually, its name, Sansuien, meant Three Green Gardens. We could see only one garden, which was a piece of utterly Japanese perfection, and when we asked about the other two we were given the very Japanese explanation that the hills at the back were regarded as another garden and so were the green banks of a small river.

This favourite inn was at Kochi.

KOCHI, on the other side of the island, not facing the Inland Sea but the Pacific Ocean, doesn't get many foreign tourists—even fewer than another place we got to, Tokushima.

As we were being driven in from the airport, through sun-bright ricefields set with stands of pluming bamboo, we noticed that the toiling women wore blouses and *mompe* trousers of a pattern quite different from the coinspots we were accustomed to seeing on Honshu. Both men and women wore a wide dish-shaped hat, *sugigasa*, made of the bark of the *sugi*-tree, the Japanese cedar. The fields were bright with coloured parasols tied to bamboo poles, to protect the newly planted seedlings from the sun. So fertile was the land the Kochi farmers got two rice crops a year.

The town (pop. 225,000) had no special character—little shops, big department stores, poster-plastered cinemas, one Western-style hotel. The Sansuien we went to had "Westernized" a room in a very heavy-handed fashion. Twin beds and overstuffed chairs stood on a thick carpet and a particularly heavy oil painting of a nude was hung right up near the ceiling. The bathroom was Edwardian and enormous. Yet you had only to walk out the door that led to the garden and you were in a different world.

The garden had stone-patterned paths that led away under old pines with twisted branches towards, in one direction, a rise that was banked with miniature azaleas; in another direction you strolled to venerable cycad palms. A low table had as its top a thick slice of a great tree's trunk, with the rind of bark still on it; and the stump of what must have been a huge cherry-tree was lovingly preserved by being covered and lapped over with beaten copper. A fine slab of grey stone that stood man-high among the greenery was carved with the ideograms of a poem. A rock-edged, water-lilied pool had the most sinuous of small dragons in greened copper, jetting a thin fountain that gave the whole garden a background of unobtrusive water sounds.

Soon after we arrived, having shed our clothes and donned light *yukata* kimono, we teetered out into the garden on *geta*. We heard the beating of a gong and rhythms of Japanese music; then the maid, whose name was Kiyoto and who spoke English, came and said, "The Odori dancers are here. You like to see?"

The dancers had come to the inn to get a donation towards the Odori (dance) Festival, a yearly event, that would begin in a few days time. For about ten minutes they danced, to a portable phonograph on a decorated lorry and the beat of a man with a gong and drum. They were all girls and they wore an attractive style of kimono and a distinctive Shikoku straw bonnet that folded to a peak and tied with a ribbon under the chin. We told Kiyoto we were sorry we would not be in Kochi for Odori time, to see more of the dancing. After she served us dinner in our room she reappeared with her own portable phonograph and records, and danced for us—and very well, for she was a teacher of dancing who served at the inn to make extra money.

Kochi people had such a variety of occupations that if you had stopped a random twelve in the street and asked what they did for a living you would have been quite likely to get, "I build ships/make paper/make bamboo blinds/make cement/pickle and dry bonito/make lacquerware/carve coral/breed fighting dogs."

The bonito dries solid as a wooden club; pieces are shaved off for soup flavouring. The coral is of a rosy red colour and hard as stone. It is worked with what looks like a dentist's drill. We watched one carver cutting intricate folds of the robes of a Buddhist-goddess figurine that would sell for around ¥50,000. You could buy small brooches for a few dollars at the Fukushima Coral Shop.

Shikoku, and along the Inland Sea 169

The Japanese make admirable papers—as the earliest Dutch traders found, and they took back to Holland Japanese paper on which Rembrandt printed some of his etchings. You can get paper impregnated with strands of silk or with leaves or, even, with the wings of butterflies, and a paper called Bonric which feels and shines like silk. So we thought it would be interesting to see at Kochi the making of hand-made paper. This turned out to be a mistake. The factory was a primitive, squalid place like a cross between a stable and an old-fashioned laundry. Middle-aged women did most of the laborious work of dipping a screen in a vat and taking it out again, over and over again. In one corner squatted a very old and dirty woman fraying rope for fibres used in some of the paper.

More interesting was Kochi Castle. The local daimyo had built himself this stronghold about three hundred years ago. It had become, like castles everywhere, a tourist attraction and museum. There was a lacquered palanquin in which milord was borne up the long road to Edo when he went to pay his tribute to the Shogun. There was a king-size kite that used to be flown when a noble son was born, and such other curiosities as a kimono made of paper, and circular snowshoes of plaited straw. Stairs as steep as ladders—they must have been hard on the castle servants—gave access to the top storey. In the foreground of a rewarding view dolphins that looked as fierce as dragons cocked up their tails from the corners of a roof of gunmetal tiles that complemented perfectly the stucco walls of white.

When the lord of Kochi was on the road to Edo any knowledgeable bystander would have known it was he from the Kochi symbol carried by his retainers. This is preserved in the castle and consists of a plaited rope about five feet long made of roosters' shining black tail-feathers.

THE ROOSTER with the longest tail in Japan, or for that matter in the world, was to be found in Kochi, for the *onagadori*, as the bird with this extraordinary growth is called, is the place's badge of fame. We were taken to see the reigning champion. Its tail was twenty-one feet (say $6\frac{3}{4}$ metres) long.

We felt sorry for this unfortunate fowl that never knew what it was to have a scratch or chase a hen. It spent its life in a tall wooden box which had a glass viewing front that doubtless made the box hotter, and the rooster was visibly sweaty when its owner removed it. In the box the rooster ate from a hopper and excreted into one compartment while its tail plumes grew and grew down into another. The farmer who bred it, Kobori-san, placed the bird on a tall display perch in the courtyard of his house. He untied string from the looped-up feathers and drew them out to their full length and let them lie along the ground, where he arranged them artistically for me to photograph.

The champion rooster was nine years old. It was, strangely, a white bird with tail feathers mainly black. Kobori-san had an all-white which, with seventeen feet of tail, gave promise of being a grand champion.

The hens of this breed lay only thirty or forty eggs a year, so it was generous of the breeder to give me one of the eggs. When our guide wasn't looking, I threw it out of the car window with the thought that the wasted egg might reduce by one the number of *onagadori* roosters shut up in boxes.

THE OTHER FORM of distinctive Kochi fauna is the fighting dog. When we returned to the inn the owner of the champion dog was waiting to show it to us.

An amiable-seeming mastiff, rather like a Labrador but with a smoother coat and more powerful build, the dog was decked with emblems of its prowess. Hanging under its neck was a scroll fringed with gold, resembling the ceremonial apron *sumo* wrestlers wear. Another, emblazoned with its name, was across its back, and a big bow-like device of stiffened white rope rose from behind its head. Its name was Koriki, meaning High Power. It had scars of battle and pitted ears. Doubtless Koriki lived a pretty good dog's life between the bouts held in spring and autumn. Its owner said that it ate, as well as meat and fish, five *go* of rice a day—about a quart, which when cooked is a lot of rice. It had to be exercised for two hours daily to maintain this weight-building appetite.

These mastiffs, and a smaller breed also, are always known as Tosa dogs; Tosa is a second name for the Kochi region. There were about two hundred such dogs and as many as eighty fought at match time in the Sumo wrestling hall.

Dog-fighting, I heard, was "under a cloud". I could not but hope that the cloud would turn to rain in the public conscience and wash the whole thing out, because I am unable to regard fight sports—from what is called "boxing" down to the cruelties of cock-fighting and the bullring—as other than uncivilized.

AT TAKAMATSU in the early hours of the morning Cyclone Wendy blew in, or maybe it was Typhoon Wendy. "Typhoon" sounds fiercer—and the feminine names meteorologists give to these devastating winds make them all sound rather innocuous. We caught only the edge of this one. It blew to tatters the *shoji* paper on the inner sliding window of our room (because I had neglected to close the outer frame of glass). Over at Kochi, the news broadcast said, Wendy had destroyed houses and sunk fishing boats.

The ferry to Shodo Island, where we were to go that day, had stopped running because of the roughened seas. Richard Hughes, doyen of foreign correspondents in the Orient had commended Shodo to me as an unspoilt island where the natives looked askance at his cigar and when he asked for whisky and soda brought him a drink with an olive in it—a Shodo olive: there are many olive groves on the island—and where there were monkeys, described in a brochure we got as "tame wild monkeys".

Anyway, if we couldn't go to Shodo because of the cyclone where could we go? I looked at the map of Shikoku and saw TOKUSHIMA—and remembered an article Peter Robinson had written for "Tiger" Saito's magazine about how at Tokushima the Bunraku puppet theatre still thrived as a folk art. Masao-san, our guide, telephoned and was all smiles: "It is most fortunate. Today is the day the people work the puppets to try out their skill in public." We just caught a train and two hours later were in Tokushima's public school assembly hall, which served as a theatre. Nobody there spoke any English but we had Masao-san with us. It was no trouble to get backstage. Bunraku people are nice people.

Most of the men backstage, who had to do with arranging and adjudicating the performances, were old—which is not surprising when you learn that it takes twenty-five years of practice to become a master manipulator of the head and right arm of a doll. It was a very hot and humid day and the old men were just in their underwear—cotton singlet and pants.

Puppets, half life-size, were hanging by the scruff on pegs, some in elaborate kimono costume, all so flaccidly lifeless you almost expected to see a heap of fallen stuffing beneath them on the floor. Heads and bodies are separate and interchangeable. The decapitated-looking heads could be disconcerting as you rounded a corner and were met by a staring warrior-type with fierce black eyebrows. There are forty-five kinds of heads, and Peter Robinson says the one that really popped his eyes was the head of an evil spirit that looked like a beautiful young woman until manipulation of internal levers changed her eyes to blood red, her mouth to a gash of jagged teeth, and two golden horns shot out of her head.

What we saw from backstage was a performance by women manipulators. Women were unknown as Bunraku puppeteers until recent years when a Mrs Rokunojo Ichimura took over, after her husband died, the direction of a troupe of performers he had headed on neighbouring Awaji Island. She taught other women, in order to keep alive an art in which the younger generation showed little interest. (But in recent years interest has revived.)

Three women brought a puppet onto the stage, which was in two parts: in front it was boarded to about the manipulators' waist height, and that represented walking level for the principal dolls. Behind this, at about shoulder height, was the level of other puppets not in the main foreground action.

The principal manipulator, the one who worked the head and right hand (with her left hand) looked a typical bespectacled Japanese housewife of about forty. She had two assistants, younger women, one to hold up the doll and the other to work the left hand (with her right hand). Mrs Spectacles, being short, had to wear, strapped to her feet like monstrous sandals, theatre clogs, which must have been about eight inches high—they look weighty but are hollow and made of light paulownia wood. She did not wear the traditional dignified dress of the puppet-master, nor did her assistants wear the usual black gown and mask; they were in everyday skirts and white blouses.

Then they brought on another puppet, an old man who was blind. The doll was walked with just the hesitant gait a blind man has, with the concentrated steadiness of the sightless head, and a stick searching the way. The audience was seeing—and so were we—not four women working a doll, but a blind man.

An old man in black kimono, squatting at one side of the stage, was the adjudicator. I don't know what points he awarded the performance, but the audience burst into great applause. When the women came off stage it was rather moving to see Mrs Spectacles, bright red in the face with effort and emotion, surrounded and being fanned by her congratulatory assistants, and almost in tears at her success.

That audience was wonderful. They were nearly all farming people; in the main, they were middle-aged to old, but some of the women fanned babies dozing on the floor mats. Hard work in the ricefields had lined and leathered their faces and had not left in their lives much room for any vanity but the cleanliness of loose white cotton undervests, which the men wore as did the women, plain women with their hair drawn back behind their ears and their faces uncoloured by any make-up.

They were so rapt, so immersed in each performance—yet it was not at

172   Inland Sea Shores

all an uncritical peasant wonder: you could feel, coming through the absorption, that sense and spirit of appreciation which is the very breath of the living theatre.

THE SHIP that was to take us from Takamatsu to Beppu in Kyushu was cancelled because of the cyclone, but there was a ship that could take us to Kobe, in the other direction, and we got on that. The ship was the *Kurenai Maru* of the Kansai Line. I was on the same vessel again in 1973—and it was an utterly different experience.

The first trip—of only four hours to Kobe—was fine. The cabins seemed quite elegant then, with their wind-down picture windows when one had rather expected portholes. Claire was in high spirits and determined not to be disheartened by the cyclone washing Kyushu off the itinerary.

A rainbow formed on a grey-silk sky and it reached right down to the sea. Then a second rainbow began to form inside the arch of the first, and the colours of this one crept down the sky until it touched the horizon where a small ship was, black in the pearly light.

The Takamatsu-Kobe trip years later was for no other purpose than to join in Kobe the JNTO man who was to accompany me through Kyushu, a young executive of the finance division, Takashi Nagaoka. His first name was commonly shortened to Tak; but he couldn't be Tak-san because that sounded exactly like the word for "enough, plenty, sufficient", *takusan*. I liked Tak at once. We had an excellent sukiyaki dinner (Kobe beef, of course) at a Japanese inn he knew, the Yama Mitsuwa, recommendable but very expensive, about $A30 for two, including ¥1,095 tax. Next morning we joined the same *Kurenai* (which means "crimson") *Maru*, now regarded as one of the old ships of the Kansai Line, and left for Beppu.

It takes thirteen hours from Kobe to Beppu. This is a long time, unless (*a*) you are travel-tired and welcome a rest, or (*b*) the trip is scenically enthralling—and it helps if the ship's facilities and service are first-class. Calm-sea conditions are the rule, making for a restful voyage. Undeniably, parts of the Inland Sea are beautiful, but expectations that are not fulfilled have been built up with hyperbolic guff such as the *"It's like a journey through a 270-mile Japanese garden"* mentioned earlier. Some pretty pine-treed islands are seen, but most are ordinary; too many have had their shores scarred by the quarrying of the granite- and gravel-getters; the shores of the Inland Sea are by no means free of industry, chimney stacks and oil storage tanks, and the amount of commercial shipping now plying on, and polluting, the strait hardly enhances what the brochure calls the "ethereal qualities of these waters". (Disastrous pollution occurred in December 1974 when a huge oil tank ruptured at Kurashiki and 50,000 barrels of oil poured into the Inland Sea, fouling a hundred miles of coastline and causing a national outcry.)

It may be that the Kansai Line does better by its passengers on its newer ships, the *Cobalt Maru* and *Murasaki Maru*; but here is what my notebook recorded about this trip on the *Kurenai Maru*: "No cabin service for drinks or anything else during the day. Teapot with tea and vacuum flask of hot water provided—that's all. Lavatories are smelly, not clean. Bar didn't open when it was supposed to at five-thirty. Seemingly wouldn't have opened at all but for insistence of few European passengers who had to round up barman, who had no English. While we downing first drink steward came and announced dining-room open. At lunch was asked to order dinner, ordered tempura. When, after second drink in bar, went to table tempura there, covered with napkin, cold. Sent it back, got it re-heated, which no way to have good tempura. No wonder so few passengers."

One of the European passengers was a Swiss girl, Helen Weibel, from whom I was glad to get information of Japan travel at a different level to what I experienced—the youth hostel way. Helen had to economize on accommodation as she had put her money into a round-the-world air ticket costing 6,000 Swiss francs (about $A2,000) that had taken her to Istanbul, Athens, Teheran, Kabul, Delhi, Katmandu, Rangoon, Bangkok, Hong Kong, Tokyo (where she worked behind the bar at Romy's in Rippongi) and she would go on to Honolulu, San Francisco, Mexico City.

Japanese hostels are, in the main, good and cheap, she said. They varied a lot: some were *ryokans*, some in temples, some were built by the Japan Youth Hostel organization, of which you needed to be a member or accommodation cost Y200 more. Average was about ¥500 a night, with supper and breakfast ¥900, extra charges for sheets and heating. You could not stay anywhere for more than three consecutive nights. A book listing all the hostels was available in English, which was spoken at the Kobe hostel Helen had just come from; but mostly there was no English and, for that reason, few foreigners were found on the hostel circuit. But, with enough language, it was quite possible to do Japan "on the cheap".

The ship got to Beppu at 9.30 p.m. At last I had made it to the Kyushu mecca of Japanese tourists and an increasing number of *gaijin* ones.

off-track in honshu

金沢 松島

Kanazawa, in its way, is another Kyoto

THE WEST COAST of Honshu gets its share, a lamb's share rather than a lion's, of tourists; but foreigners wouldn't make up more than 1 per cent of them.

If you are a Japan-going *gaijin*, one who has read enough to know where the places in his itinerary are, you may well say, "Where on the west coast is there a place worth going to?"

Kanazawa. You haven't heard of Kanazawa? Neither had I until I came across an article by the Japanese essayist Kenichi Yoshida,[35] who wrote of this west coast city (pop. 370,000) in these eyebrow-raising terms: "For the visitor to Japan who would like the illusion of Kyoto without having to push his way through all those other tourists who go to Kyoto, Kanazawa should be a preferred stop on his itinerary."

I thought: preferred to *Kyoto*—the man's mad! After spending four days in Kanazawa I still hold to the view that Yoshida-san's understandable affection for the place put a wee warp in his judgement, and would advise nobody, or nobody except the most tourist-allergic tourist, to scratch Kyoto off his itinerary in order to put Kanazawa on. But Kanazawa is worth going to. Like Kyoto, it was spared by the bombers and not scarred and transformed by war. Yoshida-san is anything but mad when he rates it highly—indeed, it is possible that if I had spent *another* four days in this seductive place I'd have endorsed his every word!

The first thing I found fascinating about Kanazawa was the very-Japanese story of how it came to be what it is. One needs to know first, though, *where* it is. If you draw a straight east-west line across the map from Tokyo to the other coast, Kanazawa is just about *there*. Being on the other side of the Japan Alps, it gets freezing winds straight off Siberia and for months of the year the place is almost buried in snow; its winter makes Tokyo's seem positively Mediterranean. Yet, difficult as the overland journey was, the daimyo, the Maeda-family lord of Kaga province whose castle was at Kanazawa, had to make his way periodically to pay his tribute and profess his loyalty to the Shogun in Edo (which turned into Tokyo, where you can now hop on an ANA plane that has you in Komatsu, where Kanazawa's airport is, in no more than one hour.)

Kyoto could be reached more easily than Edo in feudal times, although there was less reason to go to where the figurehead Emperor resided than to the Shogun's seat of power. You could sail most of the way to Kyoto—down the coast to Tsuruga and then, having crossed a neck of land to big Lake Biwa, by boat to the end of the lake, where you were almost on Kyoto's doorstep. So Kanazawa didn't exactly rusticate on the western shore—but what gave the city its character was something other than cultural cross-currents from Edo and Kyoto and from China just across the sea. Kanazawa became a kind of second Kyoto because its feudal lords, the Maedas, were not only cultured but cunning.

The Shogun knew as well as the Maedas did that Kaga was a particularly strong province that could produce yearly a million *goku* of rice (about five million bushels); so it had a considerable capacity to generate trouble for the shogunate, and, such was its isolation from the capital, an insurrection there would be hard to put down. So of course the Shogun had his spies watching the Maedas, watching particularly for any show of military muscle. Instead of this, what the spies saw was the Maeda lord devoutly restoring a temple of the Nichiren Buddhists. What they didn't see was that the temple was an innocent-looking facade for a fortress with secret doors and passages. The offering chest where the faithful threw in coins had only to be removed and there was a yawning pit which attackers rushing into the temple would fall into. A passageway led underground for 1,600 metres to the Maeda's castle.

The third Maeda lord, Toshitsune, delighted the great Ieyasu Tokugawa, first of the Tokugawa shoguns, by the attention he paid to the arts—encouraging his samurai to write *haiku* poems and practise the tea ceremony. A master potter was brought from Kyoto to make tea-bowls, and Kanazawa is famous to this day for tea ceramics. The Maedas brought ceramic artists from China to make pottery from the local blue clay, the famed Kutani ware. And they started a Noh theatre which is still functioning.

The crowning achievement of the Maedas' craftiness was the creation of a superb garden. Basically, the garden was begun in 1676 to camouflage the conduits of the town's water supply. Its enlargement in the following century and its completion in 1822 helped to enhance the reputation of the Maedas of Kanazawa of being an aesthetic lot, rather dilettante, and to be looked upon indulgently. And the garden the Maedas made as a setting for a lordly villa is rated as one of the three finest landscape gardens in Japan.

KENROKUEN PARK, as these gardens are called, was the first place I was taken to in Kanazawa. I had arrived by train from Gifu via Maibara before noon, and Kanazawa at once had something in common with Kyoto—it was a city of no distinction at all in the region of its railway station. Very close to the station was a large concrete box of a building which contained in its upper floors the Kanazawa Miyako Hotel, where I was to find myself very well accommodated, and the management could not have been more helpful in assisting my sightseeing and making my stay pleasant.

Roku is Japanese for "six" and Kenrokuen means gardens combining six features—extensiveness, quietude, artistry, the use of water to achieve effects, a relationship with history, and scenic charm. A catalogue like that can sound pretentious and off-putting, but this is a lovely place. I haven't seen the two others in Japan's top trio of gardens—the Kairakuen at Mito (the Mito that is north of Tokyo, not the one on the Izu Peninsula) and the Korakuen at Okayama, which is midway between Osaka and Hiroshima on the Shinkansen line. My standards of comparison were set by the garden round the Katsura Imperial Villa at Kyoto and Ritsurin Park at Takamatsu. Kanazawa's Kenrokuen gardens are different. They have more flowers.

The irises were in their glory when I was there in the third week of May. They were the purple ones, and specially effective blooming along the banks of a rivulet that comes out of a small lake and meanders right through the

Sand on Japanese beaches is seldom golden but it may be hot, as at Ibusuki in Kyushu, where thermal "sand baths" are claimed to have curative effects.

In the Iso Gardens at Kagoshima the starry scarlet of autumn maples frames a lovely villa built in the seventeenth century by a lord of the Shimazu clan.

Asakusa, the downtown amusement district of Tokyo with colourful shopping malls, the tourist may feel to be more Japanese than the smarter Ginza area.

At Kamakura, less than an hour by train from Tokyo, is the second-largest Buddha in Japan (and artistically better than the biggest one, at Nara). The seated bronze image 11.4 metres high was cast more than 700 years ago. It used to be housed in a hall, but that was swept away by a tidal wave in 1495.

The tea ceremony is, by Japanese definition, "an aesthetic cult in polite circles that enlightens through discipline and promotes mental composure" Men as well as women practise this ritual serving of tea. One tea master I met was the very cultivated managing director of the Hotel Hayashida Onsen in Kagoshima Prefecture, Mr. Takeshi Hara, who made the pictures reproduced below using flowers, leaves and grasses, which he gathered himself, arranged with artistry under glass and had framed for his hotel's room decoration.

park and is crossed with here an upcurved little wooden bridge and farther along a row of slabs of flat stone, no two the same shape of course.

It was also azalea time. These made a foreground of white and pink to the lakelet called Kasumigaike (Mist Pond) across which a single white swan was sailing towards a tea-house of *shibui* elegance, its wood untouched by any bright paint so that the structure did not thrust itself against the eye but merged with the shadows of the trees behind the pond. There is another pond, which is so contrived that it provides a small waterfall. And, as part of the design that was completed by a landscaper brought from Kyoto, there are three so-called hills. Up one of these knolls a path circles, like the pattern on a shell, to a resting place.

These gardens, which have many cherry-trees for springtime blossoming, have even more pines. A pine-tree to a Japanese gardener is something to be treated much as in Europe a fruit-tree is espaliered against a wall—branches are trained out and out horizontally and given wooden crutches for support. But Kanazawa has a winter problem with its pine-tree branches: so much snow weighs down on them that they could break—and only the lowest branches can be given wooden crutches. So, in winter, Kenrokuen Park has (as I've seen in photographs) many high poles and from their tops, like streamers from maypoles, hundreds of ropes stretching down to vulnerable pine branches laden with snow. Kasumigaike Pond, frozen over and with its tea-house roofs piled with snow, looks as beautiful as the pine-tree "maypoles" look strange.

SEISONKAKU is the name of a patrician villa—or one might call it a Japanese-style mansion, two-storeyed and with its outer walls of wood—that stands at one end of Kenrokuen Park. It was built for the mother of the thirteenth Lord Maeda to live in and, apart from its being classified as a "national treasure" as a building, Seisonkaku has beautiful screen and scroll paintings and richly coloured transoms that were carved in wood three centuries ago.

One of the rooms had colour such as I saw nowhere else in Japan. Only in Kanazawa, apparently, did the houses of the rich have an earthen interior wall, or walls, of cinnabar red. In his case there was also purple and olive. Sometimes there was a good deal of gold. Perhaps this indulgence in warmth of colour was to offset the winter's austerity; perhaps it reflected the closeness of China—or maybe the Maedas just liked luxurious colour. However, the architecture of the villa sacrificed nothing of Japanese elegance to flamboyancy. Its balconies were beautifully proportioned woodwork, unadorned; and at the rear of the villa there was a lovely small garden, its stone water-holder carved with the Maeda emblem, a five-petalled plum blossom.

On display was an exquisite set of dolls' furnishings. It included the tiniest mirror and combs, a writing set and, even, miniature utensils for tea ceremony. Next door to Seisonkaku is the prefectural art gallery, with fine examples of the old Kutani pottery; but this is Chinese rather than Japanese in character. The blue clay of Kanazawa was also baked into some of the loveliest roof tiles ever made in Japan or anywhere. There is, as well, a museum section to the shrine, which has a three-storey portal of a most unusual design; a Dutch engineer was its architect, in 1875. More Japanese—and better-looking to my eye—is the Ishikawa Gate set on the great stone-wall foundation of the Maedas' castle, which, except for the gate, was destroyed by fire in 1881.

Off-track in Honshu

WITH OFF-TRACK TRAVEL you find that, where English-speaking tourists are rare, English-speaking tourist guides are likely to be non-existent. So it was at Kanazawa, but the local tourist authorities came to the rescue with a very bright-minded young woman, Yukiko Minamoto, who had been in Europe where she was a governess with a Japanese family in Germany. She said her German was better, but her English proved quite adequate. However, when I went to the Noh office, the manager of the Miyako Hotel, Mr Naoe, took some hours off to accompany me. He introduced the English-speaking teacher of Noh, who said that Kanazawa's was the only public Noh theatre in Japan. The others were private in the sense that they were subscription theatres.

The teacher, Yonosuke Watanabe, had about three hundred pupils. Many were in the audience, and some of the audience had been there since eight o'clock that morning and would stay right through the day. Others were on the stage. The Kanazawa Noh company had about fifty professionals, but many of those I saw performing in this most demanding form of theatre were amateurs.

In the first piece the very dignified *shite* (principal actor) was the boilerman at the local school. In the second Noh play the leading role was taken by a dentist. In yet another the three reciters were identified to me as a doctor, a clerk and the keeper of a fish-shop. Noh solemnity is sometimes relieved by a play that is basically a farce, called a *kyogen*, and one such dealt with a robber who waylays a woman who, catching the robber off-guard, robs him. They were so good I asked Watanabe-san if they were professionals. No, he said, the robber was the owner of a supermarket and the woman ran a *ryokan*. The only part of the Noh I saw that I was able to recognize as amateurish was some of the recitative chanting, which is very difficult. For this reason nearly all the chorus were professionals. In the last play I saw called *Shakkyo* (Stone Bridge) a professional took the part of the Zen priest, but the two lions, gorgeously costumed, were played very well by a father and son who were amateurs. The Noh stage at Kanazawa was in the traditional highly stylized form and appeared to me to be exactly like the stage I had seen in Tokyo.

DURING the Edo period (1600-1867) Noh became very élitist. The common people were excluded from it and it could be enjoyed only by the samurai class. After we left the Noh my host took me to a street where there is a samurai mansion. The house was privately occupied and couldn't be inspected, but the walls that formed this narrow street were admirable. Each wall was of pale brown earth; but this *pisé's* special texture came from straw being mixed with the earth that formed it. The walls were based on three rows of stone blocks and topped with handsome grey-blue tiles.

Many of Kanazawa's back streets turn out to be blind alleys. Here again the cunning Maeda were concerned with defence capability that wouldn't obtrude or cause suspicion: *cul-de-sacs* would confuse and frustrate an enemy.

In narrow streets there are old merchants' houses and shops characterized by harmonious brown wooden facades, some identified by lovely ideographs, some with street-front curtains, *noren*, of rope or string, like the rice-malting house that was about 150 years old. There was also an admirable old medicine shop, still very much in business—and most generous with samples of its preparations to relieve upset stomach or a hangover.

As to arts and crafts, I found more interesting than the famous Kutani ceramics (which are so Chinese-derivative) the work of a living Kanazawa potter, Kosen Toshioka, whose grandfather was the founder of the gallery where I saw this potter still active at the wheel at the age of seventy-seven. His skill was amazing and so were his hands, as supple as a young man's from constantly shaping the wet white clay. Toshioka-san reminded me that the greatest of contemporary Japanese potters, Hamada, was still working at eighty. The Toshioka pot I bought is very small but, I think, very good.

The regional craft of hand-painted textiles called *Kaga-yuzen* I didn't care for at all; the patterns seemed too bright and obvious to represent the Japanese aesthetic.

My favourite *haiku*—indeed, my favourite lines in Japanese poetry—was written by Chiyo, and I did not know until I went to Kanazawa that Chiyo was a woman and she lived in a village in the area and devoted herself to writing *haiku* (poems of 17 syllables, 5:7:5) after the tragic loss of her husband, who was a samurai's footman, and her child. It is not sadness, though, but perception of beauty that comes through in her most famous lines, of which I think this is the most felicitous translation:

> *The morning glory*
> *twines around my well bucket.*
> *So I lack water.*

Noto is from an Ainu word *notto*, meaning nose, or some say jaw. Jutting out of the west coast of Honshu is a *hanto*, a peninsula, that is said to be nose-like or jaw-like. One rather wet May morning I set out in a car to see the Noto Hanto. This region, I had been told in Tokyo, was the genuine *Ura Nihon* (Back of Japan).

"They are warm-hearted, the people of Ura Nihon," says a writer about them, and adds, "They cherish the old traditions and all Japanese find in this region many arts and styles and customs to satisfy nostalgia for the past."[35]

The first place we stopped at was hardly representative. It was an extremely long beach with sand so hard that, for a distance of about eight kilometres, cars could run along it, as ours did. It was the biggest bathing beach in Ishikawa prefecture, and on a hot Sunday in August might get a hundred thousand people on its greyish sands and in its shallow waters (an Australian's judgement on beaches abroad is always harsh; we are spoilt by such good ones). The name of this beach was Chirihama. *Chiri* has to do with topography but its main meaning is "rubbish, litter"—such as a hundred thousand people leave on a hot Sunday in August. There was a prefectural move afoot to have the beach's name changed from Chirihama to Senrihama.

We drove on past fisherwomen, as well as fishermen, hauling in nets. Winter waves can be high along the Japan Sea coast, and to counter their inroads there is much backing of beaches with sand-anchoring blocks of cast *konkuriito* (concrete), ugly but effective. We were to come to a better-looking beach farther on, but it was two hours drive from Kanazawa, and in two hours a Toyota Crown such as we were in would use fifteen litres of gasoline, and gas was now twice as expensive as last year (and was ¥115 a litre, about $A1.30 a gallon, in 1975).

The coast scene was decorated with rocky islets, strangely shaped and with pine-trees pricking out of them at improbable angles. A headland called

Gammon was cut right through with a grotto. Another holed rock was one of those that gave Kuroshima (Black Islets) Beach its name. Then there were two of those "wedded" rocks sticking out of the sea and joined with a thick rope, such as I had seen before near Toba.

The land dropped steeply to the Japan Sea, and where it was cultivable it came down in a giant's staircase of rice terraces. It was the most impressive view of terraced riceland I had seen in Japan—almost comparable with the world-famous Ifugao "Stairways to the Gods" in the Philippines.

WAJIMA, a town 120 kilometres north of Kanizawa, is noted for its lacquerware. The road to it was lovely with pluming bamboos and *fuji* (wistaria) in heliotrope bloom. We passed an old man wearing the primitive raincoat of the region—a cape of straw.

By going to Wajima you can buy its top-quality lacquerware for about 30 per cent less than you would pay in Tokyo. It may still seem pricey, but what goes into it needs to be borne in mind. First the wood is dried for a year before it is shaped into, say, a bowl. The bowl is smoked for three months. Then the coats of lacquer are applied—sixty coats, even seventy on some pieces. The process takes about six months from when a bowl is shaped to when it goes on the display shelf for sale at Inachu, which is easily the principal maker and seller. I talked, through Yukiko-san, with the third-generation proprietor of Inachu, a Mr Inagaki, who was over seventy. He said, indicating some chests that were richly decorated, mainly in gold on black or vermilion, that there were 124 steps to the making of the best lacquerware. Did he export much? No, he said, because in most countries the climate was too dry and, despite all the pains that were taken in its making, lacquerware was likely to crack in dry air. Even in rainy Wajima there was a bowl of water in every display case. I still bought a small tray—black with a cut-through pattern to cinnabar red. It was done in Japanese lacquer, of which not enough is produced, so lacquer from China has to be imported. According to Inagaki-san, Chinese lacquer does not give as high a lustre.

We go farther up the road that leads to the top of Noto Peninsula and, near the town of Sosogi, come to what the usually reliable *Official Guide*[24] described as "probably the largest farmhouse in Japan". It isn't: there are larger ones in the Shirakawago valley in Gifu prefecture. But it is a most interesting rural mansion—more that than a farmhouse. It was built about 130 years ago by descendants of the Taira (or Heike), the military family that seized from the Fujiwara family the ruling power. When, early in the thirteenth century, the Taira in turn were ousted by the Minamoto family, Tokikuni Taira was exiled to the "backblocks" of Japan.

The rafters are huge and you look up to a main ceiling eighteen metres high; but one lordly room has a coffered ceiling of black lacquer edged with gold. Some of the lacquer vessels here—containers for presents and rice and sake—are said to have been made five centuries ago. One superb example is a portable wardrobe. And these were portable people—four *kago* equivalents of the sedan chair are preserved, and I was told that they were used right up to 1940.

We returned to Kanazawa by a different route that showed me the other side of Noto peninsula. There was a delay due to a smash—two trucks had collided on the winding road, where the high accident rate was evidenced

Kanazawa, in its way, is another Kyoto 183

by roadside figures of dummy policemen. These are made of plastic and are realistically painted as to uniform and face. The effect of them is salutary.

JAPAN started later than some other countries in selling tourists the "other days, other ways" attraction, usually in terms of a reconstructed village where dwellings and shops of bygone styles are assembled, and with more verisimilitude than history has in museums' glass cases and models. Near Kanazawa there is the Edo Village.

For a single village-style exhibit to express the living conditions of the Edo Period seemed too much to expect—it was an era that stretched from 1600 to 1867. In terms of English history that time-span meant from Elizabethan England to Queen Victoria's time, from Tudor cottage to Crystal Palace. But, as Tomlin puts it, "The Tokugawas brought into being a social system which was as near to being static as possible. Depending on a man's status, his living-quarters, his dress, and the degree to which he had to do honour to his superiors were all meticulously prescribed. No modern society has ever reached such a degree of 'immobility'."[5]

The overall look and layout of Edo Village is good and the buildings include samurai's mansion, temple, merchant's house, general store, peasant's house, money-lender's, warehouse, pottery, townsmen's houses, farmhouse and, of course, an inn.

Furnishings appeared to be, for the most part, valid though sparse, but the samurai's mansion was rather a mess, with its Chinese carpet, non-Japanese antiques and the worst sort of Western lampshade.

One interesting exhibit was a very large fan emblazoned with the Hinomaru, the red round of the sun. Before this became the form of the Japanese flag, the fan served as a banner and was carried into war.

My last meal in Kanazawa was at an elegant restaurant named Sekitei. As a guest, I wondered how expensive it was—particularly since we had *shabu-shabu* of Matsuzaka beef—and found out that it was ¥18,000 for five persons, including sake and beer and tax and the 15 per cent service charge that Japanese inns tack on—about A$9 a head. Everything was in very good taste, from the *hashi-uke*, the little ceramic chopstick rests, to the garden outside the private room where we ate.

Not that I didn't eat well at the Miyako Hotel, where chefs were quite important—they had so much food preparation to do for wedding banquets. On the day I left there were no less than five weddings at the hotel, which had its own Shinto chapel for the service as well as its banquet rooms for the reception. A big wedding cost up to ¥1,500,000 ($A3,750). It was arranged that I could be present in the chapel when the Shinto priest, who had an attendant shrine maiden, married Kensuke Hiroka, an industrial designer, and Harumi Fuchida, who was a very beautiful bride in the traditional finery. Hiroka-san wore Japanese dress also. All the other male guests were in morning suits. At the reception the prefecture's leading dancer performed, with six geisha playing samisens. The banquet was Western-style, but the traditional gift package each guest was handed on leaving included *tai*, the fish most highly regarded for eating in *sashimi* (raw) form.

The average age for marriage was twenty-seven for men, twenty-four for women. The trend was to marrying younger. Nearly all weddings were performed by a Shinto priest: few were civil ceremonies.

Off-track in Honshu

My flight from Kanazawa's airport at Komatsu to Tokyo's Haneda took only fifty-five minutes on a Boeing 737 of All Nippon Airways. If you carry little baggage and use the monorail from Tokyo's airport (quicker as well as cheaper than taxis) it needn't take long to get to and from Kanazawa, the off-track Kyoto.

Why the poet wrote "O! Matsushima"

THE JAPANESE are not only great lovers of nature, they are great classifiers and labellers of what they love to look at. Hokusai did Thirty-Six Views of Fuji as woodblock prints and so did Hiroshige, who also did Eight Views of Omi (Lake Biwa's province) and One Hundred Views of Edo. The foreigner could get the impression that the Japanese see a vista to rave over from every second hill. Then we find that they have gone in for the most rigorous view selection. They cut their famous views, their government-labelled "Outstanding Scenic Places", down to just *three*.

The so-called "Scenic Trio of Japan" are (i) Miyajima, the island also called Itsukushima from the famous shrine that seems to float at high tide and has its great vermilion *torii* standing in the sea; (ii) Ama-no-hashidate, the "Bridge of Heaven", which consists of a sand-bar three and a half kilometres long and lined with pine-trees that have been twisted by storms into extraordinary shapes: this bar projects into a bay on the Japan Sea side, across from Kyoto; (iii) Matsushima Bay, which this chapter is mainly about. *Matsushima* means Pine Island, and the bay has not just one but a couple of hundred islands or islets.

Miyajima, in the Inland Sea near Hiroshima, I had already been to, and it is unquestionably one of the "Outstanding Scenic Places" of Japan or anywhere. Ama-no-hashidate, on the other hand, sounded like an odd inclusion. Two of the five guidebooks I have don't even mention the place, and Fodor's says, "There is little to recommend it to the foreign visitor." You are supposed to look at the view through your legs, which, according to the *Official Guide*,[13] makes the sand-bar look as though it is suspended in mid-air, as a "heavenly bridge" that has to do with Japanese mythology. Ama-no-hashidate, in short, sounded skippable. But the more I read about Matsushima the better it sounded, and the more like the place I was looking for that had scenery such as the Inland Sea ship trip was supposed to provide, but didn't. However, I thought that anyone could be inclined to expect too much of a place that left Japan's greatest *haiku* poet, Basho, so enraptured that his verse consisted of

        O! Matsushima
        O! O! Matsushima O!
        O! Matsushima.

TO REACH Matsushima I took a northerly express from Tokyo's Ueno Station for a four-and-a-half-hour run to Sendai, from which Matsushima is another forty minutes by rail or an hour by road. Or you can go by air to Sendai: I flew back.

The Japanese rural landscape on this northern route had, as always, lots of ricelands and some nice old thatched farmhouses. There were also vineyards. And standing in the middle of one field was a memorable hoarding that said I-don't-know-what in Japanese but in English it just said, in very large letters, KINDNESS. I've no idea who put it there—a bow to him, her or them, anyway.

Before you are halfway to Sendai you are in Tohuku, which is the name of Honshu's north-east and top north. Tohuku is regarded by most Japanese as a rugged region of cold climate and warm-hearted people and impressive scenery. Of Tohuku's six prefectures the train trip shows two, Fukushima and then Miyagi, of which Sendai is the capital. With half a million people, Sendai is Honshu's biggest city north of Tokyo. During the Second World War it was of sufficient importance to get itself bombed flat. In feudal days it was a castle town, but only some ruins of the castle remain. About four kilometres from the station is the architecturally splendid Osaki Hachiman Shrine, to which one ascends by a very long flight of steps. I saw this on my way back from Matsushima, when I had an hour to spare in Sendai before being due at the airport to fly to Tokyo.

Of Sendai I saw nothing on the afternoon I arrived except the view from the hotel room of a functionally modern city. I was waiting in my room for a guide I had been told in Tokyo to expect, and who did not arrive. However, the room—a single for Y3,600—was fascinating as a triumph of Japanese ingenuity in the art of "living small". I swear that the space was under three metres long and no more than two metres wide. This included the bathroom which as well as having a shower, actually had a bath, one big enough to sit in, and made of moulded plastic, as was the basin, the lavatory, and a cabinet with two mirrors (a magnifying one for making-up). There was no clothes cupboard but some hooks in the midget hallway that led to the bedroom, which was only as wide as the bed was long. There was just enough room for a small table, and a chair that fitted under it. There was a wall-mounted television set (fourteen-inch screen), an electric alarm clock, a telephone, a hot-water jug for making tea. And a plug-in pants-presser, a flat arrangement as big as the top of the table it fitted behind. It was the economy-squeeze version of the modern hotel room complete down to a torch beside the bed and a Gideon Bible.

When it was five o'clock, with still no sign of the guide, I switched on the television. I didn't stay long with the Children's Hour TV—just long enough to see a cartoon super-villain who came flying through the air on some fiendish mission get impaled on a church steeple. With lots of agony sound and rivulets of blood splashing down—all in colour. It was *very* nasty.

I had let it be known to JNTO in Tokyo that where I wanted to spend my evening in Sendai was at an off-beat restaurant James Kirkup had written about called Robata. About six o'clock two nice men from the prefectural tourist office turned up to take me there. Neither spoke any English, but communication was restored when we were joined at Robata by a lady guide who spoke English well enough to teach it.

Robata looked less like a restaurant than a superior farmhouse, its walls hung with such things as a straw raincape and a letterbox made of a gourd shaped like a woman, and a mask or two. On display was part of the proprietor's collection of *kokeshi* dolls. Miyagi prefecture is the home of these dolls that have just a piece of cylindrical wood for the body topped by a ball of wood for the head, with an artful minimum of painting providing features, hair and kimono. Nothing is more Japanese than a kokeshi doll.

The proprietor's name was Tomiya Amae, but he was always referred to as Ogi-san. The guide said, "He is the grandfather of Robata." He not only presided over the place but his presence, more than the décor, gave it its character; I couldn't imagine the place without this kimono'd figure of a man of about sixty with short-clipped grey hair, a full-lipped mouth and the shrewdest eyes. He was squatted on a platform, with his diners seated at benches that ran round three sides of the room. There he sat and served them their sake without getting up. He had a server like a boat's paddle, but flat. On the broad end of this he stood a ceramic bottle of well-warmed sake and, with a strong and perfectly steady hand, shoved it out across the room to the diner. The food was a set menu of a number of dishes, which maids brought in.

I gathered that as Ogi-san dispensed sake he also dispensed wit and drolleries. His remarks were lost on this foreign guest, but his personality came across strongly. I was sitting at one end of a bench next to a wall cupboard. Ogi-san motioned that I should open the cupboard and see what was inside. I hardly expected what I found—another collection, not of wooden dolls but of wooden phalli. They stood much as kokeshi dolls do, but some were of remarkable dimensions, taller than a sake bottle.

The lady guide who was at Robata reappeared next morning to take me to Matsushima. She found me trying to pay my hotel bill and the Dai-Ichi saying it didn't accept TCs (travellers' cheques: and these were from Cooks and drawn on Japan's leading Sumitomo Bank, and in yen). Nowhere else in Japan had this trouble occurred, but the front-desk man here kept insisting, very politely, that I must go to the bank across the road to change my TCs. Which I finally had to do.

At the Fuji Bank a very polite young lady had me fill in a brace of forms, then said she must see my passport, which was across at the hotel and had to be fetched. Then there was a twenty-minute wait while numerous people in the bank countersigned pieces of paper. To change a TC took an hour, a wasted hour.

I told the prefecture's officials that there might be more effective ways of discouraging foreign tourists from coming to Sendai, but off-hand I couldn't think of any. They sucked in air with the hissing sound that betokens worried Japanese and said they would do something about it.

About three million tourists a year go to Matsushima, and nearly all are Japanese. The 1 per cent who are foreigners include Koreans and Hong Kong Chinese as well as Americans, Europeans, Australians. So the Westerner is such a minority that, not too surprisingly, there isn't much emphasis on catering for his needs. But that does not mean that Westerners should skip Matsushima. Fine though it is to be looked after in exemplary fashion, how you are served is not, really, as important as what you see.

MATSUSHIMA DIARY. *Day 1* is 24 May 1974. Chiba-san was the director of tourism at Sendai, Iikawa-san the director at Matsushima. The guide was Miss Sumiko Torakawa, who lived at Matsushima and taught English at Sendai.

Day 1. By car to Matsushima, via boat-busy fishing port of Shiogama, takes

188   Off-track in Honshu

an hour. Best place to stay at Matsushima, says *Fodor's* 1973 *Guide*, is the Matsushima Park Hotel, which sounds very good. Trouble is it burned down years ago and hasn't been rebuilt. I'm booked into Hotel Taikanso.

Chiba-san, Iikawa-san and guide Sumiko come up to my room, are taken aback to find it Japanese-style. Surely I want a Western-style room with bed, they say, and Sumiko gets on phone to front desk. Yes, I can have Western room, but with no view. Say I'll stay where I am. Not that it's much view — wish I had a front room. Taikanso has hilltop situation overlooking the whole famous bay prospect of sea fragmented with islands. Big hotel, old and a bit scruffy as to appointments, fun-for-young facilities and strip show at night. Three of staff speak English.

After lunch, sightseeing. But it's raining, raining. Leaden sky and sea with islands reduced to blobs on murk. Go, all the same, to the designated viewing places, by car, with umbrellas.

Poet Edmund Blunden, Prof. of English at Tokyo University in twenties, was here. Slab of rock is incised with poem he wrote about Matsushima (quoted in full in Miyagi prefecture's English-language brochure) beginning

> *Melodious is that name Matsushima,*
> *Men love the place before they travel there*
> *And when they see those islands and those pines ...*

Definitely not Blunden at his best, but it's got him memorialized in slatestone.

Apart from bay's scenic archipelago of islands, Matsushima town's chief attractions (or is it only a village?) are its Wave-Viewing House (Kanrantei) which isn't in its best viewing mood in this rain but has museum exhibits including a fine sixteenth-century screen (and a shop where I fancy a small iron teapot and buy it) and the more-important Zuiganji Temple. A "national treasure" temple, 350 years old, opulent with painted screens and carving. We approach it through a towering colonnade of *sugi*-trees. The Sendai daimyo, Masamune Date, yearned for a better castle the Shogun wouldn't permit him to build, so Masamune put a hundred-odd carpenters to work for four years at building this temple, which he used as a second house.

Chiba-san says best viewing time is winter. Clear air and Japanese very conscious of how scene can be enhanced by snow. And moonlight — some houses here have moon-viewing roofs or balconies. No moon tonight, alas.

Major reason, I think, why relatively so few foreigners go to Matsushima is that it isn't on a tour route, a circuit such as takes the tourist from Tokyo to Kyoto–Nara–Kurashiki–Takamatsu–Kobe or Osaka and back to Tokyo. It isn't on the way to anywhere else the short-stay tourists go to. It doesn't fit in the "package".

More's the pity.

Day 2. Beautiful sun-bright day. Matsushima Bay looks fine from sixth-floor dining-room as I eat Japanese-style breakfast ordered as change from Western. (Mistake.) I'm being taken to best viewing places this morning, round islands by launch in afternoon.

By car to hill called Tomiyama, then climb a track to its top. Small temple where Buddhist priest lives, with his wife. Look out across green vegetation that canopies hills to wide prospect of islanded bay.

To another viewing place called Oku (means "back of", I think) Matsushima, reached by another track, 20 km from town. Grand view from this

Why the poet wrote "O! Matsushima" 189

hilltop, too. Foreground not so good, though—dump of soft drink cans, mostly Coca-Cola.

Third viewing place has most extensive prospect yet. Different view of waterway and islands than from other hills. This one is Jiyu-ga-mori: Jiyu was name of man who gave land for lookout.

Appetite from three hilltop climbs gets assuaged with excellent luncheon I'm taken to at one of loveliest restaurants yet, Taritsu-an, at Hamada, about 5 km from Matsushima, 10 mins by car. Recommended (but closed Fridays, reservation necessary, probably expensive). Room where we lunched overlooks bay and small island with thatch of pines. Resisted eating too much of *sashimi*, oysters, clam, octopus and special Tohoku soup made from kind of potato. V.g. food but don't want to be sleepy for main sightseeing event.

THE LAUNCH set off from Matsushima waterfront near an islet called Godaido, which is so close to the shore that it is joined to it by a short wooden bridge, lacquered scarlet. Wave action has sculptured Godaido from a squareish block of palest sandstone. In contrast to the curves of a concave side there is another surface as flat as a wall's, which gets printed with shadow patterns from the pine-trees that grow round the tiny temple Godaido is crowned with.

Behind Godaido quite a long bridge of scarlet wood runs out to a much larger island, Fukuura. Another of the close-in ones, Oshima, is joined by a short bridge to Togetsuko, where, I understand, there are hollowed-out caves that contain Buddhist images and were once used by priests in retreat. I was more interested in seeing the smaller, barer, isolated islets farther out in the bay—and these were to live up to my expectations by being some of the most curious and beautiful nature carving I've ever seen.

The first of these scenic oddities the launch brought me to was Yoroijima (*jima* or *shima* being "island"). As well as a delectable small island rather like Godaido, but innocent of any man-made structure, there was curved out of the water beside it a slim rock something like a wave about to break, which was such a graceful form that one could well have admired it in the forecourt of some modern building.

More holes are to be found in these islands than in the sculptures of Henry Moore. One end of Kanejima could be a rugged try at modelling a viaduct. Another arch was of a size that let our launch go through. Kurojima is tunnelled right through at the base of a high mass of rock that has just enough soil and crevices to root half a dozen pines. Komurozaki, also curiously caverned and contoured, has but one single pine. That tree leans out at such an angle you would think a gale would have torn it loose long ago. It is at exactly the right angle to complement the line of the rock it somehow clings to—and the branches of this pine could have been designed by Hokusai. Islet after island is not so much vegetated with pines as *decorated* with them.

There is too much tagging of natural forms with names of things they are seen as resembling (guides are forever pointing out a Lion's Head or a Candlestick or The Three Kings) but there are two columnar shapes that, at the ends of two of the islands, preside over the sea as though they were stone idols.

The strangest islet shape of all is Niojima's. It is quite pineless, a bare all-rock grotesquerie that could be said to have a "head" on a well-defined "neck"; and the form of that "head" is something so arrestingly peculiar that it does rather invite the viewer to fantasize about what it is that erosion has wrought—something as absurd as "Donald Duck's Impersonation of Attila the Hun" or as surreal as "Skull of the Sphinx."

Some of the larger islands are inhabited—Katsura for one—and another that is large is Sabusawa, which forms one side of a strait. Once you pass through this strait you are in oyster-growing waters thick with stakes and rafts, and the passage is not nearly so interesting. Excursion boats take tourists among these islands, but ideally a private launch with an English-speaking guide should be hired for at least three hours. I could have taken more of this kind of off-beat scenery, which is certainly better than anything seen from the steamers plying the Inland Sea.

BACK at the Taikanso hotel I put on my *yakata* and slippers and took the lift to the fifth floor for a Japanese-style bath. Half-a-dozen men were soaking, and when I had washed myself outside the bath I joined them in it.

This was a great bath. It was big, it was round, and it revolved. Sitting just inside the rim immersed to the waist, as the bath went slowly round you could see through the glass wall the scene of the island-fretted bay, with the blue darkening as the sun went down in another sea to the west, and the beginnings of dusk thickening in the pines.

I had no doubt that I was in the best bath-with-view in Japan, and could quite understand why Basho went in for

O! O! Matsushima O!

kyushu, the south

南の九州

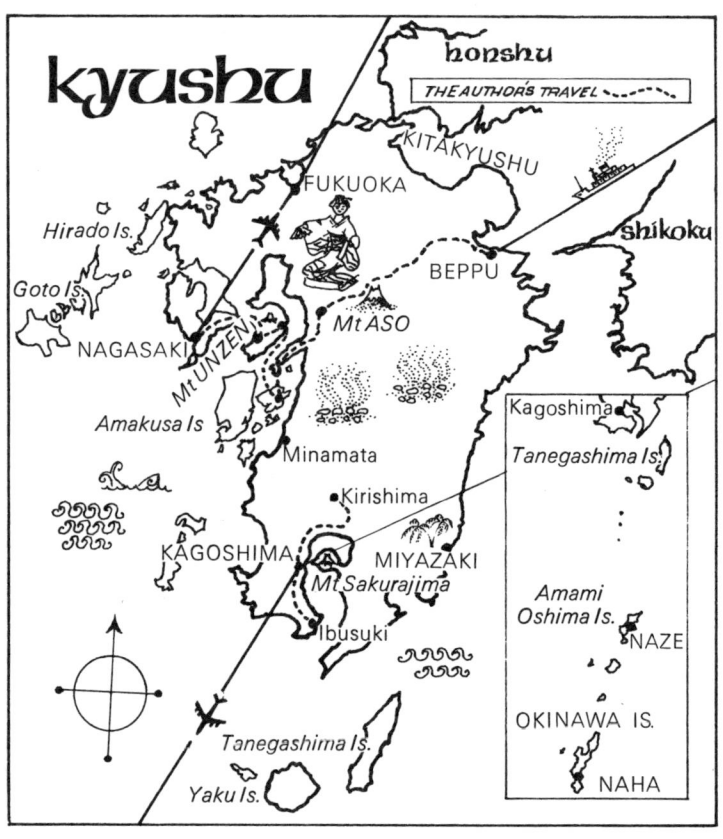

Steamy Beppu and Aso's volcano

STEAM gushed white out of the pine-dark mountainside I looked out on from my room at the biggest hotel in Beppu. Even closer at hand, just up the street, two columns of smoke rose as though, behind the pines there, two old-style locomotives were puffing at a railway station.

There were thousands of such vents in the Kyushu lid of a great subterranean cauldron. And the landscape gave the impression of having just been laundered, so cleanly bright was this eastern Kyushu air. I didn't remember it being like that at the industrial top of the island. Before this trip I had been in Japan's southernmost large island for less than a day: waiting for a plane to Tokyo in the city of Fukuoka-Hakata. (Hakata, famous for its dolls, is the city's older part on the east side of the river.) It was then the largest city in Kyushu. In 1963 five industrial cities on the northern tip of the island combined to make Kitakyushu the largest, with more than a million people.

One of the five cities of this Kitakyushu complex, Moji, was picked to be the target for the second atomic bomb the Americans dropped in August 1945. When the B-29 came over, Moji was obscured by cloud, and it was the alternative target, Nagasaki, that shared the awful fate of Hiroshima.

Although Fukuoka (pron. Foo-koo-aw-ka) is the most modern metropolis in western Japan and has a flourishing amusement quarter, it is not for that kind of thing that foreign tourists leave Tokyo. Nor are they likely to be attracted to heavy industry such as the great Yahata steelworks of Kitakyushu.

Japanese in their thousands flock to Kyushu—they know its charms—but it is never seen by most foreign tourists. The majority don't get beyond the Tokyo–Kyoto–Nara circuit. Up to now those who did get to Kyushu were likely to have come as I did, via the Inland Sea.

Since 1973 there has been a new way of getting to Kyushu or, for that matter, of getting to Japan. The opening of an international airport at Kagoshima at the southern end of the island has provided another gateway for the air traveller. Coming from Australia, this is the nearest way in. I flew from Sydney with Japan Air Lines and I went through to Tokyo, but I could have got off in Hong Kong and taken JAL's service from there to Kagoshima. Coming out, what I did was to leave from Kagoshima.

BEPPU is the biggest spa resort in Japan, which abounds in spas. It is visited by no fewer than eight million tourists a year. Catering for them were some eight hundred accommodation places, mostly *ryokans*, Japanese inns.

The vast Sugenoi Hotel, where I stayed overnight, takes two thousand guests. It is out of the city proper, set against mountains, and is so much a pleasure dome as well as a first-class hotel that many vacationers spend all their time within its complex of elaborate hot-spring bathing pools set about

194 Kyushu, the South

with luxuriant indoor jungle, the bowling alley, the ice-skating rink, the golf driving range, the performances on the stage of the theatre-restaurant, the children's amusement area with dodgem cars, and the hotel's huge hot-house of tropical plants. Room charges were reasonable and meals were distinctly cheaper than in comparable hotels in Tokyo.

The hot springs that bubble up from beneath the hotel, usually blue in colour and sulphurous of smell, are said to benefit rheumatism, respiratory ailments and just about anything from dyspepsia to asthma. But nowhere in Beppu could I find the "sand baths" the resort used to be famous for: you lay in a dug-out depression on the sea beach and attendants with shovels covered you with hot sand, which was supposed to cook all aches away. Harbourworks had taken the beach where this went on.

Beppu's situation is on a large bay and at the foot of two volcanoes, which were not worrisome; the last eruption was in the seventeenth century. As a city Beppu was hardly impressive, and from one vantage point it looked almost industrial, with smoke rising everywhere. But this was steam from some of the three thousand vents that are fitted with pipes and chimneys and provide homes with natural hot-water services.

What one goes to see are the *jigoku* or "hells", the boiling ponds and mudpool solfataras. The steaming water at the Chinoike Jigoku is, due to the iron in it, almost blood-red. Another's water is green, from iron sulphate. A pond of boiling mud is known as the Bozu (Priest) Jigoku because the bubbles rise in the shape of a Buddhist priest's shaven head.

MY SIGHTSEEING, since I am to have only six days in Kyushu, has to be selective. So I do not go by cable car to the summit of volcanic Mt Tsurumi for the view; nor do I go to see the monkeys that live on Mt Takasaki. By mid-morning we are leaving Beppu.

Takashi Nagaoka, my companion-guide from JNTO, having arranged the car hire, we head west along an excellent highway that soon has us at a resort centre called Kajima Heights. The air is cool and bright. Another big hotel, the Beppu Grand, is set beside a golf course with fairways that are end-of-summer brown. So are the mountains dry and tawny, bare-flanked more often than pine-clad, and their subtle browns under a blue sky are beautiful. The roadsides are plumed with a tall grass that leans with the breeze and shakes its head and is lovely against the light. It is with me all the way in Kyushu at this autumn season and is one of the joys of the trip, this *susuki* grass.

As we sped along the Yamanami Highway, a toll road, I reflected that the road system had improved several hundred per cent since I was first in Japan. Then I wondered whether foreign tourists could do this trip without a guide. Our driver spoke no English; but he said, through Tak, that he knew two other drivers who did. At the roadhouse where we stopped for lunch it was good to have Tak there to say, "How would you like to have the *sanzoku yaki*—that means 'mountain robbers' grill'—with vegetables that grow up here on Asahi-dai, as this plateau is called? There's this plant *zenmai* and a mountain potato, *yama-umo*."

MOUNT ASO we start to climb when we are nearly a hundred kilometres from Beppu. This is Kyushu's most active volcano, and its crater basin is the largest active one in the world.

Aerial view of volcanic Mount Akan in Hokkai

Lake Mashu in Hokkaido is said to have "an air of mystery"—and it does have a strangeness that photographs don't convey, a mood that suggests that something more than mirror-still water is cupped in the great hand of mountains.

Sapporo, a city of 800,000 people and capital of Japan's northmost island, Hokkaido, gets a lot of winter snow, from November through March. Its annual Snow Festival, held in February, has spectacular sculptures made from ice.

The Ainu headman of Shiraoi village near Noboribetsu, wearing the old regalia, told visitors how the hirsute aboriginal people of Hokkaido used to live.

This, the last of the photographs, was taken by the late Torao Saito, to whose memory the book is dedicated. Wooden utensils so aesthetically crafted to designs of such tasteful simplicity are truly Japanese, as he was.

Steamy Beppu and Aso's volcano

Mt Aso is not one peak but five. We go to Nakadake, the only peak that is active. Its summit appears to be gouged with one huge crater but, down there beneath the clouds of steam, there is one vent pooled with boiling mud and another that is constantly ejecting gas and steam and that on occasions throws out volcanic ash and rocks. Nakadake's eruption in 1958 killed six people and destroyed the cable car that used to go most of the way up. Now there is a road to the top. In case the volcano should suddenly start throwing stones again there are concrete pillboxes to take shelter in—though this is unlikely to happen without warning, because the eruptions are now predictable and if there is danger visitors are not allowed to go up to the crater.

While you are still a long way off, before the road even begins to climb the mountain, something of the menace of Aso manifests itself in the jagged line the summit draws, dark and bare, against the sky. Then the road goes up, and down again into the caldera—the volcanic basin formed by the vast original crater caving in to make a valley eighty kilometres in circumference—and there are emerald hillsides with horses and cattle grazing peacefully and children having pony rides.

We went on in the direction of the billowing smoke the wind was dragging across the summit of Nakadake, which is 1,323 metres high. The wind got keener as we ascended, and at the top it was bitterly cold on this autumn day and I was very glad I had a topcoat.

The fissure the smoke was rising from was at the bottom of what was like a great gulch. This is as deep as 160 metres and over half a kilometre across to where you see a striated grey cliff, built up by layer upon layer of lava and ash from eruptions that have been going on for thousands of years. The volume of steam was such that the bottom of the crater was obscured as by a rolling mist. It is an awesome place in a sombre way and bare as the surface of the moon.

A couple of months before there had been a minor eruption. The shivering sellers of medallions and poster-sized photographs of erupting Aso—who set out their wares on trestle tables just a few feet from the crater's edge—had had to pack and go, and no visitors were allowed for some weeks. In 1965 it belched out quantities of ash that the wind carried as far as Kumamoto, which was a half-hour's drive away, and where we would stay the night.

Kumamoto, a sexy old stronghold

KUMAMOTO came at the end of a road that ran, at first, through a valley with haystacked fields of rice harvest and a golf-coursed resort, and then had mountainsides patched with autumn colouring of rhus and maple and the *icho*-tree that glows as yellow as the brightest elm.

It was a powerful stronghold in feudal Japan, this Kumamoto, Kyushu's third city: in population it is just ahead of Nagasaki's. It is where Lafcadio Hearn came in 1890 to teach at the government college for three not-very-happy years and where, some twenty years earlier, the Emperor visited the school and the wife of an American teacher presented the Son of Heaven with a bouquet. The Japanese were horrified. A bunch of cut flowers! This, as Hearn wrote, was regarded as "a vulgar murdering of flowers...an abomination".

We were booked into a modern-looking hotel called the New Sky, which had ¥3,000 single rooms that were very small, but each had a bathroom, television (colour, of course), ice-water tap and tea-making facilities.

Seldom did we eat in a hotel, and this evening Tak found a sit-at-the-counter seafood restaurant—a recommendable place named Ohtoyo in Shimo-dori—that served excellent crab, good tempura and mussels that were very fresh-tasting. These are relatively expensive dishes. When we went later to a plushy bar called the President it cost ¥4,720 for two whiskies and a drink each for the two hostesses who had promptly joined us. Here, as in Tokyo with its rocketing prices, hostess bars seemed to be a waste of money.

We very soon left this bar, and almost immediately Kumamoto made it plain that sexual titillation was to be had much more cheaply and in far greater measure than any bar could provide. STRIP TEASE offered the sign over a doorway men were disappearing into.

"I've never seen a striptease," Tak said. I said, "Be my guest," and didn't pay more than two dollars each for us at the door.

I recollected a Japanese strip show of sorts back in 1955 with a coy lady in a kimono displaying first one poached egg and then the other. Then there was an imported performer with more bounce and bosom who wore only a G-string. Probably, I thought, a show in provincial Kumamoto would be somewhere between the two. Well, I've been wrong before.... Nowhere in Europe or Asia, not in Paris's Place Pigalle and certainly not in Tokyo, have I seen anything like what we just walked in off the street and saw at Kumamoto.

The panting simulation of orgasm that accompanied female masturbation performed on a revolving mirror was more than matched by one of the performers in a vigorous exhibition of what lesbians can do. For the rest, the girls began with some twirls of dancing, then the slow disrobe to nakedness, followed by the donning of a short transparent nightie that did not interfere with a full genital display to the customers, while sitting back on their heels, legs wide apart.

This took place on a catwalk that projected from the tiny stage, and there were some seats down either side; but most of the (all-male) audience was standing, as we were. It was, if you like, obscene: not that there is anything indecent about genitalia as such, but where female flesh is exhibited like steak in a meat market the display becomes indecent because it is degrading. At the same time it was funny—or, rather, one of the spectators was. A fat young man who peered through thick spectacles, he gave the impression that he had not only never seen a clitoral area before but feared that he might never see one again. So he was out of his seat at full stretch and craning, his eyes popping out of his flushed face—and apparently oblivious of the fact that he was causing a good deal of amusement.

The place was packed. One man I should not have wanted to be present is Bernard Rudofsky, the author of an admirable book[1] in which he wrote what used to be true: *The nude is seen in Japan but not looked at.*

KUMAMOTO was heavily bombed in the Second World War; but the castle that was pivotal to the city's power was destroyed for the most part by besieging forces in 1877. Now Kumamoto Castle looks more imposing than it ever did. In 1960 it was reconstructed in ferroconcrete. Of Japanese castles are all built to a pattern, and a very handsome pattern it is: multi-storeyed, they rise pyramidally, the roofs curved and usually gabled, to a single-roofed structure at the top. The tiles are invariably grey and the walls white. Each Castle is reared high on a very strong stone-walled base, with the kind of stone wall you see flanking the Imperial Palace in Tokyo. These walls are never vertical, always slanted. They do not come out in a straight slant but with a slight inward curvature. This strengthens the wall against the push of rain-sodden earth behind it; it also makes the stone foundation better able to withstand earthquakes. The curvature is quite pronounced in the wall of Kumamoto's Castle, which was once one of the strongpoints of a very war-minded nation.

It was only ten years after the 1945 defeat of Japanese militarism when I first came to Japan, and a common sight at places tourists thronged to, such as Tokyo's Meiji Shrine, was a band of white-clad war veterans busking with musical instruments such as the concertina. Some were blind and most were amputees with hooks for the hands that weren't holding out collection boxes, into which I used to drop coins. They didn't collect much because of their own people's rejection of them with the attitude of, "If you couldn't win the war you had no right to come back from it." This practice of ex-soldiers begging was later forbidden. In any case, in 1973 the war was a long time over and the Japanese who had been sent off to it when he was twenty was now around fifty. I never expected to see those pathetic white figures again.

Yet, as we went up the road to Kumamoto Castle under the autumnal cherry-trees, here were two of them. A standing one with the concertina and a kneeling one who had no legs below the knees, a supplicant who supported himself with his two arms forward, hands on the ground.

A tourist party of college girls was coming down the road. I didn't *see* any of them look in passing at the beggar soldiers, though an amputee with red-stockinged stumps is hard to ignore; but I had my eye in the camera's view-

198 Kyushu, the South

finder. I like to think that the picture I took is more than a portrait of a generation gap, and that if it portrays rejection it is not rejection of war's victims but of war itself.

THE CASTLE was built at Kumamoto in 1607. The daimyo was Kiyomasa Kato, lord of what was then called the province of Higo.

Kiyomasa remembered that he had won a victory in Korea because the enemy was short of food and water—so he had many wells dug in his castle grounds, and he planted gingko-trees, of which the nuts can be eaten. But the principal provender he stocked his castle with was dried potato roots. Of these papery roots, instead of reeds, he had the *tatami* mats made. In a siege emergency you could cook your flooring and eat it.

Kiyomasa found another use for *zuiki*, the dried potato roots. When he went to Edo (as Tokyo was then called) to pay tribute to the shogun he took quantities of this material with him and gave it to women of the shogun's household, who welcomed the light fibres that could be used for lining winter kimonos for warmth, instead of the heavier conventional lining which made the garments wearisome to wear.

Of this *Higo zuiki* the shogun's ladies soon had more than they needed for kimono lining—and they, through some unrecorded experimenting, found a new use for the fibres. The ladies found that *zuiki* could be fashioned into a dildo that, when moistened, felt very agreeable. They also found that the pleasures of heterosexual intercourse could be enhanced by phallic fitments in the form of rings and ticklers made from these dried potato roots.

So if you ask in Kumamoto what is the distinctive souvenir product of the place you will be told, with a smile or a giggle, "*Higo zuiki*". Which means nothing until you are shown in the shops, which have them on display in the window, the made-up articles, as fancily boxed as a cosmetics set but requiring rather more explanation.

After the end of the Kato clan's rule in Kumamoto came a daimyo who laid out, in 1632, a landscape garden that is known as Suizenji Park. Travellers who have seen Ritsurin Park at Takamatsu or Korakuen Park at Okayama should not expect their stroll through Suizenji to be as rewarding. City and commerce press in upon the garden's limited area.

Perhaps the best thing to do is simply to take tea in a pavilion that was once an adjunct of the lovely Katsura Imperial Villa in Kyoto and was transferred here. There is a small raked sand garden and a beautiful stone water holder, and the view across the peaceful pond is the nicest vista in the whole place.

THE WESTERN SIDE of Kyushu is fragmented into either islands or peninsulas that nearly sever from the mainland and become other islands. This makes for good coastal scenery, plenty of harbours, and a smaller version of the Inland Sea called the Ariake.

Going from Kumamoto to Nagasaki we reached the Ariake Sea at Misumi, where you can take a boat and reach Nagasaki sooner. But a better way is to keep driving south across the five bridges linking with the mainland five of the Amakusa Islands.

This is a route with sea views interspersing land views on the rugged islands that were cut off from the mainland until the five bridges were completed

Kumamoto, a sexy old stronghold 199

in 1966. So the gas station (which is often literally that, with so many taxis and other cars using LPG instead of petrol) and the roadside restaurant and souvenir shop have come to the islands that used to live by fishing, pearl growing, doll making, pottery and extracting oil from the seeds of camellias. Roadside ricefields are being cut into building blocks and industry is not improving the scene; but some lovely old thatched farmhouses remain.

Beads on a giant's abacus they looked like, the bobbles out on the water that were the glass buoys supporting wire trays of pearl oysters. They patterned a sea that was brilliant on this sunny blue day, and they were offshore from humpy little islands that were hairy with pines.

On the last of the bridge-joined islands we go up to a viewing place and look out over a wide vista of islanded sea. A ferry is coming in, and we take it for an hour-and-a-half's crossing to Shimabara on the big peninsula that peaks up to Mount Unzen. It is a good ferry with comfortable seats. We buy lunch boxes, complete with chopsticks, such as sustain the travelling Japanese.

Near Shimabara the seascape is lovely with islets, pine-pricked and some with beaches of that Japanese rarity, white sand. Fishing boats attested that the Ariake Sea was a great contributor of seafood to the Japanese table. But now there was fear of this fish, for the waters here had been industrially polluted and with mercury, which had given rise to the awful affliction known as Minamata Disease.

Minamata City is on Yatsushiro Bay further down the coast we left at Misumi, just south of the Sea of Ariake. Mercury went into the sea there as waste from the works making caustic soda and using mercury as a catalyst (a method now prohibited). Five hundred residents of Minamata got the disease from eating fish that had ingested mercury and become poisonous. Some were paralyzed, others went blind: sixty of the victims died. Panic swept Japan and sales of fish from Kyushu waters slumped. In 1973 there were other sufferers from Minamata Disease, and this time they were from towns and villages along the Sea of Ariake.

As the boat came in to Shimabara I could see on a small island a large white cross. It is a memorial to the Japanese Christians who died here in the seventeenth century. At Shimabara they made their last stand against the persecution of their religion by the Tokugawa shogunate. They seized the local castle and resisted valiantly for three months. The Dutch, under pressure from the shogun and fearful of having their trading privileges at Nagasaki withdrawn, did something of which Dutch historians are not proud. They sent a warship that bombarded the castle. Thirty thousand Christians were either killed in the assault or massacred after the castle had fallen.

MOUNT UNZEN is an inactive volcano that rises to 1,360 metres in the centre of the peninsula. The road to it runs alongside orchards of tangerines and oranges, vineyards and fields of vegetables. The mountain's slopes at that time were past their prime of autumn coloration but were still touched vividly with the red of rhus-trees.

The *susuki* grass by the road that ascends into pine forest is lovely against the sunlight. But the sun is hazed, and the distance appears as through a thick gauze screen. Yet there is not a cloud in the sky. Is it, then, that some industrial villainy is polluting the atmosphere, creating a sunny-day smog?

"No," our taxi-driver tells Tak. "It is from China. Sometimes the sand in the region of the Yellow River blows in on the wind from the west and dirties our air."

So, although we go up by cable car to the summit of Mt Unzen, we do not see the vaunted panorama; but the muzzy view suggests that it could be remarkable.

Coming down, the cable car is crowded, but we were among the first aboard and we get seats. Two oldish women are standing and we get up. One of the women takes Tak's seat, but before the other can take mine a man plumps his bottom into it.

Nagasaki: A flavour of foreigners

A NEWSPAPER HEADLINE that never appeared, I hope: U.S. BOMB DESTROYS LARGEST CHURCH IN FAR EAST.

Some other effects of the dropping of the atomic bomb on the city of Nagasaki (on 9 August 1945, three days after the destruction of Hiroshima) were the killing of approximately seventy-four thousand people, the injuring of as many more, and the ruin of some fifteen thousand units of housing. So it would have been indecent to headline the destruction of the Urakami Roman Catholic Cathedral, which had a seating capacity of six thousand.

Most Christians would have been surprised to learn that such a large church existed in this or any other Japanese city. Nor would they expect Nagasaki to have a large sculptural monument to Christian martyrs, twenty-six of them. They were crucified, and the Vatican has made them all saints. Twenty of the twenty-six were Japanese. The crucifixions took place in 1597.

In 1571 the first European ship, a Portuguese vessel, arrived at Nagasaki; but Christianity arrived before that, at Kagoshima, with the great Jesuit missionary Francis Xavier in 1549. It was on the four-hundredth anniversary of St Francis Xavier's arrival—May 1949—that the crucifixion site was dedicated as Nishizaka Park, where the sculptural memorial wall with twenty-six figures was to be erected; and that was only four years after the Christian enemy had dropped its atomic bombs.

It was at Nagasaki that Christianity took firmest root in Japan. By 1581 there were two hundred churches in the country, most of them in Kyushu. Eleven daimyos had become converts, and by the end of that century there were half a million Christians.

Then the crackdown came. The Shogun felt that his nobles were embracing Christianity in order to get European firearms that might be used in revolt against the shogunate; some Christian missionaries inflamed their converts against Shinto "idolatry", and Buddhist temples were burnt and priests killed. That kind of Inquisition went into reverse when the faith was banned.

After two revolts by Japanese Jesuits were suppressed, in 1639 the Portuguese were expelled. The Dutch were the only Europeans allowed henceforth to trade with Japan. And the Dutch were allowed only to occupy the harbour island of Dejima. There the Dutch traders operated for 214 years. For that time Japan was otherwise closed to the Western world.

Dejima Island has become, due to foreshore reclamations, part of the mainland. There is nothing there that is really redolent of its role as the tiny pipeline through which the Western ideas were sucked into Japan by a few ardent scholars.

At the time of the Meiji Restoration in 1868 discovery of a body of Japanese Christians who had secretly maintained their faith gave rise to the erection of the Catholic cathedral in the Nagasaki suburb of Urakami, and it became the largest Christian church in the Orient.

NAGASAKI was a prospering port of trade with China and Korea when Tokyo was little more than a fishing village. The first thing—but not the only thing—that makes Nagasaki different from other Japanese cities is that all the foreigners whose gateway to Japan it was have left their mark on it.

Chinese is the style of the oldest stone bridge in Japan, arching over a Nagasaki stream. Portuguese sponge cake is still served and there was *Portugaise* soup on the menu at the Nagasaki Grand Hotel where we stayed, and where we found in the dining-room very good food described as *Hollandi Shippoku*, a West-East combination that owed much to the Dutch. There is still a roadway called Holland Slope, the first street in Japan to have a footpath

The Americans were to come to the other coast demanding the opening of trade; but it is not generally known that in the same year (1853) as Commodore Perry did that, a Russian envoy came to Nagasaki and made the same sort of demand. The British, through a Scot named Glover, were to leave more of a mark than anyone else.

Physically, what makes Nagasaki different from other Japanese main cities is that it is stacked on three sides with hills. Between the hills the city nestles, the river debouches, the sea reaches in to make the harbour.

One of these hills is perhaps better called a mountain, and from Inasadake (Mt Inasa) there is a superb panoramic view, over the city and right out beyond the islands studding the open sea. It is well worth going to this summit by the cable car, or you can drive as we did right up the well-wooded mountainside that was still wearing some autumn vermilion in November. The view from the top is a full 360 degrees and there are few places in Japan where you will see its like.

As to Nagasaki's atomic bomb horror, our sensibilities blunt so easily. One writer (and a Japanese one at that) writes of Hiroshima having "nothing but the atom bomb to boast about" and adds, "Nagasaki could boast about *its* bomb if it felt that way, but it doesn't." Worse, I think, a well-known (Western) guidebook covers Nagasaki without mentioning the A-bomb at all.

I went to the A-bomb Museum at Nagasaki and had the same reaction as at the museum in Hiroshima: the photographs of bodies like burnt-up sausages and survivors with hideous burns were too much and I soon came away. On the way out I noticed hanging on the wall a shattered clock with its spring hanging out and the hands still pointing to two minutes past eleven. That was when, on the morning of 9 August 1945, the bomb released from the B-29 exploded when it was perhaps 500 metres above the riverside area of Nagasaki that is about of five kilometres from the Mitsubishi shipyard that was regarded as a prime target; but it did destroy Mitsubishi's arms factory and the Mitsubishi steelworks, where fourteen hundred workers died. The following day Japan announced surrender.

At least the monuments at Nagasaki and Hiroshima are peace memorials, not war memorials. However, the immense statue in Nagasaki's Peace Park is not very good as a memorial or as a sculpture. It is too pious, there is no protest in it, and it is too gesticulatory, with one hand pointing to the sky whence came the bomb and the other outstretched hand counselling peace and the eyes closed in prayer for the victims and the seated pose suggesting meditation. Still it does make its mighty presence felt (the statue is 9.7 metres high), and while I looked several Japanese stopped in front of it and prayed in the Buddhist manner.

A simple vertical slab of black marble marks the hypocentre of the explosion that destroyed about a third of the city. There is a remnant of the wall of the Urakami Catholic Cathedral. Also rebuilt, in its Gothic-spired style, was Oura Catholic Church which was partially destroyed. Near the church a souvenir shop sold dolls dressed not in kimonos but as nuns.

In the course of a taxi tour of the city I went briefly up to the Foreigner's Cemetery, as it is signboarded, where old tombstones are lettered with names as British as JEMIMA LINKLATER, as German as FRITZ VON ZANDER, and some others were French, Dutch, American and Indian.

THE GLOVER HOUSE—which is a better description than the much-used Glover Mansion—is a graceful Western-style residence with wide colonial verandas and admirably roofed with grey Japanese tiles. Single-storeyed, it is set in gardened grounds on a knoll above the harbour.

Thomas Blake Glover, a Scot who came to Nagasaki in 1859, could well have afforded to put up an ostentatious mansion, because he was making a lot of money out of being what nobody in the nineteenth century would have dreamed of calling a "merchant of death". He sold arms to the daimyos of the various clans.

In the same year as he built his fine house, 1865, he laid the first railway track in Japan, along the Nagasaki waterfront, and he imported from Shanghai a goods locomotive to run on it. As well, Glover opened a coalmine, established a shipyard and arranged for Japanese to study in England. A Japanese notice board says he "contributed in no small measure to our culture".

For some reason the Puccini opera story of *Madam Butterfly* has got itself entwined with Glover, who took a Japanese wife. There is a Madam Butterfly Garden in the vicinity, set with sentimental statuary, and Japanese guides have been known to cater to the strong streak of romanticism in their countrymen by feeding them the whole story as a true happening, with Glover as the original of Lieutenant Pinkerton.

You look across from Glover's grounds to where, on the other side of the harbour, prows and sterns rise high and, with the flicker of welders' torches and the rat-a-tat of riveting, proclaim the big Mitsubishi shipbuilding yard.

That night in a Nagasaki bar I got to talking with a young man named Hiroyuki who worked in one of the Mitsubishi shipyards—there are two, and between them they employ sixteen thousand men—and he said that they were about to build a tanker of 450,000 tons. He thought that in about five years they would be building million-tonners. Hiroyuki-san got a wage of ¥9,000 a month plus a yearly bonus equal to six months' wages, making ¥13,500 a month, which was about $A80 a week.

He said the workforce, which was covered by three trade unions, was a happy one, and Tak translated Hiroyuki as saying, "We are proud of working for a company as big as Mitsubishi."

FOREIGN businessmen who come to Nagasaki to deal with Mitsubishi Heavy Industries Ltd are sometimes entertained not in the city itself but eleven kilometres out at the little fishing port of Mogi. Getting to Mogi is a delightful drive past lushly wooded hillsides plumed with bamboo and many orchards of loquats and the sweet Satsuma oranges.

At Mogi is an unobtrusive but very good restaurant named Futami. Its private dining-rooms opening onto little balconies are right beside the water. Futami is not expensive as these places go, but the cheapest meal in a private room would cost at least ¥2,000 each. Tak and I had the meal the restaurant is famous for: it included such specialties as a delicious *hors d'oeuvre* of a seaweed found only in Nagasaki waters and grilled shellfish. As well as tempura we got a *tai* fish grilled and served with egg and warmed peanuts. The tourist without a guide who comes out to Mogi for lunch or dinner could have a problem, because nobody at Futami spoke English.

When Mitsubishi entertains executives of a foreign firm that has ordered, say, a tanker, no expense is spared. Half a dozen geisha may be brought from Nagasaki and a Japanese banquet for ten guests at Futami can cost as high as ¥250,000 (over $A600).

Nagasaki is regarded as the best city in Japan for Chinese food, because of its closeness to China-Korea and its long history of Chinese contact. The Chinese presence in the city is attested by several temples which, after Shinto shrines, seemed very gaudy. The Confucian temple built in 1967 was particularly garish.

The new gateway is Kagoshima

SUPPOSE your stay in Japan is drawing to a close and you haven't seen anything of Kyushu. You can do what I did and see Kagoshima on your way out.

As was mentioned earlier, since Kagoshima got an international airport in 1973 it is a gateway to or from Japan that is an alternative to Tokyo, provided that you fly Japan Air Lines and that you go via Hong Kong. JAL cannot fly you Tokyo–Kagoshima, but there is a good service, which I took, by ANA (All Nippon Airways) which was using Boeing 727 jets and did the direct trip in an hour and forty minutes.

No sooner was it on the international air route than Kagoshima set about getting itself on the tourist map in no half-hearted fashion. By October 1973 it had a fifty-man tourist mission in Australia led by the prefectural governor. In Sydney, Brisbane and Perth (which has become Kagoshima's "sister city" in Australia) it proclaimed the attractions of the "Naples of Japan".

The comparison was valid enough, physically at any rate: Kagoshima, too, was on a fine wide bay flanked by a large and still-active volcano. The local Vesuvius is 1,180-metres-high Sakurajima. *Jima* means island and Sakurajima was one until its 1914 eruption turned it into a peninsula by filling with lava the channel between it and the mainland. Some earnest statistician has figured that Sakurajima has now expelled three billion tons of lava. This has formed a bizarre landscape of tumbled hunks of rock, through which runs a good sealed road that extends for fifty-two kilometres right round the island. The volcano is on the other side of the harbour, right opposite the city, and is reached by a twenty-minute ferry ride.

From one of the three craters—only one is still active—there is always some smoke. The drive through the lava field is safe enough; vulcanologists monitor the volcano's moods and if it shows itself choleric road traffic in the vicinity of the summit is stopped.

There is a spa resort on one shore of Sakurajima, a town named Furusato with hotels people flock to for the hot springs—which also come bubbling up in Kagoshima City. The volcanic soil is extraordinarily fertile and produces not only loquats and oranges that are said to be particularly tasty but a *daikan* like an enormous white radish: these can grow as big as prize pumpkins and weigh as much as thirty kilos.

Sakurajima as seen from my hotel room was always a dramatic backdrop to the city, whether with the morning sunlight on its raddled slopes, or dark against the evening sky when sunset was dyeing the bay, or as a black presence barely discernible by moonlight beyond the neon-lit city's glare.

The hotel that commanded this view, the Shiroyama Kanko, had eighty-three Western-style rooms and about half as many in Japanese style. It was so popular with Japanese tourists (who filled nearly all the Western rooms) that it was being enlarged. As to foreigners, the hotel was still in process of finding out about what they required in the way of room service, but the management seemed eager to please.

WESTERNERS began coming to Kagoshima in 1549. The first Europeans to set foot on Japanese soil did so earlier on the island of Tanegashima in what is now Kagoshima prefecture. That was in 1543. The first-footers were Portuguese on a ship in charge of an adventurous trader (and writer) Fernão Mendes Pinto. The ship was bound for China when a storm drove it to Tanegashima, where Pinto sold the Japanese their first firearms. The Portuguese firearms got an enthusiastic reception, and at Kagoshima (then called Satsuma) the daimyo was all cordiality when another Portuguese ship arrived there in 1549, with the Spanish Jesuit priest who was to become St Francis Xavier. The lord of Satsuma welcomed the missionary representing a civilization that had evolved killing instruments so manifestly superior to the sword and the arrow and gave him permission to preach.

When, however, the Society of Jesus gathered some 600 converts in a matter of months, the Buddhist hierarchy began to protest, the cordiality of the lord, Takahisa Shimazu, cooled, and within a year Xavier departed for other places, where the conversions continued. Xavier felt very warmly towards the Japanese. He wrote that no other heathen race would ever be found to equal the people he called "the delight of my heart". Certainly they were quick to learn.

Japan's first blast furnace was built at Kagoshima in 1852 by the ruling Shimazu in what was still a feudal society. Predictably, among the first products of the furnace were a cannon, swords, land mines and a torpedo. The cannon can still be seen in the museum, in the building where the furnace used to be, in what were the grounds of the lord's mansion and are now the lovely Iso gardens. This progressive Nariakira Shimazu also started cotton spinning, introduced photography, ran a telegraph line from his castle to a retreat in the gardens, and put a gas lamp in one of the stone lanterns.

The Shimazu summer villa set in the Iso gardens—beside the sea and looking across to smoke-plumed Sakurajima—is where the mother of the present Empress of Japan was reared. The house was built, of Japanese cedar, in the seventeenth century, and rebuilt and redecorated in 1881. Painted wooden panels include a beautifully composed one of chrysanthemums. Anyone can look into the main reception room, but traditional wooden buildings built for nobility and their soft-footed servants would not withstand thousands of tourists trooping through. I was privileged: shoes off, I was shown through the villa by the president of Shimazu Industries, in which the still-rich Shimazu descendants hold half the shares. An offshoot company, Shimazu Kanko, operates the gardens as a tourist attraction. The gardens are backed by a lushly forested mountain, Isoyama, with a cable car running to its summit for the view.

I was there in November, and the Iso gardens had, I think, the finest display of chrysanthemums I have seen anywhere—and that is saying a great deal after two Japanese autumns, two seasons of surprise at what chrysanthemum cultivators can contrive.

These gardens are virtually a year-round joy, with plum blossom in early February, cherry-trees blooming in mid-March, tulips in April, azaleas in

May and then, after the summer show, the bright maples of October. The cruise liners *Oronsay* and *Orcades* from Australia had begun calling at Kagoshima, and their tourists were taken to the Iso gardens. Then they went shopping.

Perhaps the most noteworthy Kagoshima "buy" is Satsuma pottery, which is a highly regarded development of a Korean type of ware. I prefer the black Satsuma to the creamy-coloured kind, which usually has flowery decoration that most people find alluring. Quite distinctive is a hand-loomed fabric of a silken kind called Oshima pongee or *Oshima tsumugi* which is specially attractive in its texture and comes in some interesting patterns and colours: it can be bought by the metre or made up into such articles as purses that are affordable—but if a woman wanted a kimono made of best-quality Oshima pongee it could cost, with the *haori* coat, as much as ¥138,000 (say $A350). Bamboo ware is in great variety at Kagoshima. All special products are displayed and can be purchased at the prefectural "showcase" shop called the Sanyo Kaikan.

NOT FAR from Kagoshima are two remarkable tourist hotels. The region may still be relatively off-track for foreign tourists but it is very much on-track for Japanese. They flocked into this prefecture in 1973 to the number of nearly seven million. Kagoshima City and the hot spring resort on Sakurajima got two million; a million and a half went to the Mt Kirishima area, which has one of the two big resort hotels; and more than two million made for Ibusuki, where the other hotel is.

Kirishima National Park is about two hours by car from Kagoshima City. You go up through forest that changes from the broad-leaved evergreens to Japanese firs and red pines, and you enter a region of volcanoes, crater lakes, waterfalls and steamy hot springs. Of the hot spring areas perhaps the best scenically is Hayashida. This is where you come to a 460-room place that accommodates fourteen hundred people at a time, the Hotel Hayashida Onsen (*onsen* means hot-spring bath.)

Three things surprised me about this hotel. The first was that, although there was a beautifully decorated special suite that was ¥100,000 a day say $A250), a couple could get quite a good double room with bath and television for around ¥4,000 (in 1973). The second surprise was not its super-sized hot spring baths where hundreds of people at a time could soak, or the huge outdoor swimming pool, but its theatre-restaurant combination. Not so much because it could feed a thousand people while they watched a performance of Filipino dances, but because most of these people were sitting under very large trees—and yet they were, as we say, indoors. Above the tops of the tallest trees and over all was a roof of steel-webbing and a transparent synthetic material, covering in a whole hillside that sloped down to where the stage was.

The third surprise was the proprietor, who was not at all the hearty, glad-handing type that usually runs this kind of place. Mr Takeshi Hara, managing director of the enterprise, was a slim and diffident man of perhaps fifty with a shyly patrician air. He showed me some of the hotel's suites and rooms, and in each one was a framed picture—made of flowers, dried flowers and grasses and leaves. Hara-san had done them: collected the flowers himself in a region famous for its plants, dried them and arranged them under glass with considerable artistry. He liked his pictures best when the colours of the flowers had faded to pale and subtle hues.

Mr Hara gave me tea, in the traditional way of honouring the guest with the formal tea-ceremony. Using lovely Satsuma tea bowls, he performed the ritual with the grace and precision of the accomplished tea-master.

So it was also something of a surprise to learn that Mr Hara was the son-in-law of Kagoshima's self-made multimillionaire, Mr Yohachira Iwasaki, whom I had met very briefly in Sydney and who seemed quite a different type. Iwasaki-san was the man who had bought seventeen thousand acres of beach-fronted land on the central Queensland coast and proposed to establish—against conservationist opposition though with a lot of approval from local business interests—a $A20 million resort at Yeppoon, just north of Rockhampton.

He was the owner of the Ibusuki Iwasaki Hotel which was described in its brochure as "biggest in the Pacific".

IBUSUKI is at the entrance to Kagoshima Bay and forty-six kilometres south of the city. A brochure calls Ibusuki the "Hawaii of Japan". In Australian terms it could be the Gold Coast.

This southern tip of Kyushu makes much in its tourist publications of its being "sub-tropical." Although we tend to think of Japan as a cold country—its trademark Fujiyama is always pictured capped in snow—and as not large enough to have much variation in climate, there *is* quite a difference in the average temperature at the northern end of the main island, Honshu (barely more than 9 degrees Celsius) and that at Kagoshima (nearly 17 degrees). Ibusuki was on almost the same latitude as Cairo and more sub-tropical than I had been prepared to credit it with being. Latitude wasn't the only climatic factor: there was the warming influence of the so-called Black Current or Kuroshio that comes up from the Philippines and is the Pacific counterpart of the Gulf Stream.

What makes tropical vegetation burgeon at Ibusuki is the use of the volcanic spa water's heat to produce greenhouse conditions. Palms grow in a huge theatre-restaurant where hula dancers perform. Guests usually come in kimono, perhaps after a walk through the (indoor) Jungle Park which has trees complete with liana vines such as a Tarzan could swing on and there is even a waterfall that cascades into a pool bowered in tropical greenery. Or the guests have come from soaking in fifty-nine pools, large and small, that make up the steamy Jungle Bath, where more palms dangle their fronds and more creepers climb to the light that comes in through a roof stressed with steel webbing, and where scarlet hibiscus blooms keep odd company with white plaster statues of Venus.

Then there are "sand baths". The brochure says they are not only effective "for every kind of illness" (a statement that should be disallowed) but for removing excess fat. After lying down, kimono clad, in a trough on the beach "you can have a splendid time getting yourself covered in white sand". Actually the sand is a rather dark grey; but it is indubitably hot and, being permeated with mineral springs, could have therapeutic virtues and its heat could sweat some weight off. If high tide covers the beach, or it happens to be raining, you can take your sand bath within the hotel. What Beppu was supposed to have, but didn't have any longer, Ibusuki could undoubtedly provide.

The new gateway is Kagoshima 209

The Iwasaki establishment, already huge and planned to be bigger yet, was sited right on the beach-and-pines shore of the wide blue bay. Its entrance was flanked by twin towers that looked rather like a modern architect's idea of medieval donjons. There were 722 rooms, most of them Western-style, and those I saw were of good standard and reasonably priced. Meals were Western except in the old wing that used to be called the Ibusuki Kanko Hotel and was a building of surpassing ugliness.

There was a Swisss chef. His Steak Rossini was presented by one waiter while another filled my wine glass with something bubbly and pink. The one sip I took of the stuff confirmed that it was the sweetest sort of imitation pink champagne. Mr Shuzo Iwasaki, who was running the place while his father negotiated on the Yeppoon resort deal, said it was Starwine from Australia, where Iwasaki Senior had bought 30,000 bottles of it.

Each honeymoon couple who came to stay was presented with a bottle of Starwine, compliments of the management. They thought highly of it, usually, and ordered bottles, at ¥2,000. Some honeymoon couples stayed at Ibusuki only one night, then went on to spend other nights in the prefecture at Kirishima and Miyazaki. Japan Travel Bureau arranged five-night honeymoons on this basis.

"Sometimes we have four hundred honeymoon couples in occupancy," said Iwasaki Junior. "The place rocks a little."

On the way from Kagoshima City to this hotel at Ibusuki one of my car companions said: "In this district the people, when a daughter is born, they plant a *tsuge*-tree. This is boxwood used for making combs. When the girl has grown to marrying age, so is the tree grown up to be valuable." The Japanese wooden comb is a beautiful piece of craftwork that I hope is never entirely displaced by the manufacture of combs in plastic.

Then we come to Lake Ikeda. It is not very big as lakes go, but is the largest in Kyushu. A caldera lake of an extinct volcano, it is very deep, and only six other lakes in the world have waters more translucent. The big feature of this landscape, though, is the cone of a dormant volcano, Mt Kaimon.

At the foot of Mt Kaimon is a zoo, developed by Mr Iwasaki, and a botanical garden where sub-tropical plants are grown and where honeymoon couples from the Iwasaki hotel plant palms and camphor-trees. (Presumably they will want to return some day to see how their plantings have grown.) Near by is an eighteen-hole golf course that has been attractively landscaped and planted.

THE NIGHT BEFORE I left Japan on this '73 trip I was taken to dinner by the Kagoshima Tourist Federation people at a highly regarded restaurant called Yamachaya (Mountain Teahouse) where we were attended by two geisha. The meal was excellent and among the dishes I enjoyed was the *sashimi*, thin slices of raw fish.

I had some *shochu*, the liquor distilled from rice and sweet-potatoes, which is a special product of Kagoshima. Satsuma shochu is famous throughout Japan and at least twenty brands of it are produced in the prefecture. Some of it is aged in oak barrels for up to ten years before bottling. And some costs only ¥250 for a large bottle: it is the working man's drink. One of my Japanese companions averred that if you drink shochu you never get a hangover. I much prefer the taste of sake.

When the foreigner in Japan gets an invitation to dine it is not usually, as it is with us, for seven or eight o'clock, but it is likely to be as early as six o'clock or even five-thirty. This is not only because Japanese dining is leisurely and protracted. Commonly the guest will be taken somewhere after dinner, usually to a nightclub and sometimes to more than one.

After this dinner we went to a Kagoshima nightclub that was very tasteful as to décor and had particularly attractive hostesses, who wore kimono. At this place, Saboten, I found that I had another host, a Mr Yuzo Komaki, president of the Komaki Construction Co, whose office had made several calls to my hotel saying that Mr Komaki wanted to entertain me—for no good reason that I could think of or that was suggested by the information that Mr Komaki's main interest was in sport and that he was head of the local football association. The Japanese word for "soccer", *sakka*, is also the word for "author". Komaki-san was under the impression that I was a big man in the Australian Soccer Association. When he discovered that I was just a book-writer, he made the amiable decision to go ahead and entertain me, anyway. Although he was obviously a hard-minded businessman, Komaki-san had prepared for me a cardboard panel of hand-painted greeting in his own calligraphy.

I FLEW OUT next morning on the Japan Air Lines flight to Hong Kong. On the way to the airport the good companions who had been showing me round for several days (Masaaki Nikaido and Aishi Sumiyoshi) were insistent that I should come back to Kagoshima and stay longer. "We would like to show you," Sumiyoshi-san said, "more than you have had time to see."

One reason I should like to return to hospitable Kagoshima would be to get down to the Satsunan Islands and to the Amagi group (also called Amami) that lie about halfway to Okinawa.

The nearest island of note is Tanegashima, where the first Europeans landed in 1543 with the first firearms ever seen in Japan. It can be reached by a 45-minute flight with the Kagoshima-based airline called Toa, which in 50 minutes can fly you to Yakushima, an island with more to offer scenically. Yakushima is stacked with mountains and has forests that sound marvellous, of *sugi*-trees, Japanese cedars of such age and size that they are not allowed to be taken as timber but are conserved as National Treasures.

Farther south, the Amagi's main island is Amami Oshima, whence comes the pongee, the hand-spun silk fabric called *Oshima tsumugi*, mentioned earlier as a specially attractive "buy" at Kagoshima. These islands being truly subtropical, fruits such as papaya and pineapple grow. Two air services, ANA and Toa, fly from Kagoshima to Amami in an hour and a quarter.

It took only two and three-quarter hours to fly to Hong Kong with JAL— and elapsed time on the clock was an hour less than that because Hong Kong is an hour behind Japan and, leaving Kagoshima at 11.50 a.m. you arrived in Hong Kong at 1.35 p.m., almost in time for lunch—which you'd had on the plane. And a very first-class lunch it was of Kobe beefsteak preceded by *hors d'oeuvre* of shrimp and pâté.

hokkaido, the north

北の北海道

The top island is another Japan

HOKKAIDO is Japan's northern island. On the map it is like a scallopy kite, flying off the top of Honshu. Fewer than 6 million of the 110 million Japanese live there.

Certainly the Hokkaido winter is very severe, but in spring the northern ice-box swings open on the finest pastures the Japanese have, and some of the best cropland. From the way Hokkaido is spoken of I had begun to think of it as Japan's Alaska, but a look at lines of latitude on a globe showed that its northmost tip was well south of London and Paris. Indeed, the capital, Sapporo, was on a line with the French Riviera, the difference being that Hokkaido was beset by cold sea currents. Hokkaido's reputation was such that we lugged woollens we never wore once. We were there in the height of summer, end of July and beginning of August.

On two previous trips to Japan my interest in going to Hokkaido had been ever-so-politely discouraged. The Japanese tourist authorities just weren't ready to offer it to the foreign tourist. When that attitude changed, and they wanted to start selling Hokkaido, they didn't know how acceptable Hokkaido would be. Was it still too raw, too rough? Too Japanese in some ways, in others not Japanese enough? Suddenly I was seen as someone who could supply the answers. Would, I with my wife, travel through Hokkaido (transportation and guide provided) and afterwards tell them what I thought; and, if I considered Hokkaido was a good bet for the *gaijin* traveller, write about it? The answer was, in Japanese, "*Hai*".

On this third trip to Japan we flew by the Sydney–Tokyo service of KLM, the Dutch airline I have used to Europe more often than any other and always found very good. A few days later we were on our way to Hokkaido by the domestic service of Japan Air Lines.

As usual we had three times as much luggage as any travelling Japanese. Mr Yukio Watanabe, deputed by the Japan National Tourist Organization to be with us for eleven days, had an overnight bag.

"I am very happy to accompany you," said Watanabe-san with a bow. He was a lean thirty-five and looked younger. His English was exceptionally good: his father was a professor of English. His comprehension was quick and, shining through the most conscientious concern for our well-being, was a lively sense of humour. He said his name, Watanabe, meant Travel Place. (He was to become manager of the JNTO office in Sydney and is highly regarded in the Australian travel trade.) While I was wondering what we should call him, he added: "International name for Yukio is Jack." Thereafter he was Jack-san.

The flight takes only an hour to Chitose, the airport where we landed to go into Sapporo. The Hokkaido sun was bright, the sky bluer than I had ever seen it in Japan, and the air was fresh and winey after Tokyo. A large American car was waiting for us. Gummed to the windshield was a JTB badge with the inscription: *Welcome to Mr & Mrs Sinpsor*. The driver, on being told we were Australians, said he had never met an Australian before. When the car stopped for me to take a landscape photograph he picked a pretty spray of wild berries and presented them to Claire.

The Hokkaido landscape won us at once, but it was not typically Japanese. Instead of rice farms there were potato crops in white flower, lush fields of wheat and corn, and there were apple orchards, Holstein cows, and a boy leading a single sheep on a thin chain. Birch-trees, slim and silvery, grew among the pines. Least Japanese of all were the farmhouses and their barns.

What were those folded-over mansard roofs doing in Japan? Surely they belonged back in Iowa in the Middle West of America where I had last seen them, painted the same reds and greens and flanked by the same cylindrical silos. Why should this Hokkaido landscape look more like a set from *Oklahoma* than a Japanese print? The answer was that the architects of Hokkaido's development were Americans.

The island that had been Ezo, the home of the hairy Ainu and a place of refuge for nobles who had backed the wrong shogun, got itself in 1870 a thirty-one-year-old governor of extraordinary vision, named Kuroda. He went to the United States, saw President Ulysses S. Grant and persuaded him to agree to his plan, then persuaded Horace Capron to resign as Commissioner of Agriculture and come to Hokkaido. Capron brought in a team of other experts who, discarding the traditional rice-growing schemes, introduced everything from sheep to asparagus, put Japanese geologists to work uncovering coal, laid out Sapporo as a grid-street modern capital and got mills and factories going. One of Capron's brains-trusters, a German who had been for a walk and seen hops growing wild, brought in high-grade hop-seed from Germany and sent a Japanese brewer to study there. Today Sapporo beer is justly famous.

The modernity of Sapporo's planning makes it look materialistic and un-Japanese, but at least the plan gives it flowery park squares in the centre, whereas most Japanese cities have breathing spaces only on their outskirts. At night these pleasant squares were filled with people, and flanked with street vendors selling roasted corn-on-the-cob. Acacia-trees softened the city's angularity.

At the Sapporo Grand Hotel four officials of the Prefectural Government had turned up to greet us. None spoke English but we were made to feel very welcome and important. There was to be a Press conference. "After that," said Jack-san, translating, "they invite you to be guests at official dinner. They wish you to have food which in Hokkaido is considered height of luxury."

I hoped fervently that it wasn't anything like pickled bears'-paws or the mentioned-in-a-brochure "rare Blue Pigeons" stuffed with the local asparagus tips.

"Tell them we are deeply honoured," I said to Jack-san for translation and, as an aside, "What *is* this luxury food?"

"Mutton," he said.

Mutton. For this (I thought) we journey from the world's great sheep country; for this we fly ten thousand leagues from the land of loin chops and roast lamb to exotic Hokkaido. I demurred politely, "Oh, but Hokkaido should not kill its valuable sheep for us!"

The top island is another Japan 215

This was translated and pridefully answered: "Not Hokkaido mutton. They say Hokkaido mutton not regarded as sufficiently good quality to serve you. It will be imported *Australian* mutton."

"Yes," the good Watanabe was saying—as though I hadn't heard, "Australian mutton dinner." Then he added, "Cooked Genghis Khan style."

Genghis Khan, the Mongol conqueror, was one of history's great warrior butchers, and I have never been able to think highly of his ilk. But he certainly knew, a good four centuries ago, how to make mutton taste better than it had ever tasted to us before.

Small slices of leg of mutton (meaning lamb) are placed on the Genghis Khan griddle. This is an openwork dome of cast iron about a foot in diameter with slits formed in a Mongolian design. The dome fits on top of a brazier bowl of burning charcoal. Two of these griddled fire-bowls were placed on the table to serve our party of eight diners. It was rather like an indoor barbecue.

Using chopsticks, you lay the thin slices of meat on the griddle, along with onion rings, cut-up leeks and slices of sweet potato. These, when cooked, you lift off and dip into the cooling, delicious savour that lies in your sauce bowl. The ingredients of the sauce that works the transformation are: soy, a dash of the sweet sake called *mirin*, a little garlic, and grated orange peel.

"*Ichiban!*" I said, that being the only Japanese superlative I knew.

Claire was no less enthusiastic. The men beside her and opposite looked after her wonderfully, taking the morsels off the griddle with their own chopsticks, even dipping them in the sauce for her and then placing them on a small plate. It was odd to see Japanese men looking after a woman instead of vice versa.

FROM SAPPORO we began a trip of over eight hundred miles that was to take us right across Hokkaido and through its three finest scenic areas. It started with the train to Kamikawa.

Speeding through the valley of the island's biggest river, the Ishikari, the train shed sun-bright panoramas of rural countryside dotted with those American-style farmhouses and field workers, mainly women, in the traditional wide hats and head-scarves and patterned blue *mompe* trousers. Every house had a big firewood stack for winter, and there were piles and tumbles of great logs in timber-yards. Seven-tenths of Hokkaido was forest and the island produced much of Japan's timber as well as a third of all its fish. There were huge paper mills. As we neared Ashigawa the railside scene grew jungle-thick, its dense greenery striped with birches. In the bright mid-morning mists still trailed from the tops of the mountains.

At Kamikawa station a spanking new Ford Galaxie was waiting for us. The big car eased itself over the local potholes and ran out of the town and along a dirt road where suddenly a ten-foot policeman, a dummy wooden cut-out, loomed in the middle of the rural road, which then forked, and Jack-san announced, "We are now entering Daisetsuzan National Park. *Dai* is Great, *Setsu* is Snowy, *Zan* is Mountain."

The driver said there were still lots of bears in the forests. Their fur is blackish or dark brown and, when young, the brown bears have a white collar that disappears as they grow up. From midwinter until spring (April) they hibernate. I was told that the Hokkaido bear hibernates with honey in his claws, which he licks on waking.

Many people think of bears as vegetarians, but the Hokkaido bear not only preys on rabbits and other small animals; it takes sheep and has been known to kill horses, and bury what it does not eat at once. It will also attack humans. Bears were not protected at any season; hunters got a good price for their skins and drug manufacturers bought bears' gall bladders.

NOW THE MOUNTAINS were buttressed with rock-walls. They rose beside the road and across the stony headstream of the Ishikari. We were entering the Sounkyo Gorge. The river was spanned by a latticed wooden bridge that had a gentle Japanese up-curve in the middle. Beside this stood our inn. Its name, Sounkaku, meant "Hotel in Layers of Clouds".

A blast on the limousine's horn as it swept up the driveway brought a bowing proprietress and a scurry of kimono'd maids who fell to their knees and bowed as they said "*Irasshai mase*" ("Welcome to this inn"). Our Jack-san gave the traditional reply: "*Konnichi wa. Osewa ni nari mas,*" ("Good day. I am in your good care").

Along the polished floorboards we padded in our slippers. Mine were too small and Claire's so large that she kept losing them on the stairs that led to our room, or rather, suite. It was one of two the inn described as "semi-Western style".

At first glance through the *shoji* paper doors it looked pure Japanese. Lovely tatami, the colour of ripening wheat; a low central table; the *tokonoma* alcove, hung with its scroll, bordered with slim poles of natural wood set in an ash-grey wall. But off this main room there was—as well as a tiled bathroom—another room, and this was body-carpeted in deep cherry and had a couch and several chairs. It also had a tuckpointed brick fireplace. But no grate or chimney: you couldn't have had a fire in it.

This odd installation could not be explained by the maid who came in and announced with a kneeling bow, "*Reiko de gozaimas'. Dozo yoroshku*" ("I am Reiko. May I serve you well"), and gave us the green tea and little cakes which all good inns serve guests on arrival. We asked Jack-san about it.

"Ah, yes. Western-style fireplace. You like it, yes?"

No, I said.

Jack-san sighed. "This is a great sadness for the proprietor of this inn because I am sure he has gone to expense of installation of this fireplace for pleasing foreigners. To make them feel at home."

"But, Jack-san, we don't *want* to feel at home. We want to feel in Japan, in Hokkaido. Home is the place the tourist spends his money to get away from, in order to experience the unfamiliar."

"Ah," said Jack-san. "Do you wish removal of couch and chairs you and Mrs Simpson are sitting on, because they are making you feel too much at home?"

"No, no!" we cried together, for, while we love the good Japanese interior, one could get awfully sick of living on the floor.

I looked at the mantel of the fake fireplace. It was already littered with several books and three cameras. "Of course," I conceded, "the mantel comes in handy as a shelf."

"Then you would advise," said Jack-san without a smile, "that it is advisable to have a—mantel. What, please, is exact meaning of 'mantel'?"

"A ledge over a fireplace."

"Ah so. But, now, could not this be difficult? To have a mantel, which is a ledge over the fireplace—but not to have the fireplace?"

I groaned. "But, Jack-san, this damned silly fake fireplace is so unnecessary, and nobody's going to like it...." Then, struck by a doubt, I said, "Is there one in *your* room?" He said no it was a Japanese-style room. I said, "Would you *like* one?"

"Well," said Jack-san, grinning, "such a fireplace would be, for me, very exotic, very un-familiar. In my room I feel at home. That is bad, yes? Perhaps more *Japanese* tourists would come if—"

"Jack-san, if you advise in your report that these dreadful fireplaces be taken out of the foreigners' suites and put in the lovely Japanese rooms, I'll—"

When we stopped laughing I said, "What I want—" and he interrupted so politely with, "I think I know. Bottle of Sapporo beer. Large size, yes? I shall order immediately."

And he went to the telephone, which looked a bit odd beside the tokonoma scroll—but we would not have wanted it removed.

SOUNKYO GORGE is renowned for having two canyons, called Little Box (Kobako) and Big Box (Obako), of extraordinary formation. The rock-walls of the mountains are cracked into thin pillars of rock as angular as the sections of a crystal. The skyline is hairy with pines that often stand lonely on a pinnacle or, clutching the rocks with precarious grace, look exactly like the pines in some Japanese screen-painting. The rock-wall rising from a belt of forest breaks into clefts. Down each of these a waterfall cascades like a twisted scarf on a dark breast of stone and pine.

When we returned to the inn in the late afternoon we changed into *yukata*, the summer cotton kimonos which inns provide. We were asked not *whether* we would take a bath but at what time would we like it. The inn had an elaborate tiled bathing hall with pools from different hot mineral springs. It also had a "family bath" just big enough for a couple or a family to bathe together. Mixed bathing still prevailed in Hokkaido more than anywhere else in Japan.

I had looked in at the bathing hall with Jack-san, just before lunch. Men and women and children were in the pools or washing themselves at the side. For us: the "family" bath—and separately.

Bathed, we had dinner. We dined in our room, just as we had lunched there. Lunch had been notable for an eye-feast of a salad—the asparagus was ringed with perfectly peeled segments of mandarin. Such inns cater for a fairly prosperous Japanese clientele and pride themselves on their cuisine but do not offer a menu. However, they were most concerned to satisfy our strange tastes as foreigners. The management would ask Watanabe-san to ask us after each meal what we would fancy for the next. At the Sounkaku I said I would have the table d'hôte Japanese dinner, and knew it would be likely to be fish; but fish and Claire do not like each other much. She said, "Could I have a veal cutlet?" She got it. Next day we found out that the hotel had sent specially to Kamikawa, fifteen miles away, for that veal cutlet.

What did we wish for breakfast? Claire said she would have a boiled egg. Jack-san ordered it, boiled three minutes, and "toasted bread", butter, tea (black not green) with milk. I said I would have the Japanese breakfast, whatever it was.

In the morning we rose from our beds on the floor, glad that we had asked for an extra "mattress" each because, though they are like overstuffed eiderdowns, they are still unsprung. A man came and folded all the bed-things away into a shoji cupboard in the wall. The low lacquer table was restored to its place in the centre of the tatami. Then Reiko-san appeared bearing breakfast. Before bringing it in she had to kneel inside the door and bow and wish us "*O hayo*" ("Good morning"). True to Japanese tradition of the almighty male, she brought my breakfast first.

"What's in that fine black bowl?" Claire said.

I lifted the lid off a thickish brown soya-bean soup.

"Ugh," she said. "Soup for breakfast." Then, "What is that black stuff that looks like matted plastic?"

I bit into it and said I thought it was matted black plastic. It was a processed seaweed, which, crumbled on rice, is relished by a people whose idea of a really atrocious breakfast addition is marmalade.

I manfully drank the soup. Claire's breakfast arrived: a superb peach, four very thick slices of toast, about half a pound of butter, a cup of tea—and one for me—a quarter-pint jar of cream, and two pale-brown eggs in a china bowl.

"They've given me two eggs. Why don't you have one? And there's tons of toast." I swallowed on rice and pride. She picked up an egg and her smile faded. The eggs were stone cold.

Worse than breakfast soup, I felt, were cold soft-boiled eggs, but I opened one: it was a perfect three-minuter. You could imagine them being put into a basin of cold water to cool, maybe with ice to hurry the process. Later we told Jack-san who, distressed, took off to see the management, and came back bearing the humblest apologies. The way he told it you got the idea that he had only just been able to restrain the proprietor from rushing out and committing hara-kiri. Charge for Claire's breakfast had been taken off the bill, and would we please feel assured that no future *gaijin* guest at the Hotel Between Layers of Cloud would ever receive anything but piping hot boiled eggs?

The management also wished to express its gratitude for our drawing attention to its unforgiveable ignorance in serving butter by the half pound, cream by the jar and toast by the inch-thick slice—which, we had pointed out, was not only unnecessary but highly uneconomical.

THE CAR CLIMBED a narrow road, in brilliant sunshine, up to a plateau where we had the feeling of being on the roof of Hokkaido. We could look across to the Great Snowy Mountain, Daisetsu, its sides still streaked with snowdrifts. I wanted to feel, again, vigorous enough to climb up on to its long back—as so many Japanese students do in their university vacations—and come back with stories of strange alpine flora, and ptarmigans and the brown hare that in winter turns as white as the snow to elude the preying eyes of bears and of crested eagles sailing the heights. And the "crying" rabbits which when alarmed cried, "*Chun tsurun. Chun tsurun*".

Farther off to the south was the Tokachi Range which is said to provide the best skiing in Japan. Winter snow-sports had boomed. We often saw lanes clearned down pine-clad mountains to make ski runs. Up on this plateau there was no habitation beyond a camp of National Defence trainees, who had

The top island is another Japan   219

brown melon country-boy faces.

A mile or two farther on was a memorial. It had the statue of a Buddhist saint, like Jizo, who is the guardian of the souls of dead children. The inscription said it was *"for the repose of the spirits of the trees that had been killed by the 1954 typhoon"*.

We wound down through untouched pinewoods, and "Jack" Watanabe surprised us by suddenly quoting Longfellow's line, *"This is the forest primeval'*.

Then there was a bald-sided mountain with a long red-roofed structure running down it to a village of workers' houses at the foot, and this was Suigin, a big quicksilver mine. The deposit of cinnabar, the red sulphide ore from which quicksilver is extracted, had been found by accident. Mercury being highly poisonous, the miners could work here only four years, or their health was affected.

We came into a valley spread with some of the most beautiful cropland I have seen. Fields of yellowing wheat contrasted with the deep green rows of the beet that makes Japan's sugar. Beyond that was the bright gold of rape, the oil-seed plant, white-flowered stretches of potatoes, high corn in tassel, and peppermint—bigger in leaf than we thought peppermint could ever be. This region is the greatest peppermint producer in the world.

Beside the road was a tiny wooden shrine to Jizo, and a child from the nearby school had stopped to place in it a handful of flowers. Always the biggest building in the rural townships of Japan was the school.

Everywhere the roads were being improved. Many of the roadworkers were women, *mompe*-trousered, with broad straw hats and a coif of white cloth they wet to keep their heads cool under the midsummer sun.

ONNEYU is a small wooden spa town on a river with the Ainu name of Muka. On the river stood the sizeable Muka Hotel. Our small two-room "Western" suite had real beds. There was no attached bathroom, but the "family bath", of which we were given exclusive use, was an eight-foot tiled pool with a boy on a dolphin that spouted the water. One wall was plain glass, so that you could look at the view while you bathed.

Our room looked out on the fast-running river and across to a small field where the grass was sprinkled with summer flowers, going back to a high bank topped with trees that were full of ravens, and beautiful in silhouette when the sun went down.

Next morning we went for a walk before breakfast, wandering the little paths of the hotel's garden of shrubs and goldfish pools and stone lanterns, then going over the river bridge and up a road of farms. An old man was tending his garden of big scarlet poppies. When we stopped to admire them, he smiled and picked a bunch and, taking off his floppy straw hat, presented them to Claire.

The weather was still perfect as the car took us on, through the town of Rubeshibe, whose inhabitants are said to be entirely free of the eye disease trachoma, thanks to properties of the sulphur spa water they bathe in. Mills were slicing great logs for plywood, and smoke belched from what Jack-san described as a "telegraph post factory".

We came into Kitami—"This is a big town. The driver says it has seven movie houses". At the office of the hire-car company that owned our Ford Galaxie the driver brought out and introduced the manager and the under-manager, who bowed and presented their cards. Some children sucking ice-poles gathered to stare. Outside a shop with big paper lanterns and rows of wood-carved souvenir bears, two kimono'd housewives with babies on their backs in embroidered slings of black velvet gossiped. A strong young man strode by in a sombrero hat, green breeches and a wine-red open shirt with an armband that proclaimed him a forest ranger. A rubbish lorry came, manned by head-scarved women in gumboots. An old man trundled a handcart over the pot-holes. A very small boy peed intently in the gutter.

We drove on through a valley whose rural beauty is such that Japanese movie companies often use it as the setting for "earth" films. The landscape rolled in a lush pattern of farms and pastures in the Tokoro River's valley.

We had lunch at Bihoro, at an inn that served huge hairy Hokkaido crab. One crab makes a meal. Brown-shelled, it had legs as hairy as an Ainu's. It came on a plate without any chopsticks, and we wondered how to eat it, until Jack-san showed us how to extract the middle by using a claw as a fork. The crabmeat was delicate and delicious.

In the car I had broken an earpiece of my spectacles, which Jack-san whisked away to be mended while we lunched. We had not finished eating when the old spectacle-maker came in, bowed, knelt, and handed me a perfect repair, together with a pair of sun-goggles I had asked Jack-san to buy for me. He would not take any money for the repair.

I had bought the sun-goggles because, when I admired the pair Hashizume-san the driver had, he wanted to give them to me.

Strange lakes and the bear-cult Ainu

Now as we entered Akan National Park, we were on the threshold of Hokkaido's finest natural scenery. The island with the shaggy high head and the unexpectedly lovely rural bodice was to become a more conscious beauty, holding out its mirrors.

The first lake was Kutcharo. It spread out below us as a great blue stillness when we left the car and walked up to the viewing point at Bihoro Pass. It reached out its arms between the hills of forest, as though to reflect all of them that it could and show in double image that there was no trace of habitation. Its surface was undisturbed by so much as a fish. There have been no fish in Kutcharo since an earthquake released sulphur into the water.

I looked round from photographing the lake and saw three men squatting in a small rotunda. By their luxuriant beards and fibre-cloth kimonos and headbands of strong and distinctive pattern I knew they were Ainu, the first of the race we had seen.

At the sight of a foreigner with two cameras they got to their feet, picked up old Japanese-style swords and, hitching the robes that must once have been handsome but were now shabby, they came ambling down to me, rather like three bored bears that had scented honey. Their purpose was obviously to be photographed for tips; and it seemed churlish not to fall in with the idea. They grouped themselves round a signpost with the lake as a background and I took pictures and gave them a hundred yen each. I felt sorry for them and wanted to see them able to go away and do whatever Ainu do when they are not posing for tourist cameras or carving wooden bears for the souvenir stalls. Maybe they get drunk. My encyclopaedia says they are "a drunken people": it adds "they are intelligent, hospitable and polite".

Two of these Ainu were good-looking men. The older one's beard was quite white. The hair of the other two was black, strong and wavy. They had rather high cheekbones but their other features were not the Mongoloid ones of Japanese or Chinese, and their eyes were not slitted by the epicanthic fold. Their skins were a very light brown. Their faces and arms look most hirsute alongside the Japanese, who are relatively hairless; but other races, including our own, have markedly hirsute types who, if they let their beards and hair grow, look as hairy as the average Ainu.

Long a problem to the ethnologists—who still cannot agree on where the race originated—the Ainu are believed by most authorities to have come to Japan from Central Asia, where a people called the Gilyak, who lived near the Amur River that borders Manchuria, had a bear-cult very similar to the Ainu's.

The pudgy noses of the Ainu and their ridgy brows do remind us of features that are accentuated in the Australian Aboriginal. An authority on racial genetics, Professor Ruggles Gates, believed it probable that sometime, somewhere in Central Asia, there was a common ancestry, and then a divergence.

We wondered if any affinities showed in their art. Ainu art is not depictive, but decorative. It is design, and very good design at that, and more sophisticated design than the Australian Aboriginal ever did.

Some of the best designs we saw—apart from very old Ainu kimonos that were excellent in both pattern and colour—were the carvings on moustache-lifters. Ainu elders used these sticks, which look rather like pointed foot-rulers with one cambered side, to lift their profuse moustaches when they drank and ate (just as Victorian grandfather had his moustache cup). The moustache lifters now sold as souvenirs are not as good in design as the old ones we saw in museums at Sapporo and Abashiri.

The ubiquitous carved wooden bears are not Ainu art. Ainu craftsmen carve them skilfully enough, but only as they have been taught to do by the Japanese (or, some say, by a Swiss) as Hokkaido souvenirs.

Bihoro Pass was once a battlefield where the Ainu, who were still a bow-and-arrow people, were badly defeated by the Japanese. From there the road kept us in touch, for miles, with Lake Kutcharo. Sometimes we would glimpse the lake through white birches. Then the vegetation would mat as thickly as jungle. Against this green profusion one vine stood out, because its leaves were half pink and half white, called *matatabi*. Cats love it, and the powdered fruits are sold all over Japan as cat medicine.

Many roads are bordered with the round leaves of a rhubarb-like plant called *fuki*. It grows so large in the Teshikaga region we came to next day that people use the leaves as umbrellas.

We stopped at a beautiful picnic spot by the lakeside, where a great leaning tree dreamed over its reflection in the water. There was no one else there; but a little farther on a lot of holidaymakers were gathered round drink stands and a souvenir shop that had two young bears tethered to stakes, as tourist attractions. There was also a pathetic badger on a chain. It lay panting and looked as though it wished to die. People regarded it without any pity in their eyes.

LAKE MASHU is, in Ainu language, the Lake of the Gods. We were not due to go there until the next day, but the driver said tomorrow might not be fine. The lake is often wrapped in mist, and the car's previous passenger, the Malayan High Commissioner, had been unable to see Mashu at all.

To reach it you wind up and up the side of a mountain that, before it burst asunder, must have been as great as Fujiyama, so big is the crater. When you reach the rim the lake is far below you.

At the sight of Mashu lying deep in its dark mountain cradle I remember that I stood quite still. It is the only lake I ever saw that gave the impression of being of some substance more mysterious than water. It was so moveless, it seemed to deny all fluidity, and yet it was in no way solid like a gemstone, or a mirror. Unless perhaps, there could be a mirror—for it did hold the shadowiest reflections of its mountains' sides—that was of a colour between pewter and purple.

Directly across from where we stood one cliffy side was gashed with earth-red. The other near slopes, forested and shrubbed with rhododendrons, went so steeply down to the lake that it was virtually unapproachable. It had one cabuchon of an island, thickly wooded. The fleck of white we could see on this was a *torii*. Nowhere else in the scene was there a sign that the hand of man had touched Mashu. The lake has no inlet or outlet and goes down to a depth of 280 metres (924 feet).

The Japanese tourist literature about this lake makes reference to its "air of mystery". And, indeed, it has that air. Withdrawn from the surrounding world, as aloof down there in its mountain well as the moon is in the sky, Mashu is a sibyl of a lake whose spell forbids you to think that there could be another in the world as strange.

THAT NIGHT we spent at a hotel in Kawayu. The room at this inn was a marriage, or misalliance, of East and West. The *tokonoma* scroll, which wasn't a good one, kept uneasy company with some framed mountain-view pictures from which hung purple tassels. The *tatami* floor was three-quarters covered with a European carpet.

"Ah, so," Jack-san said sadly when we pointed a critical finger at the abomination. "There is a carpet in my room, also. To Japanese, carpet is height of luxury."

Dinner included, for our special delectation, the kind of thing the West has only itself to blame for: oyster cocktail made with tomato sauce, and mornayed fish served in (large) oyster shells. The fat Hokkaido oyster is not recommended.

Our beds being laid out—they looked right on tatami and absurd on carpet—we retired to two pillows that were so hard we replaced them with the floor cushions. The Japanese are Spartans about their pillows—wickerwork objects concave on top.

Mosquito-repellent coils were always lit by the maid as part of the bedding-down process. Claire, whose nose offends easily, considered the smell of these as "like incense you burn to a god you don't like". We used to track them down—they were usually hidden in a china pig or some more Japanese ornament—and extinguish them. We never saw or felt a mosquito.

Something went wrong with the breakfast order, though we certainly got what we asked for—plus. Claire had ordered an omelette, and I two boiled eggs. We got two king-size omelettes and four boiled eggs.

On the outskirts of the town is an active volcano, Io-san or Sulphur Mountain. Billowing sulphur vapour which was not only odorous but noisy came hissing out of holes in the ground like rabbit burrows. It was rocky ground of the strangest colours, pastel pinks and fawns and greys as well as sulphur yellow.

WE WERE AHEAD of schedule because of going to Lake Mashu yesterday instead of today. Now it was raining. Would we like to go to Abashiri?

"On the Sea of Okhotsk," Jack-san added, and I thought about how one of the rewards of travel is map names suddenly taking on reality. *Sea of Okhotsk* on the map, bounded by Russia's Far East shore and the prongy island of Sakhalin and the peninsula of Kamchatka, had seemed almost as remote as the Arctic Pole. Now it was only thirty miles away.

"Of course we want to go to Abashiri," I said.

Jack-san Watanabe smiled. "I, too, wish to go to Abashiri. But if I said that back on the mainland, people would think I was crazy. With us, to 'go to Abashiri' means to go to prison. It is like saying, to 'wear the red kimono'."

"Red kimono?" I had promised to take back to a very good friend in Sydney a kimono he would use as a dressing gown—and he wanted a red one.

"I am afraid it is not possible to buy," Jack-san said. "No man would wear it. It is convict suit."

Notorious Abashiri was a place of flowers. The grass was still scattered with pinks and yellow and the deep purple of wild iris and another flower like a magenta dog-rose. The local postcards pictured fifteen varieties of wildflowers.

The Sea of Okhotsk was as grey as the bleached, never-painted wood of the houses of the fishing villages we had passed through, poor places smelling highly of their trade. Along its brown beach sands the white gulls were sometimes outnumbered by black flocks of pecking ravens. In winter you sometimes saw icebergs that had drifted down from the Arctic, our driver Hashizume-san, said. To the south stretched the long misty arm of the Shiretoko Peninsula pointing the way to the bleak kuriles. Long-prowed fishing boats lay along the beaches. There were shrines to the spirits of fishers who had drowned in storms.

On a high hilltop behind Abashiri we ate the *bento* (box lunch) the inn had provided, sitting beside a tall slab of grey rock cut with the squiggles of fine calligraphy and set up so that all might read what Uisada, a famous *haiku* poet, had written about the sun going down in a snowstorm over the bridge at Abashiri.

Down below was the jail. We could see the cell buildings and well-kept lawns and flower beds inside the high walls, but no prisoners were in sight. It is always depressing to see a jail: the denial of freedom, the dictatorship, the discipline—they are so absolute.

Having descended to the town again, we were driving along beside the jail walls when Claire said, "Look! A festival!".

A procession of school-age girls, as pretty as powder and rouge could make them and wearing the gayest garb of patterned pants and pastel shawls, trooped, fan in hand, ahead of a brightly decorated cart with a canopy top. This was being hauled by men whose festival dress was *yukata* and a knotted handkerchief round the head. They turned up a quiet road beside the side wall of the jail and stopped before a house. The girls began to dance. On the cart was a portable phonograph.

One slimly beautiful child enchanted us. In every turn and gesture she had the grace of the born dancer. She was the daughter of one of the warders. We hoped that remote Abashiri would not prove the prison of her talent.

The governor's wife came out and gave the men a big bottle of sake and the children sweets. Then the gay cart and its bright retinue moved on, towards the prison gates.

A BRIGHT BLUE RIVER ran past a charming little garden just outside a sliding doorway of the room we had at our next inn, at Teshikaga. The blueness was caused by some mineralization of the water.

The inn was called the Mashu Grand Hotel. With a name like that you expect sewerage. But there wasn't, and Claire lost a too-big "W.C. Slipper" down a hole behind the door marked in English LADYS. The slippers you get on entering an inn are not intended to be worn into the *benjo*. Japanese Style is a seatless, floor-level, elongated china affair with one up-curved end: you are supposed to face that, not rest on it.

Strange lakes and the bear-cult Ainu

Next morning I went to see Mr Yohei Nagata, ornithologist and zoologist, author of *Animals and Birds of Hokkaido*. The rare Blue Pigeon, he said, is not blue. It is better called the Green Pigeon. The male is lime-green with a purple patch on the wing, the female is brownish. Its Ainu name means "idiot", because it was regarded as a very silly bird, and also one of ill-omen. Nagata-san had found the first recorded nest of the Green Pigeon.

Among Hokkaido's other strange birds were a woodpecker as big as a crow, with a chirp that could be heard a mile away; a bird that sucked up ants with the tip of its tongue; and the weird-voiced *etoporika*, which had a head pattern rather like a Kabuki actor's.

LAKE AKAN, the vacationists' main mecca in eastern Hokkaido, is brooded over by two mountains, whose names mean Mr and Mrs Akan (O-Akan and Me-Akan). Mrs is a quite active volcano and near its crater are two small lakes, one red and one blue.

Where we came to Lake Akan it made a small bay that was fronted with a flock of inns. Ours, the Akankose, stood to one side of a wharf where white pleasure boats kept putting in and out with loudspeakers playing Japanese tunes.

Instead of being the only foreigners on one of the tripper boats, we had a small launch to ourselves, at most moderate cost. However, with every boat goes a guide girl. Ours picked up her microphone as soon as we left the wharf and began, in English: "Lake Akan is sixteen and a half miles in circumference and thirty metres deep at the deepest part. In winter, when the All-Japan Skating Contests are held on the lake, it is frozen to the depth of fifty centimetres. Lake Akan contains twenty islands and some small ones which are floating on the surface. The water is not so clear now because of the prankton. ...."

I got Jack-san to tell the girl to relax: we would ask her what we needed to know. Then we began to enjoy Lake Akan very much.

The lake, sheened with the sun of late afternoon, was girt with growth so thick I can only describe it as alpine jungle. Among the tangle of fir and pine, with green beards of moss hanging from the branches, there were maples and lacquer-trees, which also turn bright red in autumn. From late September to mid-October Lake Akan must be a sight for the gods.

Along the water's edge were rocks, browny-gold stones, sprouting with grass and small plants. We could hardly believe that vegetation could grow out of rocks, but there it was. The volcanic stone, rich in fertilizer, must be so porous that roots can penetrate. A pocket of earth in one of the bigger rocks grew a ten-foot pine. Others were topped with small maples. Claire, who liked to make rock-gardens, pined to take home one of these garden rocks.

In one corner of the lake a small river runs out, gets lost in the greenery and eventually finds its way to the Pacific. Here there was a little archipelago of floating islands as well as rock ones.

In Lake Akan is found a weed that grows as a green ball, called *marimo*. These float about under the surface, occur at only a few places in the lake and, though the marimo we saw were quite small balls, grow up to eight inches in diameter. There were some big ones in a glass tank at the pier, under a "Do Not Touch" notice. They looked as though they would feel like the softest imaginable sponge.

The curious marimo—which are found only in another lake in Sakhalin and a couple in Europe—were being taken away in such numbers, to decorate bowls in homes and restaurants, that the government feared they would disappear. So marimo was declared a National Treasure, and people who had them were asked to return them to Lake Akan. Thousands were returned.

OUR VERY GOOD DRIVER, Hashizume-san, had to leave us now and return with the Ford Galaxie to his base at Kitami. However, the new driver, who took us from Lake Akan to Kushiro, was interesting. He saw ghosts.

"I had brought some people to the inn here and was driving back to Kushiro at night," he said, "when I saw a man sitting in the middle of the road. I braked to a stop. But the man was gone, vanished. He was probably the ghost of some man who had committed suicide hereabouts or been killed by a bear."

He related this unconcernedly as he drove, adding, "Such things happen. Other drivers I know have seen ghosts on this road."

Ghosts are seen by all kinds of people except the kind who most need to see them—writers. None of the writers I know has ever seen a ghost. But preliterate peoples who cannot use such good material—natives of Melanesia, for instance—see lots of them. It seems all wrong.

We came down through the mountains towards the Pacific coast, and through a town that was Hokkaido's biggest horse market. Then we saw cattle whose progenitors had been imported from Australia—which is where the sheep came from, too, for they are merinos. And there was a beautiful bird that is almost as big as an emu, the red-crested crane.

Kushiro was a sprawling, untidy city and it wore a frontier air. In fact it was known as the "Wild West" port of Japan. It is the port of the whaling fleet, of the fishermen who brave the foggy Kuriles, and of the hard-lipped sailors of many lands who come in freighters that empty their holds of rice and machinery and fertilizer and fill them up with processed fish and timber. It is also the city of the coal-miner and the "big smoke" of the lumber-jack and horsebreaker and they, with the sea's men, crowd the bars whose neons beckon in the pot-holey side streets and lurch out to the little quick-trade hotels with the girls who would rather do that than gut fish with the other girls, the ones we saw stacking crates at a cannery, who put their hands on their trousered hips and called out at the big car and were bolder-mannered than I had thought any Japanese women could be.

As we skirted the harbour edge I glimpsed a trawler coming in to berth, and it was so beflagged with colour I stopped the car and went along the dock towards where it was edging in to tie up alongside other vessels of the fishing fleet.

"They have big catch of salmon, so they make that signal," Jack-san said, joining me.

The flags were no fluttery pennants but big ones with lusty patterns and ideograms in red and yellow, black and blue and white. They were strung from the bow up to the foremast and right along to the bridge astern. The white hull, discoloured with sea-stain and rust, made the display look very brave and vivid. The ship tied up, the little crewmen with fatigue in their unshaven faces slung a sea anchor onto the wharf to make way for a gangplank, and the lines of the flags slacked down until the foremast was sheathed in their collapsed colours.

Strange lakes and the bear-cult Ainu 227

We went up on a hill that overlooked the city and watched the harbour shining under the sun going down a sky that seemed enormously wide. Far out the gilded clouds met a grey band of fog that is a creation of the cold current and lies always along the horizon off Kushiro.

The Fujiya Hotel, which ranked as the best Kushiro had then (it has better now, I'm assured) was a smelly place, in no way recommendable. We stayed there only for a bath and dinner and then took the night train for Sapporo.

THE TRAIN had Pullman-type sleeping cars. While I did undressing acrobatics behind the curtain of an upper berth, Japanese businessmen thought nothing of disrobing in the aisle down to their cotton one-piece underwear: it was respectable enough because, underneath, they wear a kind of breech clout. A woman suckled her child with the same unconcern. We were the only foreigners in this first-class carriage.

We were all night in the train and would have slept very well, for it was smooth and comfortable, except that our compartment contained a man who must surely have been the All-Japan Snoring Champion. His repertoire of sounds was astonishing and their range almost orchestral.

The train got to Sapporo at seven-thirty. Breakfasting at the Grand Hotel, we said, "Look! Foreigners like us!" on seeing Americans in the dining-room—the first non-Japanese faces for a week.

Then we were in a train again, a very modern stainless-steel express with seat linen as white as the flower that gave its name to the train, *Lily of the Valley*. It is a flower that is almost the emblem of Hokkaido, for it blooms across the land in spring.

We went swiftly down the line south for two hours. Then, in mid-morning, we were at Hokkaido's most famous spa, Noboribetsu.

After a week of inns we paused automatically at the entrance to the Noboribetsu Grand Hotel, ready to take off shoes and don slippers. But no, it was shoes on through the lobby with its fountain and water-lily pool and up to a room with body carpet and twin beds and bathroom attached.

When you have been eating with chopsticks for a week and knowing full well that, for all the approving smiles of maids, your performance with Japanese food is a bit hamhanded, it does your ego a power of good to see a Japanese tackling Western food with no more grace.

The family at the next table at breakfast decided me that I couldn't have done worse with the rice bowl than they were doing with the exotic dish they had ordered, eggs and bacon. Poppa-san would get a fat-slippery piece of egg on a trembling fork, then lose it. Teenage son minimized this trouble by going right down over the plate to gulp at each mouthful and suck it in. Mamma-san placed the whole egg on a slice of toast, which she held triumphantly aloft on spread fingers, and ate it that way. Junior just used two hands and a spoon.

THAT AFTERNOON we went to Hell. The place is called Valley of Hell (*Jigokudani*). The car swings up a bend in the road and there you are, faced with the most infernal scene. From cones of sinter rise clouds of steam. In those miniature craters an evil-looking grey mud bubbles into whorls with a central bubble-eye that pops. A strong smell of sulphur hangs over the place. And the background to one side of this volcanic valley is of cliffs of the brightest red clay.

If you go on through this fantastic landscape and up a hillside you find yourself on the lip of a chasm at the bottom of which is a lake of boiling water. Many Japanese were being photographed against the background of the mud craters, mostly by their friends, but some by professional photographers. One of these came up while I was taking pictures and, seeing that he could do no photographic business, began giving me information. He may have just been airing his English, or hoping to get a guide fee.

"Six hundred persons have committed suicide in here this year", he said with a bright smile.

To think of anybody plunging into that grey boiling mud was sickening. The idea of six hundred seeking death in that way, at the rate of fifty people a month, was incredible.

When I got back in the car I had Jack-san ask the driver, "When was the last suicide at this place?"

He remembered one in April, four months before. He remembered a family of five who had suicided there four years ago.

I asked myself. Would guides tell people these atrocious tales if there were not a morbid appetite for them?

AFTER DINNER that evening Jack-san and I left the Grand Hotel for the biggest bath hall, which was at the Dai-Ichi Takimoto Hotel. *Dai-Ichi* meant "Great One" and Takimoto was the name of the discoverer of this spa about a century ago: it cured his wife's disease, the story goes.

We went *scrape-clack-scrape* down the main street, which was full of other *yukata*-wrapped figures and the sound of *geta*.

The world's biggest bathroom—I cannot imagine that there is, or ever was in ancient Rome, a larger one—can take five hundred people comfortably in its twenty-five pools of ten kinds of spa water.

There must have been about two hundred women and children bathing together when I stepped out, modestly dangling a Japanese washer-towel, into this hall about the size of a large aeroplane hangar and steel-strutted like one at the side. It went grand with white pillars, blue ceiling, murals, bronze lions and about an acre of tiling set with pools of many shapes and sizes.

I saw that most, though not all, of the adult Japanese, when they walked about out of the water, used their washer-towels for modesty. In fact it was rare to see a man standing without any consciousness of nakedness. There was a good deal of crouching and sitting by the women. The children didn't bother, but there was an obvious etiquette of nudity with the grown-ups. The women bathing in my vicinity all looked like mothers, and there were those who could have been grandmothers. None was fat. Nor were the middle-aged men as thick in the middle as our men commonly are. In general, there was a relative physical comeliness. Not that Venus-san was present, or Adonis-san either.

THE AINU VILLAGE of Shiraoi is said to be the most "representative" in Hokkaido. It lies about twenty miles from Noboribetsu. We drove off a very good coastal highway into the muddy streets of a place that seemed at first glance to consist mainly of souvenir shops.

Then the car drew up beside a large hut that was oblong with walls of reeds and a pitched roof of thick thatch. Standing outside, at one rounded corner of the hut, two striking figures were being photographed by a group of Japanese tourists. The man, a head taller than the woman, had such a full beard and luxuriant moustache that his only visible mouth was a dash of lower lip. His head of hair was crowned with the Ainu ceremonial headdress: this was like that of the ancient Druids but boat-shaped and ornamented with wood-shavings. The *sabamubi*, as it is called, rested with dignity on a broad brow that was creased in a way that suggested sensibility and intelligence.

This was Tomaramu Miyamoto—he has adopted a Japanese name—the Ainu "chief" of Shiraoi. His age was fifty-three, though the beard made him look older. He wore a white-collared black short coat cut like a kimono, and under that a full kimono that was traditional in design though not in material: it showed a fine Ainu-embroidered pattern in golden-brown on black. A Japanese sword, long-handled and slim in its scabbard, was suspended at his waist. He wore a wristlet watch, and beneath his kimono the cuffs of trousers just showed above green plastic sandals.

Miyamoto's wife, in a black kimono and headband both boldly patterned in white and red Ainu design, looked distinctly more Japanese than her husband, though she, too, was said to be an Ainu full-blood.

Her mouth was tattooed. It was as though she had a moustache painted on in watery blue-black ink, but it took in the lower lip as well. To understand how the Ainu could regard this as attractive is difficult—though not more so than seeing beauty in the blackened teeth Japanese women used to have. The tattooing was a painful process. The skin was cut with flint or steel and a mixture of boiled ash-bark and soot rubbed in. The practice was discontinued a couple of generations ago. Only five women in the Shiraoi village of about four hundred people had tattooed mouths.

In girlhood the skin round the upper lip was tattooed and, at about eighteen, round the lower. Unless a young woman was tattooed she was not marriageable, she could not take part in any religious ceremonies, and when she died she would go straight to the Ainu hell.

I went into the hut with Miyamoto, the hereditary chief whose regular business was now explaining and demonstrating the Ainu way of life to tourists and posing for their cameras. The hut had a board floor, but, he said, the old Ainu floor was of reed mats and, in the winter, bearskins for warmth. There were three small windows.

"The east window is the sacred one, facing the rising of the sun, which we worshipped, with the moon and other things of nature. Through this window the meat of the bear, which was also a god, was brought into the house. Through the south window fish from the sea were brought in. The other one was just for light." Miyamoto spoke in Japnese, but the invaluable Jack-san was with me to interpret.

The bear was shot with arrows—Miyamoto fired a steel-tipped one from a short bow into a plank. The arrows were poisoned with a substance from the root of the tree called *torikabuto*. A big fish spear was used like a harpoon on tuna, and salmon were caught with a jag. The Ainu fishing boat was a dugout canoe, until they adopted the Japanese type. Never agriculturists, the Ainu lived in small communities as hunters, always near a river for drinking water. They had no rice; the wild millet was their cereal. They distilled their own potent liquors.

The Ainu did not cremate but buried their dead. When a wife died her husband burned down the house, including her utensils, Miyamoto said, and added, "Burning the house down was so that the wife could have a house in heaven."

The bear festival, called *lomante*, was the biggest ceremonial in Ainu religion, and, I gather from various sources, it was like this: A bear cub is trapped and raised in the village. It is fed choice foods and, sometimes, even human milk. The bear is really the mountain god *Kimunkamui* who has been captured by the Devils and placed on earth in the form of a bear. Only with the death of the animal whose disguise he is forced to wear can he resume his rightful form and return to the abode of the gods. Therefore he wishes the Ainu to kill the bear and set his spirit free.

So, when the bear is two or three years old, the big festival is held. The bear is elaborately dressed up in a kind of saddle and headgear. Round its cage of wooden logs there is dancing and ceremony. The bear used to be struck with small decorated arrows, as in a bullfight, before it was despatched. The torment was supposed to "make its spirit strong". That cruelty has, very rightly, been stopped. It was usually killed with an arrow in the heart. But Yohei Nagata told me that one tribe used to place heavy logs across the bear's neck and the young men jumped on the logs to kill it. All primitives have a ghastly unconsciousness of animals' sufferings.

Then the body of the bear lies in state. Offerings are made to it, including jewellery if it is a female. The festival, with much drinking and dancing, lasts for three days and nights.

Miyamoto thought there were about 200,000 Ainu in Hokkaido when the Japanese came, and about 12,000 now, mostly intermarried with Japanese. In Shiraoi there were not more than about a hundred full-blooded Ainu. And only half of those could speak the Ainu language. Miyamoto had nine children and, he said, they could not speak Ainu. It is an utterly different language from Japanese and is regarded as Aryan in construction.

"In maybe thirty years there will be no true Ainu left," Miyamoto said. "The young Ainu don't want to be Ainu. They want to be Japanese. To be an Ainu is a handicap. I am not blind, and I must think of the future of my children."

Outside a souvenir shop that sold wooden bears and postcards and stags' heads, an old Ainu man was sitting on a chair. He sat out in the hot sun so that any tourists coming into the village would see him. His trousers showed under the regalia of fibre robes that were fraying. The sun beat down on the headdress that had once been a proud ceremonial crown. He mopped his bearded face with a dirty sweat-sodden handkerchief and waited for somebody to come and take his picture, and give him a hundred yen.

THE CAR ran through beautiful countryside and along a new-paved road and stopped on the curve of a mountain. Lake Toya spread sparkling blue in the sunshine, bordered with verdant farms and virgin forest, hilled in the centre with islands and dotted with dinghies and two white sails of yachts. To one side of the lake rose the cone of Mount Usu, looking just like a lesser Fuji.

"You are getting royal suite which was occupied by Crown Prince Akihito," Jack-san announced when we arrived and shed shoes at the Manseikaku, the foremost of Lake Toya's inns, and so situated that if it were any closer to the lake it would be in it.

His Royal Highness's accommodation, which we now received, consisted of a suite of no less than five rooms, counting the one just inside the door where the maid was preparing the green tea of welcome. No carpet marred the very fine *tatami* of the main room—instead there was a huge bearskin, complete with head and paws and claws, in front of a *tokonoma* with a beautiful scroll; and this was flanked by an air-conditioner. The separate bedroom (bathroom attached) had, to our surprise, Western twin beds. The other room had odd Western parlour furnishings. Then there was the viewing-room, overlooking the lake, with a settee and chairs covered in snowy linen. This had a wall picture of a nude in white silhouette, with a profile like the late Marilyn Monroe. And a television set.

When we went out on the lake we had a small launch to ourselves and the star guide-girl of the boat company: she was charming and spoke good English, and was weaned off her microphone patter before she could say "Twenty-four miles in circumference."

We were more interested in the views of the surrounding mountains across the shining water and in the Red Pagoda of the White Serpent.

This vivid little three-tiered pagoda, with its curving roofs of scarlet and its four scarlet doors, stood out on the lake on stilts. It had been erected to appease a goddess who lived at the bottom of the lake in the form of a white serpent. If the shrine were not there the White Serpent Goddess would upset many fishing boats and many people would be drowned.

"If a woman is drowned in the lake, the body floats to the surface," we were told. "But if a man drowns, his body is never recovered. The White Serpent likes men, and when she gets one she keeps him down with her on the lake bed."

RETURNING TO SAPPORO by car we ran along by the lakeside, past campers in the birchwoods, and then turned off to see the volcanic phenomenon called Showa Shinzan, which means New Mountain of the Era of Showa.

There had been a large potato field belonging to a local farmer. On 18 December 1944, the same day as the earth tremors began, the field began to bulge. A hill began growing, at the rate of about eight inches a day. It went on growing for seven months. Then, on 23 July 1945, when it was quite a mountain, it burst into eruption—and Japan had a brand-new volcano, 400 metres high. Not much lava flowed out; mainly it filled the crater and solidified. The new volcano was proclaimed a National Treasure. The farmer had given up potato-growing and become the local postmaster.

You could walk up the New Mountain, which was ruggedly bald and purple-brown in colour. Sulphurous smoke still issued from a few blowholes. No further eruptions were expected. But the vulcanologists said that another Shinzan could happen on another nearby farm.

We climbed up from Lake Toya to a rural landscape of hillsides fluffy with asparagus, shirred with the deep green of beet, coppiced with woods, wavy with corn, limy-gold with ripened hemp.

Along the road that wound round a big mountain called Ezo-Fuji the driver suddenly said, "Here, one morning about eleven o'clock, I met a bear."

The bear had ambled off the road and back into the forest. It was not as big as one he had seen near Kitami that chased some woodcutters right into a village and poked its head through the window of a house where a woman was feeding her baby. The woman ran out of the house with the child and the bear ran after her. The woman stumbled and fell. The bear jumped right over her and went away.

The driver's other bear story was a grisly one. A few years ago two men were clearing bamboo when a large bear appeared, and it chased them. The bear caught one man. The other, who had climbed a tree, saw his companion killed by the bear and partly eaten.

The day was swelteringly hot. When we stopped to eat our box lunches we had to open the car doors to let some air through. Yet, looking up, you could see a cleft of Ezo-Fuji that still held snow.

In the winter the farmers felled timber. There was too much snow to farm, nothing else they could do. They sent the trees sliding down the hillsides on the snow.

Jack-san questioned the driver for me about the character of the hardy Hokkaido people with their broad weather-tanned faces and their strong countrymen's bodies, and what the driver said translated like this:

"They have the work-hard, play-hard pioneering temperament. They are not great money-savers—they make it and they drink it. They look on the people from the south, particularly the Osaka people, as tight-fisted. They are pretty good people."

From Sapporo, next morning, we took the JAL plane back to Tokyo.

Reference Notes

Numbers in front of the following authors' books, and other publications, are the identifying numbers which appear in the text. The reference list may also be useful as an indicator of books for further reading.

1. RUDOFSKY, Bernard, *The Kimono Mind*. Gollancz, London, 1966.
2. PORTER, Hal, *The Actors*, sub-titled *An Image of the New Japan*. Angus & Robertson, Sydney and London, 1968.
3. MARAINI, Fosco, *Meeting with Japan*, translated from the Italian by Eric Mosbacher. Hutchinson, London, 1959.
4. *Kenkyusha's New Little Japanese-English Dictionary*, edited by T. Iwasaki. Kenkyusha, Tokyo, 1960.
5. TOMLIN, E.W.F., *Japan*. Thames & Hudson, London, 1973.
6. In the *New Yorker* magazine of 12 December 1970 an editorial writer who knew Mishima made reference in the "Talk of the Town" pages to this letter and gave some details that were not in the newsagency reports of Mishima's end.
7. MICHENER, James, *The Floating World*. Random House, New York 1952.
8. MISHIMA, Sumie, *The Broader Way*. Gollancz, London, 1954.
9. HEARN, Lafcadio, *Japan: An Attempt at Interpretation*. Macmillan, New York, 1904, Tuttle, Tokyo, 1955.
10. TANAKA, Kakuei, *Building a New Japan*, English edition. Simul Press, Tokyo, 1973.
11. KAHN, Herman, *The Emerging Japanese Superstate*. André Deutsch, London, 1971.
12. In *The Australian* (whose staff correspondent in Tokyo Gregory Clark was, before taking an Australian Government post in 1975) issue of 26 October 1974.
13. *New Larousse Encyclopedia of Mythology*. Paul Hamlyn, London-New York-Sydney, 1968. (Odette Bruhl writes on Japanese mythology. Introduction is by Robert Graves.)
14. STORRY, Richard, *A History of Modern Japan*. A Pelican Original, Penguin Books, revised ed. 1972.
15. In an article "In Praise of Japanese Food" in *This is Japan* annual for 1956, Asahi Shimbun, Tokyo.
16. KIRKUP, James, *Tokyo*. Dent, London, 1966. In the chapter on Matsushima the reference is to Kirkup's writing about the Robata restaurant in Sendai in his book *These Horned Islands* (Collins, 1962) and also in the Tohuku section of *Fodor's 1973 Guide to Japan and East Asia*, Hodder & Stoughton, London, 1973.
17. Issue of 29 March 1974. Publishers and co-editors, Millard Alexander and Susan L. Scully, Tokyo.

234   References Notes

18 Robert Whymant's article also appeared in the Australian periodical *The National Times*, issue of 24-29 June 1974.
19 DeMente, Boye, *Businessman's After Hours Guide to Japan*. Phoenix Books, Phoenix, Arizona, U.S.A., 1973. (Japan Air Lines edition).
20 BENEDICT, Ruth, *The Chrysanthemum and the Sword*. Charles E. Tuttle, Tokyo, 1953.
21 BOWERS, Faubion, *Japanese Theatre*. Hermitage House, New York, 1952
22 *Japanese Noh Drama*, with translations in English of ten selected Noh plays. Nippon Gakajutsu Shinkokai (Japanese Classics Translation Committee), Tokyo, 1955.
23 REISCHAUER, Edwin O., *Japan: The Story of a Nation* (formerly entitled *Japan Past and Present*). Tuttle, Tokyo, 1971.
24 *Japan: The New Official Guide*, compiled by the Japan National Tourist Organization (JNTO), published by the Japan Travel Bureau (JTB), Tokyo, 1966. (Revised edition became available in mid-1975.)
25 HORIGUCHI, S. and HAMAGUCHI, R. in *Architectural Beauty in Japan*. Kokusai Bunka Shinkokai (Society for International Cultural Relations), Tokyo, 1955.
26 Handbook on Japan published by Mainichi Newspapers, Tokyo.
27 SUZUKI, Daisetsu, in an article in *Japan Quarterly*, no. 3,1955. Asahi Shimbun, Tokyo.
28 MOSHER, Governeur, *Kyoto: A Contemplative Guide*. Tuttle, Tokyo, 1964.
29 *We Japanese*, a compilation of customs, manners, ceremonies, etc. published by the Fujiya Hotel, Miyanoshita, Japan, comprising three books of which Book 1 was first published in 1934 and Book 3 in 1949.
30 Published by the Gifu City Office.
31 HACHIYA, Michihiko, *Hiroshima Diary: The Journal of a Japanese Physician*, edited and translated by Dr Warner Wells. Gollancz, London, 1955.
32 *The Effects of the Atomic Bombs on Hiroshima and Nagasaki*, a report by a survey team of the United States Strategic Bombing Survey which studied the effects in October-December 1945. The report, incorporating findings by the Joint Commission for the Investigation of the Atomic Bomb in Japan, was published by the U.S. Government Printing Office, Washington, D.C., in 1946.
33 NAGAOKA, Shogo, *Hiroshima* (on the title page *Hiroshima Under Atomic Bomb Attack*). Published by the A-Bomb Memorial Hall, Hiroshima, undated. (I bought it at the Memorial Hall in November 1955.)
34 February 1947 issue *Harper's Magazine*.
35 Part of a "Special Report on Ura Nihon" in *This is Japan* annual, 1967. Asahi Shimbun, Tokyo.

Index

Abashiri, 222, 223-4
Abeku hoteru, 73-5
Abortion, 11
Ago Bay, 138, 140
Agui, Frank, 50
Ainu, 28-9, 31, 181, 214, 221-2, 229-30
Airports, Chitose, 213; Haneda, 45, 108; Kagoshima, 193
Akabo, 109
Akahito, Crown Prince, 41, 230
Akan, Lake, 225-6
Akan National Park, 221
Akasaka district, Tokyo, 42-3
All Nippon Airways, 166, 205
Alps, 119, 177
Amagi Islands, 210
Amakusa Islands, 198
Ama-no-hashidate, 185
Amaterasu, 23, 24-5, 28, 144
Amida, 122
Amur River, 221
Antiques, 123
Architects and architecture, 39-40, 104-5, 109, 121, 124, 125-6, 164, 206; castles, 114-5, 143, 179, 197; commercial and hotel, 40, 129-31, 164; farmhouse, 102, 133, 182; household, 30; religious, 24, 26-7, 29, 55, 103-5, 113, 121-2; tomb, 29; villa, 115-6, 179
Arima, Cecilia, 95, 122
Art and artists, 10, 26, 29, 31, 53, 59-63, 76, 114-5, 120, 124, 185
Arts and crafts, 4, 10, 59-60, 124, 144, 165, 185. *See also* Dolls and doll-making; Lacquerware; Masks; Potters and pottery; Puppets
Asakusa district, Tokyo, 42
Ashi, Lake, 134. *See also* Hakone, Lake
Ashigawa, 215
Aso, Mount, 194-5
Atami, 135
Atomic Bomb Casualty Commission (A.B.C.C.) 163
Atomic power, 20

Atomic radiation, 160-4
Atsuta shrine, 144
Awa-Odori *see* Odori
Awazu, 119
Ayu, 146

Badgers, 222
Bakafu (tent government), 30
Bamboo, 113, 116, 207
Banks and banking, 5, 19
Bard, Ralph, 163
Basho, 185
Bath-houses, 136, 155-6
Beaches, 181
Bears, 215, 222, 229, 230, 231-2; carved, 222
Beef, 47, 49, 142
Beer, 44, 47
Benedict, Ruth, 81
Beppu, 172, 193-4
Bihoro, 220; Pass, 221
Birds, 225
Birth control *see* Family planning; Population density
Biwa, Lake, 110, 119
Black Current of Kuroshio, 208
Blunden, Edmund, 188
Bonito, 168
Bonric, 169
Bonsai, 59
Botanical gardens, 209
Bowers, Faubion, 85
Bridges, 104, 120, 166, 202
Brocade Beach, 136
Bronze casting, 124
Buddha, Shaka, Horyuji, 126; at Kamakura, 30, 101
Buddhism, 6, 23, 29, 30, 31, 49, 55, 89, 102, 103, 104, 111-2, 113, 116, 118, 121-2, 124, 125-6, 131, 167, 178, 219. *See also* Temples
Bugaku dance, 144, 157
Bunraku, puppet drama, 53, 90-3, 170-2
Byodo-in, 121

Cable cars, 119, 167
Calligraphy, 15
Camphorwood, 156, 157
Cancer, 11
Capron, Horace, General, 214
Castles, 114-5, 143, 149, 150, 159, 169, 177, 178, 197
Cats, 137, 224
Cattle, 47
Ceramics, 31, 144, 178. *See also* Potters and pottery
Cherry-blossom, 45-6, 102
Chiba, 111-12
Chikamatsu Monzaemon, 86, 90
China, cultural contact with Japan 5, 15, 26, 29, 31, 126, 157, 204; war with, 33, 157
Chinoike Jigoku, 194
Chinzan-so garden, Tokyo, 56
Chirihama, 181
Chitose airport, 213
Chiyo, 181
Chopsticks, 44, 49
Christianity, 23, 31, 199, 201-2, 203, 206
Chuo University Tea Society, 58
Civil Wars, 30, 31
Coal mining, 226
Confucianism, 6, 31, 204
Constitution (1946), 36
Coral ornaments, 168
Cormorant fishing, 146-8
Costume, 56, 157, 160; theatrical, 88, 90. *See also* Dress: Masks
Cotton industry, 206
Crabs, 122, 220
Crime, 66
Crops *see* Farming and agriculture
Currency, 31

Daibutsu (Great Buddha) figures, 124
Daikan, 205
Daimyo, 30, 31
Daisetsu, Hokkaido, 218
Daisetsuzan National Park, 215
Daiya River, 104
Dance, 83, 121, 123, 157, 168. *See also* Kabuki drama
Date, Masamure, 188
Death, 29, 32, 102, 131, 153, 159, 229-30. *See also* Suicide
Deer, 125, 158
Democratic Socialist Party, 55
Deva Kings, 104
Diet, the, 36, 55

235

236 Index

Diseases, 11-12, 132, 160-1, 163-4, 194, 199, 219
Dog fighting, 169-70
Dolls and doll-making, 131, 179, 186-7. *See also* Puppets
Dome Building, Hiroshima, 161, 162
Dragons, 105
Drain pipes, 166
Drama, 7. *See also* Theatre
Dress, 4, 8, 10, 11-12, 95, 96, 102, 109, 114, 147, 167-8, 198, 223-4, 229. *See also* Costume
Dried flowers, 207-8

Earthquakes, 130; proofing, 46
Economy, 4, 16-8, 19-20, 36
Edo, 4, 31; Great Fire of, 31; period, 180, 183; village, 183. *See also* Tokyo
Education, 5, 36
Enamel, 144
Ennosuke, 87
Enryakuji, 118-9
Etiquette, 4, 14, 83, 131
Exploration of Japan, American, 5; Dutch, 5; English, 5
Export, 5, 16
Ezo, Hokkaido, 214
Ezo-Fuji (Mount Yotei), 231

Family customs, 11
Family planning, 11
Farming and agriculture, 36, 101-2, 214, 219
Festivals, 56, 144, 224, 236
Fish and shellfish, 44, 48, 49-50, 83, 139-40, 141, 146-7
Fishing industry, 146-7, 226
Floating Pavilion, 119
Flora, 17, 25, 26
Flower arrangement, 43, 53, 81, 83
Fodor's Guide, 103
Folk-crafts, 53, 59, 165, 181, 207
Food and drink, 4, 44-5, 47-50, 83, 122, 139-40, 141, 145, 168, 183, 189, 194, 198, 202, 204, 205, 209-10, 214-5, 217-8, 220, 223. *See also* specific entries
Foxes, shrines to, 121
Fujita, Baron, 56
Fujiwara family, 121, 126
Fujiya Hotel, Kushiro, 129-33
Fujiyama (Mount Fuji), 29, 107, 119, 129, 132, 134-5
Fuki, 222

Fukuoka, kyushu, 104, 108
Fukuura, 189
Furoshiki, 109
Furusato, 205
Fushimi, 121
Futamigaura, 141

Gagaku music, 157
Gaimusho, Tokyo, 9
Games *see* Sports and games
Gardens, 113, 115, 118; landscape 117, 166, 178-9, 198; use of stone in, 120-1
Gasoline, 181
Gate of Hell (film), 157
Gates, Ruggles, Professor, 221-2
Geisha, 81-4, 122-3
Genji clan, 91
Geta, 82, 123, 135
Ghosts, 226
Gifu, Prefecture, 132, 146, 149-50
Gilyak people, 221
Ginko-tree, 55-6
Ginza, Tokyo, 45, 52-3, 66, 71
Gion district, Kyoto, 112, 122-3
Glover House, 203
Glover, Thomas Blake, 202, 203
Godaido, 189
Gods and goddesses, 24-5, 28, 113, 126, 144, 230, 231
Golf, 109-10, 132
Gorufu, 109-10
Grant, Ulysses, 214
Great Fire of Edo, 31
Great Kunto Earthquake, 34, 39, 46
Guide books and tourist literature, 102, 105, 108, 120, 161, 185, 188
Guns and ammunition, 5, 17, 31, 114, 203, 206

Hachiya, Dr Michihiko, 160
Haiku, 178, 181, 185
Hakata dolls, 82, 193
Hakone, Lake, 129, 132
Hamana Lagoon, 107
Haneda airport, 45, 108
Hara, Takeshi, 207-8
Harris, Townsend, 49
Hashi *see* Chopsticks
Hayashida, 207
Hearn, Lafcadio, 15, 135-6, 196
Heart disease, 11
Heian (Kyoto), 29, 116; period, 29-30, 124; shrine, 56, 116-7
Heike clan, 91
Hibachi, 18, 154
Hidari, Jingoro, 105
Hideyoshi, 31

Hiei, Driveway, 119; Hotel, 119; Mount, 118-9
Higashi temple, Kyoto, 112
Higo, Honganji Zuiki, 198
Hikari trains, 106-9, 110
Himoko, Queen, 29
Hinomaru, 183
Hira, Mount, 119
Hirodo, S., 56
Hirohito, Emperor, 6, 28, 40-1, 163
Hiroshige, 185
Hiroshima, 56, 159-64, 193
History, 28-32, 111, 119, 122
Hokkaido, 29, 213-20
Hokusai, Katsushika, 185
Holidays, 18
Holland, 5, 119, 201-2
Holland Slope, 202
Horiguchi, Sutemi, 121, 124
Horyuji temple, Nara, 124
Hostels, 173
Hostesses, bar, 62, 66-70
Hotels, 40, 42, 46-7, 48, 50-1, 73-5, 103, 119, 129-33, 135-6, 140, 188, 193-4, 196, 207, 209, 227, 228. *See also* Inns
Hot spring resorts, 194, 205, 207. *See also* Hotels; Spas and holiday resorts
Housing and homes, 16, 17-8, 30. *See also* Architects and architecture
Hughes, Richard, 170

Ibusuki, 208
Ichimura, Rokunojo, 171
Ikebana, 43, 53, 81, 83
Ikeda, Lake, 209
Ikeda, Prime Minister, 46
Imperial Hotel, Tokyo, 46
Imperial Palace, Tokyo, 39, 40, 54, 59
Imports, 16, 19
Inachu, 182
Inari shrine, 121
Inasa, Mount, 202
Industry, 17-20, 36, 142, 143. *See also* specific industries
Inflation, 17, 36
Inland Sea (Seto Naijai), 101, 153, 157, 165, 167
Inns, 42-5, 153-6, 166, 216, 224
International Moustache Co., 131
Inuyama, 150
Io-san volcano, 223
Ise, 25; Bay, 139; Shrine, 23-4, 125
Ise-Shima National Park, 139
Ishikari River, Hokkaido, 215

Index 237

Ishiyama, 119
Iso gardens, 206-7
Isoyama (Mount Iso), 206
Itsukushima Shrine,
    Miyajima Island,
    157-8, 185
Iwaso Inn, Miyajima, 153

Jail, 223-4
Japan Air Lines, 13
Japan Alamanac, 108
Japan Communist Party, 55
Japan National Railways, 41, 106
Japan: The New Official Guide, 101, 161
Japan Times (newspaper), 96
Japan Travel Bureau, 123, 209
Japan Youth Hostel, Inc., 173
Japanese Navy, 33, 34
Japanese Socialist Party, 17, 19, 55
Jerwood, J. M., 136
Jigoku, 194, 227-8
Jigoku-dani (Valley of Hell), 227-8
Jimmu, Emperor, 28
Jingu, 23
Jiyu-ga-mori, 187
Jizo, 102, 219
Jocho, 121
Judo, 54, 55

Kabuki drama, 85-7
Kaga province, 177
Kago, 167
Kagoshima, 108, 193, 207
Kagura, 121
Kaimon, Mount, 209
Kaira Kuen garden, Mito, 178
Kairyuyama (sumo wrestler), 97
Kamakura, 30, 101, 124
Kamikawa, 215
Kamishimo, 90
Kammu, Emperor, 116-7, 119
Kanaya Hotel, Nikko, 103
Kanazawa, 108, 177-80;
    Castle, 177; Noh Co., 180
Kanematsu company, 56
Kannon goddesses, 113-4
Kano family, 114
Kanrantei, 188
Karasaki, 119
Karate, 54-5
Kashikojima, 140
Kasuga shrine, 125-6
Kasumigaike Pond, 179
Katata, 119-20
Kato, Kiyomasa, 198
Katsura Imperial Villa, Kyoto, 101, 115-6
Katsura Island, 190

Katsura River, 113
Kawaroku Inn,
    Takamatsu, 166
Kawayu, 223
Kegon Waterfall, Nikkon, 105-6
Keio Plaza Hotel, 46
Kendo, 54
Kenrokuen Park, 178-9
Kikkaishi, 132
Kimma lacquerware, 166
Kimmei, Emperor, 126
Kimono, 4, 8, 10, 56
Kimunkamui, 230
Kinka, Mount, 149
Kinkakuji (Gold Pavilion), Kyoto, 112-3
Kirishima, Mount, 207
Kirkup, James, 53, 63, 186
Kiso River, 149, 150
Kitakyashu, 193
Kitami, 219
Kiyokuni, (sumo wrestler), 96
Kiyomizu temple, 118
Kobe beef, 47, 49
Koboke Gorge, Shikohu, 166
Kochi, 166, 167-9; Castle, 169
Kodama trains, 107, 108
Koizumi, Yakumo *see* Hearn, Lafcadio
Kokeshi dolls, 186-7
Komatsu, 177
Komei Party, 55
Korakuen Garden, Okayama, 178
Korea, 31, 126; doll-play, 90; war, 36
Kotatsu, 131
Kudara Kannon, 126
Kumamoto, 196-8
Kurashiki, 165
Kurenai Maru (ship), 172-3
Kurlie Islands, 224
Kuroda, Governor, 214
Kuroshima Beach, 182
Kusube (potter), 123
Kutani pottery, 178, 179
Kutcharo, Lake, 221
Kyogen, 180
Kyoto, 30, 45, 111 *et seq*;
    Handicraft Centre, 123;
    Hotel, 122
Kyushu, 5, 33, 50, 193

Lacquerware, 131-2, 166, 182
Lakes, 117, 119, 134, 225-6
Language and
    pronunciation, 13-6
Lanterns, 104
'League of Nations', 33
Liberal Democratic Party, 17-55
Lily of the Valley (express), 227
Literature, birth of, 29-30
Lomante, 230

Lucky Badger, 167

MacArthur, General Douglas, 36
Maeda, castle, 178;
    family, 178-9
Maibara, 110
Maiko, 82-3, 122
Manchuria, 33
Maraini, Fosco, 6, 15, 24, 105
Marimo ball-weed, 225-6
Marriage, 36, 163-4, 183-4;
    arranged, 71-2
Marunouchi district, Tokyo, 41
Marunouchi (Marunochi) Hotel, 8, 42, 45, 47
Mashu Grand Hotel, Teshikaga, 224-5
Mashu, Lake, 222
Masks, 88, 144, 157
Massage, 75-7
Matatabi vine, 222
Matsushima Bay, 185, 187-190
Matsuzakaya, Tokyo, 142;
    beef, 49, 142
Mazda, 19, 159
Medicine shop, 180
Meiji, Restoration, 5, 146, 201
Meiji Shrine, Tokyo, 55-6
Michener, James, 10
Miidera Temple, 119
Mikimoto, Kokichi, 137-9
Minamata, city, 199;
    disease, 199
Minamoto clan, 30
Minamoto, Yukiko, 180
Ministry of International Trade and Industry (M.I.T.I.), 20
Mirin, 48
Misen, Mount, 157
Mishima, Yukio, 7
Missionaries, 5, 31, 206
Mito, 178
Mitsubishi Co., 17, 202
Mitsui Co., 18, 40
Miyajima Island, 125, 153, 185
Miyako Odori *see* Odori
Miyamoto, Tomaramu, 229
Miyanoshita, 129, 131
Mogi, 204
Moji, 193
Mompe, 102, 168, 219
Monkeys, 105, 119, 170
Monks, 119
Monorail, 184
Moon-viewing, 82, 116, 188
Mosher, Gouverneur, 122
Muka Hotel, Onneyu, 219
Murofushi, Minoru, 58-9
Muromachi era, 113, 121
Music and musicians, 64, 90-3, 104, 123, 149, 157
Musical instruments, 64, 83, 88, 119, 125, 157

238 Index

Mutton, Japanese style, 214-5
Mythology, 23, 24-5, 30, 88-9, 141, 229-30

Nagaoka, Takashi, 172
Nagara River, 146
Nagaragawa, 146
Nagasaki, 5, 161, 193, 201
Nagata, Yohei, 230
Nagoya, 143-5; Castle 143-4
Nakadake, 195
Nanti, Mount, 103
Nara, 101, 116, 121, 125, 126; Hotel, 125
Nara period, 29
National Museum, Tokyo, 29
National Treasures, 144, 210, 226, 231
New Japan Hotel, Tokyo, 46
Nicheren sect, 119, 178
Nightclubs and bars, 42, 62-4, 66-72, 210
Nijo Castle, Kyoto, 114-5
Nikkatsu Hotel, Tokyo, 45
Nikko, 6, 101, 103
Ningyo-tsukai (puppet master), 90
Niojima, 189-90
Niomon, Nikko, 104
Nishikiura, 136
Nishimura, Hiro, 149
Nishimura, Richard, 163
Nishiyama, Mr, 166
Nishizaka Park, 201
Noboribetsu spa, 228
Nobunaga, Oda, 31, 119, 144
Noh drama, 31, 85, 87-9, 180
Noren, 180
Noto Hanto, 181

Obi, 10-11, 56
Occupation, Allied, 17, 35-6, 47, 54
Odawara, 131
Odori, dance, 123; Festival, 168
Official Guide, The, 120, 185
Okayama, 178
Okhotsk, Sea of, 223
Okura Hotel, Tokyo, 46
Olives, 170
Omura Bay, 140
Onagadoni roosters, 169
Onnagata, 86
Onneyu, 219
Ono, 153
Onsen *see* Hot spring resorts
Origami, 53
Osaka, 90
Osaki Hachiman Shrine, 186
Oshima Island, 189; pongee, 207, 210

Pachinko, 113
Pagodas, 125, 157
Palanquin, 169
Paper and paper goods, 53, 169, 215
Parasol dance, 83
Parasols, 83, 166
Paulownia wood, 171
Peace City (Hiroshima), 164
Peace Memorial Museum, Hiroshima, 164
Pearling industry, 136, 137-9, 140-1
Pensions, 11
Peppermint, 219
Perry, Matthew, Commodore, 4, 31, 137
Petrochemical industry, 142
Phoenix Hall, 121
Photography, 206
Physical characteristics, 9-10. *See also* Racial characteristics and origins
Physical fitness, 54-5
Pinto, Fernao Mendes, 206
Plastics industry, 108
Poets and poetry, 30, 166, 178, 181, 185, 188
Police, dummy, 182-3
Poilution, 20, 41, 108, 109, 142, 148, 172, 199; golf, 109-10
Population density, 11, 111, 124, 159, 168, 177, 213
Portuguese, 5, 30-1, 48, 114, 201, 202, 206
Potters and Pottery, 29, 31, 123, 178, 179, 181, 207
Prehistory, 28-9
Printing, 31
Prisoners of war, 35
Puppet drama, 5, 53, 90-3, 170-2

Quail, 83
Quicksilver, 219

Racial characteristics and origins, 9, 10, 28-9, 221-2
Railways, 4, 5, 6-7, 41, 101, 106-9, 203
Ramen, 47-8
Religion, 6, 23-5, 28, 124. *See also* Buddhism, Christianity, Shinto, Zen
Restaurants, 47-50, 62, 122-3, 139-40, 183, 186-7, 204, 209-10
Rice, 29, 44, 49, 101, 178
Rickshaw, 5
Rinnoji temple, Nikko, 106
Ritsurin Park, Shikoku, 166
Roads and roadworks, 16, 194, 219
Rocks gardens, 120-1
Roosters, 169
Rubeshibe, 219

Ryoanji temple, Kyoto, 120
Ryokan, 173

Sabamubi, 229
Sacred Bridge, Nikko, 104
Sacred Stable, 104-5
Sagami Bay, 136
Saito, Torao, 50
Sakamoto, 119
Sake, 45, 47, 49, 50, 83
Sakhalin, 226
Sakura (Cherry-blossom), 45-6
Sakurajima, 205
Samisen, 83
Samurai, 30, 33, 166, 178
Sand baths, 194, 208
Sanjusangen-do temple (Katsura Imperial Villa), 113
Sansuien, 167
Sapporo, Hokkaido, 108, 213-4
Sarasuwa Pond, Nara, 125
Satsuma pottery, 207
Satsunan Islands, 210
Sauna, 75
Sculptors and sculpture, 104-5, 113-4, 121-2
Seaweed, 4, 50
Seikan, tunnel, 108
Seisonkaku, 179
Sendai, 185-7
Seta, 119
Seto Naikai (Inland Sea), 165
Shabushabu (beef dish), 122
Shakuhachi (flute), 125
Shijo Street, Kyoto, 112
Shikoku, 101, 165, 166
Shima, Dr, 159
Shima, Hospital, 159
Shima, Kando Hotel, 140; Marineland, 141; Peninsula, 137, 139
Shimabara, 199
Shimazu, Nariakina, 206
Shimoda, 49
Shinkansen, 108
Shinto, 6, 23-5, 36, 40, 46, 103, 111-2, 116, 121, 125-6
Shipbuilding, 4, 5,
Shirakawago Valley, 182
Shiraoi, 228-9
Shiretoko Peninsula, 224
Sho, 157
Shochu, 209
Shodo Island, 170
Shodo (priest), 103
Shoji, 154
Shops and stores, 52-3, 123, 136-7, 207
Shotoku, Prince, 29
Showa Shinzan, Hokkaido, 231
Shrines, 23-4, 25-7, 103-4, 111-2, 116-7, 121, 125-6, 144, 157, 186

Shukkeien Garden, 164
Sight-seeing tours,
　53-7, 58-61, 63, 101
Skating, 225
Soami (painter), 120-1
Soba, 45
Social security, 11
Sosogi, 182
Soka Gakkai, 55
Sounkaku Inn, Hokkaido,
　216
Sounkyo Gorge, 216
Souvenirs, 123, 167, 198,
　222, 230; of Hiroshima,
　162. *See also* Shops and
　stores
Spas and holiday resorts,
　193-4, 208, 228. *See also*
　Hot spring resorts
Sports and games, 109-10,
　132, 210, 218, 225; at
　Geisha party, 84
Stone lanterns, 115, 125
Stones, use in garden
　landscape, 120-1
Sugar, 219
Sugi (cedar) trees,
　102-3, 104
Sugigasa, 168
Suicide, 6-7, 11, 12, 30, 228
Suiguin quicksilver mine,
　Hokkaido, 219
Suizenji Park, 198
Sukiyaki, 44
Sulphur Mountain
　(Io-san), Hokkaido, 223
Sumi-e, 60
Sumo, 95-7
Susuki grass, 194
Sutras (scripture scrolls),
　89, 158
Suzuki, Daisetsu, 112

Tabi, 83, 88
Tai, 183
Taiho (sumo wrestler), 95
Taiko, 83, 157
Taira clan, 30, 182
Taisho, Emperor, 41
Takamatsu, 75, 101, 166,
　167, 170
Tanegashima, 206, 210
Tanable Bay, 140
Tanaka, Kakuei, 16, 109
Tange, Kenzo, 55, 164
Tatami, 58, 82, 95, 116,
　120, 131
Tatooing, 229
Taxis, 9, 13, 42-3, 50
Tayu (reciter), 90, 91
Tea, 102; kettles, 178. *See
　also* Tea ceremony; Tea
　houses
Tea ceremony, 58, 81, 83,
　115; dinner, 122

Tea houses, 115
Telephones, 5, 206
Temples, 104, 111-2, 113,
　117, 118-9, 120, 121, 167,
　178, 190
Tempura, 44, 48
Tendai sect, 118-9
Ten Province Pass, 135
Teshikaga, 224
Textiles, 113, 181
Thatch, 118
Theatre, 85-9; Kokusai, 57.
　See also Dance; Drama
Thousand-Handed
　Buddha, 104
Tiles 118
Tipping, 50-1
Toba, 137
Todaiji temple, Nara, 124
Togetsuko, 189
Tohuku, 186
Tojo, General, 34
Tokachi Mountains, 218
Tokaido Highway, 5, 60
Tokonoma, 154, 216
Tokora River Valley, 220
Tokugawa, Art Museum,
　144
Tokugawa family,
　31, 39, 102, 146
Tokugawa Ieyasu, 31, 102,
　104, 105, 143, 144, 178
Tokushima, 167
Tokyo, 8, 9, 39-41, 42, 52,
　62; National Museum,
　61; tour of, 59-61;
　Tower, 41; University,
　54
Tokyo Hilton, 46
Tomito, Shiro, 95
Torii, 104, 106, 117, 121,
　125, 144, 157
Tosa dogs, 169-70
Toshioka Kosen, 181
Toshitune, 178
Toshogu Shrine, Nikko,
　103-5
Toya, Lake, 230
Toyota, 17-8
Toyotomi, Hideyoshi, 144
Trade and Commerce,
　5, 16-21
Trains, 101, 106-9, 131,
　203. *See also* Monorail;
　Railways
Tsuruga, 177
Tsurumi, Mount, 194
Turtle soup, 50

Ueno Park, Tokyo,
　45, 46, 58
Uji, 121, 149
Unions, 18-9, 36, 203
Unzen, Mount, Nagasaki,
　199-200

Urakami, 202
Ura Nihon, 181
Urushi-tree, 131-2
Usu, Mount, 230
Utaemon, Nakamura 87
Utamaro, 76
Utsukushima, 125

Valley of Hell, 227-8
Volcanoes and volcanic
　eruptions, 134, 194-5,
　199-200, 205, 223, 225,
　231

Wages, 18, 203
Wajima, 182
Waka, 167
War, 4; civil, 30-1; crimes,
　36; veterans, 197. *See also*
　World War I, World
　War II
Watanabe, Yonosuke, 180
Waterfalls, 118
Weddings, honeymoons,
　209; Shinto, 183
Whaling, 226
Whisky, 145
White Heron Castle,
　Himeji, 114
Women, 36, 41, 112, 135,
　171; writers, 29-30
World War I, 33
World War II, 17, 28, 33-6,
　39, 40, 54, 56, 102, 126,
　143, 186, 199. *See also*
　Hiroshima
Wrestling, 95-7
Wright, Frank Lloyd, 46

Xavier, St Francis,
　5, 201, 206

Yabase, 119
Yaizu, 135
Yakushido Chapel, 105
Yama-umo, 194
Yamagata, Prince, 56
Yamaguchi, family, 130
Yamashita, Zempei,
　147, 148
Yashima Plateau, 166-7
Yatsushiro Bay, 119
Yokkaichi, 142
Yomei Gate, Nikko, 105
Yoroijima, 189
Yoshida, Kenichi, 177
Yumoto Fujiya Hotel, 133
Yutakayama, 96

Zaibatsu, 17
Zen, 30, 112, 120
Zipangu, 30
Zuiganji Temple, 188
Zuiki, 198
Zoological gardens, 209